Pages *from* the Past

First Published in December 2009

Published by
Shruffaun Publishing

9 Snipe Lawn,
Newcastle,
Galway,
Ireland.
Email: tbkelly@eircom.net

Compiled and Edited by Thomas Kelly
Layout and Design: Clódóirí Lurgan, CL Print, Indreabhán, Co. na Gaillimhe.
Printed by: CL Print, Indreabhán, Co. na Gaillimhe.
Copyright: © *Shruffaun Publishing* 2009

Limited Edition 50 Copies
ISBN: 978-0-9564449-0-5

All Rights Reserved
Without limiting the rights under copyright reserved alone, no part of this publication may be reproduced, stored in or introduced into a retrieval system, or transmitted, in any form by any means (electronic, mechanical, photocopying, recording or otherwise) without the prior written permission of the above publisher of this book.

Pages from the Past

A compendium of items
gleaned from the 1929
volume of *The Tuam Herald*

Compiled by
Thomas Kelly

Pages from the Past

Introduction

This publication started by accident. I was asked to look up a particular news item which appeared in an issue of the Tuam Herald in 1929 and became engrossed by this look back in time. All items are taken directly from the pages of the Herald and represent a fairly random selection of news reports, editorials, advertisements and sundry items which appeared throughout that year. The date on which each item appeared is included and I have tried to retain, as far as possible, the chronology, style and layout in its original form.

I hope that those of you who, like me, are regular readers of the Herald will enjoy what you find here. The items are reproduced without commentary or analysis. The selection of material has neither an academic nor a political purpose but is, hopefully, a representative cross section of the bits and pieces, trivial and serious, which would catch the eye of the regular reader. If I were to make an observation it would be to the effect that some things have changed utterly whilst other things never change and that conventional wisdom does not always stand the test of time.

I have omitted death notices and court cases for reasons which, I feel, should be obvious. The only comment which I will make on the latter is that if one were to judge the Tuam of 1929 by the "crimes" reported from the courts of the time, it was an innocent community indeed by comparison with our own times.

This is a layman's look, through the eyes of the Herald, at a crucial period in an Ireland which had only recently taken on responsibility for its own affairs. In particular it is a look at Tuam and the West of Ireland through the happenings which were deemed newsworthy by the local media at the turn of the nineteen twenties. I have omitted more than I have included but hope there is sufficient here to give a reasonable flavour of the period and readers are invited to travel back and draw their own conclusions and even to read between the lines!

Those who remember that time will be able to recapture some of its atmosphere and even recall long forgotten events. More of us, who were not born then, will remember many of the people mentioned and will have been influenced by the attitudes and conventions which prevailed. I hope that the interest of younger readers may be sufficiently aroused to further research this and other periods and thereby add some more pieces to the fascinating jig-saw that makes up the history of Tuam.

There were no photographs in the Tuam Herald in 1929. The pictures of The Square and The Market Cross used are courtesy of The National Library of Ireland. The photograph on pages 156 and 157 was taken by Kilgannon Photographers, Sligo on the occasion of an excursion of Pioneers from Tuam to Sligo on Sunday 8th June, 1930 so we can be certain that those pictured were alive and well and familiar with the times depicted within these pages. The group consisted of people from Tuam town and the surrounding parishes including Cortoon and Kilbannon. That photograph was taken on the embankment beside the Great Southern Hotel near Sligo railway station. I have made a list of those whom I have been able to identify from that photograph, as indicated in the accompanying key with grid references to aid identification.

I would like to thank Alf Mac Lochlainn, former librarian of University College Galway (now NUIG), for his support when this publication was first mooted and Michael Dempsey of Clódóirí Lurgan for his advice and assistance in its production.

Finally I wish to acknowledge the role of the Tuam Herald and the people who worked there as the source and inspiration for this compilation.

Thomas Kelly, 2009

This is the form of editorial column heading used by the Tuam Herald in 1929 which contains its motto in three languages.

THE EYES OF YOUTH

OPTICIAN TO
H.H. POPE PIUS XI.

SPECIAL APPOINTMENT

Everything Seen Clearly
Distant and Near

Kryptok
GLASSES,

THE GREATEST OPTICAL INVENTION
OF ITS KIND IN MODERN TIMES.

PATRICK CAHILL
Optician to His Holiness Pope Pius XI.

13 Wellington Quay, Dublin

5/1/21

COMHAIRLE CONNDAE NA GAILLIMHE

THE BOVINE TUBERCULOSIS ORDER OF 1928.

The Galway County Council desire to notify owners that the compensation payable to the owners of animals slaughtered under the above Order shall be three-fourths of the market value of such animal when the animal is not in an advanced state, whereas if the animal shows signs that the disease in such animal is in an advanced state, he shall only receive one-fourth of its market value or Thirty Shillings whichever is the greater.

Owners or persons in charge ought therefore notify the undersigned immediately of their suspicions that any animal is Tubercular or threatened with Tuberculosis so that the animal may be inspected before it shall reduce in value and in order that if it is slaughtered he shall recover seventy-five instead of twenty-five per cent of its value.

Suspected animals must be isolated and kept apart from other animals until inspected by the Veterinary Surgeon.

The milk of suspected cows must be boiled or sterilized and not mixed with the milk of any other cow. Utensils in which such milk is placed before being so treated, must be thoroughly cleansed with boiling water before any other milk is placed therein.

Dated this 12th day of December, 1928.

PATRICK CROWE,
Acting Secretary,
Co. Council Offices, Courthouse, Galway.

HESKIN, TUAM,

begs to notify to his numerous customers that he has in addition to his already large

Stock of HARDWARE,

Timber, Iron, Coal, Cement, Slates, etc.,

which he is selling at lowest competitive prices.

Sole Agent for Raleigh Cycles, Deering Mowers

5/1/29

CARNIVAL DANCE IN TUAM.

On Thursday, Dec.27th, 1928, a Carnival Dance was held in the Mall Cinema, Tuam, commencing at 8 p.m. in aid of the Tuam Branch of the Life Boat Institution. The dance was well attended by the people of Tuam, and in addition some people came considerable distances by car, and a most cheerful and enjoyable evening was spent. The Mall Cinema was splendidly illuminated and decorated for the occasion, the decorations even including a Christmas Tree which was heavily laden with numerous prizes. These were presented by the Organizer of the Dance, Mr. R.M. Burke, Hon. Sec. of Tuam Branch of the Life Boat Institution, and included a special prize for Irish Dancing - for the best pair in "The Walls of Limerick". This was won by Mr. Nicholas Walsh and Miss D. Geoghegan. Other prizes were awarded for best fancy dress costume (won by Miss D. Leslie), fast foxtrot (won by Miss E. Flattery and Mr. Gibbons), slow foxtrot (won by Miss O'Kelly Lynch and Guard Kearney), walse (won by Miss Ena Browne and Mr. Heaslip). In addition to these a larger number of smaller prizes were awarded during "Spot Dances".

Mr. de Ross, Mr. P.M. Hosty and Mr. O'Kelly Lynch very kindly acting as Judges, did much to make the dance lively and enjoyable. A special feature was the performing of a very capable and amusing clown (Mr. E. Flaherty) twice during the dance. He was specially engaged for the occasion and his make up was very good. An excellent supper was supplied in the Mall School House, which was most kindly lent by the Very Rev. the Dean of Tuam. It had also been brightly decorated and was well illuminated. The Dean also honoured us by attending the dance, and so did Colonel The Rev.T.Ormsby, D.S.O., of Milford. Mr. J. O'Kelly Lynch, Hon.Treasurer of the Galway Bay Life Boat Branch, very kindly told us something of the splendid work done by the Life Boat Institution and received great applause. Mr. R.M. Burke, Hon.Sec. for Tuam Branch of Life Boat Institution thanked those present very heartily, not only for the splendid way in which they had supported the Life Boat, but also for the way in which Tuam had supported other excellent charitable institutions in which he was interested. He pointed out that he did not urge people to support two or three institutions and neglect others, for he knew well that there were a very large number of charitable institutions in our country which were doing splendid work and which deserved our assistance. At the same time, however, he was bound to ask for help especially for the 4 institutions for which he himself was Hon. Sec. for Tuam, namely the Life Boat, N.S.P.C.C., N.S.P.C.A., and the League of Nations Society of Ireland. Tuam had already contributed very generously to the Life Boat, N.S.P.C.C., and N.S.P.C.A., but so far the Tuam Branch of the League of Nations Society of Ireland had not received as much support as it deserved, he said, and he appealed to the people of Tuam to increase their support to this Society. The Mall Orchestra played splendidly, and at the conclusion of the dance they received three hearty cheers. Miss Flattery very kindly struck up on the piano while the Band had a short rest. We were very fortunate to have such a lively and able pianist. Another special feature of the evening were some very lively "Paul Jones" dances.

The dance was a real success financially £10 1s.0d. being the clear profit for the benefit of the Life Boat Institution, after paying expenses. Grateful thanks are due not only to all these who attended the dance but also to Mr.T.J. Mellin, who most kindly lent all the china, etc. for the supper free of charge, to Mr. Martin S.Walsh for lending boards to make tables, to those who helped with the supper, especially Mrs. Cole, to all those who helped to decorate the Cinema and School, to Mrs. Smallwood, Mr.J. Ormsby, and Mr.F. Stafford, who being unable to attend the dance, gave subscriptions, to Mr. Shearon and M.W. Allcock who most kindly sold tickets at the door, to Mr. Martin Donlan who also helped at the door, and to all others who helped in any other way.   5/1/29.

WHIST DRIVE

A Whist Drive andDance, under the auspices of Tuam Golf Club, will be held on Sunday, Jan. 6th, at the Wool Stores. The Stores will be heated and a good night's amusement is expected. Whist Drive commencing 8 o'c., sharp.

CONNACHT LADIES HOCKEY NOTES.

The Connacht Cup Competition took place during the months of November and December with the following results :

Tuam Ladies v. Galway Ladies—2-1, 3-2.
Tuam Ladies v. Galway Grammer School Girls—0-3, 2-2.
Tuam Ladies v. Athlone Ladies—7-2.
Galway Grammer School Girls v. Athlone Ladies—3-0.
Galway Grammer School Girls v. Galway Ladies—1-2, 1-1.
Galway Ladies v. Athlone Ladies---9-1.

After the first round Athlone retired from the competition.

FINAL RESULTS :

	Matches won	lost	goals for	goals against	points gained
Tuam Ladies	3	1	14	10	7
	a draw				
Galway Grammer School Girls	2	1	8	5	6
	two draws				
Galway Ladies	2	2	15	8	5
	a draw				
Athlone Ladies	0	3	2	19	0
	(retired)				

Tuam Ladies have thus won the Cup this season, Galway having held it since 1924.

The Connacht Interprovincial Ladies Hockey Trials will be held this year on the Grammer School Ground at 2.45 on Thursday, Jan. 3rd, 1929.

The teams selected are as follows :—

"Probables" —Miss Guy (Tuam), goal; Miss Sowman (Grammer School), Mrs Braund (Galway), backs ; Miss Reed (Grammer School) Miss Eraut (Galway) Miss Downing (Galway) halves; Miss P. Warner (Galway) Miss Coy (Grammer School) Miss M.Quinn (Tuam) Miss Moran (Tuam) Miss Tennant (Galway), forwards.

"Possibles" —Miss Winfield (Grammer School) goal; Miss E.Quinn, Miss Flattery (Tuam) backs ; Miss B.Strachan (Tuam) Miss P. Dowler (Grammer School) Miss E.Bailey (Galway) halves ; Miss C. Dowler (Grammer School) Miss Meagher (Tuam), Miss N.Byrnes (Galway) Miss Power (Galway) Miss M.Ryan (Galway), forwards. Miss B.Costello (Tuam) will also be tried with the "Possibles." 5/1/29

TUAM JANUARY FAIR.

TUESDAY, 8th JANUARY--- Sheep and Cattle, 2nd Tuesday.

WEDNESDAY, 16th JANUARY---Pigs, 3rd Wednesday.

Farmers bring in your Stock to this Fair. Last year there were plenty of buyers for sheep and cattle, and good prices obtained.

There is sure to be good demand for pigs, as all the leading buyers have promised to attend.

By order Tuam Town Commissioners.

JAMES DALY,
Acting Town Clerk.

TUAM TOWN COMMISSIONERS.

NOTICE TO CONTRACTORS.

The Tuam Town Commissioners will, at their next meeting to be held on Tuesday, 1st January, 1929, receive and consider tenders for cutting out a grid in ceiling, about two feet square, in the ceiling over Balcony in the Town Hall at an estimated cost of £5.

Tenders will be received by me up to the hour of 8 o'clock p.m. on the above-named day. Payment will be made on the certificate of Mr. Kennedy, B.E., Co. Surveyor, Galway.

The lowest or any tender not necessarily accepted.

By Order,

JAMES DALY,
Acting Town Clerk.

Town Hall, Tuam,
4-12-28.

"I have tried several kinds of foods," writes Mr Lewins, 7 Hawthorn Terrace, Tanfield, Durham, "but found nothing to equal Karswood Poultry Spice (containing ground insects) FOR PRODUCING EGGS GALORE." Sold in packets 2 1/2d, 7 1/2d, 1/3d. You, too, can do just as well by using Karswood. Try it NOW from:- M.S.Walsh, Hibernia Buildings, High Street, Tuam.

5/1/29

TUAM IN 1824 - ONE HUNDRED AND FOUR YEARS AGO.

Hely Dutton in his admirable work, "The Survey of the County Galway" speaks thus of Tuam in 1824. He reckons it second after Galway and writes thus:-

"TUAM - The residence of the Archbishop, is a handsome town, of considerable inland trade; it possesses several fairs, and a weekly market well supplied with excellent meat of every knd, especially veal in the proper season; also with fish from Galway, which is frequently to be had in this market when the inhabitants of Galway are without it, because the dealers in fish, called jolters or cadgers, are generally supplied before the housekeepers, as being much better customers. There is an extensive brewery kept by Mr. Blake, who supplies the country for miles round. The bread is particularly good; the town possesses a market house, and a billiard table and reading room over it, which is a great relief to many shopkeepers, as it takes away from them that great nuisance in country towns, idle loungers, who fill their shops and frighten many timid people, especially women, who cannot encounter the broad stare and second hand wit of those idlers. The Archbishop's palace, without possessing much architectural beauty, is exceedingly commodious and very spacious. It is highly ornamented by a handsome and extensive demesne and excellent gardens. There is a dispensary which, under the skill, conciliating manners and excellent management of Dr. Little, has been of infinite use to the poorer classes of society. There are also two newspapers, well edited and uninfluenced by either religious or political party. The Roman Catholic Archbishop has lately erected a handsome house which with the Catholic College of St. Jarlath (late French's Bank) adds much to the appearance of the town. An abundant and clear stream of water runs through the town, supplying the brewery, several tanneries, etc., etc., and after spoiling a good deal of choice land by the grossest neglect of the proprietors, turns a magnificient flour mill that should never have been permitted to be erected there, as throwing back water on land of ten times the value of the mill and falls intoTurloughmore from whence it runs to Lough Corrib and through the town of Galway to the sea. There are two good inns, at which the mail and canal coaches stop, which as Tuam is the entrance to the county of Mayo, is highly useful to the inhabitants of that opulent county. The town is built on a low situation, yet, I understand, is very healthy. There is a constant intercourse with Galway, from whence the shopkeepers are supplied with many articles for an extensive home trade. Much to the credit of this town religious distinctions are almost unknown to have any influence on their actions, from the Archbishop to the lowest inhabitant they live in the greatest harmony. Once for all I must say this is characteristic of every part of this extensive county and their firm adherence to a monarchial government has from the earliest period been conspicuous in every change and for which they often suffered severely. A wretched attempt has been made in the establishment of a meat and vegetable market; nothing can be more disgraceful than the appearance and site; after every shower of rain it is flooded up to the stalls and a pool of water in the centre".

Such is this careful writer's description of Tuam as he saw it one hundred and four years ago. And what changes have been wrought since. These were the days when there were no workhouses burdening the land and when the people, a fine old class, lived in harmony and knew no distinction of religion or class. The Roman Catholic Bishop of those days, who built the residence he and his three successors lived in and who built the Cathedral, the finest and first of its size in Ireland for many years, was Dr.Oliver Kelly. The Protestant Archbishop was Dr.Trench and he was the last Protestant Archbishop. His successor was Dr. Plunket, the first Protestant Bishop. The brewery established by Mr.Blake ran for nearly sixty years. The tanneries have disappeared. Tuam has lost its especial reputation for good bread made from native grown wheat. In another part of his admirable work Mr.Dutton praises the Tuam bread, when he says:- "The soil of the country generally produces every crop in abundance. The wheat, particularly that which is produced to the southward of Galway, is amongst the best in Ireland, producing the fine bread to be found in Galway,Tuam and other towns, and in almost every gentleman's house. The barley and oats, from the introduction of better kinds than were formerly sowed from the benefit of an extensive export and from the establishment of extensive business at Newcastle and Galway, have been greatly improved in their quality and the quantity astonishingly multiplied; this shows plainly if it could be doubled, the incalculable benefit of a free export of corn".

A hundred years ago a good quality of wheat was grown and used by the people in making excellent bread, but now all the bread used is made from imported American flour, not half as nutritious as the home grown article.

In Mr.Dutton's day there were breweries at Galway, Tuam, Loughrea and at Gort, and now all have disappeared.   5/1/29.

ARCHBISHOP McHALE.

Arthur Griffith wrote of Dr. MacHale as follows:

The wayside inn of Tubbernavine, a hamlet on the high road from Sligo to Ballina, was kept towards the close of the eighteenth century by a thrifty and enterprising farmer, whose superiority as well in enterprise as in stature to the mountainy farmers of the neighbourhood was hinted in his sobriquet of Padraig Mór. Padraig Mór MacHale and his wife Mary Mulkieran in their youngest son immortalised their names. John MacHale was born in the wayside inn on the 6th March, 1791, and like all the other children of the neighbourhood, of the barony - in fact, of the whole country - spoke Irish as a young child as his mother tongue. His father, indeed, was the only man in the neighbourhood who spoke any English. Padraig Mór as well as being a farmer and an inn-keeper was the transit rider who linked the country with the great towns. Evidently he was at this time one of those who, seeing English the language of the high, wealthy and influential places, inclined to the view that the teaching of that language to his children was a parental duty, and he sent his young son to learn it at the hedge-school of Lahardane - a proceeding in which he was opposed by John MacHales's grandmother - Anne Moffet, a fine old Irish woman, who strongly resented her grandchild being in any way anglicised.

Padraig Mór's young son was baptised by Father Andrew Conry of Addergoole - a priest who loved and used the Irish language on all occasions. To his grandmother and this priest, both of whom died when the child was still young, John MacHale was deeply attached. The fate of Father Conry was a tragic one. In 1798, when the French landed at Killala, and were marching by Tubbernavine, the people of that district fled up Mount Nephin. The stories current of the excesses committed in the French Revolution led them to regard the French as enemies instead of friends. Father Conry had himself been a strong denouncer of Revolutionary France, and, indeed the prejudice felt in the West and South against the French Revolution to which the Irish Brigade, practically drawn from those two provinces, was opposed, and which had injured materially the trade carried on between the South-western counties and France, was largely the cause of their comparative quiescence in 1798. Young MacHale, more daring than most of his elders, remained near his home and watched the French marching by. After the defeat of the French, Father Conry was one of those arrested and hanged. His body was carried over the mountains by the parishioners, with the women raising the piercing caoine, and the little child whom he loved kissed his cold hand before he was laid in the grave. The impression of the tragic scene never left John MacHale's mind. He was then a child of less than eight years old, but it filled him with a desire to learn all that could be learned about his country to understand how such things came to pass. For some time after the burial of the priest the little boy did nothing but weep inconsolably. Then he sought out the house of an old man, Martin Callaghan, who was reputed to know all that might be known of the history of Ireland. The old man was not unworthy of his reputation. He knew the history of his country, and he knew her songs and legends.

In them -- all in the Irish tongue -- he instructed the boy, firing in him that love of the Irish language and the old literature of the Gael which Anne Moffet had kindled. From his voluntary teacher he was sent as he grew older to the school of Patrick Staunton, in Castlebar, and his ability there attracted the attention of the Bishop of Killala, who caused him to be sent to Maynooth to be educated for the priesthood. His career in Maynooth was brilliant. He soon became lecturer, and later Professor of Dogmatic Theology, and his strong and fearless character and patriotism endeared him to the students.

Year by year Professor MacHale advanced in reputation as a Churchman, and his letters of "Heiropholos" made his name familiar in the Vatican, so that when the Bishop of Killala needed a coadjutor his appointment was at once approved. The young son of Padraig Mór returned to his native place at 34, a Bishop, and one of the objects he set before himself was to encourage and sustain the Irishism of the diocese. He insisted on all the younger generation of his own relatives who were being brought up in ignorance of how to read Irish learning to do so, and in the evening times he made one of them, in turn, read out from the Irish translation a chapter of the "Imitation of Christ," never interrupting them as they read, but afterwards reading it over himself,

Page 5

and explaining any diffucult passages. All through his long life he kept up the practice of having a chapter in Irish of the "Imitation" read to his household every night. In the evening time he encouraged the singers, story-tellers, and musicians of the neighbourhood to gather to his house, around the fireside if in winter time, and in the open at his door in the summer time. Seated in the centre he encouraged them to sing and recite in Irish and play the music of the country. To translate "Moore's Melodies," of which he was passionately fond, into Irish, and to give them to the people to sing became one of his strong desires. A little girl relative used to play them over to him on the piano, but there were times when she was not available. Bishop MacHale then played no instrument, and he solved the difficulty by getting the young girl to teach him the piano. Perhaps no incident could more illustrate the man than the fact that at the time when his name was a power in the Church, when English Ministers counted him one of the great Irish difficulties, when his days were busy with the affairs of the diocese and the defence of the poor, his evenings were spent learning the piano from a little girl, that he might put the knowledge to use for the Gael, or sitting in the midst of the peasantry, encouraging and exhorting them to retain the language, legend and music of the country, and pass them on to their children.

The political and religious activities of the great and many-sided man do not fall within this sketch of an Irish-Ireland Revivalist. It is enough to say that time has vindicated his prescience and wisdom in nearly every matter in which he was at loggerheads with his contemporaries. Monsignor O'Reilly's observation that the misfortune of this great Irishman -- if it could be called a misfortune -- was that he was always in advance of the Churchmen and statesmen who surrounded him, that his keen clear mind penetrated to the heart of things and saw clearly in the far-off future the result of the false policy of the day is wholly true. He was a great Churchman, but he did not hesitate to rebuke O'Connell for assenting to the disfranchisement of the Forty Shilling Freeholders in exchange for Catholic Emancipation. By such a bargain he told O'Connell he benefited the Catholic few, but injured the Catholic many. A statement proved tragically true in the wholesale eviction of the small land holders who then ceased to be of any political importance to the great land owners, and the restriction of the franchise for decades debarred the people at large from any real control over those who professed to represent them.

In 1834 on the death of the Archbishop of Tuam, the Bishops of the province unanimously declared for Dr. MacHale as the Metropolitan, but the English Government, which regarded him as a formidable opponent -- perhaps a more formidable opponent than O'Connell -- despatched a special messenger to the Pope, requesting him not to appoint the fearless Bishop of Killala. "Anybody but MacHale", wrote Lord Palmerston to the Holy See. But the Pope who then sat in the chair of Peter was not amenable to the influences which the British Government had successfully used before. "No place of preferment of any value ever falls vacant in Ireland," says Gregory XV1., "that I do not get an application from the British Government asking for the appointment." Pope Gregory rejected the British request and appointed Dr. MacHale Archbishop of Tuam. The news of the appointment was received with delight in Ireland, which, aware of the intrigue against the Bishop of Killala, was quivering with excitement for the result. The hills of Connaught blazed with rejoicing fires, and every fair and market echoed with songs in praise of Pope Gregory and the Archbishop he had given to Ireland. The scene when he left the Bishopric to take up his position as Metropolitan has never been surpassed in the history of the West. He was accompanied by tens of thousands of the people whom he was leaving and they were met at Pontoon Bridge by tens of thousands of those whom hence forward he was to dwell amongst. All knelt for his blessing, and the Bishop, raising up his voice until it echoed round the mountains, addressed the people in the language that was his and theirs, extolling their fidelity to their faith, and urging a similar fidelity to their country.

On his pastoral visitation and on his travels, the Archbishop always used the Irish language. His Sunday sermons were given in the same language, for as he drily observed, the rich were able to get instruction from books, but the Irish-speaking poor had to look to the pulpit.

12/1/29

THE IRISH TOURIST TRADE POSSIBILITIES.

It is not generally recognised in this country that if we only rightly availed ourselves of our many advantages and made right and proper use of our abundant opportunities we have in our unrivalled scenery, mountains, lakes, valleys, lowlands and highlands, a priceless tourist asset and a regular treasure. But we must utilise the gifts of Nature and not consider them merely as an unemployed talent. We could capture the growing American trade a hundredfold by judicious and careful consideration and regard for the comfort of our visitors -- giving them of the best, the cleanest and most comfortable accommodation and conveyance. We also should not worry our visitors with our pestilent politics, for that is the one thing they come to Europe to avoid. A great many in Ireland seem to imagine because a few Irish-Americans who come here openly profess a great interest in our political affairs that all do and accordingly every comer, whether he likes it or not, is pestered with our domestic squabbles, for such our politics are in their eyes. Now this is about the last thing Americans want or wish to be worried by. Truth to say, as every candid American will tell you, they are sick of Irish politics as they understood them for years and they would enjoy their stay here and come oftener if we simply did what they expect us now to do, settled down to steady work and let our wretched provincial, very provincial, politics alone. America has millions to spend on profitable and safe investment but not a cent will be laid out in Ireland as long and so long as it continues in a state of unrest and does not present a settled appearance, as say, Germany, France or any continental country but a few Balkan states, ever in a state of turmoil, do. As we said last week America is looking for outlets for its unemployed millions but Ireland, so far, owing to the attitude of a certain political party here, causing as it does a certain sense of uneasiness and unrest, is not looked favourably upon, and we are suffering for our folly. We could have thousands more American tourists here if we presented them what they expect and look for, a settled condition of restfulness, an ordered peacefulness and an universal disposition to work. Tourists who go to France or Germany, Switzerland or Italy, see the people there in town and country go about their ordinary business in a serious, steady, methodical way and they are impressed by their appearance. They see and read of no idle and upsetting nonsense as they are too often, if they come to Ireland, bound to be bothered with. Hundreds of tourists have informed the writer abroad that what keeps them from visiting Ireland is the unrest and the eternal political jingle and clatter which once they hear they are determined never to go in the way of listening to again. Our Hotels and conveyances have much to learn also and they are yet miles behind the ordered cleanliness and comfort of continental hotels and carriers who make it their business to please their customers. We have made some progress we admit and allow gladly but we are bound to go farther and do much more if we want to make the Tourist trade a really steady business asset. In this connection we read very pointed remarks in the "Times" of a few days ago advocating the claims of the Cross Channel tunnel and so attract tourists to these countries. There was also a letter from Professor Richardson, of University College, London, advocating the Irish Channel tunnel from Stranraer across to Larne -- a perfectly feasible undertaking -- which would certainly help the Tourist movement here and flood the country with visitors.

The tourist industry, as a whole, is one of the biggest commercial propositions in the world - and England does not get anything like her share of it, and certainly not Ireland. Exact figures about the number of visitors to any country and the amount they spend in it are not at the moment obtainable, but calculations made from different angles by British, French and American officials and those made by the League of Nations all give substantially the same results. It is calculated, says the writer, that 1,800,000 people visited France last year; and that only 412,000 visited England. The number who came to England was probably even less, for a Government return shows that during July, August, and September the number was 108,888 -- and these being holiday months the total for the year would probably be well under 400,000. Now why should the share of England be less than a quarter the share of France and Ireland a lesser share than either? A calculation made by the League of Nations in 1924 shows that the American visitors spent £70,000,000 in Europe, of which £50,000,000 went to France, the remaining £20,000,000 being divided between all of the rest of Continental Europe and Great Britain, and the United States official calculation is that American tourists in 1927 spent £180,000,000 in Europe, and on the 1924 proportions Great Britain would not get a fifth or perhaps not even a tenth of this. The tourist traffic is a potential source of an enormous addition to national income. Experienced observers say that the average expenditure of a tourist in London is about £5 a day, with an average total of about £80 for the stay. With all the historical, romantic, natural, racial, and commercial attractions of this country, what is the reason why the number of our visitors is so small -- why does our less than 400,000, not become a million, and our £20,000,000 or £30,000,000 not become £80,000,000 or £100,000,000? There are several reasons, but one of the most important, we think *the* most important, is the widespread dislike and dread of the two Channels crossing. Everyone knows from his own experience scores who for that reason do not come to England and Ireland. We have only to-day had a letter from the South of France which says:- " I can from my own experience testify to the very large number of French and Continental people who would come to Britain were it not for the repellant experience of the Channel crossing."

We are advocates for the Tunnel, for if the Tunnel were built it would double or treble our tourist business alone, and this country cannot say "No" to anything that would so enormously increase profitable business, simply because a few gentlemen are more developed in their bumps of caution -- or shall we say fear -- than in their broad judgement.

Professor Richardson, of London University College, writing on the Irish Tunnel, says :-

"I see no reason why the idea of a continuous road and rail scheme should not be extended to Northern Ireland by means of a submarine rail and road between Stranraer and Larne. Such a scheme as the roadway beneath the Channel would give this country a great outlet for its traffic. No matter what the weather - rain, snow, storm - those thirty-two miles of tunnelled roadway which my engineering friends on both sides tell me can be accomplished would always be free. It would be advantageous to have openings at intervals between the roadways and the railway, in case it became necessary to transfer any broken-down vehicle to be cleared by train. The fact that you are working four tunnels instead of one would facilitate construction, because the surplus earth could be worked out on various routes. It would be much more rapid to build four side-by-side tunnels than two or one. What is the good of merely a railway line? We want a great arterial road connecting with the great Continental roads. The scheme of a roadway beneath the Channel would place it within the reach of all, in this democratic age, to take an omnibus from anywhere to France."

TUAM GOLF CLUB.

A GRAND DANCE

Will Be Held In The

WOOL STORES, TUAM,

On

Sunday Night, Jan, 27th, 1929.

Dancing 10 p.m. Gents, 10/-, Ladies, 7/6.

HALL WILL DANCE 200 COUPLES.
DRESS OPTIONAL.

H.B. MANGAN, HON. SEC.

26/1/29

Cumann Na gCleas Luth nGaedealach.

INTER-PROVINCIAL CHAMPIONSHIPS
FOOTBALL SEMI-FINAL

CONNACHT V MUNSTER at TUAM

ON SUNDAY, 3RD FEB, 1929,
Match 3 p.m.

Referee : Mr. MARTIN O'NEILL, Sec. Leinster Council.

Admission . . 1s
Side Line, 1s Extra.

A GRAND
SELECT DANCE

will be held in

THE TOWN HALL,

Commencing at 9 o'Clock.
Tickets, 7/6---5/- Including Supper.

26/1/29

HARRIERS CONTEST IN TUAM.

Under ideal weather conditions and before a small attendance the cross-country championship of Connaught between Ballinasloe and Tuam was run off at Parkmore on Sunday last. Considering that they were practically a green team, with but little previous training, Tuam made a fairly good show, one of their number, Luke O'Brien, making a dashing third, finishing close behind the two, leading Ballinasloe men. Miko Fahy, on whom Tuam's hopes were centred to make a good fight, owing to indisposition, did not run up to his usual form. Still the Tuam boys stood the gruelling course of 6 and a quarter miles (5 times around Parkmore) quite well, and only two of the team in the last lap were forced to cry quits. The time of the winning team was 36 mins. 2 secs. and the placings for both teams were as follows :-

Ballinasloe—J.Connaughton and J.Jennings tied for 1st ; J.Crosby, 4th ; T. Connaughton, 5th ; T.Murray, 7th ; T.Tully, 9th ; J.Cunningham, 10th ; J.Cogavin, 13th ; Dn. Prat, 14th ; J.Burke, 17th ; P. Burke, 18th.

Tuam—Luke O'Brien, 3rd ; Albert Cummins, 6th ; P.Colleran, 8th ; M.Fahy, 11th ; P.Burke, 12th ; J.Martin, 15th ; M.Greally, 16th ; N. Mc Nally, 19th ; R. Whitty, 20th; F. Burke, 21st.

The Points awarded for the first six of each team were :- Ballinasloe, 1,2,4,5,7,9—Total, 28. Tuam, 2,6,8,11,12,15—Total, 55.

2/2/29

G.A.A DANCE.

A GRAND

Select Dance

will be held in

THE TOWN HALL,

ON SUNDAY NIGHT, FEBRUARY 3rd

Commencing at 9 o'Clock,
Tickets, 7/6—5/- Including Supper.

2/2/29

RUGBY FOOTBALL.

TUAM V. GALWEGIANS.

On Sunday, 20th inst. Tuam met Galwegians II, at home. The home side just managed to register a win by 3pts to nil. They missed several opportunities through hanging on to the ball too long, but then Galwegians were unlucky not to score too as they were on the whole a better side.

The return match was played in Galway on the following Sunday. The Tuam team at last showed their proper form and won by the handsome margin of 17pts. to 6pts. Galwegians opened the scoring with two unconverted tries, but by half time Glynn had equalised by two well-placed penalty goals.

Shortly after resuming play Glynn again kicked a fine penalty goal from a very difficult position near the touch line. Hehir just failed to score when he kicked the ball dead and O'Connor crossed the line again but was penalised for carrying the ball along the ground.

By this time the Tuam forwards were packing and heeling like veterans and were more than able for their opponents in both tight and loose scrums. Glynn paved the way for the next score by cross-kicking to Fox who crossed the line close to the touch. Fox again scored between the posts just before the final whistle. Glynn converted. Of the forwards O'Connor and Hehir were outstanding, while O'Brien as hooker was quite sound. The pack worked well as a whole and showed fine dash in the loose.

Of the backs, Glynn, O'Sullivan and O'Carroll were sound while Fox was easily the fastest man on the field and showed great opportunism and dash. If the team can reproduce the form it showed on Sunday last it should go far in the Cup competitions.

2/2/29

PARTWORN CLOTHING—Men's Trousers' 2/6 ; Jackets, 2s 6d ; Waistcoats, 1/- ; Overcoats, 5/6 ; New Shoes, 2s ; Suits, 7/6 ; Ladies Coats, 2/- ; Costumes, 3/- ; send stamp for list ; cheapest firm. Newman, Raines St., Blackburn.

CROSS-COUNTRY CHAMPIONSHIP.

TO THE EDITOR TUAM HERALD

SIR—In your last issue I read " Tuam is looking up in Athletics. For the first time in her history the Junior Cross-Country Championship of Connacht will be run off at Parkmore....A keen and exciting contest is anticipated." It gave me great pleasure to read this, although, unfortunately, I was unable to take part in or watch the race. On 9th July, 1928, through the medium of your valuable paper, I advocated more cross-country running in this district and I congratulate the Tuam boys who take part in this and other similar forms of sport. I do not mean to suggest that cross-country running is superior in any way to other forms of sport. I also advocate football, hockey, boxing and many other dismounted and mounted sports, for, as I have often said, I believe that athletics helps, not only to produce men and boys, strong and healthy in mind and body, but also to build up a spirit of true sportsmanship, fair play and goodwill.

I still think that too many men and boys are content to be spectators instead of taking part in sports themselves. To those I would say, " Start now while you have the chance. Don't wait till your chance is gone." I am very glad that I went in for Rugger and Boxing when I had the chance. I cannot do so any more owing to a broken nose. But this does not prevent me from playing hockey, cross-country running etc. So long as a man or boy is physically fit I don't think its ever too late to start a new form of sport, though it is better to start young. In 1927 I encouraged about 30 fellows to take up cross-country running (ages 19 to 22) some of whom had never done any before, and they thoroughly enjoyed it. It is true that some of them were already athletic, being members of a football team of which I was Hon. Sec. After taking part in 2 smaller races, 12 of us took part in a 7 mile race in which there were about 200 competitors.

I do not suggest that anyone should neglect his work for the sake of sport, but it is my humble opinion that in his spare time a boy should, in most cases, be able to take part in some form of sport.

There are many sporting organisations in Tuam, e.g. the Tuam Star Football Club, (G.A.A.), The Tuam Rugby Football Club, etc., etc. I wish them all every success and I hope that they will continue to grow and prosper.

I would also like to thank publicly the Toghermore Sports Committee who have continued the Athletic Sports meetings which I started in 1925 and 1926.

Yours, &c,

R.M.BURKE.

Toghermore, Tuam, 27-1-29

2/2/29

The Pen Hospital

Civil Servants and others in responsible clerical positions will be glad to learn that we repair in Dublin all makes of Fountain Pens and Propelling Pencils.
LIGHT CHARGES.
IMMEDIATE EXPERT WORK.
THE PEN CORNER,
12 COLLEGE GREEN, DUBLIN

ANEW Mc MASTER CO.

The above Co. started their week's programme in the Mall Cinema on yesterday (Friday) evening with "Mr. Wu." and we are asked to say that to convenience business people in town the play "The School for Scandal" billed for this (Saturday) night will not start until 9 o'clock. It is interesting to note that the costumes used in "School for Scandal" are the original ones used by Sir Herbert Tree in his production of that play at His Majesty's Theatre, London. These were designed by Percy McQuaid, R.A., and are probably the most beautiful ever seen on the stage in Tuam.

Intending patrons will be well advised to book their seats in advance, which can be obtained from 12 to 2 each day at the Cinema.

THE LEADER

THE ORIGIN OF IRISH IRELAND.
All newsagents in Tuam and the rural districts should stock The "Leader."
If unable to secure a copy please send a Post Card to The "Leader" Newspaper, 24 Pearse Street stating the name of your Newsagent.

24 Pages   Price 2d
Specimen copy on application

THE MALL CINEMA, TUAM

For 7 Nights and 2 Matinees commencing
FRIDAY, FEBRUARY 8th
At 8 o'clock.   Matinees at 3.30.
Prices (including Tax) 3/-, 2/4, 1/6 & 1/- (very limited).
NOTE—Matinee Performances by the McMaster Company are Full Versions, and exactly the same in all particulars as the Nightly ones.

Seats may be booked at the Cinema Daily.

PERSONAL VISIT (With Entire Dublin Festival Company) OF

ANEW McMASTER

(Leading Man with Gladys Cooper, Adelphi Theatre, London, 1925, Leading Man with Oscar Asche, 1923-1924) with his
INTIMATE SHAKESPEAREAN COMPANY

Friday at 8.30 Mathesan Lang's Great Chinese Play

"MR WU."

(By special arrangement with Martin Henry, Esq.)
Production an exact replica of that at the Strand Theatre, London.

Saturday at 9 sharp

THE SCHOOL FOR SCANDAL

By Brinsley Sheridan
Magnificent production of the Play which Sir H. Tree described as "Undisputedly the most brilliant Comedy that has been given to the world." The Costumes are those used by Sir Herbert Tree in his production at His Majesty's Theatre, London.

Sunday Matinee ...	ROMEO AND JULIET
Sunday Night at 8.15...	HAMLET
Monday	OTHELLO
Tuesday Matinee	THE MERCHANT OF VENICE.

Tuesday Night (The Famous Play)
DAVID GARRICK.
Wednesday   RICHARD III
(Anew McMaster in his latest great Shakespearean part).
Thursday (Goldsmith's World Famous Comedy)

SHE STOOPS TO CONQUER.

Full Company of 25 Artistes.
The Music is supplied by the Panatrope Orchestral Reproducer which is the latest Electrical Musical Invention.

SHAKESPEARE

Beautifully Acted, Beautifully Dressed, Beautifully Staged.

2/2/29

G.A.A.

At Skehanagh on Sunday last before a large crowd Tuam gave a very classical display when defeating Mountbellew by 1 goal 3 pts. to 1 goal.

Tuam were outstanding in back play when the Mountbellew forwards were overpowered and could not even send one ball over in the first half. The game began with a few rough tussles before the referee got the players under control.

From this onwards the game was first-class football with few fouls and very few touches. P. Kelly, Tuam, was the outstanding player in the centre-field during this half of the game. P. Hannon, McCormack, Mannion and Waldron were the outstanding backs. The full-back, H. Burke, got very little to do in this half. Tuam forwards were weak with the exception of H. Cunningham who played a very outstanding game throughout the whole hour, and so did T. Hughes.

The scores by Tuam in the first half were got by T. Hughes and M. Stewart, who scored a point each, and a goal by P. Walsh. Their forwards missed a few more scores in this half. The outstanding players for Mountbellew during this half were Keyes, Bannerton, and Dermody backs, and Paul Colleran forward.

The scores stood at the half time whistle—Tuam, 1 goal 2 pts.; Mountbellew, nil.

In the second half Mountbellew played much better football for 15 minutes than their opponents, but the sun was affecting the Tuam players who were easily beaten for a soft goal per McCormack for Mountbellew. This excited the game which gave Tuam still the lead of two points. Keyes for Mountbellew was playing well until nearing the end when he fell out owing to an injury to his ankle. Tuam increased their scores a few minutes after by a point per M. Stewart. Tuam forwards missed a few more scores in this half but they kept the play towards the Mountbellew goal, and when the final whistle was going Tuam were scoring their fourth point but was not counted.

The following represented Tuam :— H. Cunningham (capt.); H. Burke, T. Joyce, M. Mannion, P. Hannon, J. O'Rorke, D. McCormack, Waldron, Kelly, Birrell, Hughes, Reid, Walsh, Stewart, Nohilly.

9/2/29

MR HOGAN AT HEADFORD.

Speaking at a Cumann na nGaedheal convention at Headford, County Galway, last week, Mr. Patrick Hogan, Minister for Agriculture in the Irish Free State, said that the leaders of the Fianna Fail Party had recently been expounding their economic policy; but, as the discussions of the Economic Committee had now reached a definite stage, he did not want to deal with Mr de Valera's statement until the discussions are over. The so-called Republican programme of no exports to England did not appeal to him at all. He (Mr. Hogan) thought that the best of everything was not half good enough for the Englishman, and the only objection that he had was that the English were not paying them enough for their cattle, sheep and pigs.

The farmers of the country would agree with him that the policy of no exports would lead the country to ruin. Coupled with that policy was the one for putting tariffs on everything. What did it amount to? Most of everything that they wanted to buy should be highly paid for, and if they wanted to sell they should sell cheaply to their neighbours. If that policy were put into operation a lot of the so-called patriotic farmers would change their minds very quickly. This policy was to appeal to the long-haired, blue-eyed, pale-faced patriots who never managed a farm or a shop.

THE LAND ANNUITIES.

The only real policy that Fianna Fail had was to pay no annuities—asking the Irish people to embezzle the money lent to them for land purchase. No matter what form of government they had, if the people in bad times repudiated their debts the country would go down. Fianna Fail said the payment of the land annuities was illegal. It was open to Fianna Fail to bring an injunction against the Minister for Finance and have the matter tested in the Courts. They did not bring it, because they knew that they did not have a leg to stand on. If they repudiated the land annuities, they would have proved themselves unfit for self-government. He was willing to make that the issue in the next election, as he believed that there is enough honesty, decency and civilisation in the country to make certain that if the people understood the issue they would vote right on it.

Mr. Hogan then went on to refer to five articles which recently appeared in the "Morning Post." These articles, he said, were trying to show that since the English went away the Free State was going into decay and bankruptcy, and that neither life, limb nor property was safe. The articles were accompanied by extracts from speeches of the Fianna Fauil orators. He had read similar articles in the "Nation," the Fianna Fail organ. The "Nation" and the organ of the most die-hard English Toryism were both preaching the gospel of defeatism and decay. The object of both was to wreck the foundations laid for the Free State and neither cared twopence what happened afterwards.

COMPLETING THE BUILDING.

We have laid the foundation, concluded Mr. Hogan, of a modern civilised state, where all men are equal before the law, and we intend to complete the building, in spite of all enemies, external or internal. (Applause)

Mr. Sean Broderick, T.D.; Mr. Peter Kelly, County Councillor, who presided, and Mr. Patrick Fury, County Councillor, also spoke.

A vote of sympathy with the relatives of the late Dr. Michael Davit was passed.

9/2/29

FOOTBALL MATCH POSTPONED.

The football match between Munster and Connacht, fixed for Tuam on to-morrow (Sunday) has been postponed, pending the decision of a special meeting of the Central Council, which has been called for this (Saturday) evening.

DANCE IN TOWN HALL.

The dance announced to be held in the Town Hall after the match has not been affected by the postponement and the Committee in charge have decided that their motto will be "On With the Dance." A high class orchestra has been engaged, and other arrangements are as nearly perfect as an energetic committee can make them, so that a gala night's amusement may be anticipated.

9/2/29

MR. DE VALERA'S IMPRISONMENT.

TUAM TOWN COMMISSIONERS PROTEST.

A special meeting of the Tuam Town Commissioners was called on Monday evening to protest against the action of the Northern Government in imprisoning Mr. De Valera, T.D.

The chairman, Mr. J. Burke, presided, and the other members present were; Messrs. P. Walsh, S. Fahy, P. Dwyer, Byrne, Wilson, P. Gibbons, James Moran, M. Cooney, J.H. Corcoran, W. Holian, M.O'Keeffe.

The chairman explained that the meeting was called as a protest and condemnation of the action of the Northern Government in arresting Mr. de Valera and placing him in prison. The Commissioners joined in condemning such a bigoted and unwarranted action. Although he would not advocate reprisals - as God knows they had enough of them - people in the rest of Ireland were not so powerless that they could not let those bigots see they were not going to have it all their own way. In arresting De Valera the Northern Government had offered an insult to the people of the rest of the country who believed in his leadership and believe in Ireland a nation, and a Gaelic-speaking nation at that.

Mr. Corcoran said that Tuam was the first town to put on the trade boycott against Northern Ireland. He thought the Tuam traders should come together again and protest against travellers from the North of Ireland gettting orders. On Friday he had a traveller from a Belfast firm- a tea house- and he said to him; 'How do you expect me to give you an order when you have the leader of Fianna Fail, which is the opposition party to the present party in power, arrested and imprisoned? Until such time as you release him I will not give an order to a Belfast house.'

Mr. Holian - And the purchasers should boycott goods from that quarter.

Mr. Corcoran- Every trader should protest against giving orders to them.

Mr. Walsh - Every trader and merchant in the Free State, because it is an insult to the merchants in all Ireland.

Mr. Holian -The traders and purchasers in Tuam should boycott the goods that come from Northern Ireland.

Mr. Cooney - Considering the mission De Valera was on - it was not politics but was to help the revival of the Gaelic tongue in Belfast and Northern Ireland, it is up to every man in both the Free State and Six Counties to show they protest against the action of the Northern Government by enforcing the boycott, which should never have been lifted. It was owing to the kindness of poor Michael Collins who thought that by taking off the boycott it would be the means of gettting Catholics back to work. The Belfast boycott started in Tuam and it should be started again and spread all over Ireland and not give a single order until the Northern Government come in under the Free State altogether. Mr. De Valera will be out at the end of the month but the boycott should be kept up. They in the North pretend there is no intolerance. At social engagements they say they do not want any Border - that was all Freemasonry. He hoped the traders in the West of Ireland will endorse Mr. Corcoran's suggestion.

Mr. Fahy proposed a resolution calling for the release of Mr. De Valera within forty-eight hours and if not that the boycott should be put on. Mr. De Valera should be privileged to go to any part of Ireland where he wanted to go.

Mr. Cooney - I am sure Mr. De Valera would prefer to put in the month in jail than be released to-morrow morning.

Mr. Fahy - But I don't see why the man should be kept in suffering for no reason.

Mr. Corcoran - What Mr. Cooney suggests will have more effect. I believe Mr. De Valera is willing and prepared to put in his month, and it is a trump card for him to have to do it.

Mr. Fahy- I admit that, but at the same time I wish to demand his release and compel them to release him.

Mr. Dwyer - We all know that Mr. De Valera was never afraid to go to jail. I second Mr. Fahy's proposition, and when you speak of the Belfast boycott you must not forget that in Dublin there are branch houses of Belfast firms which should be included in the boycott.

Mr. Corcoran - They were included the last time.

Mr. Dwyer - It is a short-sighted policy. Why should Mr. De Valera be arrested any more than any man in the country? It seems they are afraid of Mr. De Valera.

Mr. Holian - I suggest that the shopkeepers of the town be asked to enforce the boycott.

Mr Fahy - If they release De Valera within forty-eight hours it is not necessary.

Chairman - We cannot enforce the boycott but we can call on the traders to enforce the boycott if Mr. De Valera is not released within forty-eight hours.

The following resolution was proposed by Mr. Simon Fahy, seconded by Mr. John H. Corcoran, and passed unanimously;-

'That we, the Town Commissioners, strongly protest against the imprisonment of Mr. De Valera, T.D. by the Northern Government of Ireland, and we demand his release within 48 hours, otherwise we will call upon the business people of Ireland to enforce the Trade Boycott against the merchants of Belfast.'

16/2/29

B. S. A. NON-EJECTOR, 11GNS.
EJECTOR, 14 GNS

Come to T. J. Mellin's for Shot Guns.

We have in stock a range of the famous B.S.A. Shot Guns—guns which have repeatedly proved their superior shooting power in the field. For all round service they are unrivalled, being exceptionally strong and well made, light, and perfectly balanced with snappy trigger pulls. All parts are interchangeable. The price is very low for such high-grade guns, each carrying the full printed B.S.A. guarantee.

Sole Agent for Tuam and District for

Cartridges and all shooting accessories supplied at reasonable prices. We guarantee satisfaction. Call or write for lists!

T.J.MELLIN
TUAM

HARWARD WADE, SON and CO., LTD.
(THE FARMER'S MILLERS).
CHARGES.

	per cwt
Wheat for "Coskeen"	1/4
Oats for Oatmeal	1/4
Wheat, Oats, Barley and Rye, Kiln Dried and Crushed	1/-

(It is a Farmer's interest to support the Mills started, owned and conducted by Farmers. Those who live at a distance can have their Corn ground in a few days by communicating with the Secretary.)

T.BRENNAN WADE,
Cregg Mills, Corrandulla,
Galway   16/2/29

COOKERY DEMONSTRATIONS.

One of the principal attractions in Tuam next week will undoubtedly be the series of practical Cookery Demonstrations which will be given on behalf of Brown & Polson Ltd., the well known makers of Corn Flour and "Raisley" (formerly named Paisley Flour) by Mrs. B.S. George, 1st Class Diplomee, Glasgow.

We understand that the Town Hall has been booked for February 18th-22nd, 1929, inclusive. Demonstrations will be given each afternoon from 3 to 4 o'clock and each evening from 7.30 to 8.30 o'clock. No charge will be made for admission and everything will be done to ensure the comfort of visitors.

Looking at the programme we must confess our surprise at the numerous, inexpensive, tempting dishes which Corn Flour makes, such as soups, sauces for fish and vegetables, savouries, hot and cold sweets.

An interesting feature of the Demonstration is a Home Baking Competition, particulars of which are given on the programme. Valuable prizes will be offered for the best cake sent in and ladies need have no fear of unfair competition as professional cooks are not allowed to compete.

16/2/29

THE IRISH ROSARY, -- Racy, Readable. The only Irish Catholic Illustrated Journal, Eminently attractive. Price 4 1/2d.

A correspondent says that over 50 couples attended the G.A.A. dance held in the Town Hall, Tuam, on Sunday night. The music was supplied by the Follies Band, Galway, and dancing was kept up until the small hours of the morning.

A much felt public want is about being supplied. Mr. W.J. Concannon proposed at the meeting of the Galway Board of Health on Wednesday, that a public latrine be erected in Tuam town. Mr. Collins, B.E., said he estimated that it would cost about £300, but he would endeavour to have it carried out more cheaply if possible. Mr Gilbert Lynch seconded the proposal, which was passed. Mr Concannon said it was principally for the benefit of country people that he had brought the matter on, and he suggested that Tuam rural district (which comprises the whole Tuam union) be fixed as the area of charge. This was agreed to.

16/2/29

LENT, 1929.

TO THE CLERGY AND LAITY OF THE ARCHDIOCESE OF TUAM.

My dear Brethren,

PART 1.

The following are the regulations for fast and abstinence during the coming Lent;-

1. There will be no black fast in future; milk may be used on all days, even days such as Ash Wednesday or Good Friday.

2. If meat is allowed at a meal, fish may be taken with it.

3. There is neither fast nor abstinence on Holy Saturday after 12 o'clock, nor on the Sundays of Lent, nor on St. Patrick's Day.

4. Flesh meat is allowed at the principal meal on all days of Lent except Wednesdays and Fridays and Ember Saturday, which falls this year on February 23rd.

5. Eggs, butter, milk foods and condiments, such as lard or dripping, are allowed at dinner on all Wednesdays and Fridays of Lent and on Ember Saturday.

6. Those between 7 and 21 years of age, and those who have completed their 59th year, are bound to abstain unless otherwise excused.

7. Those who have completed their 21st year and have not entered on their 60th year are bound both to fast and abstain unless otherwise excused. They are allowed one full meal each day and in addition a collation in the morning and a small quantity of food in the evening - the quality and quantity of the food at these meals in the morning and evening to be regulated by the custom of the place.

8. Those exempt from fasting by reason of age, infirmity or labour, are permitted to take at every meal what is allowed at the principal meal.

9. Not only Ordinaries but Parish Priests and Administrators may for a just cause dispense in paricular cases their subjects and others staying in the locality from the observance of fast and abstinence. Confessors may for a just cause dispense their penitants in Confession.

10. In compensation for these generous relaxations it is reasonably expected that the faithful will contribute according to their means to the Lenten Collection fixed for the First Sunday of Lent. The money contributed is devoted altogether to Diocesan Charities.

These regulations represent the form of penance that is usually associated with the Lenten Season. They are very mild compared with the Lent of olden times. But if the Church is willing to relax the old strict laws of fast and abstinence she must still insist on the necessity of penance. The essential idea of penance is a change of heart. In the lesson which is read in the Mass of Ash Wednesday this change of heart is thus expressed by the prophet Joel (11, 12, 13).

"Thus saith the Lord: Be converted to me with all your heart, in fasting and in weeping and in mourning. And rend your heart and not your garments, and turn to the Lord your God: for he is gracious and merciful, patient and rich in mercy, and ready to repent of the evil".

Those inspired words make it plain that conversion of the heart is the first element of penance. So much the better if there is fasting and weeping and mourning. But if there be no fasting, nor weeping, nor mourning, there must be evidence of a sincere conversion of the heart to God. This evidence is to be found in a good confession, i.e. a Confession in which all grave sins are confessed with a firm purpose of amendment, with a willingness to perform the penance and other duties enjoined by the Confessor and with a firm determination to avoid the occasions of sin. The wilful concealment of one mortal sin in Confession is evidence that there is no conversion of the heart to God. Wilful neglect to perform the penance enjoined by the Confessor for grave sin is a sign that there was no deep, sincere desire "to turn to the Lord your God". Refusal to make restitution for dishonesty or to make reparation for injury to a neighbour is clear evidence that there is no penance. And what is to be thought of a penitent who in the tribunal of Penance made a solemn promise to avoid voluntary and proximate occasions of sin and yet within a short time returned to those occasions and sold the shining garment of sanctifying grace for a base sensual pleasure? Can there be a sincere conversion to God when there is no more stable change of heart? A relapse into sin is not, thank God, proof that there was no penance, but repeated relapses caused by frequenting the same occasions of grave sin -- occasions that could be avoided -- create a strong presumption that there has been no true conversion of the heart to God.

And what pressing motives there are to make sure that our penance is genuine. For those who have turned away from God by mortal sin, penance is absolutely necessary for salvation. What was the burden of John's preaching on the banks of the Jordan? "Do penance for the Kingdom of God is at hand" (Matt. 11, 2). This is the clear teaching of Jesus Christ who said "Unless you do penance you shall all likewise perish" (Luke X111, 3). If the rich man "who died and was buried in hell" and who is still asking in vain for "a drop of water to cool his burning tongue" -- if he got a chance of coming back to earth what do you think would his penance be? Among the Saints who were remarkable for works of penance is St. Peter of Alcantara. For forty years he slept but an hour and a half of the twenty-four; for his pillow during that short sleep he had a piece of wood driven into the wall; he never covered his feet; his only garment of sackcloth; his ordinary practice was to eat once in three days. St. Teresa of Spain tells us that she was, after his death, permitted to see him in great glory, and what do you think were his first words to her. They were, she tells us, "Oh! blessed Penance which has merited so great a reward". The world would look on St. Peter of Alcantara as a fool and would pay court to Dives. But which of them was the fool?

Now you are asked to imitate the penances of St. Peter of Alcantara. The more penance you do the nearer you will be to him in the glory of Heaven. But if you do not do penance for grave sin and turn to the Lord your God, you cannot hope to escape the fate of Dives. If today your hear the Voice of God calling you to penance "do not harden your heart". Do not say I am too bad to do penance for did not Christ tell us that He came not to call the just but sinners to repentance. One drop of the blood of Christ is sufficient to atone for the blackest guilt but only on condition that the sinner does penance for his sin and makes reparation, as far as it can be done, for any injury done to his neighbour. Through penance the foulest sinner can return to God. He can return through penance from what is most base to what is most beautiful. He can return from the husks of swine to a banquet in his father's house. Through penance he can return from slavery under Satan who is waiting to drag him into hell -- from this slavery he can return to freedom and happiness in the embrace of a God "Who is gracious and merciful, patient and rich in mercy".

Most vehemently then do I exhort you all to do penance during the coming Lent. If you have not committed very grave sins, you must admit to yourselves that you have committed many venial sins. And for venial sins too there is no pardon except through penance. Easy as the laws of fast and abstinence now are, there may be some on whom they would press too hard, but then there are many other forms of self-denial both interior and exterior. Whenever from a motive of penance you do something good against your own inclination or omit doing something pleasant to nature -- not obligatory, you are practising self-denial. To bear crosses patiently is also true penance. Through both you will become the disciple of Jesus Christ Who has said "If any man will come after me, let him deny himself, take up his cross and follow me" (Matt. XVI.24).

There are two Celebrations this year in which you are invited to participate. One is the fiftieth anniversary of the Pope's ordination to the priesthood; the other is the centenary of Catholic Emancipation. As regards the first, Our Holy Father has proclaimed an extraordinary Jubilee Indulgence which can be gained on easy conditions. These conditions will, later on, be explained in detail to you by the clergy. It was a most gracious act on the part of the Vicar of Christ to make the Jubilee of his ordination to the priesthood an occasion of opening to the Faithful throughout the world the treasures of the Church, and I am sure that in taking advantage of his benevolence by gaining the Jubilee Indulgence you will not forget to pray for his intentions and also to pray in the words of the Liturgy "that the Lord may preserve and give him life, and make him blest upon the earth, and may not deliver him to the intentions of his foes".

As regards the Catholic Emancipation Centenary, the Bishops have asked the Catholic Truth Society to organise the details of this Celebration. To this request there has been a cordial response, and the following programme has been approved by the Bishops:-

1. The Celebration to begin on Sunday, 16th June, with a general Communion of Thanksgiving throughout all Ireland;

2. The Celebration to end on Sunday, 23rd June, with a Pontifical High Mass in the Phoenix Park followed by a Procession of the Most Holy Sacrament.

3. On the intermediate days papers will be read in Dublin on the long and arduous struggle for Catholic Emancipation;

4. All who take part in the Celebration beginning with the General Communion on Sunday, 16th June, are to wear badges which can be got at 1/- or 6d. and at 3d. for children.

Further information will in due time be published in the Press. I feel sure that the priests and people of this Archdiocese will not be backward in the co-operation required to make this historic occasion a triumphant success.

+ THOMAS
    Archbishop of Tuam,
        St. Jarlath's, Tuam,
        February 1929.

(Part II. will be published in next issue.)

OPERETTA AND CONCERT

In the Town Hall, Tuam, on Thursday and Friday nights, Jan 31st and Feb.1st, " The Knave of Hearts " — an operetta— was performed by the children of the Mercy Convent, Tuam.

For children under 14 years it was truly an excellent performance and the townspeople of Tuam may well feel proud of the talent displayed by the children.

The costumes were original and artistic. The singing and recitation throughout was very good and was remarkable all the more for the purity of diction. In the choruses we had good balance, richness and intelligent interpretation — the rhythm being well preserved and the entries were perfect. The soloists displayed some charming voices and their knowledge of their parts and entries testify to a painstaking preparation. The principal artistes did their parts so well that it is very hard to single out any for special praise, but Miss Kitty Burke (Knave), Miss Peggy Braye (King), and Miss Kitty Lydon (Queen), did their exacting parts in a very creditable manner.

Miss Conroy, who is responsible for the presentation of the piece as also for the training of the children, is to be congratulated on the success of her efforts— the production from such limited talent is a tribute to her genius and enthusiasm.

Miss Kitty McElgunn was an excellent accompanist.

Concert—Miss Kitty McElgunn's piano solos and Miss Lily Grealish's violin solo were well received as were also choruses by the school children, but more applause it seemed was drawn by the Tambourine Dance, (Infant School Children), six-hand reel, hornpipe, and battered jig (Misses Garvey and Ruddy). The "Frog"—a duet—by Misses Bernadette Canavan and Josephine Kelly, was really very good.

PART I.

Operetta—" The Knave of Hearts " (Somerville). Characters—King of Hearts, Miss Peggy Bray; Queen of Hearts, Miss Kitty Lydon; Knave of Hearts , Miss Kitty Burke. Cooks, The Ten of Hearts, Miss Chrissie Lydon; The Nine of Hearts, Miss Dolly Reddan; Kitchen-boy, The Ace, Miss Lily Grealish; Herald, The Eight, Miss Nellie Walsh; Bo Peep, Miss Kathleen Colleran; Queen of the Fairies, Miss Aggie Curran. Courtiers and Fairies.

PART II.

Piano Solo, Miss Kitty McElgunn ; Tambourine Dance, Infant School Children ; Violin Solo, Miss Lily Grealish ; Dance (Double-battered Jig), Misses Mabel Ruddy and Lily Grealish ; Duet (The Frog), Misses Bernadette Canavan and Josephine Kelly ; Dance (The Blackbird), Misses Lily Grealish and Gay Garvey ; Reel, Infant School Children ; Chorus, "I saw from the Beach"; Dance (Six Hand Reel), Infant School Children ; Chorus, (in Four Parts), " The Three Fishers " ; Dance (Humours of Bandon), Misses Peggy Bray , Gay Garvey, Grealish and Ruddy; Chorus, " Caitlin Ni Uallacáin."

16/2/29

LONDON FIRM extending business in Ireland, have vacancies for young men who possess push and initiative, and residing in agricultural districts, to earn assured income with prospects of promotion. Reply to box 24, HERALD Office, Tuam.

ARE YOU THIS MAN ?

The manufacturers of the famous MOLASINE MEAL have vacancies for first class commission agents in districts where not represented. Applicants must have sound connection among farmers. Write The Molassine Co., Ltd., Greenwich S.E.10.

SALESMEN CALLING on farmers required to sell well-known agricultural machine, liberal commission. Reply giving particulars, present occupation, lines (if any carried) and territory covered to :-

C.H.,
167, Downham Road,
Southgate Road,
London. N.1.

Mr W. Concannon has handed in notice of motion to the Galway Board of Health to have the salary of Miss A.G. Costelloe, Woodlands Sanatorium, increased. Miss Costelloe's present salary is £95. The Minister for Local Government has approved an increase in the remuneration of Miss K.Ryan, head nurse at Woodlands Sanatorium to £85 per annum with board, residence, etc. Paddy Nolan, of the Gate Lodge, Woodlands Sanatorium, was granted £2 for certain work he carried out in the grounds.

At the meeting of the Co. Galway Board of Health, the Secretary (M.Gallagher) submitted a return showing the number of unmarried mothers admitted to the Central Hospital last year. The total was 57.

Dr. Bartley O'Beirne, Tuberculosis Medical Officer for County Galway, is suffering from a general breakdown in health and has been ordered a two months rest and change of air.

At the meeting of the Galway Co. Council on Saturday it was decided, on the proposition of Mr. Harry O'Toole, to request the Galway Urban Council to provide seats for the women who sold the home-made stockings in Eglinton Street on market days.

The late Dr. Michael Davitt, University Road, Galway, left £2,480

Motor cars are becoming public dangers. Two cattle were killed and another injured in a collision with a motor car on the road from Partry to Ballinrobe on Monday evening. The cattle were the property of Mr. Mark Mellett, Clooneena, Ballinrobe, and were being driven on the road to Ballinrobe, when, it is alleged, a motor car travelling towards Ballinrobe ran into the cattle, with the consequences stated.

16/2/29

LALLY OF TOLLENDAL.

To the Editor of "The Irish Times."

Sir—In your leading article in to-day's "Irish Times" you state that Lally of Tollendal "fought at Fontenoy, and his services in the arms of the French Crown won him the estate of Tollendal and the Governorship of the French East Indies." You are in error in assuming "Tollendal" is a French word. It is merely a corruption of the Irish word *Tulac na dala* (the hillock of the meeting), or, as it is now called, Tullinadaly, a townland about four miles from Tuam, Co Galway, which was the seat of the Lallys. The full title of Count Lally was James Arthur Bar de Tollendal, Count de Lally. His ancestors were Barons of Tullinadaly until the Williamite Confiscation, the last to be styled Baron of Tullinadaly in Ireland being Colonel James Lally, who was Governor and Sovereign of Tuam for James II, in 1687, and a member of James' last parliament.

The Lallys originally owned large territories in Galway, which they gradually lost to the Normans until nothing was left save the property at Tullinadaly. All that now remains of their name and fame in County Galway is a ruined *leacht* on the main road from Tuam to Claremorris, which bears the following inscription:— "Pray for the soul of James Lally and his family, 1673."

Count Lally was a born fighter. He was taken to camp by his father at the age of eight "to smell powder"; at twelve he was in the trenches at Barcelona, and would have been made a colonel at eighteen but for his father's opposition. At the fight at Etlingen, in 1734, his father was wounded and about to be made a prisoner when the son covered him with his own body and succeeded in rescuing him. He saved the French Army, after the Battle of Dettingen, from destruction, as was testified by Marshal de Noailles, who wrote: "He there rallied the Army several times in its disorder, and saved it in its retreat, through the advice which he laid before the council of war after the action." It will be remembered that it was the desperate valour of the Irish exiles at Dettingen which caused George II to curse the laws which deprived him of such subjects.

The appointment of Count Lally as Commander-in Chief of the French East Indies force was opposed by the French Minister, D'Argenson, on the ground that he was too great a disciplinarian, and too straightforward a man to succeed in the conditions that were known to prevail in India. The Minister's words were an eloquent tribute to the worth of the great Irishman :- "He makes no compromise with respect to discipline, has a horror of everything that is not straightforward, is vexed with everything that does not go on rapidly, is silent upon nothing that he knows, and expresses himself in terms not to be forgotten..... They (the local people) will cause his operations to fail in order to be revenged on him." All of this was tragically true in the result. Describing the final scene at his trial, O'Callaghan, quoting from a French source, says :- " He could not," says an enemy, "bear up against the decree of infamy." Covered with fourteen scars, how hard his destiny to fall into the hands of his executioners! Accordingly then, and not before, he discovered great emotion, uncovered his head, displaying the grey locks of age, bared his breast marked with the wounds of honour, and looking upwards as if appealing from earth to heaven, exclaimed: "Here, then, is the reward of so many years' service!"

The decree of attainder was cancelled by Louis XVI in 1778, and Lally's son received the honours of his father.— Yours, etc.,
JOSEPH A. GLYNN.
Dublin,
February 1st, 1929.

16/2/29

OUR TEAS

Are The Pick of the Market, are unvarying in quality; and give universal satisfaction.

Prices, 1/8, 1/10, 2/-, 2/2, 2/4, 2/6, 2/8, 2/10, 3/-, 3/2. China Teas, at 2/-, 2/8, & 3/2.

BECKER Bros., Ltd.

8 SOUTH GREAT GEORGES STREET,
AND 17 NORTH EARL STREET,
Tel. 156   DUBLIN   Tel. 156

FREE COOKERY DEMONSTRATION

Messrs Brown & Polson, Ltd., invite all ladies interested in cookery and the preparation of food, to attend a series of free cookery lectures and demonstrations to be given by

MRS B. S. GEORGE,
1st Class Diplomee Glasgow,

at the TOWN HALL, TUAM,

from February 18th to 25th.

Afternoon — 3 to 4 p.m.   Evening — 7.30 to 8.30 p.m.

The lecturess will, during the week, prepare, cook and serve a variety of simple, economical and delicious dishes—

Soups	**Vegetables**	**Cakes**
Sauces	**Sweets**	**Puddings**
Fish	**Pastry**	**Savouries, etc.**

Bring your friends along with you.
PRIZE TEST   No entrance fee.

Brown & Polson's

Cornflour,   "Raisley,"   Custard Powder, Semolina and Ground Rice for quality.

The Road to Success and Increased Trade
GIVE YOUR CUSTOMERS THE BEST ON THE MARKET

BLACK SWAN BUTTER   **HAS NO RIVAL**

BLACK SWAN BUTTER — Rolls, Cartons, Bulk.
DOWDALL, O'MAHONY & CO., Ltd.,
Union Quay, Cork, and 29-30 Fleet Street, Dublin

THE DECEMBER RAINFALL.

From measurements taken all over Ireland at several private stations by public spirited individuals creditably inspired by Mr. Murphy of Ballinamona, Cashel, we find the heaviest fall in December in twenty-four hours was at Fofanny in Co. Down of 3.45 inches. and at Aasleagh, Co. Mayo, between 2 and 3 inches. At the Grammer School, Galway, for the month the rainfall was 3.42 inches and at University College, 4.30 inches, a strange disparity. At Ahascragh, (Clonbrock), it was 4.11 inches and at Clifden 7.49. At Delhi, Leenane, it was 13.24 and at Aasleagh, 13.94 ; Westport, 5.16; Castlebar, 4.35; Mountbellew, 3.39; Clifden, 7.49.

23/2/29

WANTED! WANTED!! WANTED!!!
any quantity of
TRAPPED RABBITS, NEW LAID EGGS
AND ALL KINDS OF POULTRY.
The following are the prices I am giving :--
BEST TRAPPED RABBITS   4/6 to 5/6
                                                  per couple.
NEW LAID EGGS   22/- per hd
ALIVE FAT FOWLS   5/- each
DEAD CHICKENS   1/8 per
                                                   pound
For particulars please apply to
ARTHUR WILSON,
EGG, RABBIT & POULTRY MERCHANT,
2 CENTRAL ROAD, LEEDS.

23/2/29

POTEEN IN CONNEMARA.

" I am pleased to record a very marked decrease in poteen-making in the Saorstat in 1928, and in many counties where it has hitherto prevailed the malpractice is now completely eradicated."

This statement was made to an "Irish Independent" representative by Gen. O'Duffy, Chief Commissioner, Garda Siochana.

He attributed the decrease to several factors—the difficulty experienced in procuring raw materials, the constant vigilance of the Garda, their better local knowledge and greater experience, and the smart penalties imposed by the District Justices. Illicit distillation, said General O'Duffy, was now practically confined to Counties Galway, Mayo, and Donegal.

In Galway the districts still affected were Oughterard and Clifden. There were 100 seizures in Connemara in 1928, but prosecutions only resulted in 50 instances. In the remaining cases the still apparatus was found on commonage. This is the usual form for evasion of the law, as in such cases no prosecution can be sustained unless the persons are actually detected in the manufacture of the spirit. In the 50 prosecutions, fines amounting to £868 were inflicted, and in two cases imprisonment was ordered. The seizures included 19 stills, 22 worms, 230 miscellaneous parts of stilling plant, 1,224 gals. of poteen, 728 gals. of "wash" and 212 cwt of controlled materials.

The Garda in Connemara performed 1,587 Revenue (poteen) patrols in 1928, and 6,780 hours were occupied in such work.

23/2/29

CREDITABLE CEMETERIES.

We are pleased to see that the burial grounds in the Diocese of Clonfert are, in the words of His Lordship the Bishop, " no longer a shame and a disgrace to a Catholic people," thanks to the enthusiastic response to the appeal made in last year's Lenten pastoral.

"Every Catholic graveyard in the diocese has been improved," writes the Bishop in this year's pastoral. "In all, without an exception, the boundary walls and gates have been repaired, old trees, briars and weeds removed, graves levelled, loose stones removed, headstones and crosses re-erected, and walks made where possible.

"This good work is to your eternal credit. The priests of the diocese tell me, when they appointed a day on which to begin the work in accordance with the scheme proposed in my pastoral, they were met in the graveyards by seventy or eighty or by even a hundred men who had assembled to improve the 'holy field' of the parish."

FLOWERS OUT OF PLACE.

His Lordship now asks the people, having put their graveyards in order, to see that they are kept in order. "The owner", he says, "must throughout the year take a deep personal interest in his plot. The work ought to be a labour of love -- and I should like to see a holy, stimulating rivalry between families as to which plot is best kept, and between parishes as to which of them has the best kept cemetery".

Emphasising that cemeteries are burial places of the dead and not pleasure gardens of the living, he says:

"It is scarcely befitting their sombre character to have them overcrowded with flowers -- especially as flowers are generally considered to be symbols of the joyousness and gaiety of life. Evergreen trees and shrubs are more appropriate than flowers.

"An edging of flowers by the walks and a few clumps of flowers scattered here and there are allowable and quite becoming, but the ideal of the Church is altogether opposed to having our graveyards a blaze and riot of colour. Flowers ought not to be grown on the graves -- and, may I add, I hope we all now realise that artificial wreaths are an abomination".

MISGUIDED SENTIMENT.

His Lordship notes that some graveyards are so crowded that they ought to be closed and new ones provided, or additions made to the existing ones. "I know", he says, "that in many cases people are opposed to this; they wish to be buried with their fathers, and they do not like the idea of being buried away from their old family burial places. This is sentiment, there is no religion or religious feeling in it. If this sentiment held sway no new graveyard could ever be opened".

In conclusion, he thanks the Galway Board of Health for their assistance in improving the cemeteries.

23/2/29.

In the March of Civilisation

Some years ago our grandmothers prided themselves on their simple feather beds but nowadays no good housewife cares to use one of these unhealthy and not too cleanly if luxurious articles. Any housekeeper wishing to dispose of one or more feather beds could not do better than communicate with

THE IRISH FEATHER CO. Ltd.,
TARA STREET, DUBLIN.

who supply Curled Hair Mattresses in part or whole exchange or purchase for cash as may be desired

ATHLONE.
IMPORTANT TO FARMERS AND OTHERS.
THE NORTHERN ADVANCE CO., Ltd.
KING STREET, ATHLONE.

The above Company beg to announce that they are prepared to grant Loans from

£5 UPWARDS.

To Farmers, Merchants, and all responsible persons all over Ireland on their own approved personal security on liberal terms.

The amount borrowed can be repaid by easy instalments, or in a bulk sum, as may be arranged, to suit the convenience of borrowers.

Loans arranged and cash sent by post if inconvenient to call.

All communications and transactions treated absolutely private and confidential.

Those requiring a temporary loan will find it to their advantage to apply to this company.

Call or write and we shall be most pleased to furnish you with full particulars without delay.

All communications to be addressed :--
MANAGER, 8 King St., Athlone

LENT, 1929.
TO THE CLERGY AND LAITY OF THE ARCHDIOCESE OF TUAM.

My dear Brethren,

PART II

In the mind of the Church, Lent is a time of Prayer and Penance. Having dealt already with Penance, I shall in this second part of the Pastoral say a word on Prayer.

One of the strange contradictions of life is that many of us wonder at what is in reality trivial and transient and don't wonder at what is most wonderful. A case in point is Prayer. Is there anything in life more wonderful than our freedom to pray which means that anyone can talk to God? To get an interview with a great personage in this world, one must have an introduction, a time must be fixed and the interview cannot be long. And even on those conditions not every person can secure this favour. But anyone who wishes it may talk with God. There is no introduction required. We may talk to God at any hour of the day or night. We may talk to Him as long as we like. And we are sure that He never tires of listening to us. This talking with God is Prayer. We may talk to God in words -- in the words, say, of the Our Father or of the many approved forms of prayer, or in our own words. This is called Vocal Prayer. But we may also commune with God within the sanctuary of the soul. This is called Mental Prayer. Again no power on earth can prevent a person from intercourse with God. The prayer of a human heart to God can pierce the strongest prison walls, can emerge from the most dismal depths of misery and in spite of all the powers of hell can pierce the clouds and make its way to the very throne of God. The Church may excommunicate a great public sinner but it could not, even if it wished, prevent that sinner from turning to his Creator to prayer. You see then that freedom to pray is one of the most wonderful things in human life.

This talking to God is of various kinds. You may adore God's infinite majesty. This is the Prayer of Adoration. You may speak or think a word of gratitude to God for favours received. This is the Prayer of Thanksgiving. You may tell God how sorry you are for your sins. This is the Prayer of Contrition. You may beg of God what you need. This is the Prayer of Petition. The Creed is the Prayer of Faith. You may firmly expect that God will give you the means of attaining eternal life. This is the Prayer of Hope. Most wonderful of all, you may talk to God as friend talks to friend, or as a child talks to a father. This is the Prayer of Charity. Not only then is there freedom to pray at all times and in all places and as long as you wish but this freedom of intercourse with God is as wide as the wants, desires and longings of the human heart.

But there is something more wonderful if possible than the freedom and range of prayer. It is the effect of prayer. Every kind of prayer made in a spirit of reverence and humility is sure to bring some gain to the soul. Every time that you bow down interiorly or exteriorly to adore the Majesty of God, you do an act that is just, and pleasing to God. God is also pleased when you thank Him for His benefits. And surely it is a gain to please God. Every sincere act of sorrow for sins will dispose God to pardon your sins and to shorten the purgatory due to them. Every petititon made to God in a spirit of Faith and confidence will get something for you. If it does not get you what you ask, it may get something better. Implicit Acts of Faith and Hope are included in all kinds of prayer. The most efficacious form of intercourse with God is love -- love of God for His own sake and love of the neighbour for the sake of God. One genuine act of love can bridge over the abyss that separates Heaven from Hell, for, as you all know, an act of perfect contrition, is an act of sorrow for sin from the motive of the love of God -- sorrow for sins because they offend God who is so good in Himself -- has the effect of remitting grave sin with, of course, the obligation of confessing the sin afterwards. All these and other effects of prayer assume that our prayer is humble and sincere. The cry of the soul like the prayer of the publican in the temple when he only said from a full heart -- "God be merciful to me a sinner" is far more likely to obtain a response from God than a long string of prayers without due attention. For this extraordinary efficacy of true prayer, we have the words of Jesus Christ Himself -- "And I say to you," He said, "Ask and it shall be given to you: seek and you shall find: Knock and it shall be opened to you. For everyone that asketh, receiveth; and he that seeketh, findeth: and to him that knocketh it shall be opened. And which of you, if he ask his father bread, will he give him a stone? or a fish, will he for a fish give him a serpent? or if he shall ask an egg, will he reach him a scorpion? If you then, being evil, know how to give good gifts to your children, how much more will your Father from heaven give the good spirit to them that ask him?" (LUKE XI.,9.13).

Now if prayer be such a wonderful thing in its freedom, in its range and in its effects, we may well ask why prayer is so often neglected especially as prayer is necessary for salvation. Why is it that theologians have to fix times when prayer is obligatory? The reason is, that the cares and the little wonders of this life obscure our vision of the great wonders of the unseen world. In one of her books the great St. Teresa of Spain says: "A time may come when even holy souls, if they would be delivered from offending God, will find it necessary to make use of the first armour of prayer, to call to mind how everything is coming to an end, that there is a heaven and a hell, and to make use of other reflections of that nature". Now if what St.Teresa calls "the first armour of prayer", i.e. reflection on the fundamental truths of religion, is necessary to keep saints in the way of salvation, how much more necessary is such reflection for the average man and woman of the world.

And how mighty and overpowering are the wonders revealed to us by Faith. In the visible creation we can see some reflection of the majesty and of the beauty of God. The three children whom God's angels protected from the flames of the fiery furnace called on all the works of creation to praise God in a canticle which will be sung to the end of time in the Liturgy of the Church. But what canticle could sum up the wonders of God's love and condescension as known to the children of the New Law? God the Son taking a body and soul such as we have -- God the Son born in a stable -- God the Son working as a carpenter in his foster-father's workshop -- God the Son going about Palestine for three years without a place whereon to lay his head, often weary and hungry, preaching the gospel of truth and liberty to all classes and healing all kinds of human misery -- God the Son taking our sins upon Himself and allowing Himself to be mocked, to be spit upon, to be scourged, to be crowned with thorns and to be crucified "that we being dead to sins, should live to justice"-- these are only a few of the wonders of God's love for men. Then, as St.Teresa so often says "All things are passing away". We are all hastening to the grave and to a judgment from which there is no appeal. "It is decreed unto man once to die and after this, judgment". Our Judge will be the God man who suffered and died in agony that we might live. What will be the sentence of the Judge not on my neighbour but on myself? Will it be "Come to Me Blessed of My Father" Or will it be "Depart from Me ye accursed". In this life all things are passing away; in the next life there is no passing away. Of all the thoughts that man can conceive, the most overpowering is the thought of eternity. You may talk of billions of years, but those figures give no idea of eternity. When all the years that figures can count are passed away eternity will not be shorter by one moment. In this world people often make great sacrifices to enjoy the pleasure of a holiday or even one night's amusement, which will quickly pass. How foolish then not to make the necessary sacrifice to secure everlasting delights of heaven, speaking of which St. Paul says: "eye hath not seen, nor ear heard, neither hath it entered into the heart of man what things God hath prepared for those who love him" (1. Cor. 11, 9.). In this life people have recourse to all kinds of sacrifice to avoid pain. How foolish then not to take all necessary measures to preclude the danger of being condemned to the everlasting pains of hell. If people thought over those fundamental truths of Catholic Faith half as much as they think over the business and amusements of life, they could not fail to turn often to God in prayer. Neither could they, with the graces obtained through prayer, fail to avoid the occasions of grave sin and to practice the self-denial which is the essential badge of the disciples of Christ. Nor need their business on this account suffer nor need their lives be dull, for honest labour is a duty imposed upon us by religion and nothing brightens life so much as the joy of sacrifice and innocence.

But some may say that it is not possible for man and woman living in the world to meditate on these profound truths. Where there is a will there is a way. It is all a question of willing to think about them. It is often a question of sitting down to read a good book. The real life of man is thought. We are what we think and we think about what we see, hear, and read in books. Hence the importance of reading good books. Hence the importance of missions and retreats. Hence the importance of good religious pictures. Hence the necessity of not looking at what is bad, nor listening to what is bad, nor reading what is bad. Hence the importance of keeping good books and papers in the home and the still greater importance of shutting out what is bad or suggestive. Is it too much to suggest that every Catholic household should get at least one Catholic Weekly published in Ireland?

In the days of persecution we know where we stood, but now we have all kinds of agencies willing to cater for our culture and amusement. Our country is invaded by a cheap and insidious Press, exhibiting at times garbled elements of truth in a background of blasphemy. One day there is a pious sermon to catch the ear of the faithful who a few days later will find in the same paper an article under big headings denying the divinity of Jesus Christ, or it may be the existence of a personal God. And we have even in Catholic Ireland prophets who deny any legal interference with the free circulation of printed matter even though that printed matter may reek with moral stench or propound doctrines subversive of the Gospel the Son of God preached for the true enlightenment of the human intellect. The fundamental remedy against all dangers to Faith, Morals, and Salvation is to walk in the light of the Life and of the Gospel of Jesus Christ by habitual meditation on the wonderful mysteries of our Catholic Faith. This kind of reflection is "the first armour of Prayer". It is the fountain of all sincere prayer. It will not be satisfied with a few routine prayers morning and evening but will pour itself forth in a melody of constant communion with God and his Saints -- what St.Paul calls "praying always in the spirit". Within the armour of this kind of prayer the soul is safe.

But we must not be content with praying only for ourselves or with praying only in private. We are one social body and within that body there are various groups of which the family is the first. The best form of family prayer is the Rosary which includes the Lord's Prayer, the Hail Mary and the Gloria oft repeated with meditations on the principal mysteries in the Life of Christ and of His Blessed Mother. Fathers and mothers should insist on all the members of the family being present at the family Rosary. We should pray that our Government may have Divine Guidance to rule wisely within its sphere and that in particular it may have the courage to protect our people against the poison of evil literature and all other corrupting influences.

We should all join as far as possible in the public celebrations which will take place next June and thank God for Catholic Emancipation. And this should remind us to pray for the Emancipation of our Cathlic brethern in Mexico. To-day and for years past amidst the callous silence of the non-Catholic world they are grimly persecuted for the same Faith and Freedom of worship for which our forefathers suffered under the penal laws.

In the freedom, range and efficacy of prayer, we have a bond of fellowship with our Creator in which all can be united and which is the most available and most powerful supernatural agency in the world for the welfare of society, for peace between nations, for the guidance of governments, for the protection of family life and for the enlightenment and exaltation of the individual soul. Prayer is always in season but Lent is a time to fan the flame which only too often lies flickering in the ashes of life's daily cares and vanities. The prayer most suitable to Lent is Meditation on the Passion of Jesus Christ. The simplest and most indulgenced form of prayer is the Stations of the Cross. I cannot conclude without repeating what I have said in former Pastorals, that to assist devoutly at the Sacrifice of the Mass is the greatest of all public religious exercises and affords the most effective way of combining the Prayer of Adoration, the Prayer of Thanksgiving, the Prayer of Atonement and Contrition, and the Prayer of Petition. On Sundays and Holydays the Acts of Faith, Hope and Charity are read before Mass. People should be in time to join in those Acts which with the prayers just mentioned make up the grand symphony of Christian Communion with God.

THOMAS,
Archbishop of Tuam,
St. Jarlath's, Tuam.
23/2/29.

A DISTINGUISHED TUAM MAN.

We perceive by the Prospectus of a new Co. just been issued, the Pye Radio, with a capital of £180,000, that among the Directorate is Sir Thomas Andrew Polson, K.B.E., C.M.G., Chairman of the Rolls Razor Co. Sir Thomas was born in Tuam where his father and family lived universally respected, and was educated at the excellent Diocesan School then conducted by the late Rev. Dr. Charles M. Murphy. After leaving Tuam Sir Thomas settled in London in business and had a successful career. For his valuable services during the War he was given a title. We are pleased, needless to say, to see Tuam men go to the front and win fame and fortune at home and abroad, and upon behalf of the old town we tender him the sincere expression of our best wishes and congratulations.

2/3/29

A BRAVE GALWAY MAN.

Captain R.L.V. Shannon, R.N., son of the Archdeacon of Clonfert, has been appointed to the command of the Discovery Expedition to the Antartic Ocean—a very perilous position but one of honour. We are glad to find the old spirit of McClintock and other brave Irishmen still survives in our midst.

2/3/29

Father Collier, the eminent Redemptorist spoke in no unmistakable terms in the Cathedral on Monday night on the new or "up to date" dances which are a travesty on the "poetry of motion" and are calculated to excite the passions of young people. He might have gone further and lamented the habit, a growing one, amongst young girls of swallowing "quick ones" to wit small whiskies to ostensibly give the Dutch courage necessary to take the floor. One has little hope for the future of the race when our young women become alcoholic dopes. The habit is not unknown in Galway— "Observer."

2/3/29

CAMOGIE.
GALWAY V TUAM.

Galway Technical Team will visit Tuam again on Sunday next to play the local team. This will be their third meeting, and up to the present the Galway team won on each occasion they have met. Tuam ladies have improved wonderful since they met the Technical Team last, and they expect to beat them on this occasion.

The game starts at 3.30 in Parkmore.

The following will represent Tuam— Misses N. Canavan, P. Canavan, M. Larkin, M. Heneghan, N. Heneghan, J. Campbell, N. Tighe, I. Campbell, I. Kenny, B. Walsh, S. Cooney, P. Morris.

2/3/29

Porter Bottles Government Stamped-- 22/4 gross. Corks and Bottlers' Fittings, Brass and Gun-metal Castings; Silver and Nickel Plating and Enamelling. Illustrated Catalogue free.--- JAMES FOX & CO. Head Office 17 William St., Dublin. Telephones (2 lines) 1765 and 601

RUGBY.

TUAM 1 PENALTY GOAL (3 PTS)
ATHENRY 1 TRY (3 PTS.)

Tuam met Athenry on Sunday at Raheen Park, Athenry, under ideal conditions. The play, however, was disappointing, and at no time reached a high standard. The Tuam forwards had the best of play, both in the loose and in the tight, and only heroic defending on the part of the Athenry backs saved their line on more than one occasion from the Tuam forwards. Both back lines, however, played badly. The Tuam backs were well served by Ashton, but made little use of the many opportunities open to them. O'Riordan, the Tuam out-half, played a good sound game, but held on the ball too much. Towards the close of the first half, Tuam forced a penalty inside the Athenry "25," and O'Sullivan landed a beautiful goal which put Tuam in the lead by 3 pts.

After the interval, the Athenry backs attacked vigorously, but were repelled again and again. Fox, the Tuam winger who, up to this, had got little of the ball, now received a pass from Ashton. He gathered the ball in his stride, and made for the Athenry line, only to throw the ball forward when a score seemed certain. From the scrum which followed the Athenry backs broke away and got well inside the Tuam "25." The Athenry supporters had now reached a frenzy of excitement, and amidst their wild cheering the Athenry out-half burst over the Tuam line. Nothing came of the resulting kick, and when the final whistle blew the scores stood at 3 pts each. For Athenry Daly and Gibson were the outstanding players. For Tuam Fox, Ashton and O'Sullivan were the best of the backs, while O'Brien, Walton and M'Guire were the pick of the forwards. HOOKER

2/3/29

G.A.A.

Tuam Star Football Club held their annual general meeting in the Town Hall on Tuesday night last, Mr. J. Ryan in the chair.

The following were elected officers for the year 1929:—

Chairman, Mr. S.Brown; Vice-chairman, Mr. J. Ryan; Treasurer, Mr. J. Burke, Secy., J.Nohilly; Captain, Mr. H. Cunningham; Vice-Captain, Mr. P. Kelly.

LOURDES AND BLESSED BERNADETTE IN YOUR HOME.
I will send a Bottle of Lourdes Water, or a picture of Blessed Bernadette, with relic attached, to all who write to me.
RT.REV.MONSIGNOR PAYNE,
ST.MARY'S, DERBY. 2/3/29

GREAT SHOW AND SALE

OF
850 PEDIGREE BULLS,
ALSO
25 IRISH LARGE WHITE BOARS,
AT
BALL'S BRIDGE, DUBLIN,
ON
MARCH 5, 6 and 7.

THE GREATEST SALES IN IRELAND.

Catalogues 2/6 (Now Ready).
Apply—EDWARD BOHANE,
Director,
Royal Dublin Society,
Ball's Bridge, Dublin.
2/3/29

TUAM GREAT MARCH FAIR.

MONDAY, 11th, PIGS—Old Fair.
TUESDAY, 12th SHEEP & CATTLE—Old Fair.
WEDNESDAY, 20th, PIGS—3rd Wednesday.

March fair last year was one of the best for 1928. Great demand, good prices obtained and all sold. So bring in your stock for above fairs, as we are sure to have a repetition of last year, as all leading buyers will be in attendance.
Pigs at the Tuam February fair made the highest price in Ireland.
By Order Tuam Town Commissioners,
JAMES DALY, Acting Town Clerk.
2/3/29

EVIL LITERATURE BILL.

The following resolution was unanimously passed at meeting of the Galway County Council held on 20th ult.

Proposed by Councillor Concannon, seconded by Councillor Kelly:— "That, whereas the poison of the mind is a greater evil than the poison of the body, we exhort the Government to resist all amendments to the Evil Literature Bill which would permit the circulation of books, papers, or other publications containing atheistical, blasphemous or obscene matter, or propagating doctrines subversive of the eternal laws of morality. 2/3/29

TUAM TOWN COMMISSIONERS.

The monthly meeting of the Tuam Town Commissioners was held on Tuesday evening last, Mr John Burke, Chairman, presiding.

Other members present—Messrs James Moran, Wm Holian, Patrick Walsh, Simon Fahy, Thomas Wilson, John Byrne, Ml.W. Cahill, P.J.Byrne, P.J. Dwyer, Malachy O'Keefe, John H. Corcoran, and Patrick Gibbons, junr.

A letter was read from the Board of Health stating that at their last meeting they adopted a proposal to have a public latrine erected in the town of Tuam on the site selected by the Tuam Town Commissioners at the Market Place, and the area of charge for the expenditure be Tuam Rural District; that the erection of this latrine be conditional on the Commissioners taking over same, when erected, and keeping it in proper order, and before instructing the Engineer to prepare the necessary contract documents they would like to know if the Commissioners are prepared to accept the Board's proposal.

The Acting Clerk was directed to inform them that the Town Sergeant would see that it was kept in order.

A letter was read from Mr Quinn, Toll Farmer, stating that a concrete shed was required to be erected in connection with the working of the scales for the weighing of the potatoes. The old box in use is past repair. That John Costello, Thomas Sloyan, and others are buying potatoes and oats at their stores and in the market and weighing them on their premises therby creating a market and depriving him of the Tolls, which is an infringement of the Commissioners rights as owners of the Tolls and Customs of Tuam. He requested the Commissioners to take action to put an end to the abuse which is going on for a long time.

Chairman—Well gentlemen what have you to say to the Toll Farmer's letter.

Mr Cahill—There's no doubt this buying outside the market is unfair to him and it should be stopped if we have power to do so.

The Acting Clerk was directed to write to the parties mentioned that the Toll Farmer is entitled to Tolls and Customs for all Produce and Stock sold and bought in the town of Tuam. That the Toll Farmer be ordered that potatoes are to be sold in the Potato Market for the next two months. That an advertisement be issued for a wooden box on wheels to be made for the Potato Market.

THE PAPAL SETTLEMENT.

Chairman—Gentlemen, I think it is only right that we should offer our congratulations to His Holiness the Pope on the happy settlement of the Roman Treaty question. I, therefore, propose the following resolution :—

"That we, the Tuam Town Commissioners, desire to offer our heartiest congratulations to His Holiness Pope Pius XI on the settlement of the Roman Treaty between the Vatican and Italian Government which restores the temporal States to the Pope, and we pray God that His Holiness may long reign to enjoy the happiness of His Kingdom as Pope and King in union with all other nations."

Mr Patrick Walsh— I have great pleasure in seconding the resolution.

EVIL LITERATURE.

Chairman—We should also call upon the Government to pass the Evil Literature Bill and stop the filthy imported books from coming into the country poisoning the minds of the young people.

Mr Cahill proposed the following resolution:

"That we, the Tuam Town Commissioners, call upon the Government and the members of the Dail to pass the Evil Literature Bill and that there be no further whittling down of the Bill to suit the susceptabilities of the free thinkers or newspaper editors."

Mr Holian—I second that.

Passed unanimously.

9/3/29

"WHEELS OF LIFE."

This week's programme at the Mall Cinema, Tuam, includes a Gaumont production, "Wheels of Life," which is now showing throughout Great Britain for the first time. Young and old of all classes should not miss this film, which owes its entire conception to the world-famous Nottingham firm, The Raleigh Cycle Co., Ltd. The story is intensely interesting and full of freshness, and the termination which shows the young couple riding away after their marriage on their "Wheels of Life" contains that spice of novelty in which all cinema goers delight.

PUBLIC BATHS.

The public baths which were opened to the people of Galway on Saturday were availed of by very large numbers of both sexes and are proving a veritable boon to the army of the great unwashed, namely, the average working man who cannot afford the luxury of a bath in the home—"Observer"

9/3/29

MINIMUM OF LABOUR WITH MAXIMUM
EFFICIENCY AND REDUCED COST.

TULLY, SONS & Co Ltd.

NEW 1927 PLANT
is
MECHANICALLY OPERATED, CHARGED, STOKED.

With or Without
WASTE HEAT BOILERS

Produces from Coke—300 B.Th.U.Gas. From Coal—350 B.Th. U.Gas, or Carburetted Gas of 500 B.Th.U.

Forming
A COMPLETE GAS GENERATING
STATION..

It is the latest and most modern Plant in the World, and is the result of experience gained in the working of over 200 Tully Gasification Plants, and Coal Carbonising experience of half a century.
Plants of from 75,000 to 2 Million Cubic Feet per day can be inspected in operation.

TULLY, SONS & CO.,
Millgate,
NEWARK-ON-TRENT.
Phone, 258 Newark. Wire, Tullcarbo, Newark.

9/3/29

THE TOWN HALL CINEMA.

As may be seen by advertisement in another column, Mr Robert Willis, the well known Manager from Dublin, has leased the Town Hall Cinema for an indefinite period and intends to show the very best of new films and all the first class companies at prices to suit the times and pockets. On this (Friday night) the famous O'Shea Dramatic Co. produce "The Ten Commandments," to be followed on Saturday night by "Falsely Accused." Two very fine plays well worth a visit to see.

SCHOLARSHIP BAN.

It is lamentable to find Galway County Council deciding to exclude Colleges which encourage the playing of foreign games from the benefits of the Scholarship Scheme. If the members only saw the immense crowd of young Irishmen who visited the International Football Match on Saturday in Dublin and the intense interest experienced all over the country in the manly sport they would not so act and thereby make themselves ridiculous.

9/3/29

TOWN HALL CINEMA, TUAM.

Lessee and Manager ... Robert Willis.

TO-NIGHT AT 8.30.
Doors open at 7.45.
THE O'SHEA DRAMATIC CO.
will play that
WONDERFUL CHRISTIAN MASTER-PIECE,

THE TEN COMMANDMENTS.

You have seen the Picture. Now come and see the Play and Hear the Actual Words Spoken.

SATURDAY NIGHT.

FALSELY ACCUSED.

A play showing you where Innocence is often proved Guilty by Modern Law.

SUNDAY AFTERNOON AT 3 P.M.
ANY SPECIAL PLAY WILL BE PRESENTED as selected by Our Patrons.
Matinee Prices : Ground Floor 4d ; Balcony 9d;
Children 2d and 4d.

SUNDAY NIGHT
A SPECIAL HEART-STIRRING PLAY THAT WILL APPEAL TO ALL. See Bills

NOTE—Night Prices for this Grand Company : Ground Floor 9d ; Balcony 1/3.

GRAND ORCHESTRA WILL PLAY ALL LATEST MUSIC.

9/3/29

A correspondent tells us that the late Tom Flatley took a leading part as an anti-Parnellite, and threw himself with vigour into the Tanner-Nolan election of 1892 which became historical by reason of the election petition which followed. Throughout his life he had the interests of the poor at heart and worked for them without the prospect of any material reward for himself. In his day he was a very successful coach builder and one of the most respected men in Tuam.

9/3/29

SPAIN AND IRELAND

Every patriotic Irishman who is a student of our History and acquainted with the close, friendly and intimate commercial relations that for centuries existed between Ireland and Spain, and who remembers that it was from that country our Milesian ancestors came, always has a brotherly feeling for Spain and the Spanish people. We are, and always were, deeply interested in that country with such a glorious past in art, literature and adventure, and in its welfare are as deeply concerned as we should be in that of an old friend in peace and constant ally in war. We have always been through our sadly chequered history on the closest terms of amity with Spain, and to-day no people in Europe are dearer or nearer to us by many ties. There we traded for centuries; there our sons and daughters went for the education denied them at home. The recent political changes in that country we have followed as well as we could, but they have been so misrepresented in the European Press, and perhaps more so in the British Press, that we do not know how they really are there. The views of such of the Irish Press that venture to deal with Spanish affairs are so largely coloured by these prejudiced presentations of the case which appeared in the London Journals that most of us are ignorant of the real facts. We, however, for our part, who want to know the real truth, and who are not afraid to publish that truth, are therefore particularly pleased with having been afforded, through the medium of an excellent English weekly, "The Sunday Referee" with a plain and manly statement of the Spanish case from General Primo de Rivera himself. He is the great man in Spain to-day, the one who has providentially come to the rescue of his country from a fate similar to that which, but for the fortunate intervention of Signor Mussolini, would, we fear, have been in store for Italy, where similar forces of disorder and disorganisation were obtaining control of the destinies of the State. There also half educated theorists and anti-religious fanatics, emboldened by the success of their black Bolshevist brethern in Russia, were acquiring a hold over the administration, which control would have meant social disorder and civil war. Italy happily spared, by the timely and firm actions of its greatest citizen and saviour, and equally so has Spain been kept from running into the abyss and kept orderly and prosperous by the manly and timely action of General Primo de Rivera. He is to-day one of the three greatest men in Europe - those three who have individually saved their beloved countries from ruin - the third being General Pilsudski in Poland. We wish that General de Rivera's plain, honest, and to us, convincing explanation of matters in Spain could be widely circulated in Ireland, and made known there. It would open the eyes of the purblind public here, those expecially who take their views of things abroad from the prejudiced Press of Great Britain, largely inspired as they are by Anti-Catholic correspondents and Jewish financiers who want to give trouble all over the world. As he points out, Spain, after the war, for although not engaged in it, she suffered by its miseries, had a terrible heritage of trouble and difficulties to face and surmount. It had too the worries of its own little war in Morocco, and but for the Generals's timely intervention in that country Spain would from military mismanagement have lost its hold of that dependency. As he remarks, the settlement he made ultimately was received with satisfaction, and the unpleasant disclosures of the muddling that went on there was equally acquiesced in. "The country (he says) demonstrated a complete serenity and a high conception of patriotism not withstanding the news of the casualties which had of necessity to occur during the operations which led to final conquest." It is clear to any observer of these affairs that, but for his being called upon providentially by the King to settle the question the Morocco affair would have been a military disaster, and it would have led to serious social and political disturbances at home. All this, fomented by the agents of disorder, would have been subversive of all orderly government. The settled progress that has undoubtedly set down since would have been impossible. The political trouble in Spain was, as elsewhere, caused and carried to extremes by unscrupulous men. Politics and business are antagonistic, particularly as the professors and the protagonists of latter day politics understand them. Carried to their logical conclusion there is no doubt that the ideals and views of the present day school of politics are opposed to any orderly and settled government, as we understand it. Most countries would be much better off if what is called politics were less prominent, if not eliminated, from the daily programme of public life. Unpractical politics should be left to the school room where immature views and half baked theories can alone with impunity be discussed. Reduced to action such politics are certain of leading to disturbance, and such crude political opinions coming from such half educated sources, can only with safety to the community be kept out of public life, for no country could prosper, or ever has prospered, with such elements of disorder and such ideas of disturbance abroad, and such socially subversive doctrines proclaimed and preached. The General, in his masterly statement of his case in the Press says, "Are politics necessary to the existence of peoples? Are they merely a form of discipline or a speculative academic study auxilary to the formation of Government in respect of law and national economy, or an essential factor indispensible to the Government of peoples? I think the former, and in consequence that a Parliament to give the greatest collaboration to the Government should not have any political colour but should be composed of eminent persons representing diverse actions of public life. Those persons should be without previous affiliation with any party organisation and without recognition of any chief, and should be able to put forward each one his own proposals, and to give or withold his approval with regard to any project in hand, and to offer the Government the benefit of their studies with complete independence of any Government action. That is my own opinion and that of the Patriotic Union, and it is this idea that will be the key note of the laws which I shall submit to the Government with the approval of His Majesty and for the consent of the people. I realise that this radical innovation in the customs and principle of Government which have been dominating the world for more than a century will not occur without resistance, but I also believe that the first half of the present century will not pass without other peoples having accepted the principles embodied in this system. When this happens I shall not be living, but in this as in all my conduct I am complacently prepared to submit my actions to the Supreme Judge of all History." Such are his views of the sort of politics he condemns and which nowhere ever succeeded. When one sees the mischievous muddle made all over the world by present day democrats, inexperienced, untaught and undisciplined and foolishly let loose to govern and vainly, trying to reconcile orderly Government with their own crude political views, when one sees what has occurred in the United States, the greatest of Democracies, and what is going on in other States, how in all corruption spreads and creeps in and threatens to infect the whole machinery of Government, one can hardly look with complacency and indifference upon what is now going on in Spain to prevent all this from occurring. We personally wish Spain, Ireland's most esteemed oldest friend and ally, the brightest future, and that she may continue to grow prosperous, peaceful and happy.

We trust Spain will continue in its present orderly course of progress to consequent prosperity, and that nothing will occur to bring about any change for the worse or to drive that gifted people into the dark, dismal and disastrous ways of, Bolshevism, which, in so many forms, is showing itself in every country to-day. We wish success to that able man who now guides Spain's destinies under its most popular Sovereign. Whether General De Rivera succeeds in dissipating the mere political elements entirely, we trust, for the sake of his country, that he will succeed in at least controlling them and keeping them within limits of legality and well ordered freedom, and so help the development and assured future of his country to which he has nobly committed himself.   16/3/29

TUAM HANDBALL COURT.

A meeting will be held in the Library of the Town Hall on Tuesday evening next, 19th inst., at 8.30 p.m. for the purpose of forming a committee to proceed with the building of a Ball Court on the site selected where the old Bridewell formerly stood at the back of the Courthouse. All interested are cordially invited.

TOWN RATE.

During the past week £90 odd was collected and lodged to the credit of the Commissioners by the new collector, Mr. James Burke.   16/3/29

TUAM TOWN CLERKSHIP.

The examination for the above took place in Dublin on Tuesday last. At least four candidates applied from Tuam, all of whom had to travel to Dublin at their own expense to contest for a position carrying a salary of £70 a year. The Appointment Commissioners did not see fit to advertise the position in any of the local papers

---

Two gifts are needed to carry us through life without unhappiness and with credit to ourselves. These gifts are compassion and humour. They are both needed. They supplement each other. Only humour can help intelligent people to tolerate so much that is senseless and wasteful in human arrangements, so much that is unintelligible and repulsive in nature. If we can smile at the spectacle of "man, poor man, dressed in a little brief authority, playing fantastic tricks before high heaven," we are saved from futile anger. If we can laugh at ourselves we are proof against worse things—fussiness, tyranny, pride. Humour keeps the intellect active. Compassion preserves the heart from being hardened. It saves us from selfishness. It prevents us from passing by on the other side. With both compassion and humour man is a little lower than the angels. Without either he is beneath the level of the beasts.

16/3/29

SHANNON POWER

—

Until Further Notice

3 - DAY

Excursion Tickets

AT SINGLE FARE

will be issued daily to

LIMERICK

from all

Stations.

—

Great Southern Rys.

P.J.FLOYD, Traffic Manager

16/3/29

INVENTOR

On Feb. 24, 1844, John Philip Holland was born at Liscannor, Co. Clare. He was a Christian Brother in Cork for some years. His discoveries and inventions revolutionised modern warfare. He was the inventor of the submarine, that deadly vessel of destruction which wrought such havoc with shipping in the World War. He died at Newark, N.J., August 12, 1914.

HONOUR FOR TUAM POSTMAN.

The Imperial Service Medal has been awarded to Arthur Kilgarriff, postman, Killaloonty, Tuam, for services before the creation of An Saorstat.

16/3/29

SEACHTAIN NA GAEDHILGE
(IRISH LANGUAGE WEEK 1929)
"Má Chailltear an Ghaedhilg, Caillfear Éire," arsa Padraig Mac Piarais. Ta an Ghaedhilg i mBaoghal fós & tá sí i muinghin cabhrac na nGaedheal atá dilis di.

On the efforts of THIS GENERATION depends the fate of the
GAELIC NATION
HELP THE GAELIC LEAGUE in the fight for **ITS TRIUMPH.**
Subscribe to the Annual Collection in aid of **THE IRISH LANGUAGE FUND** WHICH WILL BE HELD THROUGHOUT THE COUNTRY DURING
LANGUAGE WEEK
17th March--24th March.
Má's mian leat, a Ghaedhil,
ÉIRE SHAOR GHAEDHEALACH
d'ath-bhunú, chabhruigh go fial le
CISTE NA TEANGAN.

Collection material (Posters, Boxes, and Flags) will be sent to those willing to help on application to AN RUNAIDHE, 25 Parnell Sq., Ath Cliath.

Telegraphic Address } Pollexfen, Liverpool
} Steam, Sligo,
} Steam, Belmullet.

Sligo Steam Navigation Company Limited.

Weekly Sailings between Sligo and Liverpool.
Leaving Sligo every Friday, and (South Salisbury Dock) Liverpool every Tuesday.
Taking Goods etc, at Through Rates from and to all parts of England; from and to all Stations in the West of Ireland,
also
Weekly Service between Sligo and Belmullet (weather and other conditions permitting.)

Goods and livestock carried subject to conditions specified on the Company's Sailing Bills.
For further particulars apply to the Company's Offices, Union Street, Sligo, 8b Rumford Place, Liverpool, or Belmullet.

16/3/29

SWEEP IN AID OF CHARITY.

The draw for the Grand National Sweepstakes, organised in aid of the Charities of the Tuam Conference, St. Vincent de Paul Society, was held in the Town Hall Library, on Wednesday evening last. Very Rev. Father Kelly, Adm., presided, and Messrs. F.B. McDonogh, Ross and O'Connell acted as supervisors of the draw. There was a full attendance of the members of the Conference, and at the close of the proceedings Father Kelly thanked all who helped to make the sweep a success. Following is the result:— No. 4012, Rev. Father Kelly, Tuam, Kilbarn ; 442, James Glynn, Vicar St., Tuam, Kilbrain ; 1780, T.McLouglin, Dublin Road, Tuam, The Coyote ; 657, M.Tierney, Shop St., Tuam, Easy Virtue ; 5229, M.Ronaldson, Cloonthu Road, Tuam, Knight of the Wilderness; 1655, c/o D.Plenderleith, James McCaughy,Ltd.,Belfast,MountEtna ; 1231,Lawler, Ltd., Church Chandler, Dublin, Toy Bell; 3660, Paddy Farrell, Abbey, Ballyglunin, K.C.B.; 1778, Ned Byrne, Tuam, Irina; 1301, K.B.Kinnen, Galway, Sultan of Wicken ; 1649, C.J.Reid, c/o J.McCaughey, Belfast, Theorin ; 2967, Sister Priscilla, County Home, Tuam, Tipperary Tim; 775, The United Yeast Co. Dublin, Rampart; 968, Mrs. M. Cooney, Tuam, Beggars End; 1688, Twelve Hopefuls, Brothers School, Tuam, Overdraft; 1626, John Geraghty, Galway Road, Tuam, Odd Cat; 1775, Mrs. MacMahon, Circular Road, Tuam, Grakle; 1219, J.Fleming, 28 South William St., Dublin, Great Span ; 2056, Jame Kenny, 521 West St.., New York, Gree Gallach; 4284, Mrs. Kelly, P.O., Dunmore, Best Home; 920, J.Reilly, Sligo (Torney Bros.), Big Wonder; 209, Stephen Browne, Old Road, Tuam, Harewood; 66, Thos.P.Leonard, Church View, Tuam, Bright's Boy; 5235, Henry Mangan, St. Jarlath's Place, Tuam, Hawker; 159, A. O'Connell, 75 Grafton St., Dublin, Herbert's Choice; 3985, F.C.Lynch, C.C. Tuam, Lloydie; 3568, Fr. Lee, Dunmore, Gay Dog II.; 3518, Rev. Fr. McHugh, Milltown, GIBUS; 2104, No. 4 Presentation Convent, Tuam, Hop On; 964, J.Stockwell, Tuam, Lucidor; 2157, T.Byrne, Menlough, Athenry, East Africa; 3084, Martin Noonan (carpenter), Tuam, More Din ; 1668, Mrs. Hoar, Briarfield, Rosoglio ; 5232, Mrs. K. Waldron, St. Jarlath's Place, Tuam, Montaigu ; 3101, Mr. O'Malley, Dunmore, Sandyhook ; 736, Williams & Wood, Ltd., The Goslin; 472, C.J. Sheridan, Milltown, South Hill ; 1650, Miss L. Anderson (McCaughey, Belfast), Low Tide; 3500, P. Feeney, Dalgan, Milltown, Lotus Land; 103, George Nilen, Tony Lad; 211, D. and B., Tuam, Uncle Ben ; 1842, Mr. O'Malley, Dunmore, Sprig; Mary Neal, Palace View, Tuam, Stage Management; 471, C.J. Sheridan, Milltown, Tuam, Dwarf of the Forest; 2319, P. Donlan, Dublin Road,, Tuam, Shawn Golin ; 2846, Miss N. Nicholson, Shop St., Tuam, Benburb ; 960, Miss E. Griffith, Ballindine, Merryvale II ; 865, William McGrath, Tullinadaly Road, Tuam, Le Touquet ; 2913, Sisters of Mercy, Tuam, Wild Edgar; 3719, Clebborne's, Liverpool, Kwango ; 839, Mrs. O'Sullivan, Tuam, Curtain Raiser ; 811, Mrs. Connolly, Shop St., Tuam, Crypiteal ; 5173, Michael Cosgrove, Dublin Road, Tuam, Slieve Grien ; 3574, E.H. Burke, Tuam, Phosphore ; 1670, P.Murphy, Cooloo, Woodhill; 4287, Michael Howley, Dunmore, Knockir ; 1730, Bridget Ni Caitain, Casadpinien, Wild Orb ; 886, J. O'Rourke, McHale Terrace, Vasy Voir; 2895, Sisters of Mercy, Tuam, Tableau ; Sisters of Mercy, Tuam, Stash ; 1689, Twelve Hopefuls, No 2, Tuam, The Field ; 2968, Sister Priscilla, Tuam, Monduco; 3959, William Haughton, Camperdown ; 154, A. O'Carroll, Grafton St., Dublin, Billy Barton ; 2964, Sister Priscilla, Tuam, Koko ; 856, Mrs. J. Glynn, Tuam, Darrach; 3859, Anthony Keane, Oranmore, Ardunes Pride; 985, Mr. Forry, O'Keeffe's Terrace, Mabestown Pride ; 948, Michael Cooney, Tuam, Ballystockhart ; 1214, Fred Dick, 28 South William St., Dublin, Ballyharewood; 5339, J.Reidy, Tuam, Golden St., 5098, Rev. Fr. Burke Tuam, Trump Card ; 2110, John Costello, Rinkippen, Tuam, Rathory ; Rev. P. King, Tuam, Golden Rebel ; 2216, John Kelly, Dublin Road, Tuam, Maguelonne ; 1711, C.J. Sheridan, Milltown, Lordi; 2922, Mr. Rishworth, Ballymote, Miss Balscadden; 843, P.J.McMahon, Tuam, Fleet Prince ; Sister Priscilla, Tuam, Carfax; 1702, Miss O'Neill, 42 Lr. O'Connell St., Dublin, Beech Martin; 5128, Rev. Fr. Gibbons, Tuam, Richmond ; 5234, Mrs. K. Waldron, Tuam, Easter Hero ; 5099, Rev. J. Burke, College, Dinburg ; 1773, Harry Geraghty, Tuam, Drinmond ; 5051, Mrs. Beegan, College, Duke of Florence; 913, J. Trainor, Fern Bank, Sligo, Ardeen ; 2890, J. Treacy, Tuam, Stort ; 3292, H. Cunningham, Tuam, Confirmation ; 4013, Rev. Fr. Kelly, College, Soldier's Joy ; 1927, Bridie O'Reilly, Cathedral Place, Ennis, Skrun Prince; 2984, Sisters of Mercy, Tuam, Rathowen; 5005, J. Canavan, Tuam, News Boys; 5156, Katherine McDonagh, Tuam, Cloringo ; 2221, Larry Kennedy, Galway Road, Garryduff ; 3872, John Lyons, Shop St., Tuam, D.D.B. ; 3060, John Beirne, Tuam, Nanny II ; 5336, — Leonard, do., Far Flight ; 6230, Malachy Duggan, do., Melleray's Bell ; 1789, Dr. Costello, do., Master Billie ; 1914, Rosy O'Grady (Co. Clare) Kildysart, May King ; 5091, Rev. Fr. Burke, Tuam, Royal Support ; 4243, Mrs. John Quinn, Tuam, Delarne ; 3904, Mr. Gallagher, Tallaght, April Fool; 2859, Henry Madelin, Omagh, Ruddyman ; 5132, Nellie Curlin, Tuam, The Ace II.   23/3/29

ENTERTAINMENT BY ST. JARLATH'S STUDENTS.

On Wednesday evening last in the Mall Cinema, before some friends, the students of St. Jarlath's College, Tuam, gave a very enjoyable and amusing musical and dramatic entertainment. The musical items were given in a finished manner, and reflect credit on the talented teacher, Mr. Hession, Organist, while the performance of "Hyacinth Halvey" was got through as well as any professional Co. could present the piece, and that is saying a good deal.

Canon Walsh, President St. Jarlath's, at the close, thanked those who had taken part, and said that for the short time allowed for preparation the musical items and the play were very well done indeed. For that he thanked Mr. Hession, who never spared himself in his musical teaching, and Fr. Gunnigan for the excellent manner in which he "coached" the boys in their several parts in the play. He hoped before long that they would be able to stage a more ambitious programme. (Applause) 23/3/29

TOWN OF TUAM.

AUCTION OF HOUSEHOLD FURNITURE,

for Mr. James Huelett, at his residence,
THE STATION, TUAM,
ON THURSDAY, 25th March 1929,
at
12.30 o'Clock, sharp.

For items see posters.

CAHILL & CO.,
Auctioneers & Valuers, Tuam.

TUAM TOWN COMMISSIONERS.

NOTICE TO CONTRACTORS.

The Tuam Town Commissioners will, at their meeting to be held on Tuesday, 2nd April, 1929, receive and consider tenders for making and supplying 2 Wooden Ticket Boxes on wheels, according to specification to be seen at the Clerk's Office between the hours of 11 o'c. a.m. and 2 o'c. p.m.

Tenders, enclosing the names of two solvent sureties, will be received by me up to the hour of 8 o'c. p.m. on the above date.

A deposit of £1 must accompany tender.

The lowest or any tender not necessarily accepted.

By Order,
JAMES DALY, Acting Town Clerk,
Boardroom, Tuam, 22/3/29.
23/3/29

ST. PATRICK'S DAY IN TUAM.

In the Cathedral on St. Patrick's Day the usual religious celebrations associated with the Holy Festival were carried out to the full. There was Solemn High Mass at 11.30 at which his Grace the Archbishop presided. A sermon in Gaelic was preached by Rev. Fr. Moran, C.C. Headford. The celebrant of the Mass was Rev. F. Lynch, C.C., and Fathers Gunnigan and Moran, deacon and sub-deacon. Rev. Fr. King acted as master of ceremonies. At evening devotions the prayers were recited in Irish, and the children of the Convents and the Christian Brothers' Schools, to whom the nave of the Cathedral had been reserved, sang beautifully a number of Gaelic hymns. His Grace the Archbishop delivered a very interesting and inspiring sermon on the life of the Saint, and complimented the Nuns and the Christian Brothers on the excellent training they were giving to the youth of Tuam. He exhorted his hearers to be true to the teachings of St. Patrick and to the language and customs of their own country, and if they were to dance to patronise their own Irish dances, and not to give countenance to the jazz dance or the immodest costume.

Apart from the religious ceremonies in the Cathedral there were no Patrick's Day celebrations in Tuam. It is true we all wore the shamrock, but after that—. Time was, and that not so long ago either, when we had our St Patrick's Day procession in honour of our National Apostle, and a concert in the evening, which if not wholly Gaelic was at least redolent of the spirit of the Gael. Now that is all gone and dead with the men who led and inspired it, and there seems to be no one to take a lead in their place. If there is a branch of the Gaelic League in Tuam at present it seems to have gone asleep or joined the Order of Dark Brothers. 23/3/29

It is to be noticed that the new Munster and Leinster Bank premises situated at the corner of Dublin Road and Vicar St., and formerly the spacious premises of the Messrs Mc Donnell, are now almost completed. The building is on the site of a large drapery shop which was burned by the Black and Tans on the night of the sack of Tuam following the shooting of two R.I.C. men, who were killed in an ambush between Tuam and Dunmore. The lower part is built of finely cut stone of Irish quarry and workmanship, and the higher portion is brick. It is a four-storey building. The contractor was Mr. J. Mc Nally, Galway. There are four banks in Tuam: the Bank of Ireland and the Ulster Bank in Shop St., and the National Bank and Munster and Leinster in Dublin Road. 23/3/29

TUAM HANDBALL COURT.

A meeting was held in the Town Hall, on Monday evening last, with the object of forming a committee to proceed with the erection of a Ball Court on the site selected and purchased from the Co. Council, formerly occupied by the old disused bridewell at the back of the Courthouse.

Rev. P.J.Kelly, Adm., presided, and there was a agood attendance of the young men of the town.

Father Kelly explained the position as regards the building, and said the site was now practically cleared. The intention was to build two alleys, for which Mr. M.J. Kennedy had prepared plans at an estimated cost of £650. But they did not intend to go in for so ambitious a programme at once, but would proceed with the building of the main alley at present, leaving the second one and other accessories for a later period. This they expected to be able to do at an estimated cost of £200 or £250, and of that they had a substantial sum in the bank from the Town Hall burning, and they expected to be able to get the balance without much trouble. They had to-night to form a committee who would act with the three trustees, the Administrator, the Chairman of the Town Commissioners for the time being, and Mr. Pat Walsh, T.C., Chairman of the Gaelic Club. This done the plans could be altered to suit existing circumstances, the work could be advertised, and he hoped they would have the alley constructed and ready for play early in July.

Mr. W.J. Concannon, Solr., also spoke in support of the project as outlined by Father Kelly. He promised there would be no difficulty in finding the balance required. He proposed that a committee of four be elected to act with the trustees.

Mr Burke suggested six.

Father Kelly—Make it five. That will split the difference.

This was agreed to, and the following were proposed and elected to form a working committee to proceed with the building of the Ball Court :- Messrs. M.J. Byrne, Martin Cooney, Sam Browne, Sergt. Ruddy and H.Cunningham.

Messrs. J.J. Waldron and T.M. Joyce were appointed Joint Secs.

It was decided to hold the first meeting in the Town Hall on Friday evening at 8.30 so as to proceed with the work as speedily as possible.   23/3/29

The term "Whip" applied to certain members of parliamentarian bodies is derived from the "whipper in" of a hunt—men whose job it is to whip up lagging hounds and so to keep the pack together and obedient to orders.   23/3/29

CATHOLIC EMANCIPATION.

Our fellow Catholics in England are in every way manifesting their sense of the importance and value of Catholic Emancipation and publishing excellent information on the subject which enterprise stands in contrast with the very inferior literary material we are publishing. They also show their proper sense of the greatness of O'Connell, whom we regret to find some Irishmen tried to depreciate and disparage. Monsignor Howlett, D.D., P.P., of Westminster Cathedral, has just reprinted an excellent lecture which he delivered at the London Coliseum last month, and in that he very forcibly and eloquently deals with the importance of the subject and the greatness of O'Connell and the great merit of his action and the tremendous difficulties he had to surmount and the splendid ability of his conduct in surmounting them. The booklet is published by Messrs. Sands and Co. and selling at 4d.

23/3/29

ST PATRICK'S DAY.

On St. Patrick's Day every one wore the shamrock. The tradition which connects the saint with shamrock is an interesting one. It says that he enforced his preaching on the Trinity by holding up a shamrock leaf as an example of the possibility of three things in one. In certain old works of art, he is shown with a sprig of it in his hand. St. Patrick was Scottish born, studied as a monk under St. Martin at Tours, and was sent to preach in Ireland. There he is said to have founded as many churches as there are days in the year, including the cathedral at Armagh. He died on March 17 A.D. 463. Before the Irish introduced the cult of St. Patrick into England, March 17 was celebrated as the anniversary of Noah's entry into the Ark. How the date was determined, and why it should have been especially commemorated in a country where rain is, to say the least, no rare phenomenon, is difficult to say, but our mediaeval forbears missed no opportunity of holiday making. Noah's Ark Day was made the occasion for the performance of mystery plays, dramatising the Biblical record of the Flood, with Mrs. Noah as a shrewish wife to provide a touch of light relief.

"There is no improvement—it is getting worse," said Very Rev. Canon Mac Alinney, Chairman, when it was reported at the meeting of Galway Hospital and Dispensary Committee that five unmarried mothers had been admitted to the maternity hospital since the last monthly meeting.They gave their addresses as ....(one urban, four rural). Mr Martin Cooke said the country was beginning to get worse than the towns.   23/3/29

THE MEASURE OF A MAN.

Not-
   "How did he die?"
But-
   "How did he live?"
Not-
   "What did he gain?"
But-
   "What did he give?"
These are the units
   To measure the worth
Of a man as a man,
   Regardless of birth.

Not-
   "What was his station?"
But-
   "Had he a heart?"
And-
   "How did he play
   His God-given part?
Was he ever ready
   With a word of good cheer,
To bring back a smile,
   To banish a tear?"

Not-
   "What was his church?"
Nor-
   "What was his creed?"
But-
   "Had he befriended
   Those really in need?"
Not-
   "What did the sketch
   In the newspaper say?"
But-
   "How many were sorry
   When he passed away?"

23/03/29

THE SHANNON SCHEME

LECTURE BY A TUAM MAN.

Professor Frank Sharman Rishworth (a native of Tuam and the head engineer of the Shannon works), Chief Civil Engineer, Shannon Development, delivered a lecture on "The Shannon Scheme" to a large audience in the Town Hall, Rathmines, on Wednesday.

In the course of his lecture, which was illustrated with lantern slides, Professor Rishworth described some of the principal features of the civil construction works at present in progress for the hydro-electric development of the River Shannon, and referred to various model experiments which had been carried out in connection with the work. He said that in a hydro-electric scheme there must be sufficient water and a fall or head to actuate the turbines which, connected to the generators, transformed the energy into electricity. On the Shannon they had the three large lakes, Loughs Allen, Ree and Derg, and several small ones, giving them the natural storage necessary to supplement the supply during periods of drought when the ordinary river flow fell below the hydro-electric requirements, and to compensate for rainfall fluctuations. By means of the weir at Parteen Villa and the Head Race canal the series of falls in the river from Killaloe to the tidal estuary were concentrated into a single fall of 100 feet at Ardnacrusha, the site of the power-house.

By means of lantern slides, Professor Rishworth illustrated the early stages of the work and its progress, showing the canal 7 and a half miles long, diverting a part of the water across country to Ardnacrusha, where it fell 100 feet through the turbines into the tail race and rejoined the Shannon about 1 and a quarter miles further down the valley; and a great number of details in connection with the construction. Up to date, he said 10,400,000 tons of earth had been excavated and 2,400,000 tons of rock; and in both cases over 90 per cent. of the work was completed. The concrete placed amounted to 340,000 tons.

A vote of thanks was passed to the lecturer.

23/3/29

GALWAY NOTES

(From Our Own Correspondent.)

George Tully, the popular and well known actor on the London stage, has, we regret to learn, been seriously ill and obliged to go to a Nursing Home in Brighton. He is now convalescent, and about to leave for a sea trip to the Mediterranean. While he was laid up he was the recipient of countless kindnesses from his numerous friends in London and Brighton, and nothing could exceed their anxious interest in his health. The members of the celebrated Savage Club, the resort of the most cultured artists and leading literary men not only of London but of the Empire, were particularly concerned in their popular fellow member's health. Mr Tully was born in Galway, but his father, William Tully, who lived many years in Galway and died in Dublin, was born in Dunmore. It is a curious coincidence that the same little town of Dunmore, in our county, should be so closely associated with two leading actors—the best known men on the stage in their day—Thomas Mossop and George Tully. The former was a well known actor and theatre manager in Dublin over two hundred years ago, and he has left an enduring name in the theatrical annals of that once great city and in theatrical circles generally, for he went to London.

***

Jim Tully, the celebrated Irish-American writer, who contemplates coming to Ireland this summer, and is at present at Holywood, dedicated "Beggars of Life," one of his best known books, to his friends, Rupert Hughes and Charlie Chaplin, "A Mighty Vagabond." The "New York Herald" said of his work :— "Tully is without doubt the greatest writer of tramp life in America. He is never self-conscious like Jack London, and as far as reality goes he surpasses George Borrow in many respects." Rupert Hughes says of his book — "His fascinating pages make one thoroughly acquainted with the long procession of people he met. It is a book of marvellous portraits. Jim Tully is the American Gorky." The English publishers are Chatto and Windus, and the book had a great sale in these countries. It is the autobiography of an American tramp. Jim Tully took to the road as a hobo not as a poet or author on a holiday. Of his primitive and adventurous life he writes naturally, realistically and with a fine flare for vivid descriptions of vivid and thrilling experiences, of the leaping on and off moving trains, conflicts with the police, escapes from prison, blizzards, lynching and burning. In America "Beggars of Life" has already been accorded a place beside the masterpieces of tramp literature.

***

The County Courthouse in Galway as a work of architecture is greatly admired, and it is considered as fine a work of Gothic art as in Ireland can be found. It was the work of an Irish architect who was, accordng to our esteemed correspondent, Mr James Coleman, a noted Cork man of his day. It stands on the site of the ancient and venerable Abbey of Franciscans which, by the Charter of Charles II, "is to be and remains part of the County of Galway for ever." It was commenced in 1812, and on the 1st of April, 1815, it was opened for the Assizes, the going judges being Justices Fletcher and Osborne. Hardiman says of it that "it is altogether an ediface highly creditable to the county and considerably ornamental to the town." Many celebrated trials took place there. O'Connell, during his remarkable career at the Bar—unprecedented and unparallelled—came to Galway there "special" in many famous local cases, and Sir Oliver Burke, in his Anecdotes of the now defunct Connaught Bar, tells of that great man's appearance in the celebrated case of Ruttledge and Ruttledge arising out of the disputed title of David Watson Ruttledge to the estate. His house at Barbersfort was burned during our civil war, and it was, curious to say, the subject of a trial in that very same Courthouse last week. There is not one of the Ruttledge name now in the County of Galway, where at one time there were so many, so well known and so respected. David Watson Ruttledge, B.L., lived at Barbersfort, and his son Major David Ruttledge, succeeded him there. His daughter, Mrs Thompson, wife of Dr. Thompson, resides in Tuam, the only member of that family in the county. Even Mayo, where there were seven or eight distinct families of the Ruttledges, only but Mr. Ruttledge now remains a resident. Such are the ravages of time in these afflicted parts where it has done fearful destruction.

23/3/29

"An Admirable Combination"

was the expression used by a medical authority regarding the use of Holloway's famous remedies as household medicines.
They should find a place in every well ordered home.

HOLLOWAY'S
PILLS & OINTMENT.

THE PILLS are easy and agreeable to take, they rid the system of all impurities and stimulate to natural activity the Liver, Bowels and Kidneys. They promptly cure Indigestion, Biliousness, Headache, and kindred ailments, making one feel "Fit" and well, so rendering life enjoyable. Females find them of the greatest value.

THE OINTMENT in combination with the pills, is an unfailing remedy for Skin Affections, Bad Legs, Old Wounds, Sores, Boils, Cuts, Chilblains, Chapped Hands etc., cleansing before it heals, leaving the skin clear and healthy. It is also invaluable for Rheumatism and Sciatica ; and gives welcome relief in troubles of the Chest and Throat.

1/1 and 2/9 per box or pot, of all Chemists.

GAELIC FOOTBALL IN THE SCHOOLS

WESTERN JUNIOR LEAGUE.

The meeting between Tuam and Westport in the opening round of the Western Junior School's League, G.A.A., produced a spirited and well fought contest. A fast pace was maintained all through, and the tackling was very keen. The defences on both sides probably won the honours, and the forwards, especially those of Tuam, would have met with more reward had they taken the direct line to goal. St. Patrick's boys, playing with the wind, attacked from the throw-in, and Connolly scored Tuam's first point. Westport broke away from the goal kick, and McGing, on the left, scored a surprise goal. The Tuam goalie came to the rescue shortly afterwards, and Reynolds (Tuam) saved brilliantly almost immediately. Dunning, for Westport, was playing an outstanding game. Connolly placed well but nothing resulted, and the same player soon augmented Tuam's score with a well-deserved minor. Walsh and Ronan were outstanding in Tuam's forward line, but the former's effort met with poor reward. The penetrative power of the Tuam forwards after the interval was nullified by very poor marksmanship. They attacked persistently, but only one score—a point— resulted from a free by M.Murphy. Westport added two goals and a point to their half time score. H.Gill was responsible for the scores. He played a very fine game, and was ably assisted by Dunning. Westport owe their success principally to their goalie, who, time and again, brought of well timed saves. Meagher, their full back, did not make any mistakes, and came through his difficult task very well. Their right wing was certainly very clever. Both individually and as a team Tuam was good.

Tuam—J. J. Walsh (captain), C. Connolly, M.J. Murphy, F. O'Connell, D. Quinn, J. Glynn, L. Donelan, Chas. Donelan, F. Donelan, F. Keane, T. Curran, J. Rafferty (goal), T. Reynolds, M. Ronan, and P. Owens.　　　　　　　　　　　30/3/29

RETIREMENT OF MR. JAMES HULEATT.

The people of Tuam have learned with regret of the impending retirement of Mr James Huleatt from the position of Station Master at Tuam, a position which he has held practically since the amalgamation of the old Waterford & Limerick with the G.S.R., when he succeeded the late Mr Martin Egan as Station Master. Ever since his appointment Mr Huleattt has discharged his duties with such ability and courtesy as to gain not alone the approval of his superiors but the respect and esteem of the general public. Equally did his colleagues on the Railway hold him in affectionate regard and they deeply regret his severance from them. Now, after 45 years service with the railway, he retires on pension with the good wishes of all who know him and the hope that he may be long spared to enjoy his well earned leisure.

AN SAOGHAL GAEDHEALACH.

CONNRADH NA GAEDHILGE.

The annual Convention of the Gaelic League will be held at 25 Cearnóg Parnell, commencing Tuesday 2nd April, at 10 p.m.

Fleadh na Comdhála will be held in the Mansion House on Tuesday night, 2nd April, at 9 p.m.

Fleadh na Comdhála was at one time the Ceilidh par excellence of the year, but many other functions have sprung up in recent years to rival it, but as a representative gathering of the Gaels of Ireland, Fleadh na Comdhála still holds its own.

The annual collection for the language fund was made very generally on St.Patrick's day with very good results; but in many places no collection has been made yet. Of course this can be done any Sunday, and we hope no branch of the Gaelic League will neglect its duty in this respect. The Gaelic League cannot carry on the fight without money and the money can be got if looked for. Wherever collections have been made the response has been generous showing that the Irish people are always willing to help the Language movement.

Any person wishing to undertake this collection can get boxes and posters on application to the Ard-Runaidhe, 25 Cearnóg Parnell, Ath Cliath.

FEILE PADRAIC.

One of the most interesting St.Patrick's Day's celebrations was probably that held in the Hohenzollern Ober Lyceum, Berlin. A splendid programme was provided including Irish songs, dances and music, and a specially trained choir (German thoroughness).

The concert was organised by Dr. Walter Zorn and the professors and students who visited Ireland last year. Two of the students gave lectures illustrated by lantern slides on their tour in Ireland. The attendance at the concert included the Mayor of Wilmersdorf and the directors of the various Lyceums in Berlin.

In Baile Atha Cliath the two big events were the Feis Tighe organised by the Civil Service Gaelic Society, and the National Ceilidh, held on the 16th and 17th respectively. The Feis Tighe attracted over 800 people, and the National Ceilidh nearly 1,000. Interesting and interested visitors were fortunate in seeing a real Irish gathering, and they enjoyed the experience very much.

London Gaels hold what are now traditional celebrations. Mac Giolla Bride, President of the Gaelic League, presided at the Irish banquet in Paris. A splendid all-Irish concert was in the Ulster Hall, Belfast -- this was not organised by Gaels. The new Belfast Gaelic College was formally opened. A special service was given at St.Mary's Church -- a service which made one feel that he was in the heart of the Gaeltacht.

The new Belfast Gaelic College is a very spacious building, well equipped, containing a large concert hall and comfortable class rooms. Speaking at the opening ceremony, Father Fullerton thanked all who had helped in the good work, and he hoped and prayed that the hall will never be diverted from the purpose for which it was erected. Mr. Joseph Devlin said he had never been critical of any man's opinion. His indignation was with the people who had no point of view. The greatest evil that ever befell a community was stagnation. This modern age is distinctive for one thing -- the desire of men to shirk their responsibilities. There is a tendency, he said, in the North to draw us away from our national attachments; to tell us that we are not Irishmen but "Ulster men"; that we belong to something that is apart from Ireland. The more that doctrine is preached the more we must tear it to tatters. We must realise what the Gaelic League is teaching - that we belong to a country with priceless traditions; that we are custodians of glorious memories that must never die.

KNOCK PILGRIMAGES.

STATEMENT BY ARCHBISHOP.

Preaching at a confirmation service at Knock, Most Rev. Dr. Gilmartin, Archbishop of Tuam, said although there was no formal decision by the Ecclesiastical authorities on the genuineness of the alleged apparition of Our Lady at Knock, the evidence for the apparition was very arresting, and was certainly stronger than that which has created more frequented shrines in other countries.

" This is the fiftieth year since Our Lady is supposed to have appeared, as testified by a dozen witnesses, all now dead, except one or two," added his Grace, "and Father Tuffy tells me there is no falling off in the devotion of the pilgrims who each year come in increased numbers. In any case all those pilgrims come here to honour the Mother of God, and even if the apparition never took place the sacrifice they make and the fervour of the prayers will not be the less meritorious."

"I am glad to know from Father Tuffy that he has well-founded hopes that a Hospice will soon be established here, under the charge of the Sisters of Charity to accommodate pilgrims who might need hospital treatment."

6/4/29

TUAM TOWN COMMISSIONERS.

The monthly meeting of the above was held on Tuesday evening last,

Mr John Burke, Chairman, presided.

Other members present— Messrs Wm.Holian, John Byrne, Simon Fahy, Partk.Walsh, Patrick J.Dwyer, Malachy O'Keeffe, Michael W. Cahill, Patrick J. Byrne, John H. Corcoran, James Moran, Patrick Gibbons.

There were two tenders received for making and supplying 2 Ticket Boxes on wheels for the fairs and markets—one from Thomas Byrne for £14 and from David Dwyer for £19.

Mr. Walsh proposed that Thos Byrne's tender be accepted; Mr O'Keeffe seconded.

Mr T.Byrne's tender was accordingly accepted. ....

FOOTPATHS AND CHANNELS.

A letter was read from the Co. Surveyor stating that the matter of Ballygaddy Road footpath is having attention.

Chairman—Call Mr. Kennedy's attention to the state of the channel on the Galway Road which he promised to remedy some months ago.

Mr. Moran— He is going to make an application to the Co. Council for this work at the next meeting.

A letter was read from the Minister for Justice acknowledging the receipt of the Town Commissioners resolution relative to the Evil Literature Bill which would receive his attention.

LETTER FROM THE ARCHBISHOP.

The following letter was read, viz :

St.Jarlath's, Tuam,
21st March, 1929.

Dear Mr. Daly—I shall forward with great pleasure your resolution to Mgr. Hogan, our agent in Rome, whom I have already instructed to convey the congratulations for the whole Diocese to the Pope on the settlement of the Roman question. With all best wishes and thanks.

Yours sincerely,
+ T.P.Gilmartin.

The Housing Committee reported that the meat stalls were in want of repairs, especially eave gutters and slates gone.

Mr. O'Keeffe—The cost of repairs would be more than the rent you are getting.

Mr. Dwyer— It is a very long time since any repairs were done to them. I would ask the Clerk to let us know what rent we get from them.

Mr. Daly— £46 per annum.

Mr. Dwyer—I propose that repairs be carried out as recommended by the committee at a cost not to exceed £12.

Mr. Walsh—I second that.

The Clerk was directed to prepare a specification and advertise the work.

A letter from the Catholic Emancipation Centenary Committee was adjourned for consideration to next meeting. ....

A VOLUNTEER FIRE BRIGADE.

Mr. Corcoran—I wish to call attention to the necessity of keeping the fire hose and ladders in proper condition. The hose should be oiled and ready for work in the case of fire, and I suggest that about 12 young men be selected, a few from each road, to act as volunteers and be trained for the work, and that the townspeople be asked to subscribe to a fund to pay the volunteers so much per year.

Mr. Moran—The hose was taken out and oiled recently and is carefully looked after.

Mr. Cahill—Mr. Corcoran's is a very good suggestion.

Chairman—How do you propose to initiate the matter ?

Mr. O'Keeffe—It is a matter of great interest to the town, and I am sure a good many would subscribe if notified.

Mr. Dwyer—I propose that a public meeting be held this day fortnight to consider the matter of forming a Volunteer Fire Brigade for the town.

Mr. P. Byrne—I second that.

This was agreed to.

THE BELFAST BOYCOTT.

Mr. Fahy said he desired to call attention to the attitude adopted by some of the traders of Tuam with regard to the Belfast Boycott. Every town around had ceased to give orders to Northern travellers except a few in Tuam. He suggested that a list of their names be got and published. People from the 26 counties who go into the 6 counties are arrested without any cause, and on that account they should get no support.

Mr. Cahill— I saw some goods at Tuam Station the other day from Belfast which could be got equally as well in the Saorstat.

After some further discussion, Mr. Fahy proposed and Mr. Dwyer seconded, that they again call on the traders of Tuam to cease stocking goods from Belfast, and that in the event of their doing so in future that their names be published.

This was agreed to.

Mr. Toft applied for the use of the Shambles for his amusements.

Granted, but not to interfere with the potato market.

TRANSFERRED.

Supt. M. Buggy, Tuam, has been transferred to Kanturk, and will be replaced by Supt. Connolly, Swinford. 6/4/29

CONVENT OF MERCY RAFFLE.

Drawing of Prizes was held on the 3rd Inst. The Very Revd. Peter Kelly, Adm., presiding.

Winning numbers and winners were as follows:-
1st——£3 Note—7794—Kathleen Enright, Tarbert, Co. Kerry.
2nd—A Tray Cloth—1216
3rd—A Wristlet Watch—9169—Moira Quinn, Tuam.
4th—£2 Note—1307—Paddy Joe Greally, Mountrath, Leix.
5th—A Case of E.P. Spoons—11192—M. Mahoney, Monkstown.
6th—A Picture of the Sacred Heart—1256.
7th—A Fountain Pen—861—Miss Margaret Kelly, Irishtown.
8th—A Cushion—11731—J.A. Costello, Taylor's Hill, Galway.
9th—A Writing Pad and Fancy Envelopes—6023—D.B.Kirwan, Esq., Dalgan.
10th—A Tea Cosey—8649—John Martin, Ballindine.
11th— A Case of Stationery—11746—Miss Maggie Delaney, Convent of Mercy.
12th— A Cushion (No 2)—4277—Mrs J.B. Lilly, Cresson, Pa.
13th—A Child's Knitted Dress and Cap—1573—Miss J. Moran, Ballinedan.
14th— Some Squares of Toilet Soap—4245—Mrs Lilly, Cresson, U.S.A.
15th—A Jewellery Case—9151—Harry Quinn, Tuam.
16th—A Book Marker—8710—Eamon Mac Oireachtaigh, Raheny.
17th—The Life of St. Francis—2448—Mrs Timothy Waldron, High St., Tuam.
18th—Perfume and Toilet Soap—163—Thomas O'Donovan, Detroit.
19th—Friend or Foe—2069—Mr. R.F. Lynch, N.T., Ballybran.
20th—In Waste Places—097—Thomas O'Donovan, 1365 Cass Av., Detroit.

The sisters of Mercy return their most grateful thanks to the Benefactors who so kindly helped the charity.

We notice with pleasure that at the Sligo Feis Musical Competition this week Miss Ita Guy, of Hotel, Tuam, scored many successes. She got second prize in the Senior Piano Solo, 3rd prize in the Senior Piano Duet, and 1st in the Senior Quick Piano Practice—all splendid performances highly praised by the judges, deserving notice and congratulation.

In an Open Stroke Competition at Galway Golf Links on Easter Monday in which thirty-two took part, the prize was won by Mr. Paddy Noone, Dublin Road, Tuam, on a handicap of 27 with a gross of 93 and a net 66.

A correspondent informs us that some two months ago there died as a result of a motor accident in Dublin a well known and respected solicitor named Dixon. He adds, however, that his real name was Disken and that he came from these parts. He evidently thought Dixon would be less noticeable than Disken and hence adopted the other form.
6/4/29

TUAM RACE COMPANY LIMITED.

The annual meeting of the Tuam Race Company Limited, was held at the offices, Grand Stand, Parkmore, Tuam, on Wednesday, 3rd April, 1929.

Henry Concannon, Esq., Chairman, presided.

Also present—Messrs Michael W. Cahill, John Quinn, and James Daly, Shareholders.

Mr. Concannon proposed that the Report and Statement of Accounts for the year be adopted.

Mr. Cahill seconded and it was agreed to.

Mr. John Quinn proposed that Mr. James McDonnell be re-elected a Director of the Race Company. Mr. Cahill seconded and it was passed unanimously.

Mr Concannon proposed that Messrs Kevans & Son be re-elected Auditors of the company. Mr Cahill seconded it. Passed.

Mr. Concannon proposed that a dividend at the rate of two and a half per cent per annum, free of Income Tax, be paid to shareholders for the year ended 31st Dec. 1928. Mr Cahill seconded and it was passed unanimously.

Mr. John Quinn proposed, and it was passed unanimously :-   That we the shareholders of the Tuam Race Company, Ltd., congratulate Mr. James McDonnell on his almost complete recovery from the effects of the very serious accident which happened to him some months ago, and we trust that he will soon be able to come amongst us again.

Mr. Quinn also proposed a vote of thanks to the Chairman and Directors for their great interest in the affairs of the company, which was passed unanimously.
6/4/29

TUAM APRIL FAIR.

The Tuam April fair on Tuesday last was a medium cattle fair, chiefly 1st and 2nd class shorthorn stock. Buyers were well represented. All well bred stores showing condition were in good demand at firm rates. Fat stock brisk inquiry. Quotations :—

Stores, 6 to 12 months, £7 10s to £9 10s ; 1 to 2 years, £12 10s to £14 10s ; 3yrs old. £18 10s to £20.

Springing cows and heifers, £20 to £24.

Milch cows down calved, £18 to £21.

Store sheep, hoggets, £2 to £2 10s ; fat sheep £3 10s to £4 10s.

Pigs, £3 15s per cwt, l.w. ; bonhams from 30s to 45s each.

Wool, 1s 7d per lb.
6/4/29

There has been, says the "Observer," an appreciable fall in the value of licensed premises for the past three years. The licensed premises of Mr. O'Donoghue at the docks, which nearly five years ago were purchased for something like £1,200, were sold recently to Mr. Sharkey for a sum in the neighbourhood of £700.
6/4/29

HOLY WEEK IN TUAM.

The Ceremonies appropriate to this week, which brings the Lenten season to a close, and which from the liturgical point of view is the most important week of the whole year, were begun at the Cathedral on Palm Sunday at the 11.30 Mass with the blessing of the Palms and with the procession of the Palms through the Cathedral, in which His Grace the Archbishop took part. Palm Sunday commemorates the triumphal entry of Our Lord into Jerusalem on the Sunday before His death, when He was hailed by the people as the promised Messiah. "And a very great multitude spread their garment in the way; and others cut boughs from the trees, and strewed them in the way; and the multitudes that went before and that followed cried, saying; Hosanna to the Son of David; Blessed is He that cometh in the name of the Lord" (Matt.xx1).

THE TENEBRAE.

On Wednesday, Thursday and Friday evenings the office of Tenebrae was chanted in choir by a large number of priests of the Archdiocese. His Grace Most Rev. Dr. Gilmartin presided each evening. The office of Tenebrae consists of the Matins and Lauds of the three last days of Holy Week which are recited in each case on the previous evening. 'Tenebrae' which is a latin word meaning 'darkness' came to be applied to this office, because, as the office progresses, all the lights on the altar are gradually extinguished and the service ends in darkness. This darkness is expressive of the desolation of the Church at the death of her Redeemer, and symbolises also the darkness which enveloped the earth when Christ expired on Calvary. All the Antiphons, Psalms and Lessons of the Tenebrae office have a reference to the Passion of Christ, and the sad and beautiful Chants of the Lamentations of Jeremias are expressive of the grief of the Church. A notable feature of Tenebrae is the triangular candlestick with fifteen lighted candles. The topmost candle represents Christ. This candle is not extinguished but is hidden behind the altar for a brief period at the end of the office and again replaced to remind us that Our Lord died to rise again.

At the end of Tenebrae on Wednesday evening the Rev. M. Hennelly, C.C., Errismore, preached a sermon on the Blessed Eucharist. He dwelt upon the love exhibited by our Blessed Lord in the institution of this Sacrament and expounded with great clearness and force the Scriptural arguments for the Catholic Faith in the Real Presence. He concluded with a stirring appeal for an extension of the practice of frequent Communion and of frequent visits to our Heavenly King in the Sacrament of the Altar.

The clergy who attended included; Rev. M.J. Conroy, P.P. Athenry; Rev. O. Hannan, P.P., Cummer, Rev. P. Curran, P.P., Killererin; Rev.T. Lynch, P.P., Turloughmore; Rev.E.McGough, P.P., Annaghdown; Rev. P.Varden, C.C., Belclare; Rev. J. Gibbons, C.C., Monivea; Rev. E. Higgins, C.C., Kilbannon; Rev. M. Lavelle, C.C. Athenry; Rev. A. Moran, C.C., Headford; Rev. Egan, C.C., Corner Chapel; Rev. P. Cusack, C.C., Moylough;. Rev. P. King, C.C., Moore; Rev. M. Loftus, C.C. Skehanna; Rev.W. Keane, C.C., Spiddal; Rev.T. Ryan, C.C., Caherlistrane; Rev.J. Glynn, C.C., Turloughmore; Rev.J. Burke, B.D., Diocesan Inspector; Rev. M. Hennelly, C.C., Errismore; Rev. P. Kelly, C.C., Aughamore; Rev. J.T. Grealy, C.C., Balla, and the town and College priests.

The special chants on each occasion were beautifully rendered by Very Rev. Canon Walsh, President, St. Jarlath's College, and Rev. S. Blowick, C.C.

HOLY THURSDAY.

The morning ceremonies of Holy Thursday commenced at 8 o'clock with Pontifical High Mass sung by his Grace the Archbishop. The dominant note of the ceremonies on Holy Thursday morning is one of loving remembrance. For on this day the Church commemorates the Institution of the Most Holy Eucharist, which our Saviour bequeathed to us as His priceless legacy and as a perpetual memorial of His death, and to which St. John touchingly alludes in the words : "Having loved His own who were in the world He loved them to the end." The Institition of the Eucharist makes us think of Christ's love rather than His sufferings, and that is why on Holy Thursday morning the ministers at the Altar are clothed in the vestments of joy. At the Gloria in Excelsis the organ peals forth joyously and all the bells are rung. Henceforth until Holy Saturday mornn g they are silent as if the peaceful interlude of the Last Supper gave way once more to the tense atmosphere of the Passion. During the Mass of Holy Thursday the Archbishop consecrated the Holy Oils used throughout the year in the administration of the Sacraments of Baptism, Confirmation, Holy Orders and Extreme Unction. At the end of the Mass the Sacred Host, which is used in the Mass of the Presanctified on Good Friday, was borne in solemn procession from the High Altar to the Altar of Repose. Here during the day a silent crowd of devout worshippers kept vigil.

Besides the Archbishop the Ministers at the High Mass were; Rev. J. O'Reilly, deacon; Rev. P. Delaney, sub-deacon ; Rev. M. King, master of ceremonies ; Rev. J. Killeen and Rev. A. Colgan, assistant priests.

Practically the whole congregation received Holy Communion on Holy Thursday morning.

In the evening after the Tenebrae, the sermon on the Sacrifice of the Mass was preached by Rev. P. Kelly, C.C., Aughamore. The preacher took for his text the famous prophecy of Malachy and showed its magnificent fulfilment in the Mass. In simple and convincing language he explained to his hearers how the Mass superabundantly fulfils all the ends of Divine Worship and brings God's grace and mercy to those who assist at It, according to the measure of each one's faith and devotion.

GOOD FRIDAY.

The ceremonies of Good Friday began with the chanting of the Passion which was beautifully rendered by Canon Walsh, Fr. Kelly, and Fr. Blowick, assisted by the Cathedral Choir. Then followed the beautiful intercessory prayers, which are typical of the most ancient form of intercession in the Church, and which include prayers for heretics, Jews and Pagans as well as for all classes of the Faithful. Next came the unveiling, and adoration of the Cross, after which the Sacred Host was carried in procession from the Altar of Repose and the Mass of the Presanctified sung. The Vexilla Regis, the beautiful Passion hymn, which celebrates the victory of the Cross, was sung during the procession. The Mass of the Presanctified is so called because the Host which is consumed in the Mass has been consecrated previously on Holy Thursady. It is therefore not a Mass in the proper sense of the word because there is no consecration. Good Friday is in fact the only day of the year on which the Sacrifice of the Mass is not offered. The Mass of the Presanctified, however, recalls the institution of the Eucharist, and by uniting the memory of the Last Supper with the memory of Calvary gives expression to the twofold aspect of this Divine Sacrament.

The celebrant on this day was Rev. T. Gunnigan, The College; deacon, Rev. John Killeen, sub-deacon, Rev. E. Egan; master of ceremonies, Rev. M. King.

A sermon on the earlier scenes of the Passion was preached by Rev. J.T. Grealy, C.C., Balla, in which the preacher graphically depicted the sufferings and humiliations of our Saviour from the Agony in the Garden to His Condemnation by Pilate, and rounded off his discourse with an eloquent enforcement of the lesson of suffering which is to be learned from the Cross.

At 2 o'clock there was a Public Station of the Cross, at which a huge congregation attended.

The later scenes of the Passion were dealt with in the evening in a moving discourse by Fr. Gunnigan. His vivid description of the incidents of the via dolorosa and of the Sorrows of Mary, and his telling application of the Seven Last Words from the Cross, moved many of the large congregation to tears.

HOLY SATURDAY.

On Holy Saturday the ceremonies commenced at 8 o'clock with the blessing of the Paschal Candle, followed by the reading of the Prophecies, Blessing of the Baptismal Font, the chanting of the Litanies, and finally, Solemn High Mass. The celebrant of the High Mass was Rev. J. Burke, Diocesan Inspector; deacon, Rev. S. Blowick; sub-deacon, Rev. F. Lynch; master of ceremonies, Rev. M. King. The ceremonies of Holy Saturday are best understood if it be remembered that they were originally carried out on the night preceding Easter Sunday. These ceremonies are in many respects the most beautiful of all the Holy Week ceremonies. For they express with supreme dramatic effect the transition from the desolation of Calvary and the subdued sorrow of the days during which our Saviour's Body lay in the tomb to the triumphant joy of the Resurrection. The lighted Paschal candle represents the risen Christ. All the lights in the church having been first extinguished, are relighted from this candle to express the thought so prominent in the Easter Liturgy that we ought all die to sin and rise to newness of life with the Risen Saviour. The reading of the Prophecies with the beautiful prayers interspersed between, and the Blessing of the Font, recall the important ceremony of the Baptism of the Catechumens which used to take place on this day. Up to a certain point in the ceremonies the Sacred Ministers wear the vestments of mourning. But when the Solemn Mass commences they lay aside these for the white vestments symbolic of joy. Soon the statues are stripped of their veils, the organ and the church bells peal forth simultaneously, and the strains of the Grand Alleluia tells us that our Saviour is risen again.

EASTER SUNDAY.

On Easter Sunday there was a very large atendance at all the Masses, a large number of the faithful receiving the Blessed Sacrament at first Mass. At 11.30 Pontifical High Mass was celebrated, his Grace the Archbishop presiding. After the first Gospel his Grace ascended the pulpit and preached an inspiring sermon on the Resurrection. Before commencing his discourse he congratulated the people on the way they had attended the Holy Week ceremonies, and thanked the choir, the Nuns and the Christian Brothers for their good work. At the conclusion of the Mass His Grace imparted the Papal Blessing to the congregation.

THE ATTENDANCE

of the people at the various offices during the week was very large, and the numbers who approached the Blessed Sacrament of the Eucharist on Thursday was extremely large.

THE CATHEDRAL CHOIR

conducted by Mr. N. Hession, Organist, deserve the highest praise for their beautiful harmonised rendering of the week's sacred music.

6/4/29

GALWAY NOTES.

We recently celebrated in Dublin in a not too enthusiastic or befitting manner the centenary of two illustrious Irishmen -- Edmund Burke and Oliver Goldsmith. The orator who was to speak the eulogy of the greatest philosophical statesman that Great Britain ever had made a sorry mess of it and for the first time in his brilliant career did not do himself or his subject justice. Lord Birkenhead had a grand subject but he mishandled it woefully. Now Edmund Burke was connected with the County Galway and sojourned here with his aunt, Mrs.French, at Rahassane, then a fine country house, now a ruin, being burned down while owned by a Mr. Burke under such suspicious citrcumstances that the insurance was not paid. Here on the occasion of his visit the great statesman went into Loughrea and seeing a number of children standing in wonder around a puppet show he generously insisted on paying for the admission of the whole lot of admiring youngsters. When his friends remonstrated with him and offered to participate in the gift, he said, "No, no, my dear friends, this pleasure must be all my own; perhaps I shall never again have the opportunity of making many human beings happy". This incident which we can read in the "Dublin Penny Journal" of 1832, shows what a beautiful character Edmund Burke was. As a French writer said of him when he died, "There never was a more beautiful alliance between virtue and talents; all his conceptions were grand, all his sentiments generous. The great leading trait of his character and that which gave it all its energy and its colour was that strong hatred of vice which is no other than a personal love of virtue; it breathes in all his writings; it was the guide of all his actions, but even the force of his eloquence was insufficient to transfuse it into the weaker or perverted minds of his contemporaries. Mr.Burke was too superior to the age in which he lived. His prophetic genius only astonished the nation which it ought to have governed". Such was the greatest Irishman not only of his age but of all time. His aunt, Mrs. French, who lived at Rahassane, was, as his good mother was, a Roman Catholic. He is believed to have died one. After the French family left Rahassane it was occupied by a family named Joyce related to the Merview family, and they getting into financial difficulties the estate was sold in the Landed Estates Court and purchased by Walter Martin Burke, B.L., of Curraleigh, near Claremorris, who went to India early in life and made money at the Indian Bar. Returning to Ireland he got the then fashionable craze of land purchase and bought Rahassane as a speculation. He lived there some two years and on his way home one evening he and Sergeant Wallace, an Englishman and a dragoon, who was guarding him, were both shot at a turn of the road where the car necessarily should slow down. The spot where the murdered were ambushed is still pointed out. It is the wall surrounding Castle Taylor, and it is believed that old Mr. Walter Shaw Taylor saw the men and that he could recognise them, but he did not. Mr.Burke was returning from Gort, where he had gone to hand notices to quit on the tenants of the estate. He was succeeded in the estate by his brother, a doctor in London, and it was during his ownership the house was burned. The only part of the once nice house which escaped was the part which Edmund Burke's Catholic mother had got built for her use as a private chapel. A beautiful double row of beech trees which led to the house from the gate lodge was cut down by Dr. Burke and sold for a song.

13/4/29.

TUAM SENIOR SELECTION.

All followers of the game will see a good exhibition of football on Sunday next, at Galway, when Tuam senior team will travel to the opponents' grounds to give a good account of themselves against Galway and Renmore selected.

Those teams met some time ago in Parkmore, in Tuam, and without doubt it was one of the best exhibitions of Gaelic football seen for some time. Both teams have trained on since last they met, and the weather prevailing as it is, the game will prove just as interesting to the followers of the Gaelic code.

The following is a list of the Tuam players which was handed to me during the week, and to announce that the cars will leave the Square, Tuam at 12.30 for Galway :-

H.Cunningham (capt.), H. Burke, T. Joyce, M. Mannion, J. O' Rorke, P. Hannon, D. McCormack, P. Waldron, P. Kelly, T. Hughes, W. Birrell, L. O'Brien, C. Reid, J. Nohilly, M. Stewart, P. Walsh, T. Creaven, M. Rooney.

TUAM JUNIOR TEAM SELECTION.

At a meeting on Thursday evening the following were selected to play the senior schools team on Sunday next in Parkmore. Match starts at 3.15 :--

J. Farrell, W. Leahy, M. Cooney, M. Curran, W. Stockwell, J. Rooney, C. Kelly, M. Murray, T. McGough, A. Nicholson, J. Tighe, T. Leahy, J. Walsh, Jer. Walsh, J. Pierce, W. Pierce, P. Flanagan, J. Fahy, M.J. Curran.

13/4/29

WHY THE RALEIGH

THE ALL-STEEL BICYCLE IS BETTER

BECAUSE it is the only bicycle in the world built entirely of steel and guaranteed for ever.

BECAUSE it is built by special processes and plant unrivalled by any other manufacturer.

BECAUSE the Raleigh is sold at a fixed price, as distinct from alleged "cheap" bicycles sold under various names at high profits.

BECAUSE Raleigh agents put quality first and rely upon continuous sales—consult them for your needs.

From 11/6 monthly

or cash from £5 19s. 6d(no deposit)
with Dunlop tyres. Specify Sturney-Archer 3speed gear
Agents everywhere, send for "The Book of the Raleigh" free.

TUAM	Michael Heskin.
BALLINROBE	J.B.Staunton.
CAHERLISTRANE	John J.Gannon.
DUNMORE	O'Malley Bros.
MOUNTBELLEW	Mrs.B.Noone

20/4/29

At the meeting of the Galway Hospitals Committee last week, Dr. O'Malley reported that a man from Co. Mayo, had arrived suffering from the effects of drink. The Secretary pointed out that as far back as January, 1925, an order was made directing the medical staff not to admit patients suffering from alcoholism. The order stated among other things that if a person could afford the luxury of indulging in the excessive use of drink they could afford to go to a private hospital for treatment   20/4/29

TUAM PIG FAIR.

The above held on Wednesday last was without doubt the largest fair of its kind held here yet this season. Pigs kept pouring in all night and all morning, until one wondered how there could be buyers enough for the enormous quantity displayed. Nevertheless they were all disposed of, and what is much to the point, at highly remunerative prices, averaging 80s l.w. The Irish porker is coming into his own again.   20/4/29

THE THREE R'S

There was a time within the memory of living man when the essential of an education in this and kindred countries was a knowledge of the fundamental principles described and epitomized in the words "the three R's" meaning thereby that a thorough knowledge was taught and acquired of reading, writing and arithmetic. It was then believed and accepted as an axiom that no man or woman could really be educated who failed to have a thorough knowledge of these essentials. Then every person who claimed to be educated wrote a good, legible hand, spelled correctly and could add and calculate simple sums. If he or she failed in any one of these essentials he or she was by so much deemed and properly so to be uneducated. Now we have somehow modified our views on these important matters, and we are sorry to find that they are being if not neglected at least shoved aside for more ornamental if less useful subjects. The blight of the intermediate system of education and the undue training of the memory by it and by our present system of examination have certainly lowered the standard of value of these primary subjects. The Chinese, through ages past, brought examination in memory training to a high pitch of perfection and we cannot congratulate them upon thereby producing capable citizens or efficient men. The curse of the examination system is now being deplored by some of the leading educational authorities in England and they rightly regard it as calculated to unduly develop one faculty, that of mere memory, at the expense of other equally and relatively in some respects more useful and important mental faculties. A boy or girl was found by his or her gift of memory to excel and to gain the highest academic prizes and later on to win the best posts in the service of the state or in other departments of commercial or public life, and yet when they were brought to deal with the every day matters of life or the business details of their office they were discovered to be often quite unfit for the task. Their powers of reasoning and observation were deficient, their other mental qualities were underdeveloped, and all they did to get the post and all they could do to fill it was to depend on a trained memory which did not necessarily mean a trained intelligence. Take the one simple matter of handwriting. This was once deemed a prime subject of study in every primary school and as a result we had boys and girls who wrote beautiful hands and did so because a prize was attached to the proficiency and excellent models such as the Vere Foster and Christian Brothers' copy books were provided and they were made to study the examples of caligraphy therein given. There are now hundreds of young persons looking for situations for which they may be otherwise qualified who are turned down when their letters of application are seen and read. In many cases they are not only badly written and illegible scrawls but even the simplest words are badly spelled. Once if a so called educated man made a mistake in spelling or in the pronunciation of words in common use he was regarded as not educated and was so treated. Now it is too common a sight to come across letters written by presumably educated men or women for which in the old days a boy or girl would in elementary classes of a village school be severely reprimanded. Then another essential subject of education, one vitally so, is arithmetic, the trained faculty of dealing with figures in even the elementary matters of addition, subtraction, division and multiplication. How many so called educated young men and young women to-day could stand the old tests? We heard of the case where an otherwise educated young man could not off-hand calculate and add up five simple sums of money. There are hundreds we hear who cannot correctly add up, tot or make the simplest calculation, and many who for want of this training in their youth are heavily handicapped in life. We say nothing of correct and fluent speaking, for it is not so universal as it was, and the art of reading aloud or of reciting pieces of prose or poetry seems to have died out in most of the ordinary schools, and yet how necessary and how useful is that art it is needless to point out. Geography also seems to be totally neglected and the most appalling ignorance seems to prevail as to the several countries of the world, their extent, population and economic conditions. A people who want to get on in these days of universal competition must study the lives, customs and ways of other peoples and other countries and not allow their minds to provincialise and narrow down to trivial and useless matters of their own towns, district or country. In the old days all these subjects we refer to were thoroughly taught and universally learned. In girls' schools of the secondary class formerly a subject of general training was what was called deportment, or the proper way to speak, act, walk and conduct oneself. We fear that does not hold the same prominence in the programme as it did. We find women in England deplore the changed habits of the girls they now come across. They are more or less the product of the late war which brought so many curses upon these countries. Girls now cease to cultivate the qualities they once shone in and by which they were so attractive and so prized for possessing, and as a result of the change they seem less looked for by men as partners in life. They are crowding into positions men formerly held and they are not as well fitted for the posts, and worse than all they are acquiring mannish ways which in proportion as they are developed are calculated to deprive them of the special attractions of their sex which made women so fascinating. All said and ended women will never in all matters be the equal of men and as well able to bear the burdens of life or as efficiently to discharge the same duties. All these matters may be considered and deplored when one comes to study the future of the rising race of our countrymen and women, but for any man of responsibility to ignore them and try to set them aside is a fatal and foolish policy and one which no newspaper that strives to represent the public needs and to speak out the truth should ignore or neglect on any false wretched plea of expediency or any pretence of policy whatsoever.

"CEDRIC" CARRIES RECORD FIGURES FROM COBH.

The White Star Line announce that the "Cedric" which left Cobh on Sunday last (14th instant) embarked at the Irish port 336 Third Class passengers, and this is the largest number of passengers in this class carried out of Cobh by any line this year.   20/4/29

SPAIN AND IRELAND

Through the kindness and thoughtfulness of our esteemed friend, Monsignor O'Dogherty, the distinguished Rector of the Irish College of Salamanca, we are indebted for a copy of the leading daily Spanish paper of Madrid. There we notice the high compliment that great journal paid to the TUAM HERALD. It reproduced in extenso in it's influential columns a translation into Spanish of an article in TUAM HERALD of March 30 on "Spain and Ireland."

This is a great honour and compliment to us and we cannot help feeling not only proud but grateful for such distinguished recognition at it's hands of our efforts to keep alive the old friendly relations that for centuries existed between Spain and Ireland and which we trust will every year become closer, and more cordial as time goes on.

TUAM ST. JARLATH'S HURLING CLUB.

An enthusiastic and representative meeting of the above was held in the Town Hall on Monday night, 15th April, for the purpose of affiliating with the North Galway Board G.A.A.

Mr. J.Nohilly kindly consented to take the chair.

It was decided to ask Mr. S.Browne to act as Hon. Pres.

The following officers were elected for the forthcoming year :-

Capt., T.Bray; vice-capt., M.Keegan; hon.sec., F.Bray; hon.treas., J.Coughlan.

Many items concerning the future progress of the team were discussed.

It was decided to hold another meeting in the coming week for the purpose of selecting a team to meet Monard at Abbey on Sunday, 28th inst.

A motion was proposed and carried thanking the Commissioners for having kindly given the use of the hall.

20/4/29

TUAM MARKETS.

Potatoes	...	8d to 9d per stone
Chickens	...	6s 0d per pair
Ducks	...	5s 0d per pair
Hay	...	3s 6d to 4s 0d per cwt.
Oats	...	1s 2d to 1s 4d per st.
Oaten straw	...	3s 0d per cwt
Wheaten ,,	...	4s 6d per cwt
Turnips	...	1s 3d per cwt
Mangolds	...	1s 2d per cwt
Pigs	...	80s per cwt l.w.
Bonhams	...	30s to 45s each.
Wool	...	1s 7d per lb.

20/4/29

Great Southern Railways.

Big Reduction

IN

HARVESTERS' FARES

TO

STATIONS IN GREAT BRITAIN.

Until Further Notice
CHEAP THROUGH THIRD CLASS
SINGLE TICKETS
will be issued from
Achill, Ballinrobe, Ballina, Balla, Ballyhaunis, Ballymote, Ballaghadereen, Ballymoe, Ballysodare, Ballindine, Bekan, Boyle, Ballyvary, Castlebar, Castlerea, Castlegrove, Carrowmore, Charlestown, Claremorris, Collooney, Curry, Donamon, Edmondstown, Foxford, Hollymount, Islandeady, Kiltimagh, Kilfree, Killala, Leyny, Milltown (Galway), Manulla, Mallaranny, Newport, Roscommon, Sligo, Swinford, Tubbercurry, Tuam, Westport.

Particulars of the Specially Low Fares can be obtained at any of the above Stations.

P.J.FLOYD,
Traffic Manager.

20/4/29

PRIEST ARRESTED.

The Rev. John Fahy, C.C., Bullaun, was arrested on Tuesday morning last by Superintendent Doyle, Loughrea, and a number of guards and brought to Loughrea District Court, where two charges were preferred against him in connection with the alleged rescue of two head of cattle from the sheriff's bailiff.

When charged Father Fahy made a long statement in which he said that the State was guilty of high treason against the Irish nation in bringing him into that unlawful assembly (the Court) in Republican territory under the jurisdiction of an Irish Republican Government, and in direct contravention of ecclesiastical laws.

Evidence having been given Father Fahy was returned for trial on bail to the next Circuit Court in June. He refused to give bail.

20/4/29

CONNACHT DRAWS.

On the reading of the minutes at a meeting in Castlerea on Sunday last objection was made by Mr. S.Jordan, T.D. (Galway) to the draw in which Galway and Sligo were matched on the ground that the meeting was illegal and the draw, therefore, was invalid. On the appeal for peace by the Chairman, Mr. S.T.Ruane, Pres., who said that the Connacht crux was now over and they should not start quibbling about small matters, Mr. Jordan consented to allow the original draw to stand if Sligo were agreeable.

Mr. Kilcoyne (Sligo), however, declined to agree, and he moved that a redraw be made. This was seconded by Mr. Jordan, but was defeated by 6 votes to 4 in favour of a motion by Mr. Maguire (Mayo), seconded by Mr. Feely (Roscommon), that the original draw stand. The match between Sligo and Galway was then fixed for Castlerea on Sunday, April 28, with Mr. D. O'Rourke as referee, and the winners of this match will play Mayo on May 12 at Boyle : Referee, Mr. Murray (Leitrim).

20/4/29

Seasonable Farmer's Remedies.

STAFFORD'S CURD AND WOOL BALL MIXTURE FOR LAMBS.
STAFFORD'S PIG SPECIFIC for Condition
etc., 1/- per box, 1/6 double size, postage 6d extra.
STAFFORD'S POULTRY SPECIFIC, 1/- & 2/-
per box. Postage 6d extra.

Address :
STAFFORD.
CHEMIST,
VICAR STREET, TUAM.
Branches : DUNMORE & MOUNTBELLEW.

20/4/29

G.A.A. NEWS.

TUAM STARS V GALWAY CITY.

On Sunday at Galway Sports Ground, a selection from Galway City and Renmore teams beat Tuam Stars by 3 goals and 3 points (12 points) to 2 goals and 2 points (8 points), and Oranmore hurling team beat Galway City by 5 goals and 2 points (17 points) to 1 goal and 5 points (8 points).

When the teams met previously Tuam won by 4 points, and it was by this margin Galway won Sunday's game.

Galway played with the wind in the first half, and during this period the ball seldom went to the Galway end. In the first minute Gill scored a goal for Galway from a difficult angle. Galway maintained the pressure and kept on the offensive but their forwards lost several chances through erratic shooting. The Tuam backs cleared well from several attacks before Fenlon added a point to Galway's score. An attack by Tuam was easily repulsed, and MacBride from a long distance out added another point to Galway's score. Galway added another goal and a point to their score before half-time. McCarthy and MacBride were the scorers.

Although playing against the wind in the second half, Galway at the outset pressed hard. Tuam then broke away and scored a goal which was quickly followed by a second which Johnson in the Galway goal narrowly failed to save. Play was fairly even for a time, and although the Galway defence was severely tested it held until near the close when Tuam added two points from far out. The full time score was :

GALWAY—3 goals 3 points.
TUAM—2 goals 2 points.

A return game will be played in Tuam at a later date.

20/4/29

Publicans in the rural areas in Co. Galway particularly in Connemara, are properly co-operating with the members of the trade in the city of Galway to press on the Intoxicating Liquor Commission to recommend radical changes in the Intoxicating Liquor Act 1927. The law which compels publicans not to open their premises to travellers until one o'clock p.m. on Sundays and to close down at 7 p.m. is regarded as a hardship

20/4/29

20/4/29

THE LEWIS ESTATE.

The famous Lewis Estate, in this county which figured large in the old Land League days is at long last being transferred to the occupying tenantry. There is a large area of untenanted lands at Alleendarra comprising nearly 800 acres, and 14 acres of land at Gortnakila. It was on this estate the question about the percentage of reduction in rent raised a great controversy in which Lord Clanricarde appeared. He contended and rightly that the percentage of 5 to 10 per cent he allowed on his estates upon which the rent was never raised was more than equivalent to the fifteen given on the Lewis and other estates where the land was bought in the Landed Estates Court, and the owners, as they were invited to do so, raised the rents fifty per cent. This logic was not appreciated by Mr. O'Brien, and the order went out that the Plan of Campaign should be adopted on the Clanricarde estate. It unfortunately was, and the result was that the rental was increased some £5000 a year consequent on the surrender of valuable middle interests where the rent was equivalent to a small rent charge. Hundreds of farms went derelict for years and the wealth of the country by so much reduced. Scores of farmers were ruined and never recovered their old position, losing their self respect by enforced idleness. And it is now admitted that the Plan was the invention of Labouchere who wanted to prevent Home Rule and embarrass Parnell. It succeeded and delayed Home Rule for years and when it came it came to a divided Ireland which would not be the case if it was granted when Gladstone first proposed giving it and got his Bill through the Commons.

20/4/29

STREET TRADING

Street trading is becoming a nuisance and an organisation is being formed to put it down. For sometime back—it has been going on for some years—a form of street trading has come into being which has had, and is having, a penalising effect upon all classes of people living in our towns. It injuriously affects every interest, from the working man to the trader, the banker, the professional classes, and unless steps are taken immediately by the Irish Government to legitimatise trade in our towns, there can be but one ending to our town life—disaster, bankruptcy. The towns and villages have grown up under the protecting care of Parliament. From time immemorial they supplied a public requirement. The farmers till and cultivate the land and produce stock and cereals which are marketed in our towns. The two classes were dependent on each other; the farmers sold their produce and the exchange of commodities, with the trader enabled the shopkeeper to befriend the struggling farmer, when he needed temporary help and assistance. The first to admit this mutual dependence and interdependence—one upon the other—is the farmer. Speak to him and he'll tell you in confidence, that in trying years, in years of affliction and in years of requirement the town merchant was his best friend. The farmer does not want to break up or discontinue that connection. Why should he? In the hour of difficulty the farmer's best friend, if he was on good standing with him, was the townsman. But a kind of trade or street marketing is allowed to-day which is weakening the connection and breaking up the relations described. Irish towns have lost their old sense of public spirit and look upon all local men and traders with indifference. They have no local patriotism.

20/4/29

JOHN O'CONNOR POWER.

There are those still amongst us who remember John O'Connor Power as a student at St. Jarlath's College and as the eloquent and able member for Mayo. He was one of the most brilliant orators in the British Parliament and held a high place there as a speaker when he was run out of politics by a jealous gang who themselves were cast away when found out and are hardly remembered today. He was scandously treated, as Michael Davitt said, but he got little consideration from his colleagues because he would not fall in with their ways which ultimately led to ruin and disruption. T.P.O'Connor refers to him in his Recollections but is unfair to him in parts and inaccurate in some details. He says of him according to Mr. Jasper Tully's admirable review of his book :-

O'Connor Power was a remarkable figure in the early struggle waged for the Land for the People. His first election for the great County of Mayo was an outstanding event, whose influence grew with the succeeding years. It spread all over Connaught and inspired the first stages of the Land League. It was O'Connor Power's victory at the Mayo polls broke not only the power of landlordism but the power of Whiggery. The famous Irishtown meeting is always at the beginning of the Land League. Michael Davitt's name is associated by a certain legend with that meeting. The truth is that Davitt was not present at that meeting. It was O'Connor Power was the great central figure that day. He had been an old Fenian leader, and he was backed to a man by the Mayo Fenians, headed by P.W. Nally. At page 83 of his first volume, he refers to O'Connor Power as having been in his childhood an inmate of Ballinasloe Workhouse. This is paraded in derision, although at that time in the Famine Clearances some of the best of the Irish race were forced as children into Workhouses. At page 85 he stresses the "horror and contempt of his old associates for the pauper boy's name". He then refers to O'Connor Power's "tremendous defect of a very irritable and fierce temper". He continues, "O'Connor Power had a powerful but very ugly face, the ugliness accentuated by the marks of a severe attack in childhood of small-pox. Smallpox was in those days a mark or form of class inferiority; only the children of the very poor ever bore its traces. When O'Connor Power was in one of his fits of rage these little marks of smallpox would become white and his face looked ugly and ferocious".

O'Connor Power was undoubtedly a brilliant speaker in Parliament, and this is what incited against him the jealousy and rage of men, who looked upon him as an obstacle in their path. At page 84 of his first volume, T.P. says O'Connor Power had no profession; and for a while he managed to hold "the meagre job of a professor of history in a poor provincial College". Yet with all his power of impressing and moving the House of Commons, he says O'Connor Power "found a difficulty in paying for his dinner amid all the luxury-making of the Palace of Westminster". He refers to "Biggar having contempt for penniless men, and regarding O'Connor Power as no better than a traitor, and thus hounding him out of the Irish Party". "For the last twenty or thirty years of his life he was an uneasy ghost, with his great gifts unused and his heart broken. He had one piece of luck; he married the widow of a wealthy instrument maker, and hunger at least was banished from his door". He refers contemptuously to O'Connor Power disguised as a house painter, organising the Fenian movement in the North of England, and he says he had often to go from town to town on foot because he had not money for railway or tram fare. He was detected by the authorities, and had to serve some months in jail. This is T.P.'s picture of O'Connor Power, poor and unable to purchase a dinner in Parliament when he was a member of it, and once an inmate of Ballinasloe Workhouse.

20/4/29

The effort to organise a Volunteer Fire Brigade in Tuam has not succeeded. At the meeting called for the purpose in the Town Hall on Tuesday evening only about half a dozen people attended, and so the project was allowed to fall through.

The proposed improvements at Salthill---the erection of a kiosk, shelters, seats, band stand, etc., will cost £1000 which will be raised by loan.

Last week eggs were sold in the Galway market at the astonishingly low price of 1/2 per score. Later in the day the price rose to 1/9 per score.

20/4/29

MACARDLES
No. 1 STRONG ALE.

Unequalled For Bottling Or Draught.

MACARDLE, MOORE & CO., LTD.,
  THE DUNDALK BREWERY, DUNDALK.   27/4/29

ROYAL DUBLIN SOCIETY
SPRING SHOW
AT
BALLS BRIDGE,

MAY 8, 9, 10 & 11.

Support your Staple Industry by attending this great National Event.

EXCURSIONS FROM EVERYWHERE.

EDWARD BOHANE, Director.
Balls Bridge, Dublin.
27/4/29

Great Southern Railways.

V I S I T
THE SPRING SHOW
(Royal Dublin Society's)

8th, 9th, 10th & 11th May, 1929

On 7th, 8th, 9th, 10th and 11th May RETURN TICKETS will be issued at SINGLE FARES TO DUBLIN from ALL STATIONS Available for Return up to and including Monday, 13th May, and by all Trains.

See Company's Posters for full particulars.
P.J. FLOYD,   Traffic Manager.
27/4/29

TUAM TOWN COMMISSIONERS.

NOTICE TO CONTRACTORS.

The Tuam Town Commissioners will, at their meeting to be held on Tuesday, 7th May, 1929, receive and consider tenders for executing repairs to the Meat Stalls and Sheds at Circular Road, according to specification to be seen at the office of the Town Clerk.

A Deposit of £1 must accompany the tender and will be forfeited in the event of the contractor not perfecting his bond.

Tenders, enclosing the names of two solvent sureties, will be received by me up to the hour of 8 o'clock, p.m. on the above-named day.

The lowest or any tender not necessarily accepted.

By Order,
JAMES DALY,
Acting Town Clerk.

TUAM HANDBALL COMMITTEE.

Tenders are invited for the building of a Handball Court on the site at the rear of the Courthouse, Tuam.

Tenders received after Saturday, 4th May, will not be considered.

Lowest tender not necessarily accepted.

Specification and plan can be seen any day between 2 and 3 o'c. p.m. on application to
T. JOYCE,
  Hon. Secretary,
    c/o Central Hotel,
      Tuam.

27/4/29

The Tuam Herald

SATURDAY, MAY 4, 1929

OUR ECONOMIC CONDITION

Two important pronouncements from two authoritative sources were made on Monday on the actual economic condition of the Free State which are of more than ordinary importance and significance. The facts therein stated should give the Irish people grounds for hopefulness and inspire a greater degree of confidence in them in the future of their country than would seem to generally exist. We regret to find in too many cases a sense of national inferiority, a slavish submission to the racial inferiority complex which is the result of past conditions and should now, if we are ever to advance, give place to a more self reliant spirit and a self respecting feeling of confidence in ourselves. We do not want now to give instances of this deplorable national self depreciation and this want of confidence in ourselves and our country and future, but they are very patent and persistent and prevalent. Combined with that is a sense of political insecurity and uncertainty for which there are or need be no grounds if we only do our duty. All this discouraging of ourselves tends to induce those of us who have money to invest to put it into every enterprise but a native one. It was this want of confidence in ourselves and in our future which was commented upon by Mr. Colbert, the Chairman of the Agricultural Credit Corporation, and for which he conclusively showed we have no real grounds, in his thoughtful address at the Rotary Club. He pointed out that Ireland's financial status stands high and that the Free State, according to a London financial journal recently, stood fourth on a list of thirty-four Government borrowers. He further pointed out that the Free State credit in New York stands in the very front rank of foreign Government borrowers and took precedence of such sound and solvent European borrowers as Holland, Sweden and Switzerland. He stated that the Free State National Debt is both absolutely and relatively amongst the smallest in the world, and that a third of the National Debt is counterbalanced by invested capital assets which are and will be revenue producing, while the whole debt is underpinned and reinforced by an exceptionally strong annual sinking fund. A comparison of our financial position even with that of Great Britain, with a debt burden exceeding seven thousand millions sterling, with an annual Budget expenditure exceeding eight hundred million pounds, with all three parties seeking instead of retrenchment and economy new sources of revenue with which to finance new vote-catching projects and with over a million unemployed who have to be carried on the backs of the rest of the population is not, he contends, as comfortable a financial position as the Free State. These statements are made by a financial expert and therefore they should be carefully considered by our people and they should, if dispassionately viewed, give them greater confidence in the future of their country and make them more resolute in their efforts to increase the productive revenues of the country. The other important statement made on Monday was the speech delivered at Cork by President Cosgrave. This also dealt with the economic situation. He pointed out how sound and hopeful it was and he stated that a stable basis had been reached in the national finances; that there were no undetermined liabilities hanging over our heads, and that the period of violent fluctuations in prices, wages and cost of living had come to an end. He also said that, allowing for abnormal items, the approximate cost of running the State was about twenty-four millions; that this figure was likely to remain constant for some time, and that the downward trend would be gradual, unless the abolition of some of the services was agreed to. He dealt upon these and many other encouraging circumstances, and in conclusion he rightly said that it was high time that some one sounded a cheerful note about our future based not on foolish optimism but upon a sense of reality. This he truly said was the only sound policy upon which the prosperity of the State could be built up and maintained. We seldom come across more important and significant statements than those made by President Cosgrave and Mr. Colbert. Both were speaking authoritatively upon questions they were competent to deal with and both were speaking with the calm assurance of fact and reality and basing their statements upon absolute and unquestioned statistics and figures that cannot be controverted and that eloquently speak for themselves and that require to be but plainly and clearly stated to carry conviction with them. There is no manner of doubt but that the actual economic condition of the Free State is sound and hopeful and that it can be further improved if the people only do their part by producing more and talking less, by discrediting any and every effort to undermine or prejudice the stability of things or by encouraging, aiding or abetting disorder or unrest or giving countenance to those who do so.

The syllabus of Tuam Feis is printed. It embraces 37 competitions covering every branch of Gaelic culture. Upwards of £100 are being offered in prizes. Last year Tuam Feis was one of the most successful Feiseanna in the county, and it is hoped to make this year's even a greater success.   4/5/29

GALWAY NOTES.

In the current number of "Studies"- a well known Dublin quarterly - Mr. Michael Tierney, Professor of Greek at the University of Dublin and a native of this county, writes a very learned and interesting article on "Tarsus, the Birth place of St. Paul". When rescued from an excited mob at Jerusalem by the Roman Tribune, Lysias, St. Paul astonished that officer by asking in eloquent Greek for permission to speak to the people. "What,", said Lysias, as we read in the Acts of the Apostles, "you know Greek"? "I am a Jew," said Paul, "a Tarsian from Cilicia, a citizen of no mean city". Mr. Tierney gives a brief but connected account of that once great city, now a mere collection of huts. It attained fame under the Greeks and Romans, but gradually, like other once important places, declined into obscurity. It had once a famed University, one only inferior to those of Alexandria and Athens - its curriculum being a "rounded education". Mr. Tierney is a prominent member of the Dail, and a useful and active parliamentarian. He was born at Ballymacward in this county, and there his parents live. He got his early education at Galway College, and is an accomplished Greek scholar and professor of that wonderful language

***

"Printing at Ballinrobe" is the title of a very interesting paper by Mr. E. McDix. His inquiries into this question are, as usual, very exhaustive and very comprehensive, and are characterised by his usual accuracy. He tells us that in 1846 there was a Michael Connolly a Letter Press Printer in Abbey Street, Ballinrobe, and that in 1850 at Mr. Gore Kelly's general Printing Office was printed "A Special Report of the Trial of the Rev. David Mylotte, R.C.C., against the Rev. John Callaghan". There was also in 1866 printed there the newspaper the "Ballinrobe Chronicle and Mayo Advertiser". It was a weekly 6 columns to a page paper and is stored at the British Museum. It was suspended in 1866 for a few months owing to a fire which broke out and destroyed a valuable and highly appointed printing office but the publication of the paper was resumed and continued until 1900 when it was dropped consequent on the death of Mr. Kelly. Here was printed the first edition of the Commentaries on the Epistles by the Very Rev. John McEvilly, then President of St. Jarlath's College and afterwards Bishop of Galway and ultimately Archbishop of Tuam. It was a wonderfully printed work, remarkably and creditably so, for a local printing office to turn out, and it was greatly praised for the admirable style of its get up. Mr. John Feerick, after Mr. Kelly's death, continued the "Chronicle" printing office and runs it successfully to this day. He is a native of Tuam.

***

We are sorry to see by "Observer" that in Galway the craze for gambling on racehorses is not confined exclusively to the sterner sex. There are women in the city who are as well posted about the "form" of the "gee gees" as the most inveterate male punter. And now comes the news that a certain trio of the fair sex in Galway have been able to secure a half-dozen of the London Stock Exchange Sweep tickets on the Derby. This is something of an achievement when it is stated that influential business men have been unable to secure these tickets at any price. It is scandalous for the London Stock Exchange to be encouraging betting. 4/5/29

***

A resolution congratulating Mr. John Duckette on his appointment as stationmaster at Tuam was passed by his fellow townsmen of the Killarney U.D.C.

***

Mrs Smallwood has taken Quarry House, Galway, for the summer months.

***

The Barnaderg Barracks are to be rebuilt at a cost of £1,450

TUAM TOWN CLERKSHIP.

We understand that intimation has been received by the Tuam Town Commissioners from the Local Appointments Commissioners that they recommend Mr. John Peter Whyte, Ballinastack, Ballyglunin, as Clerk to the Town Commissioners. Mr. Whyte is 24 years of age and his recommendations are that he has had a good secondary education, Commercial and Secretarial training in the City of Galway Technical Institute, and is a fluent native Irish speaker.

4/5/29

IRISH MUSIC.

TO THE EDITOR TUAM HERALD.

SIR--I would feel very grateful if you would kindly insert the enclosed short article on "Irish Music" by Mr. A.M. Gifford and also the enclosed programme of a concert organised by him recently, as I think many of your readers will read them with interest and pleasure. I have the honour to know Mr. Gifford personally and I think we should be grateful to him for his work for Irish Music.

IRISH MUSIC.
By A.M.Gifford.

Irish music is totally unknown in England, the apalling parodies which pass as such being neither English, Irish, nor even Chinese. To speak of Irish music in England conjures up memories of "The Minstrel Boy" and "Killarney," which Mr Sean O'Casey has scathingly described as a sentimental song about an Irish lake. The "Londonderry Air" has at last "caught on" in England, but it has taken 46 years to do so, and at this rate we are not likely to learn more than one or two before we die. The greatest misfortune that has befallen Irish music in England has been to Anglicise it to suit English ears which, 40 years ago, could not tolerate the flat seventh, and we have the beautiful air, "The Foggy Dew," mutilated with C sharp in the key of D minor or with D sharp in the key of E minor. A violinist hearing me play C natural instead of C sharp in this air, told me she should never again play the arrangement she had got.

The Irish scale contains no sharp seventh or leading note, but is built upon modes which cannot be produced, except approximately, upon a keyboard instrument.

English ears are trained almost exclusively on the major keys. That is why English singers sing out of tune. Ears should be trained on the natural notes of the pianoforte—G-G (with F natural): A-A; B-B; and so on, avoiding starting any scale on its key note. If only singers would adopt this system, false intonation would soon disappear. We in England possess a wealth of music undreamt of by any other nation, for we have the music of four nations (England, Ireland, Scotland and Wales) to draw upon; yet it is so utterly unknown today that I question whether there is a child or even adult from John O'Groats to Land's End who can sing even six national songs without the music and words.

We have exploited foreign music of all kinds to such an extent that we have forgotten that we possess any of our own.

MOST POETICAL IN THE WORLD.

Here is what Dr. Percival Graves says of Irish music : " Irish music is probably the most human, most varied, most poetical in the world, and is particularly rich in tunes which imply sympathetic sensitiveness. Here is theme after theme suitable for treatment in oratorio or opera, sonata or song."

What are our schools of music doing with this inestimable legacy ? How many of their professors and teachers are even alive to its existence ? If so, how is their knowledge of it influencing the studies of their pupils ? How often does it operate upon the programmes of concerts ?

The greatest living authority on Irish music, Carl Gilbert Hardebeck, under whose influence I was fortunate enough to learn it, made me understand not only Irish music, but opened my ears to Grieg, Debussy, and Ravel in a way I little dreamed of.

Although blind, he has accomplished a task that would appal the most courageous musician blessed with sight, for he has taken down from the lips of the Irish peasants hundreds of beautiful melodies which would otherwise have been lost to the world, and added his own wonderful harmonies. These are published in four volumes in both Irish and English languages by Messrs Pigott and Co., Dublin.

IRISH MUSIC.
Irish Concert on St. Patrick's Eve at Catford.
Programme.

1. Choir—"Song of Our Land,"—Alicia Needham; "O Erin, my Mother,"—Hardebeck.
2. Songs—" The Snowy Breasted Pearl," "Norah, The Pride of Kildare,"—arr. Gifford.
3. Violin—"Fantasia on Irish Airs,"—Roche—Hardebeck.
4. Songs—"Erin, the Tear and the Smile," "The Lark in the Clear Air," "Savourneen Dheelish,"—Hardebeck.
5. Songs—"Song of Glen Dhun," "Haste to Weddin',"—Hardebeck
6. Pianoforte—Twelve Preludes,—Hardebeck.
7. Songs—"Let Erin Remember," "Meeting of the Waters," arr. Balfe.
8. Songs—"Fair Hills of Eire," "Old Donegal,"—Hardebeck.
9. Irish Jig—Hardebeck.
10. Viola—" The Unspoken Farewell," "Ned of the Hills,"—Hardebeck.
11. Duets—"Kate Kearney,"—arr. Gifford; "To My First Love."—Hermann Lohr.
12. Songs—"My Mary," "Mary Griffin,"—Hardebeck.
13. Violin - "Munster Reel," "Devil's Jig", "Maloney's Reel,"- Hardebeck.
14. Trio - "Has Sorrow Thy Young Days Shaded," - Joseph Smith.
15. Songs - "The Bells of Shandon," - Arr. Gifford; "Tho the Last Glimpse of Erin," - arr. Balfe.
16. Choir and Audience - "Here's a Health unto His Majesty," - Jeremiah Saville 1678.   4/5/29.

"THE LORD MAYOR."

On Sunday and Monday nights next the Tuam Dramatic Society will produce in the Town Hall the three-act comedy, "The Lord Mayor," to be followed by a concert in which some of Tuam's most popular singers are billed to appear. To mention the Tuam Dramatic Society is sufficient guarantee that the play will be worthily produced, for their previous performances have met with general praise and they promise to excel themselves on the present occasion. The proceeds are to be given to the good working, benevolent institution, the Tuam I.N.F.

11/5/29

TUAM TOWN COMMISSIONERS.

MEETING ADJOURNED.

At meeting of above on Tuesday evening last there were present—Messrs. John Burke, Chairman (presiding), P.J.Byrne, Pat Walsh, J.H.Corcoran, M.O'Keeffe, S.Fahy, John Byrne, T.Wilson, P.J.Gibbons, W.Holian.

Immediately after the minutes were read and finance business transacted, Mr. Fahy proposed that they adjourn the meeting as a protest against the imprisonment of Rev. Father Fahy, C.C., Bullaun.

Mr. Wilson seconded, and the motion was passed unanimously.

Mr. Fahy handed in the following resolution :-

Whereas the Irish people are the lawful owners of the soil of Ireland ; and whereas the lawful owners of the soil of Ireland are being robbed by the British Exchequer and by the remnant of the British Garrison in Ireland, the levy of a yearly tribute by a so-called Irish Government is the definition of slavery. I propose that we transact no further business and adjourn this meeting as a protest against the arrest of Father Fahy. Also to show our whole-hearted sympathy with his patriotic action in his heroic and practical gesture to the enslaved and oppressed farmers of Ireland. That with deep respect we tender our congratulations to Father Fahy, the worthy comrade of Father Griffin. That we forward copies of this resolution to "Honesty" and "The Nation" newspapers as Ireland is, unfortunately, without an Irish daily paper.

11/5/29

EMANCIPATION BADGE

SEVERAL UNOFFICIAL ISSUES IN CIRCULATION.

The Catholic Emancipation Centenary Committee wishes to direct the attention of the public to the fact that several so-called "Emancipation Badges" are on sale for private gain throughout the country. The only Emancipation Badge having official recognition is that illustrated herewith. It is made in bronze (brooches, pins and studs) for adults, and is procurable through the Churches as a receipt for subscriptions of 6d and upwards to the Emancipation Fund. The same

design forms one side of a badge in aluminium specially struck for children, which is procurable at 3d through the schools. The reverse side of the children's badge is a representation of St. Patrick. The bell design depicted has been registered as copyright by the Emancipation Committee. It has been brought to the Committee's notice, nevertheless that it has been copied and incorporated in designs produced for private profit. Legal action to restrain such persons from infringing on the Committee's rights is being instituted. The public in the meantime are warned that only the official badge will entitle them to the privileges of Emancipation Week. The entire proceeds of the sale of the badges will go to defray the heavy expenses of the Celebrations

18/5/29

ORANMORE.

A remarkable freak of nature recently occurred in Oranmore. A local resident, a well-known breeder of fowl, had an early brood of ducks. One of these emerged from its shell not as a biped but as aquadruped, for it had four legs. As it began to waddle about, it was found that it was only using the two hind legs, carrying the two fore legs suspended from its breast in the air. The phenomenon was shown to Mr T. Mac Dermott Kelly, M.R.C.V.S, Athenry, who immediately operated upon the duck, cutting away the portion of the breast to which the useless legs were attached. The operation was quite successful and the duck is now thriving.

11/5/29

TUAM PIONEERS.

The half-yearly general meeting of the Tuam Pioneer T.A.Association was held in the Cathedral on Sunday evening. The nave of the Cathedral, which was specially reserved for the Pioneers, was crowded on the occasion. Rev. Father Fergus, Spiritual Director of the Association, addressed the congregation and read the report of the Association, showing the great progress the Society had made for the last half-year. He congratulated the members on the continued success of their organisation and said the Tuam Centre had now a membership of over 1,000. He then preached a very interesting sermon on the Gospel of the day.

His Grace the Archbishop also addressed the congregation. He congratulated the Pioneers on the strength of their organisation in Tuam, and stressed the point that of all the Temperance movements started in Ireland so far the Pioneer movement was most potent for good. He blessed the members and their organisation and hoped it would continue to grow in strength from day to day.

At the conclusion Benediction of the Most Holy Sacrament was imparted to all present.

18/5/29

G.A.A.

TUAM STAR FOOTBALL CLUB.

A meeting of the Senior and Junior teams was held in the Commissioners Room on Thursday evening.

Mr. John Ryan was moved to the chair.

The minutes of the last meeting were read and signed.

A discussion as to a Treasurer election for a separate finance of the Club took place and it was decided to leave the matter over for a special meeting to be called by the secretary.

The following were selected to represent Tuam in the Senior contest for the first round of the North Galway Championship to be held in Parkmore on Sunday next—H.Cunningham, (captain) ; H.Burke, T.Joyce, P.Hannon, M.Mannion, D.McCormack, P.Waldron, J.O'Rorke, T.Hughes, P.Kelly, C.Reide, J.Nohilly, M.Stewart, P.Walsh, W.Birrell, M.Rooney, T.Creaven, J.Collins.

The junior team to meet Corofin on the same day was selected as follows—J.Farrell, P.Fleming, J.Rooney, W.Pierce, W.Stockwell, J.Walsh, C.Kelly, F.Burke, J.Fahy, T.Connor, W.Lohan, J.Reilly, M.Cooney, P.Quinn, P.Fleming, M.Curran, J.Tighe, W.Leahy, T.Leahy, A.Nicholson, T.Hopkins.

18/5/29

CATHOLIC TRUTH SOCIETY OF IRELAND.
CASTLEBAR BRANCH.

7th May, 1929.

Dear Sir—We have been directed by His Grace the Archbishop of Tuam to send to you for publication the following letter from Mr. F.O'Reilly, Executive Secretary of the Catholic Truth Society of Ireland :-

"I desire to call attention to the dishonest methods of an elderly colporteur, who, last week, was operating in certain towns in County Longford. He is, presumably, an Agent of one of the numerous non-Catholic Bible Societies, and is offering for sale, (Price 6d.) and as suitable reading for Catholics, a book which is described on the cover as "The Douay Testament." The book measures 4 and a quarter inches x 7 and is bound in green cloth boards. It is a reprint of the Rhemes Bible, printed in Dublin by Coyne in 1820. The present (1929) printers are the firm of Messrs. Sealy Bryers & Walker, Crow Street, Dublin, who, however, are not responsible for its distribution. Their name is mentioned in order to enable the book to be identified.

" The version of the New Testament above is that prepared by the late Archbishop Troy who had it ready *with notes* when he died. The edition above referred to has been published *without notes*. The English translation of the Old Testament was made at Douay, and of the New Testament at Rheims. The whole is called the Douay version of the Bible ; but Catholics are not permitted to read the Bible in vernacular editions, without notes, although they are permitted to read it in the original without notes. This regulation seems to date from the period of Pope Benedict XIV, (1740-1758). Pope Gregory XVI (Encycl. Inter Praecipuas 6th May, 1844) speaks of it as a new restriction, introduced by Benedict XIV, and states that these popular editions should be approved either by the Holy See, or be furnished with notes from the Fathers of the Catholic Church, or from learned Catholic men ; and as a reason for this regulation he gives 'the persistent frauds of heretics.' The present law is found in Canon 1391 of the new code of Canon Law, which states that editions of the Bible, without notes, require the approval of the Holy See; editions with notes can be published if approved by the Ordinary .

"Catholics are therefore forbidden to read the book in question (1) because it is published without ecclesiastical approval; and (2) because it is published without notes; and those who have purchased copies should destroy them."

The above letter speaks for itself. It remains for me only to add that the hawkers of these unauthorised versions of the Scriptures are agents of the notorious Souper organisation, the Irish Church Missions whose avowed object is to flout Catholic authority. They are at present active in Co. Mayo and the West generally. Catholics would be well advised not to give them any encouragement by engaging in conversation of any kind with them.

Yours faithfully,

J.P. Ryan , Hon. Secretary.

The Editor TUAM HERALD, Tuam.   18/5/29

GALWAY NOTES.

(From Our Own Correspondent.)

Some fifty years ago there were excellent clay pipes made in Galway by a Mr. O'Gorman and all classes of people smoked them. Also at Knockcroghery in the Co. Roscommon, near the town, were pipes so famous that they were known all over the world. They are now not to be seen. Maid and boy, man and woman smoke cigarettes to the undoubted injury of their health, for by such way of smoking they imbibe all the nicotine of the tobacco which, when undoubtedly taken in large quantities, is a poison, and the cigarette is no protection from its infection.

In a back lane in Waterford are to be found also all that remained of a one-time flourishing Irish industry. It was the last stronghold of the clay pipe in Ireland. When I pushed open the door of the office I found the proprietor, with a clay pipe in his mouth, sitting among a remarkable collection of pipes. They were all made of clay. Some were white, some black, polished and unpolished, plain and fancy. One pipe, a two-and -a -half-feet-long monster, dated from the time of the Danish occupation of Waterford, and was found fifty years ago when excavations were being made for the laying of a water main.

Mr. Patrick O'Neill is the oldest manufacturer of clay pipes in Ireland, and has been making them for the last sixty years. His pipes are being smoked not only in most parts of Great Britain but in America and South Africa.

He has successfully overcome the difficulty that wiped out similar firms, and is still hopeful of the old clay pipe's return to favour.

"It deserves to come back," he said. "It has fought a great battle. Its greatest enemy has always been the cigarette. They could not provide pipes for the men on active service during the war, and they gave them cigarettes. The formed the habit there and they have stuck to the cigarettes ever since. If they had to cling to the old clay pipe," he declared, " half the people who are dead since they took on the cigarette habit would be alive to-day. Of course, the young people think of nothing but fashion now-a-days, and they do not realise they are cutting their lives short. They cannot live as long as the smokers of the clay , many of whom—men and women—I have known to live to 105 years. The clay absorbs most of the nicotine in the tobacco and thus provides a cool, clean smoke. That is the reason why the average life of the clay is only a week."
18/5/29

PLAIN CHANT.

A writer in the "Irish Times" last week speaking of the recent Feis says—"The delight and joy which Sir Richard Terry expressed at the growth of the plain chant movement in Irish music reminds me of the efforts made by the late Mr. Edward Martyn, of Tullyra Castle, County Galway, in establishing a Palestrina Choir in Dublin. Dr Terry remarked that not since Palestrina's time has such a wonderful musical movement arisen as that which Ireland is establishing to-day. What a joy would have been that of Mr. Edward Martyn, who lived for this great idea. He gave his money generously to advance Chamber music, and the Palestrina Choir in Marlborough street when his enthusiasm and that of Mr. Vincent O'Brien were the driving force in musical Dublin."

This is painfully true of Edward Martyn. How few remember what he did to set up a proper plain chant style—how nobly he strove, how generously he backed up his views, how ungratefully he is now remembered. Some admirers of his should subscribe between them a small sum and therewith establish a Martyn Cup for competition at the Feis and so perpetuate his name and his inestimable services to Irish music. It would not cost much to do so, and it should be done while there are persons alive who remember Edward Martyn. He actually gave some £9,000 or £10,000 of his income to establish the Palestrina Choir at Marlboro St. Catholic Church. It was then thought a quixotic and a vain idea but now it is recognised as the saving of the plain chant and under the conductor Mr. Martyn himself selected it is doing marvels and well earned the praise bestowed upon it last week by one of the greatest of living musicians in these countries.
18/05/29

A woman rate collector came before the Galway Council on Saturday and stated that she found it impossible to collect rates on the islands off the Galway coast. No one would take her to the islands. When the Civic Guards supplied a boat and arranged to take her the boat was stolen by the islanders. No rates had been paid for several years. The Council decided to ask the Government to supply a boat.
18/5/29

Although only sixteen years of age, Patrick A. Fleming, of Gortaleam, Dunmore, supposed to be the youngest wireless operator in the world, has been appointed to the Laurentic.
18/5/29

ENTERTAINMENT IN AID OF TUAM I.N.F.

On Sunday and Monday evenings last in the Town Hall before large audiences the Tuam Dramatic Society presented the 3-Act Comedy, "The Lord Mayor." The proceeds were given over to the Tuam Branch I.N.F. for whom the performance had been got up. The play was splendidly staged and acted and each of the ladies and gentlemen engaged displayed remarkable histrionic talent and acted their parts as if "to the manner born."

Mr. P.J.Dwyer, as the pussilanimous and weak-minded Lord Mayor, but withal strong enough to refuse a knighthood and a lucrative position rather than betray the people, did his part to perfection, while Mr. J. Cunningham, as the bullying Gaffney was equally good in his part; Mr. Martin McGrath, as Kelly, the cynical patriot, acted with great adroitness and coolness throughout ; Mrs O'Brien, as the Lady Mayoress, looked and acted her difficult part with consummate skill ; while Miss Mae Leonard, as Moira the Lord Mayor's daughter, and incidentally a fire-eating rebel, was all that could be desired, and as one whose first appearance this was, her acting was wonderfully natural and lifelike, and richly deserved the praise given her; Miss K.Bain as the shrewish creditor, got unstinted applause for the capable manner in which she portrayed the grasping Mrs. Moran, and Mr. J. Fahy, who would have his " pound of flesh," and Mr. J.Bain, (who always said "ditto") as the greedy creditors, played their parts extremely well ; Mr. J. Heneghan, as the dashing military attache from the Viceregal Lodge intent on making the Lord Mayor receive the King, acted with surprising aplomb and self-assurance. How shall I describe the two Mansion House charwomen, Mrs. Murphy and Mrs. Malowney, (Messrs. E. Cooley and Ger Shine), whose very appearance and make-up was sufficient to evoke roars of laughter. Mr. Cooley is an old favourite with Tuam audiences, but on this occasion he excelled even himself, his humorous interpretation of the Dublin charwoman and her Dublin accent, putting the house into kinks of laughter again and again. In Ger. Shine he had a capable counterfoil as Mrs Malowney, and he too acted his part right well indeed. If humour is " the spice of life," we had quite a feast of it on Sunday night, thanks to Messrs. Cooley and Shine.

Taking it all in all the play was as capably acted and staged as any amateur society in Ireland could produce it, and it is no spirit of local favouritism that prompts me to say that if ever the Tuam Dramatic Society are induced to compete for dramatic honours with other such societies in Dublin or elsewhere, they will give a good account of themselves and bring honour to this old town.

THE CONCERT.

In the concert which followed, Mr. Johnny Bain led off by singing a very up-to-date poetic skit on the "Commissioners' Fire Brigade", which took so well that at "special request" he had to give a "repeat" performance the next evening. Mr. E.O'Brien next gave "Columba's Lament" in fine style, for which he was deservedly encored. Mr. John Dwyer's fine baritone was heard to great effect in "True till Death" and "Nancy Lee". A four-hand reel danced by four pretty little tots dressed in Cumann-na-mBan costume was the theme of deserved praise.

On Monday night the performance was repeated with equal success and we had in addition songs in Gaelic (which shows the national language was not left out) by Mr. M. Bray, a Feis prize winner, and again a four-hand reel, by the pretty little dancers —Misses Greally, Ruddy, Bray and Garvey. Miss Ciss Geddes also danced a reel which was very well done indeed and secured a deserved encore. And then as the last item on the programme we had a hornpipe from Mr. M. Keegan, who has done so much in Tuam and district to popularise the Gaelic language and Gaelic dancing, which was danced only as he can dance it. Late as the time was and tired as the audience must have been, not one stirred from their seats until he had to come again and give an encore dance.

Miss Ita Guy capably presided at the piano. After each evening's performance, Mr. James Coogan the popular Chief Ranger of the Tuam I.N.F., in a neat speech thanked the audience and the artistes on behalf of the Tuam I.N.F.

18/5/29

ANNUAL HOLIDAY.

In accordance with what is now becoming a time-honoured custom all business houses in town will be closed on Monday next (Whit Monday) to give the shop assistants their annual holiday. 18/5/29

TUAM TOWN COMMISSIONERS.

An adjourned meeting of the above body was held on Tuesday, 14th instant, Mr. John Burke, chairman, presided.

Other members present - Messrs. Patrick Gibbons, Patrick Walsh, Simon Fahy, John Byrne, James Moran, Patrick Byrne, and John H. Corcoran.

The Acting Clerk reported that there was only one tender received for repairs to Meat Stalls, viz., from Mr. David Dwyer.

Mr. P.J. Byrne proposed that Mr. Dwyer's tender for 4 and a half inch eave runs be accepted at £7.5s.6d.

Mr. Walsh seconded and it was passed.

APPOINTMENT OF TOWN CLERK.

Chairman - The next business is a letter from the Local Appointments Commissioners recommending Mr. John P. Whyte, of Ballinastack, as Town Clerk. Whilst I have no objection to Mr. Whyte coming on, still I think it is only right in the interests of the town that we should ask the Minister of Local Government to sanction the continuance of Mr. Daly as Town Clerk, especially as he has given satisfaction, and since his appointment the finances of the Board have been greatly improved. I propose that the Minister of Local Government be requested to sanction the appointment of Mr. James Daly as Town Clerk in view of his experience of Local Government and Municipal work, and in the interests of the town and on account of the general satisfaction he has given.

Mr. Moran - I have great pleasure in seconding the chairman's resolution. When Mr. Daly came on we were in a dilemma, but by his great knowledge of Local Government and Municipal work he took us out of the mess and he has put the accounts of the Board in a very satisfactory position. It is strange that they recommended a young man with no knowledge of L.G. or Municipal work.

Mr. P. Byrne - The time is past for that now. We could have saved money if the appointment was made sooner. We are paying £3 a week, and I propose that we adopt the recommendation of the Local Appointments Commissioners.

Chairman - Does any one second Mr. Byrne's proposition?

As there was no seconder to Mr. Byrne, the chairman declared the resolution passed, Mr. Patrick Byrne dissenting.

Mr. Daly - I don't see how you are losing money. You paid the late Clerk at the rate of £3 per week and Mr. Byrne who was on the Finance Committee should have looked after matters. I am quite willing to leave at any time, to-morrow if you like.

Chairman - We are not responsible for the delays of the Local Government or the Appointments Commissioners and the members of the Board know that quite well. In Ballina it took them nearly 12 months to get their clerk appointed, although they were paying a substitute clerk £5 per week.

Mr. Walsh - I would be glad to see Mr. Daly get the position. Since his appointment he has given great satisfaction and the townspeople are very thankful to him.

Mr. Fahy - I, too, am in favour of Mr. Daly being appointed.

Mr. John Byrne - I agree with the remarks of Messrs. Walsh and Fahy and hope the Minister will sanction his appointment for the welfare of the town.

THE LIBRARY ROOM.

Chairman - I wish to call the attention of the Board to the fact that it is a great inconvenience to the people to have the Library Room closed up, and I think some arrangement should be made by the Committee with the Commissioners to have the room opened. I propose that the clerk be requested to write to Mr. O'Connell to ask the Library Committee to call a meeting and discuss the matter with a deputation of the Town Commissioners.

Mr. Walsh agreed with the chairman's remarks. When the room was let as a Public Library it was on the distinct understanding that meetings of the townspeople should be allowed to be held there.

Mr. Moran and the other members agreed and after some little discussion, the clerk was instructed to ask the Secretary of the Library Committee to call a meeting of that committee to meet a deputation of the Commissioners to arrange about the matter—the chairman, Mr. Walsh and Mr. Moran being appointed to meet them on behalf of the Board.   18/5/29

CORPUS CHRISTI.

A meeting of the townspeople was held in the Town Hall on Tuesday evening to make arrangements for the Procession on Corpus Christi.

Rev. P. Kelly, Adm., presided.

Also present—F.B. McDonagh, M.W. Cahill, T.C.; H.B. Mangan, Patk. Walsh, T.C.; John Burke, T.C.; M.J. Walsh, Malachy Duggan, R.K. Browne, Sean O'Hehir, D.J. Butler, T. Hayden, Joe Cloonan, James Daly, Frank Walsh, Wm. Stapleton, Ml. O'Connell.

It was decided not to have any bunting or trees through the town, except to put up the scrolls with sacred mottoes and to decorate the Square around the Altar. If the people desire to decorate their houses with flags or sacred pictures it is to be a matter for themselves.

Mr. Fredk. McDonagh, Solr., was appointed Chief Marshall to be in charge of the Procession.

Mr. M.J. Walsh proposed a resolution expressing regret at the illness of Mr. P.M. Hosty, and hoped he would be soon amongst them again.

The resolution was unanimously adopted.

Mr. Daly said there was a balance to credit and probably it might be sufficient to pay the expenses.

The meeting adjourned to Friday evening next at 8 o'c p.m.

25/5/29

TULLINADALY FAIR.

This old established fair—the oldest it is believed in Ireland—held on Wednesday last, was well supplied with first-class stock, which is only to be expected coming from a sound country, and prices ruled high. Tullinadaly seems to be the only country fair holding its own in prices and stock and of late years is making an improvement. Quotations :-

Ewes and lambs single, from £4 10s to £5 ; hoggets from £2 10s to £3. Cattle, one to two years old, from £10 to £14 ; 3 years old and upwards, from £15 to £19 10s ; springers up to £24.

25/5/29

PARS. OF LOCAL INTEREST.
(From Our Own Correspondent)

RELAYING TUAM RAILWAY YARD.
For the past month quite a number of men have been employed relaying Tuam Railway Yard. The rails have all been taken up and re-arranged and a number of new rails laid down and additions made to the existing lines. A fair amount of local labour has been absorbed while the work is progressing.

***

POLITICS BARRED.
The deputation appointed by the Town Commissioners (Messrs. Burke, Moran and Walsh) waited on the members of the Library Committee on Monday evening with a view to having the room made available for meetings of any description called by the townspeople from time to time. Permission was secured to hold meetings of the G.A.A. and kindred organisations, but the Committee decided that on no account would political meetings be allowed in the Library Room.

***

TUAM BALL ALLEY.
Advertisement may be seen in this issue for the construction of the Tuam Ball Court. The work had been advertised previously and a tender accepted but the gentleman selected backed out when called on to sign his bond. This time a deposit of £2 must accompany each tender to be forfeited if the declared contractor does not sign his bond within a specified time.

***

UNDESIRABLE VISITORS.
On Saturday evening last a number of tinkers with something like a couple of hundred asses in their train invaded Tuam and remained in and around the Square until a late hour in the evening. Needless to say they made the welkin ring and some choice language was indulged in. And to make matters worse the streets in and around the Square on Sunday morning were in a filthy condition as a result of their visit. This is not fair to the men employed cleaning the streets who often work overtime to have them presentable on Sunday mornings. Next time the tinkers visit Tuam en masse they should be made continue their trek with a shorter period for recuperation.

***

ANOTHER CHEAP TRIP TO GALWAY.
As may be seen by advertisement in this page the G.S.R. are giving another cheap trip to Galway on to-morrow (Sunday). This time there is the added attraction of a great Corpus Christi procession through the streets of Galway, so a large number should avail themselves of the opportunity to visit the "Citie of the Tribes" on that day.

***

TURF CUTTING.
Not for many seasons past was the weather as favourable for turf cutting as this one. On all sides of the town people are busy cutting the winter's supply of turf and are blessed with ideal weather. The crops, too, are doing well, and the weather so far, please God, promises a golden harvest.

1/6/29

Stands the weight of Ten Men

RALEIGH
THE ALL-STEEL BICYCLE

That is the weight it is built to carry. This enormous strength—far ahead of ordinary bicycles—is due to the unique all-steel construction, the careful design & the patent low—temperature brazing.

From 11/6 monthly. (no deposit) or cash from £5 19s. 6d. with Dunlop tyres. Specify Sturney-Archer 3 speed gear. Agents everywhere. Send to the Raleigh Cycle Co., Ltd., Nottingham for the address of the nearest to show you the wonderful Raleigh

Or ask for "The Book of the Raleigh" free.

TUAM	Michael Heskin.
BALLINROBE	J.B. Staunton.
CAHERLISTRANE	John J. Gannon.
DUNMORE	O'Malley Bros.
MOUNTBELLEW	Mrs. B. Noone

1/6/29

A GHAEDHEALA BEIDH
FEIS THUAMA,
15adh agus 16adh MEITHEAMH.

Language competitions go leor as well as Competitions in Singing, Dancing and Music.

Prize-winners Concert and Ceilidhe on Sunday night. Look out for later list of Tailteann Prize-winners in Music and Dancing who will contribute.

Entries close on 1st June.
Clár le fághail ó

MICHEÁL MAC AODHAGÁIN,
Tuaim.

1/6/29

TUAM HANDBALL COMMITTEE.

Tenders are invited for the building of a Handball Court on the site at the rear of the Courthouse, Tuam.

Tenders received after 7 p.m., Friday, June 7th, will not be considered.

Each tender must be accompanied by a deposit of £2.

Lowest tender not necessarily accepted.

Specification and plan can be seen any day between 2 and 3 o'c. p.m. on application to
T. JOYCE,
Hon. Secretary,
c/o Central Hotel,
Tuam.

1/6/29

THE CORPUS CHRISTI PROCESSION.

This year the weather was somewhat boisterous at the start but calmed wonderfully while the procession was in progress. The people of the town as usual put forth their best efforts in the matter of decoration, and the procession exceeded in dimensions any ever held in Tuam before. The large number in the Men's Sacred Heart Sodality and in the Pioneers attracted a good deal of attention.

The route was through the grounds of the Mercy Convent, Dublin Road, Vicar Street, The Mall, High Street, Foster Row and back to the Square where the altar was erected under the shadow of the historic Tuam Cross. At the various vantage points sacred scrolls and bunting spanned the streets and fluttered in the breeze.

The procession was led by the band of the Galway Industrial School playing sacred airs. Next came the school children of the Mercy and Presentation Convents with their white costumes and veils and bouquets of flowers. The various women's sodalities followed—the Children of Mary, the Women Pioneers, the Women's Sacred Heart Sodality, etc. These were followed by the various men's sodalities and societies—the Pioneers, the Men's Sacred Heart Sodality, Civic Guards, etc. Next came the unison and harmony choirs of the Cathedral, the Presentation and Mercy Convents, The Christian Brothers' Schools, and St. Jarlath's College, under the capable direction of Mr. Hession. The Town Commissioners formed a bodyguard for the Most Blessed Sacrament, which was carried by the Rev. Father Blowick. His Grace the Archbishop wearing the Cappa Magna brought up the rear.

When the huge procession had reached the altar at the Market Square and had been closely packed into every available space, Father Blowick imparted Solemn Benediction to the kneeling thousands. It was at this solemn moment when young and old, rich and poor, bowed their heads low in adoration, that one realised the inner meaning of all the festive decorations and how much Jesus in the Blessed Sacrament means to the people of Tuam.

After this the procession returned to the Cathedral where Benediction was again imparted by Father Blowick. 1/6/29.

TUAM FEIS.

Tuam Feis, which last year was the most successful Feis in Connaught, from every point of view, promises to be even still better this year. Competitions are more numerous, prizes are better and everything which can be done to eliminate causes for complaint is being done.

Some of the best known figures in the Irish-Ireland movement are volunteering their services. Tailteann and other artistes of outstanding merit are being engaged for the Concert, whilst the Céilidhe will be the best ever held in Tuam.

Already entries are pouring in from all sides. Competitors will be more numerous than last year and the competition in all branches on a higher plane. Everything promises that the 15th and 16th of June will be two of the most enjoyable days of the year. So everybody with a drop of Irish blood in his veins should give every assistance he can to the movement which has for its object the upholding of the tradition of the Gaelic race in song and in story, in dance and in music, and above all the revival of the Gaelic Tongue as the spoken language of Erin. This he can do by encouraging the youth and the teachers who are striving so hard and so earnestly against heavy odds. We cannot all become fluent Irish speakers, but we can at least lend our sympathy.

At a meeting of the Feis Committee, held on Sunday, it was decided to appeal to the people of Tuam for funds. A house-to-house collection will be made and it is hoped everybody who can do so will contribute some little help to the ideal of a Gaelic Ireland.

1/6/29

FIRE IN THE TOWN HALL.

On Wednesday evening last what might have been a very serious fire, were it not for the promptitude of some of the townspeople and the Civic Guard, occurred in the Town Hall Cinema at about 8.30 p.m. It appears that the operator in the cinema box had just switched on the current when a red glare was seen on the screen, then the arc lamp fell out, and immediately the operating room was a blaze of fire. The audience, which was small, having noticed the glare of fire on the screen at once left the hall, and there was no panic nor was any person injured. Great credit is due to Mr. Martin Rooney and Mr. John Daly, jnr., who brought up five Minnemax extinguishers, and with the assistance of some townspeople and the Civic Guard, under the directions of Sergeant Ruddy, the fire was quickly got under control. Messrs. Shine and McCoy were also promptly on the scene with the fire hose and in about half an hour the fire was completely extinguished. The fire escape ladder recently erected by the Town Commissioners outside the hall was of great use as it enabled the hose to be played directly on to the operating room where the fire originated and had its strongest hold. This propably saved the hall from being burned to the ground.

1/6/29

WHITE STAR
COBH TO U.S.A. & CANADA

Largest Steamers from Ireland.

Facilities provided on board for celebration of Holy Mass.

COBH to BOSTON & NEW YORK.

Cedric	Sun June 9	*Adriatic	Sun June 30
*Baltic	Sun June 16	Cedric	Sun.July 7
*+Arabic	Sun June 23	*Baltic	Sun July 14

*Not calling Boston.   +Via Halifax, N.S.

COBH to QUEBEC & MONTREAL

Calgaric Wed. June 12   Magantic Sun June 30

For further particulars apply WHITE STAR LINE, 31/37, Victoria Street, Belfast, Liverpool, Southampton, Bristol, Birmingham; London : 1, Cockspur Street, S.W.1., and 33 Leadenhall Street, E.C.3.

1 & 2, Eden Quay, Dublin.
SCOTT & CO, Cobh, Queenstown,
OR LOCAL AGENTS

8/6/29

CUNARD LINE

LARGE MODERN LINERS FOR STEADINESS AND COMFORT.

COBH TO NEW YORK.

Samaria	June 9	Samaria	July 7
Franconia	June 16	Laconia	July 14
Laconia	June 23	Scythia	July 28
Scythia	June 30	Samaria	Aug 4

COBH TO BOSTON.

Franconia	June 16	Laconia	July 14
Scythia	June 23	Scythia	July 28

COBH TO QUEBEC & MONTREAL.

Aurania	June 8	Aurania	July 7
Ascania	June 22	Ascania	July 21

For further particulars apply CUNARD LINE, CUNARD WHARF, COBH or 6 LOWER ABBEY STREET, DUBLIN, CUNARD BUILDING, LIVERPOOL, or Local Agents.   8/6/29

O'CONNELL.

As was said by a writer in the "Spectator"— O'Connell fascinated and dazzled his generation. Lecky said of him that "he filled a space in the thoughts of men that no Irishman and very few Englishmen have equalled." "In Kerry they'd say he's the full of the door," sang the rhymester of the Dublin Streets. Gladstone thought him "the greatest popular leader the world has ever seen." Thackeray, not altogether uninfluenced by the current opinion in certain fashionable circles that he was " a bully , a blackguard, and a buffoon," made the interesting admission "he may be a humbug, but he is a great man and we owe him Catholic Emancipation."

Mr. MacDonagh throws a light upon the conflicting verdicts which puzzled the novelist. O'Connell, he says, had, like so many of his countrymen, "a want of the sense of the incongruous, an obliviousness to the line where things noble and solemn verge on things puerile and ridiculous." The author has a wonderful power of showing his reader scenes of Irish rejoicing, noble in their aspiration, ridiculous in their expression, as when "forty-two bands filled the air with discordant melody," or when a large tree was planted (or stuck in) during the night opposite his (O'Connell's) window and filled with an orchestra playing fiddles and flutes by whose strains he was awakened. A Celt and a Catholic, O'Connell was always a stranger when he was in England. He had remained with his foster-parents longer than was usual even then. He belonged in a sense to the peasantry, in whom racial pecularities are always marked. On his deathbed the priest records that he was saying his prayers "in the sort of rude Irish dialect" in which he had first learned them.

Not the least graphic chapter in the whole book describes O'Connell's duel with D'Esterre. Duelling was at its height in Ireland, and O'Connell drove out from Dublin to the appointed place in a coach and four. He mortally wounded his opponent, to the wild delight of a crowd of spectators who seemed to have behaved like men at a race meeting. But the death of D'Esterre, which occurred many hours afterwards, shocked O'Connell terribly. Of the kind of remorse which in an Englishman is usually connected with secrecy, however, he knew nothing. He always lifted his hat and murmured a prayer for his adversary's soul and his own forgiveness when he passed the house where D'Esterre died. He wore a black glove always on his right hand when he received the Sacrament of Communion. " That hand," he said, " took a fellow-creature's life, and I shall never bare it in the presence of my Redeemer." The incident probably was not without effect in his determined opposition to political bloodshed. Indeed he said in the House of Commons that this was so.   8/6/29

See IRELAND First

Holidays HERE this year!

INFORMATION FREE
Where to go--How to travel. What it will cost. Make your arrangements now. Write for free information to the I.T.A.

(L.)

MEATH and LOUTH

The Boyne Valley Trip is one of the most interesting and most popular tours in Ireland. Tara, the ancient capital; Newgrange, the burial place of kings 3,000 years ago; Monasterboice and Mellifont, historic abbeys of other days--and then the scene of the famous Battle of the Boyne. If you have not done this trip there are ample facilities this year.

On the coast Omeath, Carlingford, Greenore, Blackrock, Laytown and Bettystown are bright comfortable seaside resorts with good accommodation at moderate charges.

We will gladly send you an Illustrated guide.

IRISH TOURIST ASSOCIATION (Inc.)
American Chambers, Lower O'Connell St.,
Dublin.

K.A.A.

Mr. Hogan.

Mr. P. Hogan, Minister for Agriculture, who addressed four meetings during Sunday, dealt in Sligo with the subject of land annuities. He pointed out that farmers who bought out under the 1909 Act got a loan of the money at three per cent., to be repaid in 67 years. This money was obtained from banks, insurance companies, the Protestant Church in England, the Catholic Church in Ireland, convents, and ordinary citizens in Great Britain, America and elsewhere. The Government had yet to complete land purchase, and this would cost twenty million pounds. If the land annuities were not paid back to the people who lent the money, would they be able to borrow a hundred pence again? The British Treasury did not get a penny of that money, and every member of Fianna Fail knew it. That question was put before them, because Fianna Fail believed them to be more dishonest than honest men in the country. The Government believed otherwise. The law by which these annuities was due was that of the Seventh Commandment.

Pontoon.

Pontoon is a beautiful spot and a good place for sport. With the Rev. Joseph Jackson, M.A., as president, the Pontoon Anglers' Association has been formed, the object being to improve trout fishing on Lough Conn. With the aid of a £500 grant, secured through the medium of the Tourist Development Association, the road fro Castlebar to Pontoon has been considerably improved. 8/6/29

Galway Notes.

There recently appeared in the "Spectator" an admirable article by a well-known Irish writer, Mr Lett, a Wexford man. He described therein his meeting with Lady Moffatt, a charming old lady, who for nearly fifty years was a popular resident in Galway. She has, since her popular husband's death, been living in Dublin and is a resident at present at Herbert Park, Donnybrook. She is a strikingly attractive personality, one of the graceful old ladies we see in prints of those of the early Victorian age. Although in her 92nd year, she is full of vitality, energy and intelligence. She remembers the many eventful happenings of her life and never forgets her countless friends in Galway. Whenever the name is mentioned she brightens up and hastens to bring back to her wonderful memory some things of the past which at such an interval of time one naturally forgets. It is marvellous how well she wears her years, what vivacity she shows, and what bright intelligence she displays. One speaking to her could not imagine that she is within eight years of the century. She can move about with almost all the activity and grace of former days. Time and again she says she can never forget dear old Galway, its kind people of every class and creed and the countless happy days she spent there. Galway certainly has a large part of her affections and recollections.

Her distinguished husband, Sir Thomas Moffatt, LL.D, was first Professor of English Literature at Galway College, and certainly no one could be better fitted for the post. He was a polished speaker and a writer of excellent English and a lover of its classics. His addresses to his classes were marvels of taste and wide reading. He was familiar with all the best English classics, and particularly deeply read in the Elizabethan and early Victorian writers. T.P. O'Connor always speaks and writes with rapture of his old Professor in Galway for whom he entertained a positive affection and to whose training he attributes much of the facile style of writing he acquired and can use so well. There are few writers of the present day with such a finished and yet ready pen, with such a pleasing style, and that T.P. acquired at Galway under Dr. Moffatt. Dr. Moffatt succeeded Dr. Berwick, who came after Dr. Kirwan. He was the first President of Galway Queen's College, and, by the way, was P.P. of Oranmore. This appointment was made to conciliate Catholics and to make popular the College. In addition to making a Catholic the first President, he was in addition a Priest. Yet that was not all. Half the professorial staff was Catholic, and there was a provision in the Act to appoint a Catholic Dean of Residence to look after the young students of that religion. All this did not please the Hierarchy, or rather a bare majority of them, for at the Synod of Thurles, by a majority of one only, were the Colleges condemned and Catholics forbidden to attend them. This was afterwards deplored as a mistake, for the College could have been more Catholic than it is today and used by the Catholics of Connaught instead of being as it was, mainly used by the Presbyterians of Ulster. That class were largely educated there and took all the prizes, for there was no valid or vigorous competition. The Catholic who could win a prize was kept away and the prize was won by an Ulsterman. Of course several Catholics did nevertheless attend and to that fact they owe it that they were able to win high professional positions at home and abroad. Galway men flooded the medical profession and in England thousands found employment. In the Indian Civil Service they secured the highest posts. So did Sir Anthony Mc Donnell, who owes his title and distinction all to Galway. It would be impossible to enumerate the men who went out from Galway and won fame, position and wealth abroad. Galway is now a Gaelic University and as such its activities must necessarily be resrtricted. In the medical line it is not what it was, or in the law and engineering. During Mr. Morley's Chief Secretaryship it was determined to force Sir Thomas Moffatt to resign under the 65 rule and he was accordingly dismissed. But Mr. Morley was badly advised in so doing. Sergeant Campion, Professor of Law at Galway at the time and a leading jurist at the Irish Bar, advised that the act was unconstitutional and illegal and that the President could only be dismissed under the King's sealed order and that for special faults, such as neglect or serious moral mistakes. This ssue was so decided and Sir Thomas remained on in Galway until he died. Mr. Morley, it was said and believed, intended appointing as President Professor Pye. He was a Clifden man and an able man in every respect, but the illegality of the dismissal or removal of Sir Thomas destroyed his chances and he died not long after. Sir Thomas Moffatt's successor was Dr. Srarkie, who was not a popular President. Dr. Berwick, Sir Thomas's predecessor, had a daughter, who was of great height, being over 6 feet. She was a great favourite. Her relatively superior height, six feet in a girl, made her look much taller than she really was. A Professor at the College then was also a six-footer. His cousin is Canon Stoney, of Dublin, who was also educated at Galway.

***

A Galway man, one who is a credit to the place where he was born and reared and whose people lived for generations and usefully contributed to its public life, is Harry Persse, son of the late Henry Persse, Esq., of Glenard. He is the most famous trainer of the day, and he is now training the Derby favourite, and of him and his horse a writer in a London paper says: "The Derby candidate, Mr. Jinks, whose public form shows him to be one of the best horses in the race is evidently enjoying his preparation. This frisky, pleasure-loving grandson of The Tetrarch is ready to make friends with anybody. There is no trace of sourness in his sunny disposition. This would not be such good proof of his contentment with his preparation if he were naturally energetic; but, Mr Jinks, like many others born since the war, quadruped and biped, has some of the laziness of the natural aristocrat. I have just spent a night and a sparkling May morning with Mr. Jinks at his home on the great hills above the old Hampshire village of Stockbridge. One expects on entering the sacrosanct stables which house a Derby favourite to find a state of exaggerated tension and the favourite himself treated with Royal honours, guarded by detectives, unapproachable by any. One does not sense that atmosphere or see any detectives at Stockbridge. Mr. Jinks is treated exactly the same as each of the fifty-two racehorses which Mr. H.S. Persse has in training. He is cared for night and day in exactly the same way as all the others. This does not mean he is any less a Derby favourite with his popular owner, Major McCalmont, or his trainer or the lads at the stables; rather he is as general a home favourite because of his looks, his disposition, and his achievements, as he is with the British public, who only know him as the winner of the Two Thousand, the first classic of the year, and other important races to the tune of £20,000 or so. If you were so fortunate, as I was, to obtain Major Mc Calmont's permission for an introduction to Mr. Jinks, the ceremony would not be complete until Mr, Jinks had made his own contribution, which he did in my case.

***

The Claddagh, the seaside and fishing suburb of Galway, is well known to every visitor. It is about being rebuilt, so the following graphic sketch of that romantic spot in the "Towns and Cities of Ireland," by Mr. Stephen Gwynn, is worth reading. He says :-

At the quay in Galway you can see, too, the slow but gradual transformation which is altering the methods of taking fish. The Claddagh is to-day what it has always been - an Irish-speaking fishing village, lying outside the limits of the city proper, and living its own life apart. Outside every Anglo-Norman town there grew up an "Irish town" beyond the walls, beyond the city pale; and at Galway its people were fishers, who have probably, since the beginning of time, complained that "the fish are not in it as they used to be." At all events, a bye-law of 1585 enacted that no fisherman "do take in hand the plough or spade that would barr them from fishing." But if the harvester of the sea was forbidden to seek labour on the land or in the town, the community recognised that the fisher needed help in his precarious job; and they enacted that fishers or their wives "be reasonably served before others with all necessary sustenance and food, whereby they might have the better hope". To-day in Galway, as anywhere else, there is the complaint of the trawlers; and now the local sailing trawlers, of which the Claddagh complains, are, in their turn, complaining of the steam trawlers which sweep their grounds mercilessly. The Claddagh men, or the older of them, cling to their old, high-sided boats, beautiful sea-craft; yet side by side with these you will find the larger flush-decked "nobbies" and "Zulus", which the Congested Districts Board have introduced on the Connemara shore and in Aran. Claddagh has never taken kindly to these; but it has gone a step beyond them, and a motor boat, the "Claddagh King," now follows the sign of herring all round the Irish coast. So we get on, even in Claddagh. Sail has got to give way, whether to steam or to oil, just as surely as hand-looms are bound to yield to power-looms; and Galway should be a true centre for a big fishing trade, with its outpost at the Isles of Aran, nearer to the grounds. Aran has always closely connected with the city, and the Mayor of Galway's jurisdiction as Admiral of the port was extended to the mouth of Galway Bay and as far as the Isles of Aran. A little steamer now connects the islands with the city by a regular service; here, too, sail is superseded.

Yet, for pleasure at least, I think, sails will always be there, and I know no pleasanter place to spend a summer day than that superb stretch of water with the hills of Burren south of you, the hills of Connemara to the north. You can spin for mackerel to heart's content, and if you see a shark's fin, as often happens, you can mount a mackerel on some powerful gimp tackle and spin for shark, one of my friends killed thirteen of these creatures in a day. Or if lake and river please you better than sea, there is Corrib river and lake at your command. Those who planted one of the Queen's Colleges down in Galway made a fine choice, and the building quadrangular like our Oxford Colleges, is dignified and beautiful.

But very unlike the Oxford life is the life of students here. Galway is essentially a poor man's college - and the better for that. Removed within the last few years from Government control, self-governing now in a self-governed National University, it begins to play its part in reshaping the life of Connaught. Connaught students are more than a hundred where they used to be less than fifty; and the College which, in one brilliant year, sent out Antony MacDonnell to be the ablest Indian statesman since the Lawrences and T.P. O'Connor to become head and front of English journalists, may turn out other Connaught men, not less gifted, to as great a career at home in Ireland.

Near by to the building of 1840 stands another of more recent date, less costly, less elaborate, yet to my mind, of quite as much artistic interest. This is the new diocesan college which, in one long facade, rises like a cliff dominating the hill westward. It is like a cliff and not like a shop front, because by skilful variations, what looks uniform is, in reality, skilfully modulated. The Irish architect who planned it had a large sense of decorative effect; and as you slip on the flood tide in the quiet dark of a summer evening through the shadowy glimmer of water with the quay's lights reflected on it, that long, craggy outline up against the remnants of western glow in the sky is a fine link that carries up the profile of the town to the heights on the Connemara side. So seen, with the velvety dusk flung about it like a Spaniard's cloak, there is no place in Ireland more romantically beautiful than Galway.

8/6/29

TOWN HALL CINEMA , TUAM.
TO THE EDITOR TUAM HERALD.

Sir---Mr Willis wishes to publicly thank all the helpers who extinguished the fire in the operating box with the marvellous " Minimax" extinguishers. He also wishes to thank all his esteemed patrons for their sympathy and offers of help and assistance. He wishes it to be made known that the children's picnic he promised them will be duly carried out at a later date. Will everyone please accept his grateful thanks.

Yours sincerely,
R.WILLIS   8/6/29

CATHOLIC EMANCIPATION.

TO THE EDITOR TUAM HERALD.

Sir—I think that the views of members of the Protestant Church of Ireland are liable to be misunderstood by some people on this important subject, and I would, therefore, feel grateful if you would kindly allow me a little of your valuable space to deal briefly with the subject. In this letter I am *not* officially acting as spokesman of the Protestant Church of Ireland but I feel sure that many members of that Church would agree with my views. I believe that the passing of the "Catholic Relief Act" in 1829 was, indeed, a landmark in Irish history, and that the Irish Protestants can combine with Irish Roman Catholics in commemorating what was an act of obvious justice. I rejoice at "Catholic Emancipation" just as much as any Roman Catholic.

I am convinced that the system of excluding men from political rights on account of the religious views which they hold is utterly unjust, un-Christian and indefensible. I heartily wish that the history of Ireland was not besmirched with the Penal Laws.

We must remember, however, that we live in an enlightened time, and that many things that were done 100 years ago, would never be done in these days. It is wholly untrue to suppose that the members of the Protestant Church who were against Catholic Emancipation were the only wrong-doers. Equally terrible wrongs were perpetrated by members of the Roman Catholic Church in those dark days of long ago. Take, for example, the records of the Spanish Inquisition.

But thank God that is all over now. In those dark days there was very little tolerance. Few of us understood the true meaning of the teachings of our Blessed Lord and Saviour Jesus Christ. I was talking to a Roman Catholic friend of mine lately on this subject and he expressed his agreement with me. We are all sorry for the evil ways of some of our ancestors. (But we can all thank God that there were also some great and good men in those days though they may have been few in number).

Let us, however, return to the present and rejoice together that the injustices of the past are gone.

Irish Roman Catholics and Irish Protestants can now work together for the common good and for the welfare of our country. I have lived happily among them for a long time, and if God spares me, I hope to live and work happily with them for many more years. And when our work on this earth is finished I look forward to meeting them again later on in Heaven.

I am convinced that we will not be divided there. In Heaven there will be no sign posts saying - "Roman Catholics this way"- "Protestants that way"! We will, I am sure, all be together in Heaven and we will then understand many things which may not be quite clear to us now. We all serve the same God, and we have the same Lord and Saviour Jesus Christ, and some day we shall all be united in the service of our God and Saviour.

Let us, therefore, work together with a spirit of peace and goodwill, while we remain down here on earth, and let us all thank God for all His goodness to us.

Yours, etc.,
"Protestant Irishman".

P.S. I think I should also mention, for the benefit of those who are ignorant of the fact, that even in 1829 very many Irish Protestants rejoiced when the "Catholic Relief Act" was passed, and there were not a few who had given long and strenuous efforts to bring it about - for example Grattan, and again Edmund Burke who worked and struggled for it, down to the day of his death. God will reward them for their work whatever man may say.

8/6/29

"FARMERS' GAZETTE".

Ireland's Agricultural Journal.

Every Saturday ... 2d
Subscription Rates :—
12 Months, 13/-
6 Months, 6/6
3 ,, , 3/3
On sale at all newsagents and Bookstalls.
Publishers,
THE BRUNSWICK PRESS, LTD.
Brunswick House, Pearse St., Dublin.

8/6/29

We learn from the "Observer" that the School Attendance Guard went to a house in Bohermore and interviewed the woman bending over the washtub. "And how many children have you got altogether?" "Well, there's Lucy and Alice and Olive and Charlie and Willie and Nell and Mary and Tom and Michael and Joe and Patrick and James and Maggie and Timothy and---" "Er---Madam, it will be sufficient if you just give me the number." "Number, indeed," replied the proud mother, wiping her dripping hands on her apron; "we haven't got to numbering them yet. We haven't run out of names yet by a long way."

15/6/29

"RECIPE FOR A NATIONAL THEATRE"

In the June issue of that excellent monthly publication, "The Realist," appears an article on "Recipe for a National Theatre," written by Mr. Lennox Robinson, the well-known playwright and Manager of the Abbey Theatre in Dublin. It gives an account of the birth of the National Theatre Movement in Ireland which led to the production of many clever plays and to the appearance of many talented native actors. For to the Abbey we owe the first appearance on the stage of the two Fays, Sinclair, Kerrigan, McCormack, Sarah Allgood, Maureen Moloney, Renee Kelly, Margaret Nicholls and others who have acquired fame. Mr Robinson truly says that much is due to two Galway persons who gave the Abbey its first push into the forefront and made the theatre an actuality, not a dream. These two are Edward Martyn and Lady Gregory. The money required for producing plays and running the place in its early years was generously supplied by Edward Martyn. Lady Gregory supplied some excellent little humorous plays and gave the place her best attention. William Boyle also did his part and his three plays were excellent comedies. Mr Yeats undoubtedly lent a hand in selecting plays and in writing one or two of merit and popularity. But one cannot help thinking that without Martyn's money and Gregory's humorous plays one fails to see what could be done by the poet or others. Miss Horniman, an English lady, whose parent made a fortune by selling tea, gave great and valuable aid to the national theatre in Ireland. Synge came along with some excellent plays, but his "Playboy of the Western World" nearly wrecked the movement. We never could see any literary or other merit in that play which made a hero out of a man who was supposed to kill his father and who with the women became unpopular when it was to their disgust found out that he had not been a paricide. There were countless other playwrights of varying merit. The Abbey has endured and by the aid of the Government subsidy it seems destined to endure. Mr Robinson who, as we said, wrote several good plays that appeared on its stage, has given a fair account of the origin, growth and evolution of the Theatre. It won favour with the literary few left in the country, and George Moore and George Bernard Shaw, the two Georges, lent it their beneficient countenance, not that such aid helped it materially at first. But all said and ended it was Edward Martyn's money that gave the Abbey Theatre its first real shove into actuality and got it over the dangerous time of its feeble infancy. It is now, thanks to that generous-souled and well-meaning Irishman, an established institution, and if there were any gratitude in the present management and friends of a successful movement they ought to put up in the Theatre some lasting memorial to Edward Martyn. A bust or a marble tablet telling future generations what he was and what he did would be a fitting memorial.

As one goes into the entrance hall one sees several framed theatre programmes and one particularly noticeable in Czeck. It tells us that Synge's play, "The Well of the Saints," was produced in Prague in the National Theatre under the direction of the late Mr. Charles Musek, the clever actor-director of the Czeck National Theatre. The original play was in English and it was sent to Prague by Mr. R.J. Kelly, K.C., who twice visited that city and who knew Mr Musek well. He translated the play into Czeck and took a part in its production. He came once to see Lady Gregory at Coole Park, Gort, and he also visited Mr. Martyn at his hospitable home at Tullyra, then and for years, indeed all through his life, the resort of countless visitors. Indeed for over thirty years Tullyra was never without a party of friends enjoying the converse and society of a cultured and hospitable Irishman of the old school.

A constant visitor to Tullyra in these days was Claude Chevasse, an English man converted to Irish ways and what he thinks is the Irish dress. His uncle was Protestant Bishop of Liverpool and died recently, 82 years of age. His biography is published and he is described as a saintly and kindly man. His nephew gained notoriety, if not fame, in Ireland, and so attachable is he to the country that he married an Irish girl, Miss Mary Fox, and bought and lives at Furbough, near Barna, once the home of the Blakes. One of them, John Blake, was Lord Clanricarde's agent and was shot dead on a holiday when going into Mass in Loughrea. He is buried in a kind of family tomb which was erected by his father and where several of the Blakes are buried. It is beside the public road to Spiddal—a melancholy mortuary monument.

22/6/29

Great Southern Railways.
CATHOLIC EMANCIPATION
CENTENARY CELEBRATIONS
at DUBLIN
19th to 23rd June, 1929.

—

On 18th, 19th, 20th, 21st and 22nd June
RETURN TICKETS AT SINGLE FARE
will be issued
TO DUBLIN
from
ALL STATIONS
available for return within one week
from date of issue.

—

SUNDAY, 23rd JUNE,
SPECIAL EXCURSION TRAIN

			3RD Cl. Return Fares
			s. d.
Tuam	dep.	6.30 a.m.	8. 6.
Ballyglunin	„	6.45 „	8. 0.
Athenry	„	7.15 „	7. 0.
Broadstone	arr.	10.45 „	

Returning at 7.45 p.m.
Tickets available date of issue only.

P.J.FLOYD, Traffic Manager

15/6/29

THE BANK OF IRELAND RAMP.

The learned Editor of the "Irish Rosary" for June has the following article on the above subject:—

"The list of the Bank of Ireland's directors and officials, as set forth in Thom's Directory for 1929, reads like the roll-call of Cromwell's army. Consider the names which follow, and remember that we are now in the centenary year of Catholic Emancipation:—

Stanmore Nutting—Miller—Brabazon—Smith Clark—Amphlett Goulding—Henry—Hogg—Jameson—Broadhurst Pollock; these, with that millitant Ascendancy man, Sir John Keane, form the great majority of the directorate, while only two Catholic names are faintly discernible in the helpless minority.

Among the chief officials at the head office in College Green, we find these names:—Foster—Stewart—Johnston—Pratt—Etherton—Christie—Dobbs—Rutherford—Joy—Franklin—Wells—West—Parke—Lyndon—Hill—Diver—Notley—Dudgeon.

Four or five Irish names are omitted, for the simple reason that they may possibly be borne by Freemasons; while, on the other hand, a very few of the un-Irish names above given may possibly belong to members of the depressed Catholic minority in this quasi-State Bank of the Irish Free State. What public or private influence led the Presbyterian Mr. Blythe to select this Freemason Bank as practically the State Bank of this nation? It would be rather interesting to know.

Now we come to the Cromwellian names among the agents or managers:—Symes—Stuart—Leggett—Hall---Montgomery—Bassett—Smythe—Hinds—Beatt—Craig—Chestnut—Nixon—Osborne—Hosford—Bassett—Good—Symes—Johnston—Allen—Wade—Hunter—Starkey—Jackson—Heron—Kimmitt—Matthews—Mussen—Anderson—Aldwell—Stone—Clear—Gibson—Jackson—Brabazon—Johnston—Franklin—Vernon—Richey—Stephenson—Simpson—Ross—Johnstone—Sloane—Dickenson—Topp—Gray—Orr—Elliott—Evans—Elliott—Jones—Foxall—Hopkins—Devitt—Ashe—Osborne—Stoney—Gardiner—Lloyd—Crosbie.

These form the great majority of the branch managers of this quasi-State Bank throughout Ireland. Side by side with them, we find a few neutral names, such as Barrett—Fleming—Carr—Morris—Blake—Hackett—Norris—Moore—Shaw. These are followed by a tiny residue of common Irish names, such as Lennane, Mahon, Joyce, McGuire, Gowan, Shea, and a very few others, — these, of course, may possibly be the names of Freemasons; while among the Cromwellian and neutral names, a stray Catholic may be found.

Turn we now to the names of the sub-agents (sub-managers). Line after line, they march like Cromwell's Puritans;—Alston—White—Rooke—Harding—Smye—Morrow - Lendrum - Smythe—Gifford—Swayne—Vanston—Gray—Frazer—Hodges—Adams—Fullerton—Smythe—King—Henning—Tucker—Outon—Crosbie—Jones—Longstaff—Prentice—West—Johnstone—Johnston—Gibson—Beveridge—Purdon—Chambers -White—Ashe—Armstrong—White—Evans—Alley—Williamson—Robertson—Hutchinson—Twigg—Carleton—Searight—Frazer—Lowry—James—Lebas—Peard—Odbert—Alexander—Drought—Franch—Fryer—Vernon—Exshaw—Cranston—De Rosse—Lawrence—Johnson—Bredin—Meyers.

The number of Irish and neutral names among the sub-agents is so few as to be practically negligible. There is a larger proportion of Cromwellian names among the sub-agents than among the present agents of this Bank. In other words, when the present agents (or managers) retire, in a few years' time the agents or managers of the Bank of Ireland's branches throughout the country will be more Cromwellian—and more Freemason—than they are even now, which is saying a great deal.

It is exceedingly instructive for an Irish Catholic a member of the 93 per cent majority, whose money enriches the Bank of Ireland—to look through a list of 2,000 or 3,000 Freemasons in this country. He will note, with a feeling of unpleasant surprise, the ominous frequency with which the "Bank of Ireland" is given as the address of a Freemason bank official in all manner of towns throughout the country. Of course, you may say that the Provincial Bank, the Royal Bank, the Ulster Bank, the Northern Bank, and the Belfast Bank are no better, possibly a shade or two worse. But six or seven blacks do not make a white; and the bigoted Freemasonry of certain other Banks affords no shadow of excuse for the very bigoted Freemasonry of the Bank of Ireland.

For a considerable time past, it has been a matter of current rumour in Dublin that the Freemason Bank of Ireland has been promoting a Bill which will enable it to swallow the Hibernian Bank, even so it has already chewed and digested the National Lane Bank. Rumour also has it that, when the Hibernian Bank has been devoured, the National Bank (founded by O'Connell as an offset to the bigotry of the Bank of Ireland) will become the next victim; while the Munster and Leinster Bank will fight to the bitter end for its existence and independence.

The attitude of the Government, in the recent debate on private bill procedure, was distinctly ominous. It seems clear that the Government party will not hinder the Freemason Bank of Ireland in its desire to gobble up two of the three distinctively Catholic Banks, that is to say, the Hibernian Bank and the National Bank,—and possibly the Munster and Leinster Bank as well. It will be a charming way of celebrating the centenary year of Catholic Emancipation!

Fancy the scorn and contumely which the great O'Connell would have poured upon the pigmy creatures who aid and abet his old enemy, the bigoted Bank of Ireland, to capture his own National Bank,—and that in the centenary year of Catholic Emancipation! Fancy how nobly he would rage against the puny politicians who are, apparently, ready to perpetrate this growing act of treason!

Are the directors and shareholders of the Hibernian Bank—are they ready to acquiesce in the ignoble bargain? Are they ready—for a consideration—to betray their distinctively Catholic Bank into the hands of a bigoted Freemason concern? The thing seems incredible. The directors of the Hibernian Bank are Messrs. Martin F. Mahony, Thomas Moore, Senator P. J. Brady, William R. Nolan, Charles E. Lambkin, and Charles H. O'Connor—practically all Catholics—with Alfred Tenison Collins (whose name often appears in Freemason lists) as general manager. Can it be possible that these gentlemen, and the bulk of the Catholic shareholders, have acquiesced in the sale of their Catholic Bank to its intolerant, Freemason rival? We cannot believe them capable of such a deed.

The Catholic public of Ireland—93 per cent, of the population of the Irish Free State—has looked in vain to the Murphy Press for instruction and direction in regard to the Censorship Bill and the Bank of Ireland Bill. The Murphy Press, supremely intent on money-making, cares for nothing that might jeopardise its earnings. So we are left without guidance from the Murphy Press as to the inner meaning of many things.

The Censorship Bill proved to be an acid test of the sincerity of our politicians. Under that test they wilted, they failed ignominiously. Judged by the Catholic standards which most of them acknowledge in theory, their conduct has been ignoble. Hard on the heels of the first, now comes a second test of their quality. The Bank of Ireland Bill will be a second acid test by which our present race of politicians may be judged. The omens are all unfavourable.

Perhaps in fifty of a hundred years' time some future Sir Jonah Barrington may be writing a history of The Rise and Fall of the Irish Free State. Or it may be some keen Fitzpatrick, writing of some present-day Sham Squire, or some present-day traitor MacNally. In either case, the future historian may be able to explain why some of our Deputies and Senators exhibited such white-hot zeal for the interests of the Putrid Press; and why the politicians of every party showed so little regard for the moral interests of the nation, and so readily obeyed the crack of the Freemason whip, in connection with the Censorship Bill.

In like manner, the future historian may possibly explain why our Free State Government proposes, apparently, to celebrate the centenary of Catholic Emancipation by enabling the Freemason Bank of Ireland to gobble up O'Connell's National Bank and the Hibernian Bank as well. It is enough to make O'Connell turn in his grave. It bids fair to be one of the greatest betrayals since the Act of Union was passed by a corrupt Protestant Parliament.

Our present Government deserves ample praise for its bold resistance to Freemason bluff and intrigue in such matters as the Shannon Scheme, certain tariffs on imported wares, compulsory Irish, the Merrion Square Bill, and sundry other measures. Why, then, should the Government have shown the white feather in the matter of Evil Literature? And why should it now seem willing to connive at the machinations of the Freemason Bank of Ireland? Freemasonry stands for Evil Literature, and for the octopus-like operations of the Bank of Ireland. Why should the Government capitulate to Freemasonry.

Delta. 22/6/29

GREAT UNITED CIRCUS.

The Great United Circus Limited, will pay a visit to Tuam on Wednesday, June 26th. The Show is direct from America, and landed at the North Wall on March 25th last year, all the motors and horses causing endless trouble through customs, freightage etc.

The Show is an all-motor Show; everyone connected with the concern are supplied with Pullman sleepers so there is no early rising, consequently all are in the best of form to give an artistic performance.

The horses are also equine artistes and travel by motor, as they are all very valuable animals.

The performance is the same that has been given in America up to last February and has been running continuously through the States for years with only one break, when coming over by White Star liner.

22/6/29

SUNDAY'S HISTORIC DISPLAY.

The marvellous popular display on Sunday in the Phoenix Park, Dublin, was one worthy of the occasion and of the people who took part in it. It was on every side and by every class of people described as most impressive and was carried out with admirable precision and faultless exactitude - almost incredibly so. The arrangements were perfect and the cordial cooperation of the thousands that attended from not only all parts of Ireland but from the neighbouring English and Scotch countries, particularly from Glasgow and Liverpool, made things move with almost mechanical completeness. The weather was particularly favourable and the imposing display of all the Irish bishops and other robed ecclesiastics and Church dignitaries were such as only Catholic display could so fittingly lend itself to. All this with the groups of the young of both sexes in their several confraternities and societies, all of them marching with such splendid regularity and in the style that only military displays could equal, was most picturesque and impressive. The testimony of every eye-witness and every observant participator, all without a single exception, unite in proclaimning Sunday's demonstration as magnificient, impressive and stimulating. A people and the professors of a creed that so spontaneously could gather together and show forth such a magnificient attitude of reverence and belief in their faith has a great future of hopefulness before it if only they were to realise the fact and act on the inspiration of such a belief. The once down trodden Irish Catholic has, like a giant aroused, risen up after centuries of suppression to display all his strength and do so with the dignity of democratic strength and not aggressively or overbearingly but with the simple consciousness of power in his numbers and faith in his destiny. A nation that can on such an occasion and in such a way so well acquit itself is one not only to be proud of but one to hope much for. A religion that can bring its followers of their own free will without any compulsion or pressure together to the number of nearly a half a million of its faithful adherents and so collect them in a single city and upon a single day has great possibilities and much to be proud of and to rejoice in. The vast, orderly well-behaved crowd that marched into the Park on Sunday, and deployed into their allotted place as a regiment would do on parade, acted also with a spirit of devotion and reverence as they took part in the religious ceremonies, constituted a grand sight for not only a Catholic, one of the common belief, but for any other Christian in these days of growing infidelity, agnosticism and unbelief, to be proud of. Across the Church of England is reft by dissension and even its very bishops and deans are proclaiming doctrines subversive of Christianity itself and absolute treason to their own calling. The same Church, in the days of its strength and supremacy, backed up by the authority and power of the State, it was that held the people of this country in chains because only they were Catholic and were such men and women as their descendants were to-day in this great celebration. For centuries the Irish Catholic was held in subjection and slavery but now he is free and the submerged and subject creed has risen up and asserted itself in all the might which numbers and sincerity of belief gives it. The people who so demonstrated are not, however, going to retaliate and to revenge themselves for such cruel treatment but to continue their course of orderly Christian lives under the inspiration and strengthening doctrines of that Faith which consoled their forefathers and alone enabled them to survive and in the end prevail. Only a faith with divine authority behind it could have brought forth its people from the systematic, cruel and organised slavery and prosecution which their ancestors sustained and which their fortunate descendants lived to triumph over, as Truth always sooner or later triumphs over Injustice and Error. Every English newspaper correspondent, every one who came with open minds and honest intention to see the realities and to tell the simple truth, with one voice, praised Sunday's demonstration. Catholic Ireland has reason to be proud of itself and to congratulate itself upon such a happy ending to a great undertaking. The arrangements were excellent and in every detail worked out admirably. The streets of dear old Dublin looked simply beautiful and with a curious strangeness the poorest parts were those that strove to outdo themselves in their tasteful display of the Papal flag which never before in Ireland was so universally shown and so widely respected. It seemed as if Catholic Ireland were not only celebrating the centenary of our liberation from slavery and from State subjection which a hundred years ago was brought about under God by the one great Irishman all united in honouring and to whom all the Catholic world this week fitly paid tribute of respect, but as if Catholic Ireland also were at the same time, celebrating the liberation of the revered head of their Church from the subjection of a Temporal power that unjustly deprived the Pope of his Patrimony and possessed itself of the territory which was given him and which was his as the head of the Church, for his welcome liberation also just providentially brought about this very month. The O'Connell celebration in Dublin was a magnificent demonstration and a remarkable display of Catholic faith and we trust its lessons will not be lost upon us but that in the spirit and according to the teaching of that faith, our loyalty to which so proclaimed, we may continue to live Christian and Catholic lives, obey the great behests of our Church and continue worthy of being called sons of the Church founded by St. Patrick and which through the ages has given such evidence of the strength and sublimity, the faith which the Apostle of Ireland preached and for which so many generations of the Irish people have suffered and in the profession of which same faith so many hundred thousand, nearly half a million, on Sunday last so decorously demonstrated in the Phoenix Park in Dublin.

29/6/29

Mr Kenna, teller, National Bank, Tuam, has been promoted chief teller, O'Connell St. Branch, Limerick, and is replaced in Tuam by Mr. Harkin, Crossmolina.

Last week the German liner Karlsruhe, from New York to Boston, landed 300 passengers at Galway.

29/6/29

TUAM AND THE O'CONNELL CENTENARY CELEBRATIONS.

On Friday, in accordance with the plans of the Emancipation Centenary celebrations, was the day of the Diocese of Tuam.

Dr. Gilmartin again presided at the public meeting at the Mansion House, and delivered a speech on the position of the Roman Catholic Church in Ireland. Papers were read at the afternoon and night meetings, and the Mansion House on both occasions was filled.

The Church ceremonies in connection with the celebration of the Centenary of the Catholic Emancipation were continued on Friday, when a solemn Votive Mass of the Holy Ghost was offered up in the Church of St. Andrew, Westland Row, Dublin. It might be described as a Tuam festival, as the presiding dignitary was His Grace Dr. Gilmartin, Archbishop of Tuam, and there was a good representation from the West. The spacious church was crowded with clergy and laity, and the arrangements for regulating the convenience of a big assemblage were perfect. As on the previous day at the Pro-Cathedral, the Boy Scouts were a valuable aid to the police in keeping order in the street in front of the church.

The celebrant of the High Mass was the Right Rev. Monsignor Macken, P.P., V.G., Claremorris; the deacon, the Rev. P.J. Moane, C.C., Ballyhaunis; the sub-deacon, the Rev. H. Curley, C.C., Louisburgh, Westport. The assistant-priest was the Rev. Canon McDonald, P.P., V.F., Newport, and the Master of Ceremonies was the Rev. P. Rafter, C.C., St. Andrew's, Dublin. The assistants at the throne were the Very Rev. Canon Monahan, P.P., St. Audeon's, Dublin, and Very Rev. P. Canon Boylan, M.A., St. Patrick's College Maynooth.

In the afternoon at a largely attended meeting, the Archbishop of Tuam said he wished to re-echo the sentiment of His Grace the Archbishop of Dublin, that the object of the celebrations was not to create resentment or ill-feeling towards their non-Catholic brethern. They were not responsible for the evil deeds of Elizabeth and Cromwell, and he assumed that the great majority of them had no sympathy with religious persecution. Their object in recalling the tortures inflicted on their forefathers was to keep alive the spirit of faith through which victory was won, and to thank God for rescuing them from annihilation as a Catholic nation. The mission of the Catholic Church was a continuation of the mission of Christ, and, as the Gospel and ideals of Christ were opposed to the passions and prejudices of human nature they could well understand how the life of the Church had been a history of opposition, and at times malignant persecution. Even in the natural order unjust compulsion created a reaction of courage and resistance.

His Grace proceeded to read, amid applause and laughter, from Joyce's history references to the policy of the Tudors in trying to Anglicise Ireland, the legislators undertaking to regulate how the hair was to be worn, the beard clipped, and for women the colour of their dresses, the number of yards of material that they were to use and the hats that they were to wear.

"But," said his Grace, "if many of our people have given up most of the distinctly national features of Irish social life, and, if too many have shown lamentable weakness in imitating foreign fashions, there are, thank God, no signs of weakening in adhesion to and practice of the Irish faith which was tried as gold in a furnace." (Applause). "Instead of growing dim, let us hope that this gold will shine brighter in the brighter days to come." (Applause).

The celebrations of this week, his Grace continued, including the splendour of Catholic liturgy carried out in the churches of the capital, the reading of instructive papers and the open air service and procession fixed for next Sunday should do much to make them realise that the Faith of Christ was man's greatest possession, and that this inheritance which had been handed down to them, sealed with the blood of Irish martyrs, should be guarded as the geatest treasure of the Irish nation. (Applause.) It had been said that history was a conspiracy against truth. That was certainly true of many of the histories of the so-called Protestant Reformation, the fundamental fact of which in these islands was the rebellion of Henry VIII against the authority in spiritual matters of St. Peter's successor. When the Pope refused him an impossible licence to divorce his lawful wife, the English King simply revolted against his authority and made himself a Pope within his own dominions. This was the beginning of the tragedy which reached its culmination in the reign of his illegitimate daughter. How unnatural a form the persecution by Elizabeth of the old Church took in Ireland Father Gannon had told them in his eloquent and logical paper.

"It is to be hoped," said His Grace, "that after this week we shall hear no more about the laughable claims of the so-called 'Church of Ireland' to be regarded as the descendant of the so-called 'non-Roman Church' of St. Patrick. Before its disestablishment in 1869, the Protestant Church in Ireland was one with the Established Church in England, called the Anglican Church, whose distinguishing charactristic is the usurped right of the civil power to all ecclesiastical jurisdiction, and to be supreme judge of her doctrine. If mere mechanical succession to the material buildings and ecclesiastical revenues, of which we were despoiled in the sixteenth century, could make it the Church of St Patrick, it can show ample title to that claim. (Laughter and applause). But succession of this kind does not confer a succession to orders and spiritual jurisdiction. The continuity both in orders and jurisdiction in the Church founded by Christ and the Apostles was ruthlessly broken by the rebellion against Papal authority and the rejection of the essential tenets of the old Catholic doctrine and liturgy. And this continuity can only be restored by a reunion with the church to which Henry VIII was loyal before the Pope resisted his unlawful desires—the church of the Mass and the Seven Sacraments, the Church of St. Patrick, Brigid and Columbkille, the Church which alone in the world to-day has the marks of Unity, Apostolicity, Catholicity and Sanctity. (Loud Applause.)

"I do not wish to assert that there are no sinners in the Catholic Church," said his Grace, amid laughter. There are, unfortunately, too many, which is the Church's greatest trial. Nor do I mean to say that all without the Catholic Church are sinners. I believe there are thousands of good men who, through no fault of their own, do not belong to the body of the Church. And this is exactly the reason why all the facts connected with the revolt against the Catholic Church in the sixteenth century ought to be constantly kept in their proper historical perspective. The reading of such accurate history will, under the influence of the Grace of God, be a revelation to the good souls outside the Church who are humbly seeking the truth, many of whom are daily finding their way into the true fold." (Applause.)

The Archbishop referred to the recent history by Monsignor D'alton, of the Archdiocese of Tuam, in which the unprejudiced reader would find not only a graphic picture of the Elizabethan persecution in the West of Ireland, but also of the persecution of proselytism and souperism. If Ireland, as a whole, deserved to be publicly congratulated on the victory of faith over dungeon, rack and sword, the West of Ireland deserved to be congratulated on the victory of faith over souperism. Souperism was a system of inducing hungry people to sell their faith for food and clothes. He assumed of course that enlightened Protestants looked upon such a system with horror, but the fact remained that fabulous sums of money were contributed to seduce the people of Achill and Connemara from their allegiance to the faith. The system which was inaugurated by Nangle in Achill shortly after the passing of the Emancipation Act took on its most active operations in the days following the famine, when the people of the Western seaboard were dying of hunger. Churches were built to accommodate the unfortunate weaklings who pretended to sell their faith for a mess of pottage; but today only decaying buildings remain to witness the failure of souperism, while new churches and schools had sprung up to witness the victory of the faith over this insidious form of religious persecution. While they sang their paean of victory over spoliation, persecution and souperism, it was wise to take measures that success might not become failure.

It was by a living faith that Jesus Christ was the son of God that their forefathers conquered the forces of hell, and it was by the same living faith that their children could maintain and extend the inheritance so dearly bought.

"Recriminations or desires of revenge are absolutely alien to the Christian ideal," said His Grace. "The greatest weapon of the Christian missionary is charity. The Protestants of the twenty-six counties have paid numerous tributes to the fairness of the Government of the Free State and to the civility of their Catholic neighbours. Will the day come when the Catholics of the North will be able to pay the same testimony to the Government of Northern Ireland? When that day comes we may hope to see vanish the last remnants of unnatural persecution, when North and South united may enter upon an era of the fullest religious and political liberty.

29/6/29

TUAM MARKET.

New potatoes were sold at Tuam market on Saturday at 3s. per stone, and on Wednesday at 2s. 6d.

29/6/29

FISHING AT OUGHTERARD.

The fishing at Oughterard, says " Observer," during the dapping season has eclipsed that of previous years. The Corrib has been dotted over with boats everyday. The hotel Corrib catered for seventy Waltonians. The famous Angler's hotel, the home of the sportsman as well as the old established Darcy's Lough Corrib hotel were also overcrowded. Since the opening of the season many other sports men are camping on the shores of the Corrib and taking up rooms in private houses situate in picturesque spots along the Corrib shore. The catches were beyond the most sanguine expectations. It goes without saying that the fishing inspectors were on the alert and poaching is now almost a thing of the past.

29/6/29

LORD DEWAR.

Undoubtedly the wittiest speaker we have to-day is Lord Dewar, a Scottish peer, and a peerless wit. In fact in our honest opinion the wittiest men we come across in reading and intercourse are the Scotch. We, Irish, once supposed to be witty have, perhaps, got too serious or at any rate we have lost the art and no one ever hears or reads of any clever Irish sayings since Father Healy and Lord Morris died. Our modern system of education so largely based upon examination and memory have driven all original thinking out of our heads, and certainly in the literary line we have fallen far behind other nations. Recently there died in Dublin an excellent raconteur, Sir James Percy, and the light seems to have gone with him. He was a good after dinner speaker and collected a lot of humourous sayings and anecdotes mostly of the past generation and printed them under the title " Irish Bulls." They sold well, but he had to call upon the fast fading generation of Irishmen for his wise sayings and modern instances.

Lord Dewar serves to keep alive the spirit of humour, and long may he live to brighten our present sadly drab, dull, deadly dull, lives. We recently came across a few of his sayings in a speech he delivered to a delighted audience in London at a dinner of the Poultry Club.

Received with merited applause, Lord Dewar thus delivered himself :-

My feelings, he said, might be compared with those of a swallow in its delirious glide through the air until it suddenly strikes a telegraph wire.

I do not know the rudiments of this subject—man's anthem—woman. When a bachelor flatters himself he knows a woman—he flatters himself.

Never having experienced the echo of the call of joy or the high ideals and noble aspirations of the marital problem—domestic felicity, the evolution of faith and hope—I have therefore no place in this discussion. I stand before you a man of keen susceptability— a subpoenaed witness to the hand of fate.

I do not exactly admit that I have an extraordinary shrinking from the fair sex. I have to communicate to you, in the bonds of confidence, that I venerate and have always thrown bouquets of forget-me-nots at the beloved shrine of the petticoat—an article which I am credibly informed is now obsolete. The dresses to-day begin anywhere and leave off abruptly. There is more latitude than longitude about them. There is many a safety pin that carries more responsibility than the chairman of a bank. The snap of a burst suspender foretells a downfall. What the world needs to-day is more permanent wives and less permanent waves.

Although I take only an academic interest in this momentous question of the ladies it is worthy of a little introspection and retrospection. If you reach out through the darkness of forgotten days and stretch away down our long genealogical aniseed trail there you find the first woman Eve collaborating with the serpent over a sour apple, and ever since she hankered for fig-leaves men have been continuously paying large dressmakers' bills. Eating apples may keep doctors away, but it started dressmakers in business.

I am certain there is not a man present here to-night who does not appreciate those beautiful lines :-

> Here's to the Garden of Eden,
> That Adam was always a weedin'.
> Till Eve by mistake
> Got bit by a snake
> That on a ripe apple was feedin'.
> A longing seemed then to possess her
> For clothing sufficient to dress her,
> And ever since then
> It's been pleasure to men
> To pay for her dresses, God bless her!

To-day women display more backbone than men. When a man exposes himself he catches a cold, and a girl catches a husband. In prehistoric times girls caught men with their bare hands—to-day they catch them by their bare shoulders.

Brevity to-day is the soul of the frock business. If a little boy wants to hide behind his mother's skirt to-day he has to get in his high chair to do it.

Everyone will admit that woman's dress to-day is the most rational and hygeinic that has ever been worn since the day that Samson had his hair bobbed. That is why the women of to-day are healthier, handsomer, and more beautiful than in any other generation, from away down the ages ever since the time that Solomon chased the Queen of Sheba. Solomon didn't believe in taking presents home—a word to the wives was sufficient.

Train up a housemaid to the way she should go, and the first thing you know she's gone.

When some of us feel we are getting mellowed with age. creeping on to the silver twilight of our days, and our chins are beginning to lead double lives, Cupid passes by with a frosty salute.

A husband should tell his wife everything that he is sure she will find out and before anyone else does.

29/6/29

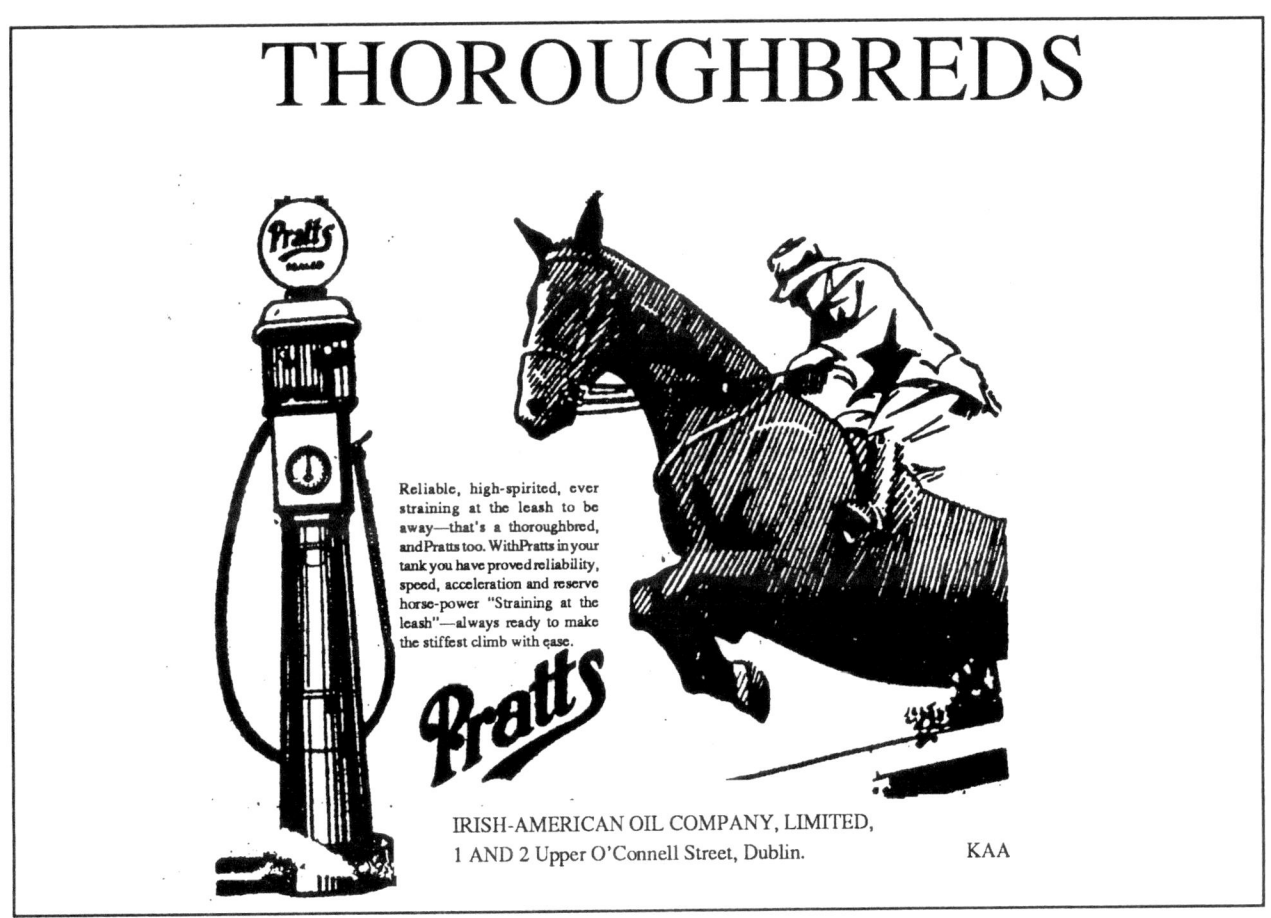

THE CENTENARY CELEBRATIONS.

The arrangements for the Centenary Celebrations in the Phoenix Park were excellent and reflect great credit upon all concerned. We are pleased to see that three Connaught men took a prominent part in the affair and creditably contributed to make it the splendid success even the splenetic scorner who never sees any good in what an Irishman, and above all a Catholic, does, is silent on the occasion. He wanted confusion, scuffle and squabbling and not having got that treat, so often characteristic of our Donnybrook performances, he is driven to dumb disappointment and disgust. These three men were Sir Joseph Glynn, a Gort native, Mr Charles O'Connor, a son of the late O'Connor Don and a grandson of O'Connell's best friend, and Mr. Monaghan, a son of the late Dr. Monaghan of London and grandson of Mr. Monaghan of Gardenfield, Tuam, who had control of the arrangements for the electrical transmission of the voices engaged in the ceremonies.

29/6/29

THREATENED STRIKE.

The threatened strike on the Great Southern Railway in regard to wages and working hours of the shopmen employed at Broadstone and Inchicore, Dublin has been averted. It is understood that the company set a reduction in wages of 12 and a half per cent, while the men were prepared to accept a 7 and a half per cent reduction. An arbitration board was appointed and its findings, which were issued on Wednesday, are for an all-round reduction of 10 per cent to be made from the earnings for a five-day week. The award is agreed to upon the understanding that the Great Southern Railway Company will, during the period of operation of this award, guarantee to the several classes of operative workers affected a five-days week of 42 and a half hours. Hitherto the men had been employed on four-days of the week only, the works being closed Friday and Saturday, as well as Sunday.

29/6/29

THE ST. GEORGE ESTATE SOLD.

THE LANDS OF CAHERLISTRANE DISPOSED OF.

The estate of (which) Catherine St. George (widow) of Kingstown, and Oswald Browne of Tuam are the owners, and which are situate in the Barony of Clare and Co. Galway, and formerly formed part of what (was) known as the estate of Christopher St George, D.L., of Tyrone House, Oranmore, extending over thousands of acres.

The present land(s) are at Caherlistrane near this town, and are now being finally disposed of, and thus close the chapter of the St George ownership. We give a few details of the transactions at last accomplished. The names of the principal tenants to whom their holdings have been transferred under the Land Act are as follows :- John Joseph and Ulick McDonnell of Cloverhill, Ballinrobe, 134 acres; Michael Reilly of Ummoon, Caherlistrane, 18 acres; Thomas Roche, Patrick Curran, and Patrick McDonnell, of Ummoon, Moonaragh, and New Village, 18, 5, and 20 acres; John Kean, 24 acres; Thomas Haughton, 10 acres; Michael Haughton, 33 acres; James Nally, 42 acres; Michael Keane, 34 acres; all of New Village.

Sarah Burke, 35; John Gibbons, 5; Julia Burke, 66; Edward Corless, 27; Michael Meagher, 13.

Cloonaskia, Carragh and Beaghmore—William Connor, 29; Mattie Keane, 37; William Crowe, 43; Mary Devilly, 44; James Halty, 44; James Nalty, 41; James Reilly, 42; Oswald Browne, Beaghmore, 13 acres; Arthur Benedict O'Connor of Beaghmore, 125 acres; Ulick McDonnell of Cloverhill, 5 acres; Michael Keane, 22 acres; Thomas Moran, 26; John Shaughnessy, 26; Bartly Higgins.

At Carragh Mary Moran, 33; Edward Comer, 33; John Moran, 35; Michael Walsh, 39; James Walsh, 16, and Patrick Farragher, 40 acres.

These lands were since Mr. St. George's death run by the agent, Mr. Kirwan of Tuam, and he and the tenants never had any disputes or unpleasant relations. The lands are situate at Beaghmore and adjoining townlands which are six miles from Tua At Derryhiveney, Loughrea, in the Barony of Longford in this County, 471 acres the property of David England Young, deceased, and continued in the name of Marie Young widow, and Rev. Golding Maddison Fry, have been acquired by the Land Commission at a fixed price of £4,500 payable in 4 and a half percent bonds.

(From a Correspondent).

The St George estate at Caherlistrane, in this neighbourhood, has just been taken over (on 9th inst.) by the Land Commission and the price paid to the owner determined and fixed upon. The various former tenants and the sums applotted are set out in the schedule. In the case of John Joseph McDonnell, the owner, gets £1030 in Land Bonds; in John Egan's case, £1,540 ; in case of Arthur Benedict O'Connor, of Beaghmore, £1399 ; Myles McDonnell, £139; Michael Naughton, £157. The total amount payable to the landlord, Catherine St. George (widow) and Oswald Browne is £8,291 payable in Land Bonds.
29/6/29

THE LATE SIR THOMAS MOFFETT, L.L.D.

Mr. R.J. Kelly, K.C., has received the following interesting letter from Lady Moffett, widow of the lamented and universally esteemed President of the old Queen's College of Galway and now in her 92nd year :--

Herbert Park, Dublin,
June 21st, 1929.

Dear Mr. Kelly---Many thanks for your kind courtesy in sending me the TUAM HERALD touching so pleasantly on my unworthy self.

There was one great mistake with regard to Sir Thomas Moffett. He was not dismissed but asked to resign under the 65 Rule, which he refused to do to the satisfaction of all the professors, except the one man, the result being summed up in the words of the College Porter : "Och, the President was a grand man, for he not only bate the Government but he bate the Queen---the whole of Galway rejoicing."

Again thanking you, with kind regards,
Yours Truly,.
EMILY M. MOFFETT.
R.J. Kelly, Esq.

TUAM JULY GREAT LAMB FAIR.

WEDNESDAY, 3rd—PIGS (Old Fair)
THURSDAY, 4th—Lambs, Sheep and Cattle
(Old Fair)
WEDNESDAY, 17th—Pigs, 3rd Wednesday

Farmers would be well advised to bring in their Lambs, Sheep and Cattle to this fair, as stock are in good demand at the present time. Lambs at the June Fair realised high prices, so at this fair record prices are expected.

By order Tuam Town Commissioners.
JOHN P. WHYTE,
Town Clerk.
29/6/29

TUAM SPORTS.

A very representative crowd assembled in the Town Hall on Friday evening for the purpose of getting up a Sports in Tuam during August.

Mr W.J.Concannon, Solicitor, was unanimously elected to the chair.

It is now certain that with the progress which has been made up to the present Tuam will have an excellent Sports during August. The date is not certain yet, but there are hopes of having the Sports either on Sunday, 11th or 18th August.

A meeting was called for Thursday evening at 8.30 in the Town Hall, at which correspondence was read from N.A.C.A. Offices, Dublin.

The programme of events was drawn up and the probable prizes to be given.
29/6/29

O'CONNELL AND TUAM.

It may be interesting to old Tuam folk to recall the fact that some sixty years ago there lived here a charming lady, Mrs.O'Connell Redmond. She was a niece of the Liberator. Her husband was William K. Redmond, the popular R.M. He got that position by merit in recognition of his bravery in connection with a Fenian encounter, he being then a District Inspector of the Constabulary. He followed an escaping prisoner out into the river, into which he had jumped to get away, and would have escaped but for Mr.Redmond's pluck and courageous act. Mr.Redmond lived, greatly respected, in Tuam for some years and was changed to Waterford where he died. His grandson, Dr.Henry O'C. Redmond, is a well known medical doctor, whose father and brothers were educated at the Christian Brothers' School here. 6/7/29.

GALWAY COLLEGE.

We observe that last week a bill was introduced in Dail Eireann to increase from £12,000 to £28,000 the annual grant to University College, Galway, and to secure that, in future, persons appointed to offices or situations in the College shall be competent to discharge their duties through the medium of the Irish language. According to the preamble of the bill these provisions are being made by reason of the fact that lately the Governing Body of the University made statutory provision to secure that certain professors and lecturers should deliver their lectures in Irish, and propose now "to take such further steps as circumstances may permit to secure that an increasing proportion of the academic and administrative functions of the College shall be performed through the medium of the same language. The second and final reason for the bill is that the Governing Body, having lately reduced student fees - as well as having undertaken to establish a scholarship scheme for native-speaking undergraduates- now finds that the depreciating value of money in recent years has made the annual grant of £12,000 inadequate for the needs of the College". 6/7/29

TUAM GOLF CLUB.

A most successful open meeting was held last Sunday, 7th July. The Open Stroke Competition was won by H.B.Mangan (16) 65 nett, D.Cummins (20), 67 nett, being 2nd. Supt. D.Connolly won best gross with 79.

In the Fourball Rev. Fr. Gunnigan and Fr. Loftus, Dr. Nohilly and H.Quinn tied with 6 up.

The prizes were presented by Mr. John Quinn, who thanked the visitors for their attendance. The meeting was not as large as last September when the new Golf House was opened. Nine of their members were on holidays, but they had 11 clubs represented there—Ballinasloe, Galway, Gort, Loughrea, Ennis, Balla, Westport, Castlerea, Nenagh and Clontarf. The prizes were won by the Tuam Club but he was sure the visitors did not grudge them the winning. He hoped the visitors would come again and they would have a hearty welcome. (hear, hear.)

13/7/29

TUAM TOWN COMMISSIONERS.

SPECIAL MEETING.

A special meeting was held on Tuesday evening to appoint a Rent and Rate Collector and consider tenders for repairs to Town Hall.

Mr. P.J. Byrne, C.T.C., presided.

The names of the other members present will be found in the division lists below.

Applications were received for the position of Rent and Rate Collector, etc., from—Messrs. A. Griffin, J. Geddes, B. O'Donnell, — Clancy.

Mr. Walsh proposed the appointment of O'Donnell and Mr. O'Keeffe seconded.

Mr. J. Byrne proposed Anthony Griffin and Mr. Dwyer seconded.

Mr. Fahy proposed J. Geddes and Mr. Holian seconded.

Clancy was not proposed.

A poll was then taken as follows :-

For O'Donnell—Wilson, O'Keeffe, Cooney, Walsh—4.

For Geddes—Holian, Moran, Fahy, Corcoran, Byrne P.—5

For Griffin—Dwyer, Byrne J, O'Brien, Gibbons, Burke—5.

O'Donnell then dropped out and a second poll resulted as follows :—

Geddes—Holian, Moran, Fahy, Corcoran, Byrne P., Wilson, Walsh—7.

Griffin—Dwyer, Byrne J., O'Brien, Gibbons, Burke, O'Keeffe, Cooney—7.

There being a tie, the Chairman declined to give his casting vote and suggested the selection of one of the two be left to the L.G.D., and this was agreed to.

REPAIRS TO TOWN HALL.

There were two tenders for repairs to Town Hall, viz. :-

Mr. David Dwyer, £92 17s 6d.

Mr. Martin Burke, £115.

Mr. Dwyer's tender was accepted.

SELLING THE NEW HOUSES.

The Chairman announced that the contractor Mr. Moggan, had completed six of the new houses and was ready to hand over the keys. He has the engineer's certificate and he (Chairman) suggested that the Housing Committee visit the houses and after that they could be advertised for sale immediately.

This was agreed to and it was also agreed that the Finance Committee should meet and go into the figures so as to arrive at the minimum amount to be accepted for each house.

The Board adjourned. 13/7/29

The Tuam Herald.

Fiat Justitia Ruat Coelum.

Bidheadh cóir déanta dá d-tuitfeadh neamh.

LET JUSTICE BE DONE THOUGH THE HEAVENS FALL.

Guaranteed to be the best Provincial Advertising Medium in Ireland.

SATURDAY, JULY 13, 1929.

LEAVING THE LAND.

All over the civilised world the people who lived on and by the land and helped to produce the food which enabled others to live in towns and cities and follow other pursuits are leaving the land and ceasing to be food producers, are becoming food consumers and thereby intensifying the problems of living. But for the fortuitous discovery of a certain frost resisting wheat which enabled the limitless plains of Canada to be cultivated we would be in a bad way for the chief article of life — our daily bread, being relatively cheap, for the general production of food is not keeping pace with the growth of civic populations. Agriculture is not keeping pace with the imperious needs of the times and is everywhere lagging behind in the race. A very able observer and economist writing on this subject, Dr. Bernhard, writing in the 'Sunday Observer' of May 5th says:- "There is hardly a purely agricultural village in Switzerland that has not fewer inhabitants than it had 50 years ago. In Austria most of the communities with fewer than 5,000 inhabitants show a steady decrease. In 1871, 63.9 per cent. Germans lived in places with fewer than 2,000 inhabitants, now only 35.6 per cent. so live. The Agricultural population of France has gone back from three quarters to just over one half. In Belgium from 14.6 per cent. to 6.3 per cent; in England, between 1871-1920, from 38 per cent. to 20 per cent., and in the United States, between 1890 and 1920, from 64 to 48."

These are remarkable and significant figures and they give us food for serious thought. We must apply the lesson and its application to ourselves and see how we fare in that respect. We have not exact figures to go upon or statistics available that will illustrate the problem as to whether we are agriculturally an advancing people and whether more people are to-day on the land than were to be found on it twenty years ago. We have had the annual drain of emigration which, although restrained by the American laws, yet is too serious and weighty to be lightly turned aside and not minded.

We have had a complete agrarian revolution, the complete transformation of an occupying peasantry to an owning peasantry. Landlordism, in the old form, is dead. Every tenant is practically owner of his farm and owns no submission to a superior. Rent is no longer the crux here as it once was, but the increasing rates and taxes are taking its place in the account and swelling the total. This is all very well if we were on our part meeting the strain and stress of existence by producing more food, as in proportion to the extent we do so will we be prospering or the reverse. In the old days of comparative comfort and quiet in many respects, the ordinary country household in Ireland grew nearly all its own food and made at home, or got from neighbours, nearly all the articles it required. They only wanted from outside tea, sugar, wine, if of a superior class, and the rest, eaten or worn or used, was produced at home. As late as sixty years ago no house of the farmer class ever bought bakers' bread or even flour, for they all grew, or their neighbours did, their own wheat or oats and they were all ground at the local mills which have all stopped now except in some few cases. The clothes worn, linen or woolen, were locally produced. Now all this is changed. The ever expanding grass is taking the place of the tillage and it is a less profitable form of farming. Our food problem is a serious one and as tillage goes out of fashion it is becoming every year more serious. No imposts will ever reduce our present food prices - the only way to meet it is by increased cultivation. As now carried on stock raising is the most primitive, most precarious and least profitable form of farming, and yet we are embarking on it more and more. Our young men and women are getting discontented and are leaving the country - some going to America and in lesser numbers to Canada and Australia, or flocking into our few cities and big towns. Dublin is expanding from this inroad from the country and is at present in a very unsatisfactory condition, economically, for she cannot absorb the crowds coming in and find profitable employment for them - a very serious outlook when the pressure of penury comes to be felt. The industries in Dublin capable of absorbing this immigration are few and have not the business to do to justify expansion, even assuming the persons coming into her area wish for such employment and would not prefer the more genteel work of clerkships or tobacco factory hands for the girls. The United States, with its immense resources of land and money, are agriculturally in such a plight that no longer can they export food and must look to Canada for a large part of its beef and corn. Australia is only a country of four overgrown cities and an unexpanding country and they are most feeling the want of the farmer who will grow in numbers with the growth of the cities and so keep pace with its imperative demand for food. Hitherto Ireland, despite the ravages of a Famine whose effects could have been alleviated if properly dealt with, as was the case in India in our time, and a preternatural bleeding to very death by emigration, was hitherto a food producing country, not only able to supply its own wants in that respect, as all the continental countries were, but to export quantities to feed the factory workers in England. It is fast falling away from that position and it is now so imperfectly fulfilling its trust as food producer that the Danes send us butter and bacon, and even New Zealand mutton. We have in proportion to our population in the Free State and Ireland generally more persons depending on outside supplies of food than ever and more than any other country but England, which in that respect of dependance is in a most alarming condition.

Various expedients have been suggested to meet and correct this very unsatisfactory and unpromising state of things, and undoubtedly the Department of Agriculture, through Mr. Hogan, is doing giant work in improving the output of food in the shape of livestock for exportation and eggs and butter for consumption in Great Britain. But for that improvement and its results we would be bankrupt and unable to pay our way, for the native demand for food if we could supply it to-morrow would not pay our farmers. Our system of education is faulty and requires revision and overhauling. No agricultural country that we know of takes less trouble in its schools to teach the children of the farmer what he and she should know- how plants grow, what suits various sorts of land and how best they can be cultivated - how to make bread, butter, clothes and provide all necessaries of the household, as their fathers and mothers well knew how to do. How few girls growing up in a farm can milk a cow, make butter and bread and properly dress themselves. How few young men know a single thing about the farm, than the Dane, the French, the German, and all progressive people, teach their youths and insist upon their being taught before anything else. We have our own destiny in our own hands- to sink or swim, to grow rich or grow poor, to be good or bad citizens - the fashioning of the future is in our own hands and God help us if we neglect our duty and giving to empty politics and talk what was meant for work, to fall behind the race of life and lag along weary wastrels, with no spirit to get on, no ambition to move ahead, no desire to utilise our opportunities and advantages. Never had a people such a chance to get on as we have now, if rulers and people only face the problem like men determined to succeed and if all classes do but combine to help the movement for regeneration and advance. If we lag behind we shall lose the race and forfeit our place in the ranks and never be able to regain it.

13/7/29.

Great Southern Railways.

PILGRIMAGE
TO CROAGH PATRICK
SUNDAY, 28th JULY, 1929.

SPECIAL EXCURSION TRAIN

			3rd Cl. Ret. Fares.
			s. d.
Galway	dep.	6.30 a.m.	5 6
Athenry	"	7.0 "	4 0
Tuam	"	7.30 "	3 6
Westport	arr.	9.15 "	

Returning at 6.40 p.m.

Proportionately reduced fares will be charged from intermediate Stations at which Special Train will call.

Tickets available for date of issue only.

P.J. FLOYD,
Traffic Manager.
20/7/29

PARS. OF LOCAL INTEREST
(From Our Own Correspondent.)

Tuam Sports.

The Sports Committee are leaving nothing undone to make the forthcoming sports a great success. Already several members of the Committee have promised to provide valuable cups, and an appeal is being made to the business people of the town to do their part in support of the event. The course has been mapped out in one of the finest enclosures in Ireland in Parkmore, and given fine weather the Sports on the 11th August promises to be one of the best held in the West for some time past.

Aeroplane over Tuam.

The Hon A.E. Guinness left Dun Laoghaire on Tuesday afternoon in his triple-engined seaplane, and was seen flying very high to the west of Tuam. His destination was Cong, in this county. Mr. Guinness was accompanied by his pilot and two passengers.

Improving our Streets.

During the week the Co.Council steam roller was engaged rolling the corner at the Galway Road which has been widened considerably where indeed it was much required. The road along the new set of houses built by the Town Commissioners has also been steam rolled and widened considerably, so that when the work is completed the new St.Bridget's Terrace will be one of the prettiest streets in Tuam, a welcome addition to the housing accommodation of the town and a credit to the Town Board under whose aegis the housing scheme was undertaken. The road outside the Munster and Leinster Bank at the corner of Vicar Street and Dublin Road has also been widened and is presently being steam rolled.

Tuam Ball Court.

After considerable delay the contract for above work has been secured by Mr. Martin Burke, contractor, at the sum of £230. The work is to be commenced immediately and when completed it is expected that Tuam will be in possession of as fine a ball alley as exists in Ireland. If the hopes of the Committee are realised it is expected later on to build a second alley adjoining and a stand capable of accommodating anything up to 1,000 spectators. The site is an ideal one at the back of the Courthouse where the old disused bridewell once stood.

Pioneer Hall.

The Pioneer T.A. Association are going ahead with the work of improving their new hall adjoining the Cathedral gate. A bagatelle table has been secured and the Council are laying down a new floor in a room where they expect to install a billiard table before the long nights come. With a membership of over 1,000 the Tuam Pioneer Hall is an assured success.

Tuam Excursions.

Tuam has nothing to complain about in the matter of railway excursions this year, and the general public eagerly avail of the opportunities offered them. On Sunday 270 left Tuam for Galway, and in addition to the Sunday excursions to Galway a cheap excursion (as may be seen by advertisement in this issue) is to be run. 20/7/29.

BUS ACCIDENTS.

Bus accidents are more and more frequent and in nearly every case they are more or less fatal. The greatest carelessness is shown by the class of reckless young men who are allowed to drive these dangerous vehicles. The State should oblige a strict examination into the competency of any person who has committed to him so dangerous a machine. The mentality of most motorists is positively scandalous and criminal. They seem to think that all they need do is at some time or in some circumstances to sound their abominable hoot and that is alone sufficient. They need not abate one jot of their reckless speed or in any other way take precautions. In every case of death from motor accidents the fatal result could have been avoided if the delinquent driver took ordinary care, while it is laid down as the law in England that he must take redoubled care, for he has committed to him a deadly, dangerous machine.

20/7/29

Tuam Races

—

FRIDAY, 2nd AUGUST.

Flat, Hurdle and Steeplechases.

LARGE ENTRIES FOR 6 EVENTS.

SPECIAL TRAINS FROM ALL PARTS AT CHEAP FARES.

Admission to Grand Stand :-
Gents ... 10s   Ladies ... 5s
Admission to Course, 1s
Motor Cars parked, 5s.

20/7/29

MALL CINEMA, TUAM.

SUNDAY & MONDAY, JULY 21st & 22nd.
at 8 p.m.

THE GREAT IRISH-AMERICAN SHOW.

ON THE SCREEN—
EMMET MOORE presents the wonderful
Irish Picture, "ERIN'S ISLE."

10,000 Feet Motion Picture, including
Episode 9—VULTURES OF THE SEA.

ON THE STAGE—
EMMETT MOORE HIMSELF.
Hear his Golden Voice. Also MAE FITZGERALD,
Leading Lady of Emmett Moore
Attractions from the Irish Playhouse,
New York.

Don't Miss This Splendid Treat.
Prices of Admission—2s and 1s., inc.tax.
20/7/29

Great Southern Railways.

GALWAY RACES
31st JULY & 1st AUGUST.

On each day Return Tickets at Single Fares
will be issued to Galway, available for return
up to 3rd August.
The usual 2 Day Excursion Tickets
will also be issued.

AUGUST BANK HOLIDAY
EXCURSION ARRANGEMENTS.
On FRIDAY, SATURDAY AND SUNDAY
2nd, 3rd and 4th AUGUST.

EXCURSION TICKETS AT SLIGHTLY OVER SINGLE
FARES will be issued between ALL STATIONS,
where train service suits, available for return
up to and including Saturday, 10th August
(Express Mails G.S.& W. Sections Excepted).
27/7/29

GALWAY NOTES.

(From our own Correspondent).

We referred last week to Mr. Anthony E. Malone's excellent work on the Irish Drama (1896 to 1928) and we gave particular prominence as it deserved, to his account of the late Edward Martyn - so well and so familiarly known in his native county, as indeed all over Ireland. We felt bound, in justice to his memory, to correct some few unintentional inaccuracies. Speaking as we did from a life long and intimate knowledge of that true Irishman - one who was a credit to his country and one whose memory ought to be perpetuated by some fitting memorial in Galway - the county and people his ancestors lived so long in and were so closely identified with and which he himself loved. It is sad to think that one who gave away so much money, probably some fifty thousand pounds in his lifetime to every object and every person, one so deserving of recognition, should have no memorial, however small and modest, to his memory. A marble tablet in the church of Ardrahan, which he and his mother did so much for, would be a suitable and fitting tribute to him, and it would be, we are sure, widely subscribed to. We venture to make the suggestion now while his memory is still fresh in the people's minds and ere he is entirely forgotten.

Mr. Malone gives equal space and notice in his book on the Drama to the work of another native of this county, Lady Gregory. She is a daughter of the late Mr. Dudley Persse, of Roxboro, and a sister of Mrs. Lane, and of Mrs. Shaw Taylor - all three clever and gifted women. The sons of two of them, Mrs. Lane and Mrs. Taylor, will long be remembered for their public spirited services. Captain Shaw Taylor did two memorable things in his short but useful life which alone should serve to keep his memory green in the public mind. He initiated the movement for stopping the scandously indiscriminate spread of public house licenses, and in this connection he said publicly in Dublin at a meeting of the magistrates of all Ireland that he first took the matter of this abuse from articles which appeared in the TUAM HERALD, from the pen of his friend, Mr. R.J. Kelly, K.C., then and still its chief writer. It was, in the fitness of things right, that another Galway man, the late Mr. John J. Clancy, K.C., M.P., should have introduced and got passed a bill in the British Parliament, called after him the "Clancy Act", preventing any new license being given for a drink shop until and unless a former license lapsed. It did great good, and to the late Captain Shawe Taylor Ireland is indebted for that good. But a greater service he rendered was by bringing together landlord and tenant and so paving the way for the famous Wyndham Act, which was the work of a great statesman and one who was the best Chief Secretary Ireland ever had. To Shawe Taylor we owe that great boon which unfortunately later on was allowed to be crippled by the Birrell Act, because it was too successful and costing too much to the Exchequer. Had the Wyndham Act not been hamstrung by the amending Act of Birrell, not an acre in Ireland would have been unsold in five years.

The next of the two noted nephews of Lady Gregory was Sir Hugh Lane, a real genius for discovering the merit of pictures and who made thousands by this peculiar gift. He went down in the Lusitania, universally deplored.

Mr. Malone says of Lady Augusta Gregory that she " gave to the dreams and aspirations of W.B.Yeates and Edward Martyn for the creation of a literary theatre the practical shape which they seemed unable to give them themselves. It was she who suggested the start of a literary theatre in Ireland, and it was she who secured the interest of her very large and influential circle of friends and acquaintances for the project. She was born at Roxborough, Co.Galway (now a sad ruin), a member of the Persse family which has given so many notable personalities to both England and Ireland. The family was of English extraction, its culture was English, and its outlook and symnpathies were English, and its politics Unionist. Her near neighbour was Edward Martyn, who lived at Tullyra Castle, and a little more distant at Moore Hall lived George Moore. Thus it will be noted that all the four founders of the Irish Literary Theatre and of the national drama which derived from that Theatre were ultimately associated by birth and family with the province of Connacht. Of the four two were members of Catholic families and two of Protestant, but all four were of the Anglo-Irish rather than of the Gaelic tradition, though doubtless there was considerable Gaelic blood intermixed with the original English or Norman. Connaught is very mixed in its blood, but it is nevertheless still the most Gaelic in thought and speech of the four provinces. Lady Gregory had lived among the peasantry of her native Galway for the greater part of her life and never has been away from it for any very prolonged period. In her early life she was attracted by the folk stories and folk songs of the cottagers, and she commenced that systematic collection which has since been presented to the world in many forms, not the least is the material which is used in many of her plays. In this way her love for the people grew until it became almost a passion, and she in her turn became the beloved of her people. Her life became part of the life of the district and her thoughts and speech became those of the people." He says later on that "she was in her fortieth year when in 1898 she drafted the circular letter which initiated the movement and of Lady Gregory more than any other single one of the four who founded the theatre, it may be said the Irish Theatre, is hers and she made it. Because not only did she provide the necessary organising ability in the initial stages but she also moulded its policy and its plays. She has been a Director from the first and she remains to-day as keenly and as actively interested in its management and in its welfare as she was in the beginning." The Abbey Theatre opened on the 27th of Dec. 1904, and one of its plays was "The Spreading of the News," a play that always attracts and delights. Then followed a series of successful plays from her prolific pen and numbering some 30 or 40 - the chief being Hyacinth Halvey, The Gaol Gate, The Rising of the Moon, Kincora, Dirgovilla, The Canavans, The Jackdaw, The Workhouse Ward and countless others. It is a wonderful collection of really clever and popular plays anyone of which could be reproduced again and again and listened to with interest. In political satire Mr. Malone says "Lady Gregory is especially strong. Her best comic efforts are satirical and the majority of her plays are capable of political interpretation. Indeed her work might almost be used as a continuous commentary upon the Irish political scene during her life time. Her best three act comedy "The Image,"1904, is based on a story related by the poet A.E. which has also been used by George A.Bermingham for his popular play, General John Regan". In every sense Lady Gregory is a very able writer and it is surprising neither of our two Universities which ought to recognise native literary merit should not confer their honorary degree upon her except that they always seem to give the distinction to people whom every one but their friends and academic backers seems to know no earthly reason why they should be so honoured. Honour coming from indiscriminating sources is of course no honour, but Trinity and the National ought to be abreast of the times and try to recognise and honour native talent as all such well run institutions do. Lady Gregory long since should have been so honoured, and so in his day ought Edward Martyn, far more so than some of the dull dug-outs that are so distinguished. Then there is Katherine Tynan Hinkson. She also deserves recognition but like Lady Gregory she will have to wait. 27/7/29

The Calvary attached to Ballinrobe Catholic Church, one of the most artistic in the West, has recently been renovated by Mr. De Guieney, Dublin, son of an Italian artist, who first erected the Calvary. 27/7/29

JIM TULLY

"Jim Tully," the famous Hobo writer, is an Irish-American. In his very popular work, "Beggars of Life," he describes his early years of adventure as a hobo or tramp and his many adventures riding on railways without a ticket and living with the tramps in all sorts of places and under all sorts of conditions. Yet he always had a taste for reading, always indulged in that taste and seems always to have read the best books and so acquired a style that would put to shame half our so-called educated writers who hail from universities but cannot write grammatical English. This is how he writes:- "I, a throwback to the ancient Irish tellers of fairy tales, was at last on the way to high adventure. Sad and miserable men, broken on the wheel of labour, tired, nerve-torn women too weary to look at the stars -- these would be the inhabitants of the dream country I was going to. What a picture I must have made -- a heavy-jowled, red-headed youth with a crooked smile and a freckled face and clad in the cast-off clothing of more fortunate working boys. Everything seemed to pass through my mind - I was a beggar at the gates of life. I would return to St.Mary's a rich man. I would show the aristocratic girls who snubbed me on Spring street that I was not what they thought I was. I would not come back until every one had heard of me and when I did come back and walked along the streets people would say: "There goes Jimmy Tully, he used to be a little drunkard and hang round and look at him now - huh - that shows what a fellow can do in this country if he works hard and saves his money." Even then dreaming of some day being a writer, I would write great stories, and my name would be in the magazines. Some day the natives in St.Mary's would wake up and see my name spread across the front page of the 'Saturday Evening Post' - by God, I'd show them I would. As the train gathered speed my thoughts came more swiftly."

Thus vividly and graphically he describes his start in hobo life, his first trek as a tramp. He went out unknown and he now returns with his name as a writer on every man's mouth. 27/7/29

We are pleased to see that Mr. J.J.MacKeown, Inspector of Taxes, Dublin, has been appointed assessor of public departments, Dublin Castle, in succession to the late Mr. Thomas Hogan. Mr MacKeown, who is a native of Newry, is the author of the successful comedy of Irish life, "The Real McCoy," which was produced by the Irish Players at the Olympia Theatre last year, and which has completed its initial tour of more than 250 performances. Mr. Mackeown has also written two other successful plays, "Still Running," and "The Pension." He is a nephew of the late popular P.P. of Collooney, Archdeacon O'Rorke, and the distinguished Historian of Sligo. 27/7/29

DUBLIN HORSE SHOW
AUGUST 6,7,8,9, 1929.
EXCURSIONS FROM ALL PARTS.
BALL'S BRIDGE,   EDWARD BOHANE,
DUBLIN   DIRECTOR
27/7/29

GALWAY RACES.

The Annual Racing Carnival of the West,
on
31st JULY & 1st AUGUST, 1929.

RECORD ENTRIES.

EXCURSIONS FROM EVERYWHERE.

Charges down to Pre-war level.
27/7/29

TUAM TOWN COMMISSIONERS.

NOTICE OF APPOINTMENT OF RATES AND RENT COLLECTOR, TOWN SURVEYOR AND TOWN HALL CARETAKER.

The Tuam Town Commissioners will, at their meeting to be held on Tuesday, August 6th, 1929, proceed to appoint a competent person to the position of Collector of Rates and Rents at a commission of one Shilling in the Pound on all monies collected and lodged provided that all sums collectable in any week or part of a week are duly accounted for each week or part of a week. The person appointed Rents and Rates Collector must also discharge the duties of Town Surveyor and Town Hall Caretaker at a salary of £25 per annum. Applicants for the position will be required to submit themselves to an oral test in Irish (prior to the meeting). Applications, enclosing the names of two solvent surities, willing to join in a bond of £700 for the due and faithful performance of the duties of the office, will be received by me up to 7 p.m. on the above named day. By Order,
JOHN P. WHYTE, Town Clerk. 23/7/29

The Tuam Herald.

Fiat Justitia Ruat Coelum.

Bidheadh cóir déanta dá d-tuitfeadh neamh.

LET JUSTICE BE DONE THOUGH THE HEAVENS FALL.

Guaranteed to be the best Provincial Advertising Medium in Ireland.

SATURDAY, JULY 27, 1929.

THE SHANNON SCHEME.

On Monday, amid the most impressive religious scenes, the first phase of the great Shannon hydro-electric work was inaugurated. It was most fitting that a gigantic undertaking, such as this undoubtedly is, should be blessed by God and by the singularly beautiful prayer that the Bishop of Killaloe offered up to Almighty God imploring His blessing on the work and that it would in due course eventuate in success. It is certainly a magnificent undertaking and we would be wanting in all sense of national pride and all conception of its importance and magnitude if we did not feel genuinely proud of the project and pray God that it would be crowned with merited success. It is the most extensive hydroelectric work in these countries, we doubt if there is in Europe another can be found to equal it. It as we fervently hope it may realise the expectations of the Government and promoters it will be an enduring proof of their enterprise and public spirit and a great thing for this new country, now entering on its career of nationhood. We sincerely hope and pray it may turn out to fulfil the high hopes entertained of it and if it should happen to do so it will be a great act of achievement, one which any Government may well glory in. It is a colossal enterprise but its greatness and its magnificient magnitude do not detract from its ultimate merit and utility. Mr.Cosgrave went down specially to speed on the great work and in the course of his apt remarks on its cost he confirmed a statement made in the Senate last week that a five per cent. margin will cover the difference between the actual and the estimated costs of the scheme. We gladly welcome that cheering announcement, for there were the usual crowd of croakers talking of excessive expense and improbable success if not failure.No country has a greater crop of such detestable persons as Ireland has, men always picking holes in every effort and always out of their crass ignorance taking the most gloomy view of every thing and every one. These pessimists are a pest in any society and we do not know any country where they so universally abound as here. Such persons are the clogs on enterprise and a public nuisance, their dispiriting disparagement and doleful foreboding take the soul out of many enterprises that otherwise should prosper. These critics and croakers of the Shannon Scheme will, we believe, be disappointed and much to their surprise it will succeed. Its splendid success will be an enduring monument to the energy and spirit of the Government of the Free Stae and a creditable proof of its efficiency. We cannot do better in this connection than to repeat for our part and fervently endorse Dr. Fogarty's impressive prayer and with him and all who wish well to Ireland join in the beautiful aspiration and blessing that most fitly was pronounced by him under every circumstance of solemnity. We may well say with him:-

"O Almighty and Everlasting God, by Whose high providence all things are governed, deign we beseech Thee to bless from on high these newly erected gates to control the inflow of the Shannon's waves; so that, protected by Thy arm, they may rightly fulfil their purpose for Thy greater glory and the good of the people of Ireland; and grant that we Thy servants, illumined by the light of grace, may regulate our lives according to Thy holy will in all things, and after the darkness of this world be admitted through Thy mercy within the gates of eternal light. Through Christ our Lord. Amen".

This prayer for the blessing of the canal, and subsequently this final prayer of blessing on the whole scheme we may well reiterate -
"O Almighty and eternal God, Who alone disposeth all things rightly, and without Whose aid the grandest designs of men and nations must come to nought, graciously hear our prayers,and send Thy angel from Heaven to watch over, defend and protect these vast works, now happily completed by Thy favour, and keep them ever safe, and make them ever more fruitful for the glory of Thy name and profit the people of Ireland. Through Christ our Lord. Amen".
"And may the Queen of Heaven and St.Michael the Archangel, and all the saints of Ireland, make intercession for us, and present our petitions before the Throne of God, in the name of the Father, Son and Holy Ghost. Amen".

SIGNS OF RETURNING PROSPERITY.

The addresses of the Chairmen of the National, Provincial and Munster and Leinster Banks on Wednesday and Thursday show that in the opinion of these capable and experienced judges there is a decided improvement in the condition of things in this country. There are no better or more reliable tests of the real state of a country than its bank returns. Sir Stanley Harrington said that there was no doubt the country was more prosperous, and Mr.Trotter, the

Provincial Chairman, stated that "encouraging features in the position of the country to-day are the expanding figures of our export with a proportionate lessening of the advance balance, the extent of which a few years ago was disconcerting and was the subject of unfavourable comment." The Chairman of the National Bank was equally emphatic in his testimony to the improved and improving condition of the country. All banks had to report a falling off in their respective circulation due to the new currency arrangements but all had to participate in that disadvantage. It is therefore plain that the prevailing tendency is towards a better and more stable state of things and this will undoubtedly continue so long and as long as peace and order prevail and a consequent sense of security encourage the people to put more energy into their business and devote more thought and time to the serious business of life-leaving politics and petty, pestiferous wrangling and internecine quarrelling alone. The country has a bright future before it while the people keep on these lines of moderation and common sense and leave aside all those tactics of terrorism or disorder which hamper enterprise and retard progress. Our native industries are capable of expansion and development and more new sources of employment and of resourceful labour might be explored with advantage. Thus in and about the bog lands of Athlone it has been found profitable to establish a new industry in the growth of seed potatoes of the best kind. The wonder is not so much why this should now be discovered, but why it was not found out years ago and turned to advantage and why other places with abundant bog do not utilise the advantage similarly. It is a small thing in its way, but it is by such small things universally adopted and utilised throughout the country, by making every acre profitable, that the national resources generally can be appreciably added to, prosperity brought about and with it the blessings that follow from comfort and content.

27/7/29

The Universe,
Founded in the year 1850,
WEEKLY CATHOLIC NEWSPAPER.
Offices :
1, ARUNDEL STREET, LONDON, W.C.2.
Telephone : Central 8776.

Women keep their good looks by taking Beecham's Pills

FACTS AND FIGURES

Regarding the oldest Irish Life Assurance Company :--

Income per annum	£100,000
Assets exceed	£130,000
Claims paid to date exceed	£150,000
Claims paid during 1927	£34,000
Deposited with Saorstat Government in accordance with Statuary Requirements	£20,000

Support an Irish Office that employs Irish Labour, whose policies bear the Revenue Stamp of Saorstat Eireann, and whose funds are all invested in Irish Securities. 27/7/29

300 MASSES Annually :--One alms of 1s will secure you a share in these during life and after death,--St. Peter Claver Sodality at Benedictine Priory, Princethorpe, Rugby, England.

IRISH INDUSTRIAL REVIVAL.

Write any of the following to-day for their prices.
(MENTION THIS PAPER.)

A WORD TO FARMERS - We buy all Classes of Accident or Mortality Hides or Skins at Tanners' Prices. Irish Feather Co.Ltd. Tara Street, Dublin.

About Used Sacks and Bags. We are large Buyers of all Classes and allow Highest Prices. J.P.Keogh & Co., 2 George's Quay, Dublin.

Anti-Corrosive Oxide Paints. Paints, Colours, Varnishes (spirit and oil) Distempers, Printing Inks, Wholesale from A.E. Derrington, St.Kevin's Paint Works, Lower Clanbrasil St., Dublin.

A BIG TIP - We are largest cleaners and exporters of sheep casings to the U.S.A.; enquiries and consignments solicited, Irish Casing Co.,Arbour Hill, Dublin, also at Kilkenny, Telephone: 2705; Telegrams: "Edible, Dublin".

ASTHMA, Bronchitis and Nasal Catarrh. Dr.Palmer's papers are an instant and effective remedy for Chest Complaints. Manufactured now by us from the original recipe. In boxes 2/2 post free. Brown and Son, Chemists, 139 Stephen's Green, Dublin.

A WELDING Firm of repute; specialists in repairing Boilers, Chassis; Iron and Steel Work generally - South of Ireland Electric (Arc) Welding Co. Ltd., 7 St. Barnabas' Gardens, Dublin.

BRASS and REED BAND Instruments, Bagpipes, Drums and Jazz Effects and Fittings stocked. We have supplied all the leading Bands, including the famous No.1 Army Band. Repairs to any Instrument. Pianos by all the leading makers at keenest prices. Tunings anywhere. Prices on application. McCulloughs, 58 Dawson Street, Dublin.

ENGINEERS' CASTINGS, Clean Castings, Keen Prices, Quick Delivery, Brass, Gun Metal, Aluminium, Phosphor-Bronze, Nickel Plating, Enamelling, also General Repair Work - Fox's Brass Foundry, 18 and 19 Wellington Quay, Dublin,

FRUIT - If you want the best selling lines in Fruit, send your orders to Thomas H. Seaman, 16 Little Green Street, Dublin. Personal attention to all orders. Cash or reference with first order,

Feathers and Feather Beds bought for cash. Send postal sample; we pay carriage. Hair Mattresses and springs supplied. Irish Feather Co.Ltd., Tara Street, Dublin.

Factory Equipment and all classes Shafting, Machinery, Boilermaking, Brassfounding, Repair Work, Motor Cars and Agricultural Implements Overhauled. Wireless Outfits Supplied. Geo Watt Ltd., Mechanical and Electrical Engineering Works, Bridgefoot St., Dublin. Enquiries Solicited - Wires, Wall, Dublin. Phone 4268.

FISH - Thomas Murphy, (Dublin), Ltd., Wholesale Fish Market, Dublin. Country Fish Merchants Supplied with Herrings, Salt Herrings, Reds, Kippers, etc. Prices, terms on application. Telegrams:- Thomas Murphy, Fishmarket, Dublin.

Grey Hair Restored to its Original Colour by Using Dr.King's Hair Restorer, Bottles 1s.6d. Postage 6d. extra. Made in Dublin by Leonard's, Apothecaries, North Earl Street, Dublin.

ICE - Increase your sales by selling Ice Cream, but be sure you get the best ice from National Ice & Cold Storage Co., 28 Sir John Rogerson's Quay, Dublin.

PORTER Bottles Government Stamped - 22/4 gross. Corks and Bottlers' Fittings, Brass and Gun-metal Castings; Silver and Nickel Plating and Enamelling. Illustrated Catalogue free - JAMES FOX & CO., Head Office, 17 William St., Dublin. Telephone (2 lines) 1765 and 601.

MANOR MILL LAUNDRY CO., Ltd., Dundrum, Co.Dublin. Special arrangements for washings sent per parcel post; Gentlemen's Collars finished in unique style. If you give us a trial we think you will become a regular customer.

MATCHES - Use only Patterson's Irish Match and keep your Money in Circulation in Your Own Country. Refuse All Foreign Brands.

McCULLOUGHS Music Salons, 56 Dawson Street, Dublin. (late of 39 Grafton Street) for Drums, Bagpipes, Banners, of our own manufacture. Brass and Reed Band Instruments. Pianos by the Leading Makers at keenest possible prices. Write for Lists today. Phone 4829. Wires, "Music," Dublin.

M.M.L.- Lace Curtains washed and finished with our Dust Resisting Surface; lasts clean a long time. Send them by rail or post - Manor Mill Laundry, Dundrum, Co.Dublin.

"TOGHER"

Sir — I think that many of your readers who do not already know Togher well would probably be interested in some information about this beautiful place, which is such a boon to Tuam in many ways. It might well be described as "The Phoenix Park of Tuam", for the handsome avenues through Togher are open to the public (cyclists and pedestrians) every day of the week, and no charge whatsoever is made for admission.

On most fine evenings after work hours (7 p.m. to 10 p.m.), and especially on Sunday evenings, large numbers of pedestrians and cyclists pass along the avenues and their merry peals of laughter may often be heard. Here they are far from the dust and noise of the public road, and they are surrounded by handsome woods, and pasture lands on which horses, cattle, sheep and donkeys may be seen grazing. They should certainly be grateful for the privilege of using these beautiful grounds, towards the upkeep of which they are not asked to contribute one penny. It is unfortunate that some untidy persons sometimes disfigure the grounds by throwing about papers, cigarette boxes, etc. Men and girls cycling to and from Tuam on any day of the week also have the privilege of passing through Togher, instead of going along the uneven, muddy or dusty road.

There is, however, no right of way through Togher. Cyclists and pedestrians should certainly be grateful for the privilege of making use of the Togher avenues.

Togher, however, is not only a picturesque place, but is also a lively business concern. About 350 statute acres are farmed (excluding woods and bogs) on progressive lines, and many up to date machines are used. These include a Fordson Tractor, a double-furrow tractor plow and a potato digger. Work is given to about ten men throughout the year. With the aid of the Tractor and saw bench some of them cut timber into boards, stakes and fire wood on wet days in winter, and all this is done in a large shed under cover. Others do painting and sundry jobs. The employees at Togher are really given quite a good time. Their work is not monotonous and their wages are comparatively good. All the employees are provided with a good house which is kept in repair for them and a garden is given with every house, and also the grass of a cow, calf and donkey, and a turf bank for their own use. All rent, rates and taxes are paid for them. There are nine dwelling houses on Togher Farm, and well over £100 has been spent on repairs and improvements during the past two or three years. These nine houses accommodate seven families and two single persons.

Togher Sports, which has been much talked about in the district, (and judging from what I hear, much appreciated by all who come to them) ever since they were started in 1925, are not by any means the only outstanding event in the year at Togher. In addition to these popular and healthy athletic and cycling sports, two other annual entertainments take place. First there is the tea, dance, concert and Christmas Tree to which all employees and local people are cordially invited. Tea and cakes, etc., are supplied at 6 p.m. and then presents are given from a Christmas Tree to about 40 boys and girls of Togher and Coolrea. Then the Concert and Dance begins and continues till about 10.30 p.m. Irish Dances and Irish Songs are a special feature. Last Christmas between 80 and 100 people (including boys and girls) attended this function and were all heartily welcome.

The second event is the annual excursion to Galway by train. Those entitled to come are not only given free return tickets, accommodated in a special car on the train, but also two good meals in Galway, and bus rides. Swimming at Salthill is usually one of the chief attractions, and these excursions also seem to be very much appreciated.

On the whole, therefore, I think that most people would agree that Togher is a very pleasant place at which to live.

The work at Togher, however, is not at a standstill. It is progressing — not very rapidly we must admit, but surely and steadily. Things are getting a bit better every year and progress is being made. We have great hopes for the future. The day will come, we hope, if we live so long, when Togher will give employment to far larger numbers than it does to-day, when they will all have really good, useful, up-to-date and pleasant houses to live in, (lit up with electric light from the Shannon Scheme!!), when they will all be able to get really good wages, when the very best cattle, sheep, pigs and poultry which the country can produce will be reared annually, and when every deserving person for many miles around will be supplied with all that is best for him or her.

If, however, we do not live to see these days of peace and prosperity — if we die before these times come — what matter. It merely means that we pass on to higher service in a far better place than this wonderful world in which we live to-day. And we must then leave it to those left behind to carry on the work at which we have laboured so hard here on earth. We must merely say "Carry on, friends, God bless the work; and God be with you till we meet again". Yours, etc.,

"Progress". 30/7/'29.

3/8/29

CHRISTIAN SCHOOLS TUAM.

Examination Successes, 1929.

EASTER SCHOLARSHIPS :
- JOHN HARDIMAN
- JOHN MULLINS
- MICHAEL KELLY
- JAMES O'KEANE
- PATRICK FLEMING
- JOHN WALSH
- JOHN NESTOR
- MATTHEW MACKEN

LEAVING CERTIFICATE--SECONDARY EDUCATION :
- FRANCIS BURKE
- HUBERT J. CUNNINGHAM
- MICHAEL CONCANNON
- JOHN NESTOR
- MATTHEW MACKEN
- JAMES MOONEY.

PUPIL TEACHERSHIP. ENTRANCE TO TRAINING COLLEGE.
- FRANCIS BURKE
- HUBERT J. CUNNINGHAM
- MICHAEL CONCANNON
- JAMES MOONEY.

NATIONAL UNIVERSITY OF IRELAND. MATRICULATION.
- FRANCIS BURKE
- HUBERT J. CUNNINGHAM
- ALBERT COMMINS
- MICHAEL CONCANNON
- PATRICK COLLERAN
- JAMES HESSION
- JOHN HUGHES
- PATRICK FLEMING
- PATRICK QUINN.

Schools re-open on Mon. Aug. 5th.
Senior pupils return on Aug. 19th.

It is stated that the Great Southern Railway have decided, in the interests of economy, to abolish one of the signal-boxes at Tuam station-that near the gates at Churchview-which has been operating since the line was laid between Tuam and Claremorris. It is proposed to operate the points near the cross-level gates from the second box above the loco yard.

3/8/29

TOGHER SPORTS.

(5th Annual Meeting)
AUGUST 4th, 1929.

EVENTS:
1. Boys Race under 16.
2. Girls Race ,, ,,
3. 100 Yards Open
4. 220 ,, ,,
5. 440 ,, ,,
6. 880 ,, ,,
7. 1 Mile ,,
8. 120 Hurdles ,,
9. High Jump ,,
10. Long Jump ,,
11. Bag Race
12. Obstacle Race
13. 3-Legged Race
14. 1 Mile Cycle Race
15. 2 Miles ,, ,,
16. 3 Miles ,, ,,
17. Ladies' ,, ,,
18. Tug-o'-War
19. Camogie Match

FIRST EVENT 2 P.M. SHARP (Summer Time).
ADMISSION TO FIELD—6d.
Entry free for all events.
Committee—M.J.BUTLER, H.FENTON, M.J.RYAN.
3/8/29

TUAM SPORTS.

CUP PRIZES IN MARATHON RACE.

LARGE ENTRY OF COMPETITORS.

As may be seen in our sports advertising column Tuam Sports will be held on Sunday 11th inst. The energetic committee in charge has left nothing undone to make the Sports a success from every point of view, and particularly an enjoyable day's outing for spectators. The track has been well prepared on the football ground in Parkmore, and so situated that spectators will have a splendid view from all sides.

Amongst the valuable prizes to be presented are 3 silver cups to the 1st, 2nd and 3rd in the Marathon Race from Dunmore to Tuam. This race has been announced to start at 12.30, but to meet train arrangements the Committee has decided to hold it over until 1.30 p.m. This race is to finish in the Sports ground in Parkmore. There is a large entry of competitors for all events, and prominent athletes will attend from Dublin, Limerick, Ennis, Ballinasloe, Castlebar, Westport, Belmullet, Claremorris, etc. Special trains will run from Athlone, Claremorris and Galway.

St. Patrick's Band, Galway, will attend.

10/8/29

TOGHER ATHLETIC AND CYCLING SPORTS.

The fifth annual Athletic and Cycling Sports meeting was held at Togher on August 4th. First of all we must thank God for giving us a splendid day. Bright sunshine and absence of rain make a very great difference at an Athletic Sports meeting. This year we had three new events, all of which proved to be extremely popular and enjoyable. These were (i) Camogie Match, (ii) Obstacle Race, (iii) Race open to men who work on Togher Farm only. About 10 men were eligible to enter. One of the competitors in this race was Mr. Martin Corcoran, one of the tallest men in the district. The Obstacle Race contained many formidable and amusing obstacles, the most popular of which was a series of motor tyres suspended from a horizontal bar so that their centres were about 5 ft. from the ground. They had to leap or climb through these.

As a result of all entries being free this year there were more competitors in some of the events than last year especially in the 100 yards open and 120 yard hurdles. Our idea in wishing to have more competitors is to encourage all able-bodied boys and young men to take an active part in Athletic Sports, and thus raise the standard of athletics and physical fitness in the district.

In proportion to the numbers of young men who merely act as spectators, however, the number of competitors in most events (especially the longer distance foot races and the cycle races) is still lamentably low. We hope that there will be more next year if we live so long.

We are most grateful to the Tuam people for their continued support, and we wish them every success at their own Sports arranged for August 11th. We were very sorry, however, not to have Mr. P.M.Hosty with us this year. He has always been a great help to us and we missed him very much. It would be difficult to find such a fine all-round sportsman, and his kindly and cheery manner was always much appreciated. We hope that he will soon be well enough to be back amongst us again.

The following were the prize-winners :—

Event	1st Prize	2nd Prize
100 Yards,	T.Hughes,	W.Melia
220 Yards,	P.King,	W.Melia
120 Yds Hurdles,	M.Dunleavy,	M.O'Sullivan
440 Yards	W.Melia,	W.Kelly.
1 Mile (Foot),	P.King,	W.Melia.
2 Mile Cycle,	M.Connelly,	M.Collins.
3 Mile Cycle,	M.Connelly,	M.Costello.
Ladies Cycle,	Miss Stevens,	Miss Commins.
High Jump,	M.O'Sullivan,	M.Kelly.
Long Jump,	M.O'Sullivan,	P.King.
Boys Race,	P.Gormally,	J.Gormally.
Girls Race,	Miss D.Costello,	Miss Canavan.
Obstacle Race	W.Kelly,	T.Mullins.
3-Legged Race	{King and P.Hession}	{C.Martin, J.Gormally}
Bag Race,	W.Kelly,	J.Coleman
Togher Race,	J.Ryan,	W.Cunningham

(3rd M.Corcoran)

Tug-o'-War, Togher v Dublin Road, latter won.
Camogie Match, Togher v Tuam, former won.

10/8/29

TUAM TOWN COMMISSIONERS.

The monthly meeting was held on Tuesday, Mr. P.J.Byrne, Chairman presiding. (For names of other members see division lists below.)

APPOINTMENT OF RENT AND RATE COLLECTOR ETC.

There were two applicants for the above position, Messrs. J.Hession and B.O'Donnell, and on being called before the Board both passed the necessary oral test in Irish.

Mr. Pat Walsh proposed and Mr. T. Wilson seconded the appointment of O'Donnell.

Mr. James Moran proposed and Mr. J. Byrne seconded the appointment of John Hession.

A poll was taken and resulted as follows:-

For O'Donnell—Walsh, Corcoran, Cahill, Wilson, O'Keeffe, Cooney, Gibbons—7.

For Hession— Holian, Moran, Byrne, Fahy, Dwyer, Burke, and the Chairman—7.

The polling having resulted in a tie the Chairman gave his casting vote in favour of Hession who was thereupon declared elected.

FIVE HOUSES SOLD.

The following applications were received for the new houses :— Mr. Jame Coogan £210 for No. 1, Mr. Pat Costelloe, Galway Road, £210 for No. 3, Mr. T.Cottle £210 for No. 2, Mrs. Regan £210 for No. 5 and Mr. John Hession , Galway Road, £212 10s for No. 6.

Five out of the six cottages having been thus purchased it was decided to advertise the remaining one with the four now under construction for sale at next meeting.

ST. PAUL'S TERRACE.

It was decided to name the new street of houses leading from the corner of Galway Road towards the Railway Station, St. Paul's Terrace.

10/8/29

GALWAY NOTES.

A Tuam man, Mr Joseph Hanly, is the organising inspector of rural science in the schools of the Free State. He must feel well satisfied with the progress of his subject; I see it stated in the report of the Department of Education that the rural science course is taught now in four hundred and twenty schools, all of which have demonstration plots. The nature study course for boys and for mixed schools under a master is taught in five hundred and eighty schools, while the nature study course for girls, or for mixed schools under a mistress, is taught in 1200 schools. Thus, in two thousand two hundred schools rural science and nature study are established. This message of progress owes much to Mr Hanly's energy and zeal. Last year he addressed county conferences in fourteen counties, with an average attendance of fifty-two teachers..

Mr. Hanly was born at Barnaderg near Tuam. He is son of the late Mr. John Hanly of Hillsbrook, who for years was a well known figure in Tuam and district. His brother was Patrick Hanly of Carrowmanagh, and his sister Mrs Commins of Barnaderg. A son of Mr John Hanly still occupies the old homestead at Barnaderg. Mr. Patrick Hanly and family went to Canada about forty years ago and settled there. At one time the brothers, Patrick Hanly and John Hanly, who were strong farmers, were Poor Law Guardians and took an active part in public life. They were fine, tall men, over six foot in height. Mr John Hanly became Relieving Officer of the Killererin District of the Tuam Union, succeeding Mr. Charles Kelly of Ardskeagh. He held the post with credit till he died.   17/8/29.

THE HORSE SHOW.

The great national event opened on Tuesday under depressing conditions—the rain coming down heavily, but next three days were fine. The attendance was very large and representtative and the international military competition keenly watched— the success of the American horse on Wednesday being remarkable. A fine show of horses were to be seen and excellent prices obtained— the first day's sales totalling over thirty thousand pounds. Galway held its own in the hunting competition, thanks to Mrs. Darcy's entries and plucky riding. The whole affair was a brilliant and creditable success.

The whole show ended on a brilliant note on Friday last when the greatest spectacle and the most moving moments of the whole week were provided by the military horse jumping competition for the Aga Khan Cup, which after the most thrilling and representative riding and jumping contest staged even in the famous Ballsbridge enclosure was won by France by one point on a rejump with Ireland after a tie. Sweden was third.

WHAT IS A FRIEND ?

What is a Friend ? I will tell you. It is a person with whom you dare be yourself. Your soul can go naked with him. He seems to ask of you to put on nothing, only to be what you are. He does not want you to be better or worse. When you are with him, you feel as a prisoner feels who has been declared innocent. You do not have to be on your guard.

You can say what you think, so long as it is genuinely you. He understands those contradictions in your nature that lead others to misjudge you. With him you breathe free. You can take off your coat and loosen your collar. You can avow your little vanities and envies, and hates and vicious sparks, your meanness and absurdities, and in opening them up to him they are lost, dissolved on the white ocean of his loyalty. He understands. You do not have to be careful.

You can abuse him, neglect him, tolerate him. It makes no matter. He likes you. He is like fire that purifies all you say. He is like wine, that warms you to the bone. He understands, he understands. You can weep with him, laugh with him, pray with him. Through and underneath it all he sees, knows, and loves you. A friend, I repeat, is one with whom you dare be yourself.   17/8/89

CHARITY.

By its very nature, charity is a social virtue. Wherever a social group is formed- in the home, the community, the civic association- good will is a necessity. It is charity rather than justice that overcomes selfishness, casts out rancour, forbids hatred, clears away misunderstanding, leads to reconciliation. After justice has rendered impartial decision, it is charity that brings men back to fellowship. And if at times it be fitting that mercy should season justice, the quality of mercy itself is but charity touched by compassion

TUAM RACES.

Tuam Races last week were a success. The stand was crowded as was also the general course. Over 30 horses ran in the six events. There was only one race with three horses, the other events having from five to nine horses. One jockey was thrown at the water fence in the second race and received a fractured shoulder.   17/8/29

PADRAIG O'CONAIRE.

Who down here did not know that well known character so familiar to us all in the West, for years past, particularly in Galway. A strange stroller was Padraic O'Conaire. He was a veritable Bohemian and loved to loll about as did many other famous men, but behind that apparent disregard for the conventions a strong sense of humour, a racy love of fun and frolic, and could tell a good story and enjoy one. In the town he was a familiar figure, and he has passed away with little or no literary record of his worth as he was not among the "crowd of celebrities" who live on publicity and trade on it. The "Dublin Magazine", an admirable publication that deserves success if merit is any claim, however contains some splendid lines on Padraic from the pen of a fellow Connachtman, F.R.Higgins, which deserve notice and commendation. We are sorry we cannot reprint the poem for it is a beautiful tribute to the dead, but a few lines will give an idea of how well the writer expresses his admiration of the dead. "Dear Padraic of the wide and seacold eyes, so lovable, so courteous and noble, The very West was in his soft replies." Opening with the lines, "They've paid the last respects in sad tobacco, And silent is the wakehouse in its haze, They've paid the last respects and now the whiskey flings laughing words on mouths of praise and prayer." The writer adds :-

"They'll miss his heavy stick and stride in Wicklow,
His story talking down Winetavern Street,
Where old men sitting in the wizen daylight
Have kept an edge upon his gentle wit;
While women on the grassy streets of Galway
Who hearken for his passing but in vain,
Shall hardly tell his step as vanish shadows
Through archways of forgotten Spain."

And so on in praise of Padraic sung by an old friend with whom we say, God rest his soul. Before we leave this sad subject may we say a word for the "Dublin Magazine." It is a quarterly, well edited, well written, and should be well supported if we have any appreciation of literary merit and really want to have a sound, good magazine as fifty years ago our fathers had and supported, for they knew the value of good books and not the tedious trash that passes muster for literature to-day. 17/8/29

REVIVAL OF ATHLETICS IN TUAM.

President - Reverend Peter Kelly, Adm., Vice President - Very Reverend J.S.Canon Walsh. Chairman of Committee - Wm. J.Concannon, Solicitor. Hon.Treasurer - Daniel Sheeran.

Hon. Secs. - P.T.J.O'Grady and James Nohilly. Handicapper and Starter - P.G.Lennon.

Judges of Athletics - P.Crean, P.Walsh, H.Ruddy, H.Mangan, M.Cooney.

Judges of Cycling - F.Stafford, M.Cahill, L.Strahan.

Lap Keepers - R.Walsh, M.Kelly, H.Cunningham, J.O'Rorke, T.Burke, H.Burke, D.MacCormack.

Marksmen - .T.F.Dempsey, J.O'Connell, J.Fahy. Call Steward - D.Creedon.

Ticket and Gate Stewards - Hon.Secs. Hon.Treasurer. J.Moloney, J.Ryan, J.Hurley, R.Whitty, M.J.Byrne, J.Moran, T.McLoughlin, P.Biggins.

Field Stewards - The Judges of Athletics and Cycling.

Judges of Tug of War —F.Stafford, P.Walsh, J. O'Brien, H.Ruddy, P.Crean.

A very enjoyable Athletic Meeting was held in Tuam on Sunday, 11th inst., comprising cycling, foot races, etc. The venue was the famous Race Course of Parkmore where some of the best Chasers and Hurdlers have carried their owners colours to victory. The success of this Athletic Meeting is mainly due to the Rev. Peter Kelly. Adm.; Very Rev. J.S.Canon Walsh, and to a Committee of Gentlemen of the Town presided over by Mr.William J.Concannon, LL.B., Solr. Events which aroused the greater interest were the 10 Mile Marathon Race from Dunmore to Tuam. Tug of War, won after a wonderful contest by the Tuam team. In the evening a Dance was held in the Town Hall which was very largely attended, the music being excellent.

It is thirty-five years ago since such a successful Sports Meeting was held in this Town, and the able Committee have a large balance in hands to make even a greater success of the Tuam Sports next year.

ATHLETIC EVENTS.

100 Yards - F.Fox (Dunmore) and B.P.Canavan (Tuam) dead-heated. Fox won run-off.
220 Yards - F.Fox, 1; P.Flannelly (Castlebar), 2.
440 Yards - F.Fox, 1; J.P.Gilligan (Claremorris), 2.
880 Yards - M.O'Malley (Westport), 1; M.Roche (Caherlistrane), 2.
Mile - M.O'Malley,1; M.Roche, 2.
10 Miles - D.Donnellan (Ballinasloe), 1; T.Daly (Athlone), 2; M.J.Kennedy (Galway), 3.
100 Yards (Choir Boys Race) - P.O'Rorke, 1st; M.Bray 2nd.
220 Yards (Boys Race) - B.Denn, 1st; J.Quinn 2nd.
Putting 16 lbs. Shot - Gd.Ruddy, 1st; Gd.Talbot, 2nd.
880 Yards (confined)- M.Roche, 1st.; Luke O'Brien, 2nd.
220 Yards (confined)- P.Walsh, 1st; Dan McCormack, 2nd.
High Jump - M.Nolan, 1st; J.Manley, 2nd.
Long Jump - Nolan, 1st; Manley, 2nd.
1 Mile Relay Race - Dunmore 1st; Corofin 2nd.
Sack Race (confined) - W.Kelly, 1st; Jack Quinn, 2nd.
Tug of War - Tuam, 1st.
Clock Golf - D.D.Denehy.

CYCLE RACES.

1 Mile Cycle (open handicap)- F.Williams 1st; Forde 2nd.
2 Miles Cycle (confined) - Forde, 1st; Duffy, 2nd.
3 Miles Cycle (open handicap) - Williams, 1st; Forde 2nd.
5 Miles Cycle (open handicap)- J.Kavanagh 1st; Forde 2nd; Duffy 3rd.

17/8/29.

THE GERMAN REPUBLIC.

Ten years ago the German Republic, under many disadvantages and difficulties, was established. Thanks to the wise provisions made for its stability and its excellent democratic constitution then settled upon it has continued to grow in strength, status and popularity. Next week we shall have the pleasure and privilege of publishing an exceedingly interesting and well reasoned article on the entire question of the new German state, by a leading German, which we commend to our readers' most careful consideration. We all in Ireland wish well to the New German State and we cordially extend to the German people our best wishes for the future prosperity and peace of their country. In Dublin the interests of the German State are fortunately in the hands of a very popular representative, Herr von Dehn. He is a gentleman of wide culture and experience of the world and he is one who has already made himself universally respected since his advent here. He is also a great sportsman, a plucky rider and intensely fond of horses and horsemanship. The "Irish Times" in its issue of Monday has this proper appreciation of this gentleman:-

"I had the pleasure of attending an 'At Home' at the house of the German Consul-General to the Free State in Dublin yesterday, in commemoration of the signing of the Weimar Constitution exactly ten years ago. Herr von Dehn is renowned for his hospitality, and a large crowd of prominent citizens accepted his invitation. The Governor-General of the Free State and Mrs. McNeill were present, as well as a number of well-known politicians; and as the weather was fine, the guests adjourned to the garden after tea. I always enjoy a visit to Herr von Dehn's house; for he is a connoisseur of uncommon taste, and his rooms are furnished almost exclusively with antiques. He has some magnificient Louis XVI pieces, one room being furnished entirely in this period, and some of his old Gothic antiques from the twelfth century must be priceless. He also has a fine collection of old silver, including some Irish loving cups; while his family China comprises some beautiful specimens of Meissen ware, one old ink-stand, which has been in his family for generations, being a wonderful piece of work. Every year Herr von Dehn makes a point of 'dragging' the antique shops of Southern Germany in search of new treasures, and his Dublin house contains one of the finest collections that I have seen for some time.'

17/8/29

KNOCK PILGRIMAGE.

Inspiring scenes were witnessed at Knock on Sunday last when the first organised pilgrimage in the fifty years since the apparitions were reported, was made to the Shrine.

The pilgrimage from Dublin was organised by St. Michan's Conference of the St. Vincent de Paul Society, and was received by Most Rev. Dr. Gilmartin, Archbishop of Tuam, who was accompanied by Right Rev. Monsignor Macken, P.P., V.G., Dean, and Rev. J.J. Tuffy, P.P., Knock.

The day, which was gloriously fine, proved what Knock means in the religious life of the people of the West, and there was general satisfaction amongst them that the capital should have joined them in honouring our Blessed Lady.

Dublin girls, in short skirts and silk stockings contrasted with the homely attire of the West. All went about the Stations with Rosary beads in hands engaged in devout prayer.

Although all the Connaught counties were represented in the gathering, the Dublin pilgrimage was the principal one. The pilgrims left Dublin by special train, accompanied by the St. James's Brass and Reed Band, which rendered sacred music at Broadstone, Mullingar, and Athlone whilst the pilgrims sang hymns. At 4 p.m. a procession in honour of the Blessed Virgin was formed, headed by a statue of the Virgin. Over a thousand people marched. A feature was the rendering of the hymns in plain chant by the Dublin section. The St. James's Band also played at intervals.

Solemn Benediction, at which Most Rev. Dr. Gilmartin presided, was given from an altar in the church grounds by Rev. T. Jennings, M.A., St. Jarlath's College, Tuam, assisted by Rev. P. Blowick and Rev. T.A. Owens, C.C., Knock.

THE APPARITIONS - WHAT THE CHURCH TEACHES.

Most Rev. Dr. Gilmartin, addressing the pilgrims, said his presence was not to be taken as giving any official sanction to the apparitions alleged to have taken place there some 50 years ago. The Commission appointed at the time to investigate the matter came to no definite conclusion. Ecclesiastics were taught to be suspicious about alleged visions or apparitions, and not to give encouragement except they were certainly supernatural.

The faith of the Catholic Church did not depend on visions or apparitions, nor were pilgrimages an essential part of Catholic worship. There had been several cases of fraud in connection with supposed supernatural phenomena, but as far as he knew nobody had discovered any fraud or abuse in connection with the Knock apparition.

It was another matter if this might not be ocular deception, but in the absence of an authoritative ecclesiastical decision, a Catholic was free to follow his own views about these apparitions.

The same was to be said about alleged miraculous cures. Lourdes had advantages over Knock, that in Lourdes there was a Medical Bureau to examine and report miraculous cures. There had been no such proviso for a juridical inquiry into alleged numerous cures at Knock. Individuals were left free to follow their own judgment.

It was from the angle of devotion to the Mother of God that he wished to be associated with the zealous and enlightened pastor of Knock in bidding the pilgrims a hearty welcome. Devotion to the Blessed Virgin was independent of all shrines, no matter how highly privileged they may be. The solid basis of all true devotion to Mary was the dogmatic truth that she was the Mother of God the Son made Man. Apparitions and cures were not required to confirm the sons and daughters of St.Patrick to the Faith. If at times there were such supernatural manifestations, they may be designed by God to rescue his children from slavery of yielding inordinately to the allurements of the world and the flesh.

PRESENTATION TO THE CHURCH.

Rev. M.Tuffy, M.A., C.C., St.Michan's, presented to the church a beautiful candelabrum to mark the first Dublin pilgrimage. The day, he said, was a memorable one, and had been a pilgrimage of prayer and devotion to the Mother of God. The presentation would serve as a small appreciation of their esteem for the splendid work Fr.Tuffy had done for Knock. Fr.Tuffy associated himself with his Grace in welcoming the pilgrims, and thanked Dublin for its gift. Knock was not, he said, well organised to receive pilgrims, and this was the first organised pilgrimage to come to Knock. He hoped to provide better facilities for the future, and he also hoped, if the plans he and other friends of Knock had in mind matured, to have a religious house established there, whose special work would be to cater for pilgrims

Dr.Gilmartin concluded the ceremonies by offering the Rosary for fine weather for the harvest. He also laid his hand on the brows of a number of invalids, who were under the care of members of the St.John Ambulance Brigade and nurses.

Amongst the clergy present were:- Rev.G.Sheridan, Rev.T.Mahon, Sligo College; Rev. Fr.Jarlath, O.Cist., Roscrea Abbey; Rev. Fr.Bruno, O.Cist., Duluque,Iowa, U.S.A.; Rev.Fr.Angelus, O.S.F.C., Dublin; Rev. S.J. Walsh, P.P., Aughamore; Rev. P.Kelly, C.C., do.; Rev. M.Walsh, C.C., Achill; Rev.W .Kipp, Denver, U.S.A.; Rev.E.Whelan, C.C., Claremorris; Rev.C.J.Whyte, P.P., Bekan; Rev.J.Mulrennan, B.D.,C.C.,do.; Rev.M.S.Conlon, O.P., Black Abbey, Kilkenny.

The pilgrims on Sunday, writes a newspaper representative, were keyed up to a high pitch by a reported cure on the night of the 14th-15th inst., when some hundreds of people spent the night in prayer in the church and grounds, 2,000 receiving Communion on the Feast of the Assumption, when six Masses were celebrated in the church.

Several people came with crutches, and in the morning it was discovered that a crutch had been added to those already resting beneath the shadow of the Shrine.

The discovery quickened the feelings of the people in a remarkable way, for the crutch was recognised as one which had been used by a man on the previous night. On feeling that he could again use his limbs without aid, it is stated that the man requested that his name should not be disclosed for the present, or that the facts of his case should not be made known. 24/8/29

PARS OF LOCAL INTEREST.
PUBLIC MEETING.

A public meeting under the auspices of Fianna Fail is to be held in Tuam on Sunday, 8th September. Mr Seaghan Lemass, T.D., and a number of other prominent T.D's it is announced will attend and speak.

* *

TUAM LIBRARY FURNITURE.

The furniture of the Tuam Library, (tables, chairs, etc.,) was purchased last week by Mr. P.J. Byrne and Mr. M.W. Cahill, who had been deputed to act on behalf of the Tuam Town Commissioners and thereby save them for use of the town. Thus ends the ill-starred attempt to establish a Public Library in Tuam, which, from the start, whatever the cause, somehow never seemed to get going properly.

**

TUAM PIG FAIR.

Notwithstanding announcements in the daily press that there had been an increase in pork and pig prices the Tuam Pig Fair on Wednesday was not a very satisfactory one. In the early morning buying was a bit lively, but when it was found that there were no Northern buyers in attendance buying slacked off and prices dropped, and some pigs were left on the streets for hours unsold. This usually happens when the Northern buyers are absent and the others find they have it all their own way. Rather a suicidal policy, one would imagine, for those buyers to adopt, for sooner or later the Western farmer, long suffering though he may be, is bound to awaken and try the efficacy of combination and co-operation and so teach their exploiters a much needed lesson. Prices averaged from 63s to 65s per cwt. 24/8/29

THE FUTURE OF IRISH TOWNS.

There is not the slightest doubt about the fact that modern means of intercommunication are revolutionizing our country and fast changing the whole social organism, particularly in rural parts. What will be the ultimate result of the facilities now afforded for locomotion no one can accurately foretell, but that the changes will be vast and serious no one can venture to doubt. People are now travelling who rarely moved from home before and the omnipresent bus is everywhere inviting and inducing persons to travel. Rates and fares are relatively cheap and speed is attained at danger to the inmates not infrequently. A Belgian student, a keen observer, in the last issue of "Irish Trade" deals very carefully and intelligently with this subject and he is under no illusions. He is of opinion that whether Irish towns will prosper or decay in the future depends neither on the continuance nor on the abolition of the bus traffic but "entirely on how far the merchants and people generally concerned in them will rouse themselves and endeavour to avail of, before its too late, the possibilities and advantages that are at hand." "If one half of the time (he says) and attention, one half of the personal expense and one half of the energy so unreservedly given by our leading citizens to Local Government affairs were given to local industrial development the future of our towns and villages would be assured. There are limitless opportunities in the urban areas of Ireland for the creation of small industries, but there are obstacles also. The possibility of extinction may, however, be the 'good out of evil,' or the goad to urge us on to do things quite unthought of in the calm prosperity and undiscovered exclusiveness of these areas in pre-motor days. The chief obstacles to industrial development include lack of confidence and lack of belief in ourselves; a prejudice against homemade goods; a feeling that success in industry is the offspring of a generation of industrial activities; a false notion that technical skill is inherited and not acquired; and a belief, amounting almost to delusion, that Ireland can never be more than a country of export for agricultural produce and human beings. Conditions which ensure success and which are present in practically all our chief towns are : an ample market within an economic distributing radius, unlimited supply of labour ; no scarcity of factory sites; numerous buildings capable of conversion to factory purposes at low costs ; and sufficient people with ample spare capital for the requirements of one small industry for each town."

This is his view and there is a great deal of truth in it. We have only to look around us and see what industries started here, and once thriving, have failed, and that largely through a want of local support and the deplorable absence of that spirit of local patriotism which is not so robust and vigorous in our midst as it should be and as it must be if our local industries are to endure and those dependant on them are not driven away for want of employment and our town consequently decay. Living conditions, so far as house accommodation are concerned have undoubtedly improved, but good houses won't keep people when they have no employment to depend upon. Once Tuam was a busy town of industry. It had a bobbin and wood factory at the Curragh, a woollen factory at the Mercy Convent, two well-equipped printing offices giving employment to nearly twenty men and boys. Now the factory is closed, the woollen factory abandoned, and one printing office alone here, while the work in advertising and printing, which kept two offices running at full speed, is sent elsewhere and it is considered the best policy to do so. The Belgian observer recommends the opening up of local industries in our rural towns, and he thinks there is no town where a small industry cannot successfully be established and carried on by a system of local federation and by a grouping of small towns and above all by a healthy spirit in the people to support, encourage, aid and uphold by every possible means such local industry. Above and before all must be encouraged a system of technical education, one suitable for our towns and for our people who ought to be as well able to acquit themselves in these matters as are the inhabitants of the small towns on the continent which are all centres of thriving industry. He adds these sensible remarks on this important subject and we cannot too highly commend his suggestion for the establishment of a progressive, up-to-date technical school in every town of the size, importance and natural advantages, as Tuam for instance. For want of a practical scheme of public education the old trades and crafts have died out here and our young people are growing up with the equipment of only a literary knowledge that fits them abroad for mere clerical employment. They have lost the aptitude and taste for mechanical work and consequently are fast falling behind in the race for life which is now for the mechanic and not the clerk. The remarks of this intelligent observer on this point are worth notice and repetition and we give his views in his own words. He says :-

"Technical educaton, the utility of which is often publicly questioned, can be dove-tailed exquisitely into a scheme of this sort. Each town would have its Technical School, catering for every subject for which there was a demand, but paying particular attention to the preparation of young people for the employment in its local factory. One might agree with those who cry down Technical Education in its present form on the grounds that it prepares people for occupations and industries that do not exist, were it not that we know so many of our young people are obliged to emigrate, and surely it is better to send them out technically trained, so that they may effectively take their places with the highly trained youth of other countries, than to send them out technically ignorant and fit only for the lowly positions of crossing-sweepers."

We must bear in mind that a town to exist must have some industry to depend on. Shops cannot be carried on if people are induced by better prices to go elsewhere and can do so more readily now than ever. Some think the ultimate effect of the present social change will be that fifty years hence Ireland will be a country of some five or six large, overcrowded cities or towns with factories of a kind giving employment of a kind with a relatively overteeming population of the unemployed and often unemployable, and the rural villages parts largely divested of their inhabitants. We trust that will not be so but we cannot shut our eyes to what is fast going on around and about us at every moment. The tendency townwards is fast growing and may become so intense as to become a regular exodus. Dublin is being quickly filled up with a large accession of country folk, and these being a class of persons who hitherto lived in the country, some in the large houses or mansions now fast falling into ruin. Added to this increase in population is a disproportionate inflow of more or less undesirable foreigners so that its population at the next Census, if it reveals all those facts, will be an eye opener to some of our complacent public men. To meet the objection to his scheme for starting local industrial development the "Belgian Student" we refer to says what we will conclude by reprinting :-

"Opposition to any scheme of industrial development may be expected and must be lived down determinedly. It comes usually from all sorts of Dismal Jimmies, who will always remind the pioneer that every local industry failed, and that as soon as it was going on well it was killed by strikes ; they blame every cause except the right one ; they give no help, physical or financial, and they act the proverbial wet blanket to other people's efforts; but if one town gives the lead in the creation of a local factory other towns will follow, a federation of industries will come into existence with surprising rapidity, and prosperity for the whole area will follow the establishment of factories. It might be appropriate to quote here an Americanism :-

" It is not position, nor wealth, nor state,
But 'Get up and git' that makes a town great."
24/8/29

WATER TROUGH FOR TUAM.

TO THE EDITOR TUAM HERALD.

Sir—Would you kindly insert this short letter in order to correct a slight error which appeared in your issue of yesterday, 17th inst.? It was stated in the TUAM HERALD that "The All-Ireland Donkey Protection Society" has made an offer to the Tuam Town Commissioners to erect, free of charge, a donkey water trough in the town of Tuam for animals. It was, as a matter of fact, myself who wrote to the Town Commissioners on the subject on behalf of the "Connacht Society for Prevention of Cruelty to Animals"—not the A.I.D.P.S.

But as the C.S.P.C.A. and A.I.D.P.S. work in co-operation, both approve of this offer. Mr. John Whyte, Town Clerk, kindly replied that "the Roads Committee of the Tuam Town Commissioners will determine a suitable place for the erection of the trough." I would like to have this trough made in Tuam in order to give employment to local men. I thank my many friends in Tuam who have already renewed their annual subscriptions to C.S.P.C.A.; (and I hope others will do so soon!).

Any contributions sent to me for C.S.P.C.A. no matter how small will be most gratefully received.
Yours, etc.,   R.M.Burke,
Hon. Collector for Co. Galway and
Local Hon. Sec. C.S.P.C.A.   18/8/29

24/8/29

TUAM SCHOOLS.

Tuam schools figure prominently in the results of the leaving certificate examinations under the Intermediate Education Board. St. Jarlath's College takes a leading place, seventh with fifteen successes out of seventeen pupils presented; nine of their successful pupils obtained honours. The Christian Brothers Schools presented nine pupils of whom seven passed, one, Herbert Cunningham, Shop Street, Tuam, obtained honours and got first place in the Free State in Irish, having obtained 362 marks out of a possible 400. Out of 89 schools competing in the examinations, Mr. Cunningham scored the highest marks in the national language. The Presentation convent sent forward six candidates and the six passed, three of them with honours. The Tuam Presentation Convent takes seventh place amongst 68 girl schools of the Free State that competed at the examinations.
24/8/29

Advertised goods are cheaper goods. Read the advertisements and make your money go farther.

GROWING OLD.

The following interesting poem is written by Rev. Sister Smith, a cloistered nun in the community of the Hotel Dieu, Kingston, Ont., now in the 93rd year of her age. She is a convert, and has been a member of her community for over 68 years and recently celebrated her diamond jubilee in her convent home and is very active :-

GROWING OLD.

A little more gray in the lessening hair,
    Each day as the years go by;
A little more stooping in the form,
    A little more dim in the eye.
A little more faltering of the step
    As we tread life's pathway o'er,
A little nearer every day
    To the ones who have gone before.

A little more halting of the gait,
    And a dullness of the ear;
A growing weariness in the frame
    With each swift passing year.
A fading of hopes, and ambitions, too,
    A faltering in life's quest,
And a little nearer every day
    To a sweet and peaceful rest.

A little more loneliness in life
    As the dear ones pass away;
A bigger claim on the heavenly land
    With every passing day.
A little further from toil and care,
    A little less way to roam;
A drawing near to a peaceful voyage
    And a happy welcome home.

24/8/29

REPORTED KNOCK CURE.

Two days after the return from a pilgrimage to the church of Our Lady at Knock, on August 18th, a Dublin woman, who had been deaf in the left ear for 50 years, was able to hear perfectly with both ears. Describing her experience to a representative of "The Standard," she said that after the pilgrimage prayers she felt "a kind of cold breeze" going into her left ear. Two days later, while lying in bed on her right side, she heard the clock ticking with her left ear.

24/8/29

The Texas Petrol and Oil Co. were given a licence by the Tuam Town Commissioners for a storage tank to be erected by them in Bishop St., Tuam.

24/8/29

"TUAM UNITED ATHLETIC AND SOCIAL CLUB."

TO THE EDITOR TUAM HERALD.

Sir—I am sure that your readers were pleased to read the account of "The Revival of Athletics in Tuam" in the last issue of the TUAM HERALD. Certainly the President, Vice-President and Committee, and all those who assisted them have done a great thing. It may be said that Tuam has a fine past on which to look back. So far so good, but let us all unite, with God's help, to give Tuam an even brighter and more glorious furure! I think, therefore, that this would be a suitable moment to place a humble suggestion before the people of Tuam for their consideration.

I suggest that an Institution should be formed called the "Tuam United Athletic and Social Club," or, if some one can think of a better name, so much the better. I believe that this Institution, if properly managed, could be a great power for good. It could do fine work for the Glory of God and for the present and future welfare of the people of Tuam and district. It should be a democratic institution, run on Christian principles, and open to people of every creed and of every honest occupation.

COMPOSITION.

I firmly believe in the old saying "Unity is Strength," and this institution should therefore unite every already existing club or society in Tuam. All these clubs and societies could then work together in co-operation for the common good.

This is, of course, no new idea. Many somewhat similar institutions are in existence, and they do good work and prosper. I have some practical experience of the working of such a club on a small scale, for I have served on the committee for some time, and was, about two months ago, elected (every member of the club having an equal vote) as President, for the year, of the "U.A.S.C." United Athletic and Social Club.

Of course, if such a club was to be a success in a large place like Tuam, prominent men should be elected as officers of the club. I feel sure that the Rev. Peter Kelly, Adm., and the Very Rev. J.S.Canon Walsh would be unanimously elected as President and Vice-President respectively. And the committee would probably contain men like Messrs. P.M.Hosty, T.J.Mellin, J.O'Brien, M.Cahill, F.Stafford, and H.J.de Rosse. If they offered themselves for election, I expect that Messrs. H.J.Concannon and Wm. J. Concannon would also be elected on to the committee.

The u/m already existing clubs, etc., could each elect one member of their committee to represent them at meetings of the Tuam United Club:—"Tuam Club," "Tuam Star Football Club," "Tuam Rugby Football Club," Tuam "Hurley," "Hockey," and "Camogie" Clubs, Tuam "Race Committee," Tuam "Tennis" and "Golf" Clubs, Tuam "Dramatic Society," etc. Organizations such as the "Pioneers" and the "Foresters" could also send a representative to the United Club meetings. Charitable organizations such as the "St. Vincent de Paul Society," and the Tuam Branches of the "N.S.P.C.C," the C.S.P.C.A," the "Life Boat Institution," etc., could also be represented; and so could the Tuam Branch of the "League of Nations Society of Ireland," and of course "Tuam Sports Committee."

All these clubs and societies could remain independent as far as their internal working was concerned, but in matters of common interest and common welfare they could work together. Each minor club could continue its own President and Committee and its own annual subscription for members.

Membership of "Tuam United Athletic and Social Club" could be open to any man in Tuam and District provided that (i). He was believed to be a sober, honest and respectable citizen, and (ii). that he paid an annual subscription of one shilling, to be devoted to charitable purposes in the town of Tuam at the discretion of the committee.

An annual subs. of one shilling would make possible for the least wealthy men in Tuam to become members. If we had, say 1,000 members, that would mean at least £50 a year for charitable purposes, which would be a great help. Members who were better off financially would probably subscribe 5/-, 10/-, £1, or even £5 annually and thus several hundred pounds a year might be raised.

All members who could afford to do so might be asked periodically to subscribe to special objects for the welfare of their fellowmen.

THE WORK OF THE UNITED CLUB.

The Tuam United Athletic and Social Club might give themselves a programme such as this:-

(i.) To assist Tuam Town Commissioners to (a) Build more houses in suitable places and remove some of the terrible houses that still exist in places like Tierboy Road. (b) To provide, before Tuam expands any further, as near the centre of the town as possible, a public garden for the use of the old people in summer, and also a public playground for children, instead of allowing them to obstruct the streets and be run over by motor vehicles. (c) To provide suitable fields for football, etc., in addition to Parkmore, as near the town as possible, and to prevent houses being built on them.

(ii.) To build a Public Swimming Bath and also a Gymnasium for Tuam. (I am glad to hear that these schemes are already under consideration).

(iii.) To assist the Town Commissioners to keep the streets, pavements, etc., in good order and clean, and to make Tuam the finest town of its size in the whole of the Irish Free State.

(iv.) To see that all new houses built should not be ugly, should be built in a suitable place, and if possible, possess a garden of a reasonable size.

(v.) To assist all minor clubs, societies or individuals to raise funds for charitable purposes by means of theatricals, concerts, dances, whist drives, collections or other suitable methods. (An entertainments committee might be formed to give support to any deserving institution which endeavours to raise funds by right and reasonable methods).

(vi.) To do everything possible to reduce poverty, and unemployment in Tuam and district.

The above are only a few of the many possible activities of "Tuam United Athletic and Social Club." When the Swimming Bath and Gymnasium are erected two more minor clubs might be formed called "Tuam Diving and Swimming Club" and "Tuam Gymnastic Club."

It would take up too much of your valuable space to mention further details of the above scheme, but I am convinced that it is possible and would be beneficial to all concerned. If the people of Tuam wish to start this United Club without further delay I shall be pleased to help in any way I can. If not, we must merely wait, but I can continue to hope and pray that this scheme or something similar will one day be achieved, to the Glory of God, and for the welfare and prosperity of the people of Tuam.

Yours etc.,
R.M.Burke,   Toghermore, Tuam.
Sunday, 18/6/'29.
P.S.—Perhaps "Tuam United Improvement Club" would be a better name for this new Institution.
24/8/29

GALWAY HOSPITAL.

It was reported at Galway Hospital and Dispensaries Committee on Wednesday that six unmarried mothers had been admitted to the maternity department of the Galway Central Hospital since the last monthly meeting. A discussion took place on the advisability of having such cases treated in future in the Children's Home, Tuam, and Mr. Eamon Corbett remarked that an investigation into the matter would be discussed at the next meeting of the Homes and Home Assistance Committee.

24/8/29

Your Urine Warns You!

If you experience a burning, smarting pain during urination, or if the urine is thick and cloudy, evil smelling, sandy or blood-streaked, there can be no doubt that your kidneys are weak.

Examine the urine for quantity, also. If too much is passed each time, or if there is too little, and if you urinate too frequently — or too seldom— you can feel definitely warned of kidney weakness. Nothing could be more serious; you are in danger of blood poisoning, and its injurious effect upon every tissue, nerve and muscle of the body.

Don't delay! Take Doan's Backache Kidney Pills. There is no better known remedy for kidney weakness, urinary troubles, backache, lumbago, dropsical swellings, rheumatism and sciatica.

All dealers sell Doan's, 2/9 per box.

Sole Proprietors: Foster-McClellan Co., London, W.1.

24/08/89

LOURDES AND BLESSED BERNADETTE IN YOUR HOME.

I will send a bottle of Lourdes Water, or a picture of Blessed Bernadette, with relic attached, to all who write to me.

RT. REV. MONSIGNOR PAYNE,
ST. MARY'S DERBY.

LIGHTING THE BOROUGH OF TUAM.

The Tuam Town Commissioners will at their meeting to be held at the Town Hall, Tuam, on Tuesday, 3rd Sept., 1929, at the hour of 8 o'clock, p.m., receive and consider Tenders for the Lighting of the following Street Lamps, in the Town of Tuam, from the 15th August, 1929, to the 1st May, 1930:

49 or more Lamps at   per lamp to be lighted from sunset to 11 o'clock, p.m. Candle power per lamp to be specified.

Cost of putting up Lamps and keeping them in repair to be borne by contractor, and that all Lamps are to remain lighted all night for the October, November, December, and January Fairs.

Two Lamps on the Catholic Cathedral grounds which must be lighted on every Saturday and Sunday nights, and on such other nights as there may be special Devotions at said Cathedral (Notice of same will be given by the Parish Clerk) at   per lamp.

Two Lamps at the Protestant Cathedral grounds, said lamps to be lighted on each Sunday night between 6 o'clock and eight o'clock, and on such other nights as shall be notified to the Contractor by the Sexton of said Cathedral at   per lamp.

The Lamp at the Square to be an all night lamp and the clock to be lit all night.

The Contractor will be required to enter into a Contract and Bond with two solvent sureties, same to be prepared by the Solicitor to the Board at the expense of the Contractor and to contain a clause that should any of the lamps be unlighted for any period for which the contract required them to be lighted, the Contractor shall pay a sum to be agreed upon and deducted from amount of contract in case any lamp be left unlighted. Said fine to be deducted from the contract price as agreed upon. The Town Clerk shall inform the Contractor on such occasion that any of the said lamps shall be out and on such intimation being given the said fine shall be payable.

By Order Tuam Town Commissioners,
JOHN P. WHYTE,
Town Clerk.

24/8/29

ANNUAL EXCURSION FROM TOGHER TO GALWAY AND SALTHILL.

This annual event seems to be becoming more popular every year, judging by the numbers who avail themselves of the opportunity. Between 8 a.m. and 9.30 a.m. on Wednesday, 21st August, people—not only boys and girls but grown up men and women—were hastening towards Tuam from almost all directions! Not only from Togher did they come, but also from Coolrea and Grange, and even from Lavally and Kilconly.

And how did they come? Answer "Everyway!" Anyhow they came in motor cars, donkey carts, motor bikes, push bikes and on foot. The well known Togher Ford—purchased 1924 and still going strong—was buzzing to and from Tuam almost continuously from 8.30 to 9.30 a.m. (It also travelled twice to and from Galway, and several times round Galway and to Salthill during the day—ably driven throughout by Mr. Michael Darcy—and goodness knows how many different people it carried!).

The Southern Railway, as usual, did everything possible to make us all happy and comfortable, and they succeeded. The majority of the party travelled to Galway by train, but there were some who, for various reasons, were not able to be in time for the train. These followed to Galway in motor cars and by motor bus, and all arrived safely—altogether over 120 persons.

This year, not only the boys, but some of the girls were brave enough to hurl themselves in to the waters of Galway Bay. Swimming and diving (in moderation) are excellent pastimes for boys and girls who are sufficiently hardy and healthy to do such things.

An excellent lunch and tea were supplied at 1 p.m. and 4.30 p.m. respectively, to over 100 persons at MacDonnell's Restaurant. After lunch 105 people were brought to Salthill by buses and more swimming and diving took place.

In spite of the long day, we danced up and down the corridor, (excellent music was supplied by a melodian) and sang songs etc., most of the way home! Certainly we Irish are very jovial people! If you travelled round the world, it would be hard to find a more cheery crowd than we were!

The organiser of these excursions (R.M.Burke of Togher) is most grateful to the Great Southern Railway and MacDonnell's Restaurant, Galway, for their excellent service, and their most reasonable charges. If their charges had been excessive he could not afford to pay for an annual excursion for so large a number of people. If anyone else is organising excursions to Galway, he would have much pleasure in recommending the Great Southern Railway for Transport and MacDonnell's Restaurant for the Catering.

He would also like to thank the Galway Buses for their transport services, and the players of the melodian for their excellent music which did much to make the journey enjoyable—and also the singers and the jig-dancers!

Last, but by no means least, thanks are due to the Dean of Tuam and Mr. and Mrs. Eraut of the Grammer School, Galway, who not only gave us the use of their car and buildings respectively, but also helped us in many other ways.

And thank God we all got home again safely without any serious mishap.

31/8/29

"WATER TROUGH FOR TUAM."

"A donkey water trough for animals" referred to in our last issue was a misprint. It should have read "A *drinking* water trough for animals."

31/8/29

ST JARLATH'S COLLEGE, TUAM.
Tenders are invited for the supply of all necessities (including house shoes). Quotations to be sent before 3rd September to

THE BURSAR.

31/8/29

ST KEVIN'S.
42 PARNELL SQUARE, DUBLIN.
Under the Management of the Dominican Fathers. A Residence for Catholic Business Ladies and Ladies Visiting Town. Hot and Cold Baths, Cubicles and Private Bedrooms, Special Study Hall for Students, Careful Supervision of Young Girls, Very best quality Food supplied. Terms Extremely Moderate. Apply :-

LADY SUPERINTENDENT.

31/8/29

U.S. MAILS BY AIR.

IRELAND—LONDON HUSTLE.

36 HOURS SAVED.

The "Daily Mail" says:—

The first Galway to London air mail journey of more than 400 miles was completed yesterday in 3 and a quarter hours.

The aeroplane, piloted by Colonel Charles Russell, formerly the head of the Irish Free State Air Force, left Oranmore, County Galway, shortly after 8 a.m. with a large consignment of American and local mails, and landed at Croydon Aerodrome at 11.38.

Among the letters were greetings from Galway citizens to the "Daily Mail" which were delivered at 4.30 p.m.

The American mails were landed from the North German Lloyd liner Karlsruhe by motor launch at 6 a.m. and rushed to Oranmore, where with the local letters they were placed in the aeroplane.

The Irish letters which were delivered in London would normally have reached their destination this afternoon. The American mails would have been delivered to-morrow morning. Thus 24 hours were saved on local mails and 36 hours on American mails.

31/8/29

COUNT O'KELLY.

TO EDITOR TUAM HERALD.

Gurtray, Portumna,

25th August, 1929.

Dear Sir,—I thank you much for having kindly sent me the extract from the TUAM HERALD, relating to my son, Gerald. Will you kindly allow me to correct two inaccuracies in the article :— Gerald is my 3rd son not the eldest; 2nd., The title Count of the Holy Roman Empire was conferred in 1776 on my great great grand uncle, John Dillon O'Kelly of Gallagh, by the Empress Maria Therese for reward of military service in her army, so is thus transmitted to our family through my father.

Yours Sincerely,

John A. O'Kelly.

31/8/29

FORD CAR FOR SALE

For further information apply to
R.M.BURKE,
Toghermore,
Tuam.

Proposed Woollen Factory For Tuam.

In accordance with a requisition of the Tuam Town Commissioners a public meeting of the townspeople was held at the Town Hall on Monday, 26th instant, for the purpose of discussing the advisability of starting a Woollen Factory in Tuam.

Mr. Patrick J.Dwyer, Vice-Chairman of the Town Commissioners, presided.

And there were present—

Very Rev. Canon Walsh, President, St. Jarlath's College; Mr and Mrs Cloonan of New York; M.W.Cahill, T.C.; Joe O'Brien, T.C.; Wm. Holian, T.C.; Thos. Wilson, T.C.; J.H.Corcoran, T.C.; Simon Fahy, T.C.; Malachy O'Keeffe, T.C.; Anthony O'Malley, Thos. J. Cahill, Timothy Hayden, James Daly, Ml. Heskin, Tim Cotter, Sean O'Hehir, Patrick Farrell, Ml. Farrell, Patk. Mannion, Ml. Finucane, J. Mc Cormack, Patk. Walsh, T.C., P.Gibbons, T.C.; Jas. Moran, T.C. etc.

The Chairman said— You all know the object for which the meeting was called, it is a worthy one, and he hoped it would receive support so as to give employment and keep our young boys and girls at home. He would be glad to hear the views of the gentlemen present.

Mr. Thos. J. Cahill—As the initiator of the meeting, I think it is only right I should explain how it arose. I met Mr. and Mrs. Cloonan occasionally in Dublin, and we were discussing the question of industries for Ireland, when we were joined in the discussion by the Hon. Judge Kilbarry, who said he was in Ireland at present for the purpose of helping the promotion of industries, and he would be glad to do anything for Tuam, as he had some old friends in Tuam. Mr. and Mrs. Cloonan told him they would be glad to go to Tuam and discuss the matter with the people if they desired. So I asked the Commissioners to call this meeting, and it is for the people to decide for themselves as I consider that it would be a good thing for Tuam.

He felt much pleasure in introducing Mrs. Cloonan, who would speak on the matter.

Mr. Corcoran favoured a boot factory as more desirable and less expensive.

Mrs. C. Cloonan—I thank you for your reception. The facts are as stated by Mr. Cahill, and when you consider the large number of young boys and girls who have to leave every year for New York for want of work in their own country, because agriculture is the chief industry of Ireland, it shows clearly that industries are required, and if the Irish people had faith in themselves I have no doubt that the people of Tuam would succeed in putting up a woollen factory.

In America there is a good demand for Irish tweeds and blankets and it is surprising how they pay more for the Irish goods so as to help them on. Should you go on with this project I will do all in my power at the other side to get the capital subscribed.

Mr. Daly suggested that a committee be formed to inquire into the project as it would probably cost over £40,000.

Mr. O'Malley said he thought the proper course would be to refer the matter to a committee and let them take the necessary steps to find out all information as to cost of machinery for carding, weaving and spinning looms, and then let another meeting be summoned when they have the information.

Mr. Michael Cahill said that in Clery's they had not a single Irish blanket to sell and that if there were more woollen mills working that would not be the case. In Foxford they were sending out the most of their stuff to America. If you had a woolen factory in Tuam it would give employment to about 200 people and keep the young people at home.

Mrs Cloonan announced that she would take £500 shares, Mr. Cloonan £500, Mr. T.J.Cahill, £500, Mr. M.W.Cahill, £500.

Mr. O'Malley proposed that a committee be formed to enquire into the matter, Canon Walsh seconded.

Mr. Hayden proposed that Mr. Daly act as secretary and Canon Walsh seconded.

The following were appointed a committee— Canon Walsh, Mr. O'Malley, J. O'Brien, T.J. Cahill, Fr. Kelly, Adm., T.Hayden, M. Heskin, W.J.Concannon, H.Concannon, J.Quinn, F. McDonagh, P.M.Hosty, J.Cooney, M.Finucane, W.Purcell, J.McCormack, Dr. Costello, D.J.Butler, P.Byrne, P.J.Dwyer, James Mc Donnell.

Canon Walsh—I have great pleasure in proposing a vote of thanks to Mr. and Mrs. Cloonan for the interest they have shown in the project. (Applause.) Mr. Dwyer—I beg to second that.

Mrs. Cloonan thanked the meeting for the vote of thanks, and assured them she would do all in her power to help the project. 31/8/29

St Patrick's Training College
DRUMCONDRA, DUBLIN.

Applications may now be made by those who wish to present themselves at the next Easter Scholarship Examination, with a view to entering the above College or the course of Training beginning in September, 1929. No application will be received after the 16th January next. Applications (with stamped addressed envelope) should be made at once to :-
THE REV. PRINCIPAL,
Saint Patrick's Training College,
Drumcondra, Dublin.

"INADEQUATE PENALTIES FOR CRUELTY TO ANIMALS ?"
TO THE EDITOR TUAM HERALD.

Sir—May I use your valuable paper to bring this matter before your readers ? I regret to have to do so, but I feel it to be my duty.

First of all, here is an extract from the annual report of the D.S.P.C.A., of which I am a member:

"INADEQUATE PENALTIES."

"The following list of cases speak for themselves and give an unpleasant impression of the attitude of some District Justices to this question. Under the circumstances it is very much to the credit of the Civic Guard that they are so active.

"Co. Galway. At Mountbellew D.C. on 13/6/28 Guard John Dolan 2624 summoned John Ward for putting a ring for a pig in a dog's nose. The D.J. dismissed the case under the Probation of Offenders Act.

"Co. Mayo. At Ballyhaunis D.C. on 21/3/28, Patrick Kearns was cautioned for beating a horse with a flail.

"Numerous cases of horses and donkeys found working by the Civic Guard with sore breasts or unshod were dismissed by the D.J. These are clear cases of cruelty—no possible doubt as to the suffering caused to the animal and they are caused by deliberate cruelty or carelessness and not the result of an accident."

The above is all the extract from the D.S.P.C.A. Report. Similar cases of "inadequate penalties" are quoted from Co. Monaghan, Co. Kilkenny, Co. Donegal, Co. Kerry, Co. Tipperary, and Co. Cork.

Perhaps the D.J's will reply that their penalties are quite adequate. If so, I would earnestly ask them to reconsider the matter. Do they realise that they may cause people all over the world to say that the Irish are cruel and brutal people and thus give a bad name to Ireland throughout the world? It is a very serious matter. I would humbly suggest that the D.J's. and all patriotic Irishmen, and in fact all Christian people should read a book entitled "Kindness to Animals" by E.M.Grange, printed and published by O'Gorman, Printinghouse, Galway, (price 6d I think) and especially the letter in it in the name of His Holiness Benedict XV. by Cardinal Gasparri for the Roman S.P.C.A.

Yours etc.,
R.M.Burke,
Hon. Collector C.S.P.C.A.,
and Member D.S.P.C.A.
Toghermore, Tuam, Sunday, 25/8/'29.
31/8/29

TOURMAKEADY.

It is not often one finds in the London papers descriptions of our picturesque spots in this country, yet there are countless such lately to be found. This occurred to us when a few days ago we came across the following very fair account of Tourmakeady, situate in the adjoining county of Mayo. It is in many senses out of the beaten track. It is remote from the ordinary tripper and, therefore rarely finds notice in guide books. Yet it has a beauty of its own. It is situated in a really romantic region surrounded by the Partry mountains. There as a pastor at one time, nearly 100 years ago now, lived and laboured a vigorous, and in his early days, a valiant defender of the endangered faith of the people, the celebrated Father Pat Lavelle. He subsequently became P.P. of Cong, and died as such. There in Partry he fought souperism and squashed it by exposing its inherent malignancy and mischief and now owing to his manly exposure and defence of the old faith, souperism and its off-shoots have disappeared and left not a wrack behind.

Like a green jewel amidst the bleakness of the bog country of County Mayo, the tiny tree-clad village of Tourmakeady lies near Lough Mask, unspoilt and unknown. No one who has ever seen the village on Lough Mask with its rugged, rocky shores, its stretches of silver sand, its brown mountain streams fringed with fern, forget-me-not, and meadow-sweet, can ever forget this corner of Ireland. The air is fragrant with aromatic bog myrtle, sweet briar and wild thyme. To-day, Mask may lie like a mirror; to-morrow the south wind sweeps up the water and lashes the rocks and sands, the foam flying in a fury. If you love a walk in a forest you can follow the Tourmakeady River with its dark, shady trout pools, through towering bracken and fern of tropical luxuriance till you come to the magic beauty of the waterfall. Here the water foams over the rocks under the trees and swirls away in a brawling lake. These, with utter peace are the charms of Tourmakeady, and to me they are perfection.

31/8/29

LABOUR SAVING SCHEME.

To the Editor Tuam Herald.

Sir-- I would be grateful if you would allow me to use your valuable paper to inform your readers that I have thought of a simple scheme for saving them time, money and trouble! Every cheque one writes means not only two pence but also time and trouble - not to mention ink and depreciation on the fountain pen!

In future I will be pleased to receive one cheque annually from kind persons who wish to help any number of the six institutions for which I am Hon. Sec. Collector instead of several separate cheques. I will be pleased to send them separate receipts. Several people who subscribe to 5 or 6 of them have already adopted this scheme. I would like to point out that only members of the Protestant Church of Ireland are expected to subscribe to the Co. Galway Protestant Orphan Society, for which I collect.

All the other Societies, however, are interdenominational and are subscribed to generously by all creeds. They are all, however, in need of funds, and I would therefore earnestly ask those persons who do not already subscribe to start now. Now is the time!

To those who do subscribe I would say "Thank you very much. You are doing splendid work and helping to make the world a better place, and I feel sure you are doing what is right in the sight of Almighty God. Please persuade your friends to help also." Yours, etc.,

R.M. Burke.

Hon.Sec. Life Boat Institution (Tuam Branch).
Joint Hon.Sec. N.S.P.C.C. (Tuam Branch).
Hon.Collector for Co.Galway C.S.P.C.A.
Hon.Sec. League of Nations Society of Ireland (Tuam Branch).
Hon.Collector Co.Galway Protestant Orphans Society (Tuam Branch).
Hon.Collector Soldiers and Sailors Help Society, Co.Galway Branch, Tuam District.

P.S. - The last mentioned Society does a great deal to help Irish ex-service men in Co.Galway, and so does the Soldiers, Sailors and Airmen's Families Association for which I also collect.

Ireland has a reputation for being generous in supporting deserving causes. Patriotic Irishmen! Help us to keep up that reputation!

Business Men of Tuam! We need your help. Sportsmen of Tuam! We need your help. Every contribution, no matter how small, will be gratefully received.

R.M.B. Toghermore, Tuam, Sunday, 1st Sept., 1929.   7/9/29

MARTYRED IRISH PRIEST.

His Grace, Most Rev.Dr.Gilmartin, Archbishop of Tuam, in a letter to Rev. John Blowick, Director of the Chinese Missions, pays tribute to the memory of the late Rev.T.Leonard, who was murdered by Chinese bandits. He writes:-

"Allow me to send you a word of most sincere sympathy with you all on the murder of Father Leonard. But if, as it seems, it is martyrdom, then the martyr's halo of glory will take the place of what would be the darkness of a great tragedy in the natural order.

"In any case, we must remember him, as I did in my Mass (giving him my plenary indulgence), feeling sure that he will remember us".

Most Rev. Dr.Fogarty, Bishop of Killaloe, writes:-

"His, no matter what the circumstances, is the first Irish blood shed in your missionary field. I remember him well - a single-minded, honest-hearted and devout priest, whose ambitions were all with God".   7/9/29

DECENT DRESS DECREE.

The Archbishop has just issued a circular letter, read in all the churches of his diocese on Sunday, in which he expresses grave disapproval of modern fashions in women's dress, and prescribes that women are never to assist at church services in low necks, sleeveless dresses or skirts not well below the knee. In a sermon on Sunday in the Tuam Cathedral his Grace explained that his circular was not called for by anything like a prevailing abuse, but because there were individuals who might at times forget the reverence due to the worship of God. He recalled the expressed wish of His Holiness the Pope that not only should Bishops insist on this minimum of decorum in the churches but that they should warn their children against all fashions that border on immodesty. Hence the Irish Bishops had given their approval to the modest dress and deportment crusade, the principal rule of which is that skirts should be worn well below the knees. He felt sure that the clergy would carry out the wish of the Church in all these matters with prudence, charity and firmness without giving offence to anyone.

7/9/29

A pike caught by Mr. J. Barrett in the Lake at Loughrea weighed 22 lbs. Inside the fish were two large perch and a water hen.

7/9/29

AN SAEGHAL GAEDHEALACH.
(Irish Ireland Notes).
Fior Mholadh.

"From a national, economic and moral point of view, the work of the Gaelic League cannot be overestimated. Everyone in Ireland should be a Gaelic Leaguer — not perhaps as active members but the principles and aims of the Gaelic League should be an influence in their lives. It is a grand thing to think that the next generation would be able to speak in the native tongue, when the language of the Church, the Courts, the home and family life would be Irish".-(Most Rev. Dr.O'Doighneain).

RANGANNA GAEDHILGE.

Another month and the clerk of the weather will have given up his pretence of providing summer weather. He will give us the long nights to return to our studies and hobbies and now is the time to map out our programme for the winter months. How are we going to spend them? Are we going to continue as some of us has been doing - our useless time passing pursuits? Or are we going to devote at least some of our time to bettering ourselves - and incidentally our country?

The vast majority of our people believe in an Irish Ireland, but it is not sufficient to say "I believe," one must also say "I Serve". It is not sufficient for us - who call ourselves Irish Irelanders - to attend Gaelic matches and Ceilidhs, and to wear Irish made clothes; these things are all good, and if more people did even these few things, Ireland would be healthier, cleaner and more prosperous, but to build up a real Gaelic Nation, one of the greatest essentials is the restoration of the language.

To restore a language long neglected is not an unheard of proposition; other countries have done it, and what other countries have done Ireland can do.

It is a great pity that the Irish people do not know how much Irish history has influenced the history of Europe. Great German politicians and soldiers have acknowledged that the Irish Land War inspired the German people, and we know in our own day how much the Gaelic League is admired in Wales, Scotland, Brittany, Belgium and in other small countries fighting for their native language.

No matter what cynics and pessimists may say the language movement in Ireland has made remarkable progress. Irish is being restored much quicker than it was being killed, and to-day we have the consolation of knowing that every child we meet in Saorstat Eireann is learning Irish, and that a great many of them are already good Irish speakers.

This again is all very good but we must not leave the whole burden of the restoration on the shoulders of the youngsters - we grown-ups must do our share, and we have plenty of opportunities and facilities for that share.

In September most of the Irish classes throughout the country will be opening; these classes are most under the control of the local or County Technical Committee; first class teachers are provided, and in order to lighten the burden of study, singing and music are very often included in the curriculum of the class. Dancing is not, of course, on the programme, but as a rule the Irish teacher manages to have a special time for learning our graceful, clean dances.

As a rule, classes can be formed wherever at least twelve persons sign a request and promise to attend, but only adults -- those over 14 years of age, are eligible to attend these classes.

When your class is formed, and a good membership is recruited, your next job is to affiliate your class as a branch of the Gaelic League. This is not only allowed by the Department of Education, but it is recommended because it is recognised that good work will be done in a class whose members are good Gaelic Leaguers.   7/9/29

FIRE IN TUAM.

It is stated that over £300 worth of damage was caused by a fire which broke out on Sunday evening last in a store on the Mall, owned by Mrs. Carroll, High Street, Tuam. The first to notice the fire were the Misses Walsh of High Street, who were in their garden, and gave the alarm. Mr.Tom Moran, Garage Proprietor, quickly was on the scene and entering the burning building at considerable risk removed any inflammable material that was inside. In this he was willingly helped by the Civic Guards under Sergeant Ruddy and several civilians, including Messrs. Martin Rooney and Paddy Mooney, who gave valuable help. Mr.John Shine, Supt.Waterworks, had the hose on the spot immediately and with the aid of the willing workers mentioned and others, the fire was got under control, but not until a motor van that was stored in the building was consumed and a large amount of provisions destroyed. The store where the fire occurred is right beside and adjoining the Mall Cinema, and had the fire progressed much further, it is thought there could be no saving that building.
14/9/29

A dance was held in Athenry Town Hall on Monday night. The band of the Galway Empire Theatre was engaged.

14/9/29

DEPLORABLE BAD MANNERS IN GALWAY.

We regret that an English Catholic gentleman, Mr. Gibbons, who travelled on foot last year from Calais to Lourdes—700 miles—and recounted his pleasing experiences in a London Magazine and subsequently republished them in book form, has had a very different experience to recount in Ireland this year and that it should be in this county. He has been going through Ireland for some days and giving very readable and excellent accounts to the "Daily Express" of the places he has visited and the people he has met. Everywhere, but not so alas we regret to say in Galway, he was received with the innate and characteristic courtesy of the Irish people—but particularly of the old generation now passing, all ladies and gentlemen by instinct. In Galway, however, he unfortunately happened to meet with a discreditable exhibition of vulgarity and bad manners. In the hope that such occurrences will not take place again and that the youth of this county, if this be so, will learn to behave themselves, we give Mr. Gibbons' description of the yahoos he happened to come across in the bus from Galway to Spiddal. We are inclined to think that these misbehaving fellows were not natives but visitors or sojourners, as we never heard of the Galway people, young or old, peasant or otherwise, ever treating strangers except with native courtesy, kindliness or good manners. However whether native or visitor, Mr. Gibbons happened to strike on a deplorably unmannerly crew. He tells his experience as follows in Tuesday's "Daily Express" :-

Perhaps, though, I am over-critical, for when the other day I did strike a bit of Irish humour I didn't enjoy it. It was just out of Galway. I think I'd seen everything I ought to see—Lynch Castle and the Lynch Window, the great old medieval church (with, incidentally, the Catholic bishop inside it, inspecting the monuments now in Protestant hands), the enormous station that they put up years ago when they thought that Galway was going to capture Liverpool's Transatlantic trade, and the modern aerodrome, which they hope now is going to bring about something of the same result.

They have just begun rushing the American mails over by airplane to London, and if it works it will save 48 hours from New York. Then they might do the trick with passengers.

It would be a grand thing, they told me, to have London dependent on Galway.

I think I'd seen it all, and there was an omnibus just starting for Spiddal, so I might as well pay my 3s return. In it were half-a-dozen young men with the high spirits that in London we see on Bank Holidays. Only there public opinion is against them. Here it is with them.

And the louder they blew through paper trumpets and gave cat-calls the better pleased everyone seemed to be. Then seeing me two of them began a conversation in a caricature of an exaggerated "English" voice. "Magnif-ic-ent scen-ery, dear fellow! What ! What !" That sort of thing. And everybody was awfully amused. Except , of course, me.

Two girls, quite pretty enough to have known better, positively beamed upon them, and a dear old lady next to me nudged me joyously in the ribs at the more poignant hits. When one of the lads held a half-crown in his eye she nearly went into convulsions. And , confound her, I do not wear a monocle.

Then, quite suddenly, the entire atmosphere changed. The young women looked stonily away. The old lady told me she didn't like such manners at all, and the conductor, hitherto obviously only a neutral by virtue of his official position, bluntly told the lads to make less row.

You may think, of course, that all these people had suddenly awakened to the majesty of myself and the British Empire, but you will think wrong. The fact was that we had passed a church door, and while every one else had raised their hats or crossed themselves, these wretched young men, intoxicated by their own wit, had overlooked their duty and gone on shouting and cat-calling.

In that second they had alienated an entire busload of Irish sympathies. No, this Irish humour is not quite as simple as it seems in the English novels of Irish life.

14/9/29

Miss Nora McDonagh, daughter of Mr. Michael McDonagh, Headford, and Miss May Cunliske, daughter of Mr James Cunliske, Balyfruit, Headford, passed with honours in the intermediate certificate examination. The are pupils of the Secondary School Presentation Convent. Tuam.

Rev. Fr. Blake, Liverpool archdiocese, is at present on a visit to his sister, Mrs Kennedy, O'Keeffe's Terrace, Tuam.

We regret the death of the Very Rev. Fr. Mc Cormack, O.P. of the Dominican Order. He was a native of Tuam, a son of Patrick Mc Cormack, Esq., Terryland, Galway, a well known gentleman in these parts, one of his brothers living at Queensfort and another is a doctor at Liverpool. He was an eloquent, distinguished preacher and a hard working , zealous priest.

14/9/29

PARTRY AND CORBETT.

Mr. Gibbons who is tramping through Ireland and recounting his experiences in the "Daily Express" —most readable and excellently well done— visited Partry recently. As we last week referred to Jim Corbett's connection with that place we give the correspondent's account of how Jim is now treated in Partry, where once his uncle, Father James Corbett, was up to his death the respected P.P. Mr. Gibbons writes of the place thus :-

Then yesterday I passed a place that might have a moral. A very tiny place it was by English ideas, just a collection of whitewashed cottages. But it gave itself airs that would have been insufferable in a world capital. For it had two great prides. It *had* two, I said. Now it has only one, that born there was a child who afterwards became a great and famous cardinal in the United States. For year after year the old gentleman, they said, would cross the seas to visit his native land and look at the graves of his father and mother. The other pride? They don't talk about it now. But born in that village was a man who afterwards became one of the world's champion heavyweights. When he was at the height of his fame and making his thousands of pounds, he sent over to the Irish hamlet the money (a great deal of it) for two great pillars to be erected for the adornment of the church. Some day the hero was coming over himself to see them. The village was very proud. Then fell the blow. It is a little difficult to explain in England, but the Irish haven't got any divorce problem to write books and plays about. They just call it by a short name, ever so simply. So when the cables flashed across the Atlantic that poor Jim Corbett, for all his six feet of bone and muscle, had fallen into sin, the village just pulled down his grand pillars, erased his name from them, and wrote and said he needn't come back after all. Now I, at least, see nothing so riotously humourous about that story.

14/9/29

FIANNA FAIL MEETING IN TUAM.

A largely attended meeting under the auspices of Fianna Fail was held in the Square, Tuam on Sunday last.

Mr. P.J.Dwyer, Vice-Chairman Tuam Town Commissioners, presided and introduced the speakers.

Mr. Sean Lemass, addressing the meeting, said Fianna Fail was endeavouring to abolish past dissensions and attain complete independence and unity by peaceful political means. It was the policy of Cumann na nGaedheal spokesmen to represent Fianna Fail as a sort of secret society and an organisation that had only adopted peaceful methods for a time, until a suitable opportunity arises to overthrow existing conditions by force. Fianna Fail stood for a Republican Government in Ireland in their day. They had never made a secret of that, and their aims and activities were directed towards convincing the people that only in complete independence lay the possibility of economic prosperity and full national development. They recognised, however, that any attempt to abolish by force the barriers erected by the Treaty would probably fail under the circumstances that exist, and would in any case, so weaken the nation that it would be unable to gather the fruits, or to resist renewed British aggression.

In 1925 Treaty No 2 was signed by which the Government agreed to permanent partition, and to the payment of a lump sum of £5,000,000 to the British Treasury. Three months later Mr. Blythe signed a new secret financial agreement in London by which the Free State agreed to pay £6,000,000 that year and £5,000,000 every year thereafter.

That was never ratified by the Dail, and never submitted to the British Parliament. It therefore had no legal binding force.

Mr. Lemass repeated his arguments in support of the retention of the Land Annuities. Another portion of the money, he said, represented the contribution towards the pensions of the R.I.C. and Black and Tans for careering through this country in their campaign of murder, loot and raiding. The money was paid, although there was nothing in the Treaty to compel them to pay it.

They had been led to believe that the Treaty was their economic salvation, but it had led to nothing but unemployment, emigration, and a drain on the resources of the country. (Applause).

Mr. Mark Killilea next addressed the meeting, and in the course of his remarks emphasised the urgent necessity of having the land now in the hands of the Land Commission distributed amongst the people and vested in the agricultural owners as quickly as possible. Some of that land was in the possession of the Land Commission for nearly 20 years and there was still no sign of it being vested in the people. The Land Commission was costing the country £80,000 a year, and it was the intention of the Fianna Fail party when they got into power to so speed up Land Purchase and land distribution as to save the greater portion of that £80,000 and to turn it to some more useful purpose for the people. He exhorted his hearers to join the local Fianna Fail Club, so that when an election came—and it might come sooner than was expected—they would return the party to power who were anxious and capable of doing some good for the plain people (applause).

14/9/29

THE FREE STATE ARMY.

From the interesting and informative address delivered at the Rotary Club in Dublin on Monday we learn much of the creation, development and ultimate establishment of the Army of the Free State upon a settled basis that is eminently satisfactory. The conditions of the country in 1922 rendered a large armed force necessary and, unwilling as they were, the Government were forced to establish a force of dimensions capable of dealing with the situation of difficulty and peril to public peace which it had to face. An army of 50,000 was then enrolled at a cost of ten millions. That is part of the heavy expense forced on the country by the tactics of terrorism and unlimited lawlessness that were adopted as a policy by men who had little if any regard for the best interests of the nation which had to bear the cost of their action and foot the bill of the tremendous expense incurred in consequence. The total cost in money consequent on that policy of disorder would, if available for useful purposes, have carried out the entire cost of the Shannon Hydro Electric Scheme, constructed a deep water harbour at Galway for a Transatlantic service and met all the expenses incurred on roads and buildings and reconstruction and leave us with no need for a public debt and with less burden in taxation, by one half, to that which we must now bear. An army is essential in any event and we must, as practical people, look upon such a force as an unpleasant necessity. Its being therefore demonstrably necessary one must contemplate the fact with complacency and resignation and be satisfied when we see that, as Mr. Fitzgerald conclusively proved, the army is reduced to the lowest possible figure and, as it stands, is undoubtedly an efficient and economically run force. It certainly can in training, in appearance, in physique and general get up compare favourably with any other such armed force elsewhere. It presents a very creditable appearance and the young men in it are as fine, well behaved a lot of soldiers as one could wish. Two departments of the army are specially good—its small but excellent cavalry and its band. This latter, under the able direction of Colonel Brase, who was head of the Imperial band in Berlin, has been brought to a high state of perfection and we trust its merits and accomplishments will be suitably recognised by the authorities of the Royal Dublin Society and its efficient services utilised in future in place of imported bands. Now that we happen to have a thoroughly trained and excellent band of our own citizens we do not require or need the importation of outsiders. Mr. Fitzgerald said that he realised that some may urge that there should be no army maintained here, and that consequently the citizen owed no duty to the army. He pointed out that every government in every country found it advisable to maintain an armed force. When they read that this or that country proposed to disarm they would find that such proposals merely tended to approximate more or less to the Saorstat army proposals. He regarded it as certain that the army will be maintained by any government that the Irish people may from time to time put in charge of national affairs. The end for which the army exists is not war but peace. It is a purely defensive force. The existence of the army is a natural corollary to the right of the state to exist and to the right of citizens to live their lives in security. Some years ago ordered security did not exist. The circumstances of those years necessitated a large and comparitively expensive army. Only with the restoration of security could they attempt to establish a proper and normal balance between the army and the other state services. On the matter of economy, he pointed out that the standing army had been reduced from 55,500 in 1923 to 5,418 now, and while the cost in the financial year 1922-23 was £10,461,401, it was estimated for the current year at £1,442,521. Though the army existed pre-eminently for the purpose of national defence this estimate includes matters which have other aspects of utility. He referred to the Army bands, which were a decided asset to the musical amenities and the musical culture of the country; and to the horse jumping team, which he was assured by many better able to judge than he was, not only brought credit to the country and Army, but was a decided asset to the horse breeding industry of the country.

This is a very satisfactory state of things, one highly creditable and commendable. If we are to have an Army, and no one disputes or doubts that fact, it is well that it should be an efficient one, run on economical and proper lines and be found capable of properly discharging any duties entrusted to it. We have in the Free State to have an Army as every state—even the new Vatican state has—and it is comforting to know that it is a good one and worth the money it costs.

14/9/29

BREVITIES.

The Choir Boys and Mass Servers of the Christian Schools, Tuam, had their annual outing on Thursday last. This year the venue was Westport, and the boys had a most enjoyable day in that pretty little town.

A Sports is announced to be held in Kilconly on Sunday, 22nd inst. A very good programme has been prepared.

14/9/29

WEDDING.

There was a large congregation at St. Thomas of Canterbury Church, St. Leonard's last Tuesday afternoon, when Angela, daughter of Mr. and Mrs. Rupert Wontner, 3 Cumberland Gardens, St. Leonards, was married to Doctor Edward J. Glynn, son of Sir Joseph Glynn, St. Jarlath's, Ailesbury Road, Dublin. The bride, who entered the church on the arm of her father, wore a gown of white satin crepe made in medieval style, and trimmed with pearl and diamante, while the girdle was a rope of pearls. The beautiful train was of old Limerick lace, and the tulle veil, which fell in billowy masses about her shoulders, was held in place by a wreath of orange blossoms. She carried a sheaf of Harrissi lilies. Her attendants were the Misses Enid Langham, Mary O'Neill Donnellon, Dorothy and Phyllis Chubb, Ruth Redmayne and Violet Hall. They formed a charming picture in their medieval gowns of peach taffetas and Juliet caps of peach net trimmed with pearls to tone. Their shoes were of peach colour, and they carried chrysanthemums, while each wore a necklace of Bengal opals, the gifts of the bridegroom. Mr P. Glynn (brother of the bridegroom) acted as best man. After the ceremony, which was performed by the Very Rev. Canon Segresser, a reception was held at 3 Cumberland Gardens. Later Dr. and Mrs Glynn left en route for Paris, where the honeymoon is being spent, the bride travelling in a brown cloth tailor-made costume, with brown hat ornamented with diamante brooch and brown python skin shoes.

14/9/29

IRISH PREPARATORY COLLEGE, LETTERKENNY.

The great success of this College at the Intermediate Cert. Exam. in topping the lists of all the schools of Ireland and gaining 1st place in Maths. (with max.marks) and English, calls for congratulation from the people of the West, as it is the Sisters of Mercy, Tuam, who have charge of the College.

Two years ago the School was established in temporary quarters at Rockhill House, Letterkenny; both Sisters and pupils are looking forward to being in their new College at Tourmakeady next September, as it is expected that it will be ready for residence by that time.

We tender, therefore, our hearty congratulations to the good Sisters who have taken up this great work "for the glory of God and the honour of Ireland".

21/9/29

HARNESSING THE SHANNON.

By J.S. Bainbridge, M.Sc.,
In "Overseas."

The Irish Free State, the youngest Member of the British Commonwealth of Nations, is sometimes regarded also as being one of the most backward, but a scheme has now almost been completed which will place the Free State in a remarkable and unique position. The scheme aims at nothing less than providing the whole State with electric light, heat and power from one vast hydro-electric generating station, using the waters of the Shannon as the motive power. It is one of the most remarkable engineering projects with an economic purpose which has ever been planned. The expenditure on the first part of the scheme, which, according to calculations, will meet the present needs of the State of 150,000,000 units of electricity per year, has been nearly £6,000,000, and since the population of the Irish Free State is only 3,000,000 it is obvious that Mr.Cosgrave and his cabinet must possess not only courage, but vision and faith in the future of their country

At present only about 700,000 of Ireland's 3,000,000 inhabitants live in districts where a supply of electricity is available. Distribution of electricity from the Shannon power station is expected to start sometime in December, and thereafter every town and village which has a population of more than 500 will be supplied. At present nearly 60 per cent. of the fuel requirements of Ireland are met by imported fuel, in spite of the vast reserves of peat which the country possesses. If the Shannon electricity scheme is a success the importation of coal will fall to a negligible figure.

How is this possible? Only because the position of Ireland and the configuration of the country through which the River Shannon runs offer natural advantages which cannot be equalled anywhere else in the world. The annual rainfall is high, the catchment area is large, a series of natural lakes provides a huge storage capacity and, the most vital part of the scheme, at one point a head of water of nearly 100 feet can be obtained. The average rainfall for the last thirty years has been 37 and a quarter inches, and the catchment area of the Shannon is over 4,000 square miles. About three quarters of the rain falling on this 4,000 square miles is discharged into the river, and if any reader of "Overseas" cares to work out the calculation he will find that this means an average of 54,000 gallons per second. During the first part of the scheme only Lough Derg is to be used as a storage lake, but when the full scheme is in operation the levels of all three of the largest lakes of the river -- Lough Derg, Lough Ree and Lough Allen -- will be raised, on the average, 6 feet above their present levels, giving a total storage capacity of nearly 200,000,000,000 gallons. It is estimated that this will be sufficient to keep six 30,000 h.p. turbines permanently at work, with annual output of 425,000,000 units, which is three times the present power needs of the country.

The water for the power station is taken out of the river near O'Brien's Bridge, at which point it passes into a head-race canal about 7.5 miles long, 300 feet wide and 30 feet deep, the entrance to which is provided with six electrically-operated sluice-gates, each of which weighs 85 tons. The head-race canal conveys the water to Ardnacrusha, three miles north of Limerick, where the main power house - a wonderful building with its massive stonework and intricate equipment - is situated. At the power house there is a fall of nearly 100 feet, and the water is then led back to the river by a tail-race canal about a mile long.

The power generated at Ardnacrusha will be distributed throughout the State by a vast network of cables, which is itself one of the marvels of the scheme. The electricity is to be transmitted to Dublin and Cork along 100,000 volt cables, the main transmission cables for the rest of the country will operate at 35,000 volts, hundreds of subsidiary cables will carry 10,000 volts, and there are elaborate arrangements for stepping-down the current to the low voltages required for domestic use, etc. and for preventing leaks. Some of the cables are 225 miles long, and it is estimated that the annual expenditure on the first part of the scheme will be nearly £500,000 of which 90 per cent. will consist of interest and amortisation charges and expenditure on the elaborate transmission network and complicated transformer appliances. This works out at 0.38d. to 0.85d. per unit according to the distance from the power station.

The power station itself is in one sense only a minor part of the scheme. Parts of the river bed had to be deepened and a ship lift and other works have to be carried out. When these are complete every county from Cavan to Limerick will have a direct outlet to sea for their produce. Precautions have also to be taken to avoid flooding the country-side. The land near the Shannon has always been liable to flooding, and the steps taken to avoid this have involved or will involve the construction of 150 miles of embankment. It is, indeed, hinted that the provisions made may later form the basis of an extensive draining system which will make many thousands of acres of land now liable to flooding available for agricultural or industrial developments.

The huge sluice-gates which admit the river to the head-race canal were opened by President Cosgrave on July 22nd in the presence of 500 distinguished guests. The filling of the canal for the first time must be done with great care, the embankments being watched carefully the whole time in case constructional defects manifest themselves, and the water is not being allowed to rise in the canal by more than three inches a day. This means that the final testing of the turbines and generators cannot take place until about the middle of September. Should the final test be satisfactory - and there is no reason to fear otherwise - distribution of electricity throughout the Irish Free State can be started in the early winter.

Concluding his speech at the opening ceremony, President Cosgrave said: "This scheme lays a firm foundation for confidence both at home and abroad in our capacity to realise those economic developments of wide national scope and efficiency to which we look forward. It is certain that even so great a plant as this will in a comparatively few years prove insufficient for our needs, and that other developments to increase our power will have to be undertaken".

To that the only comment possible is: "Bravo, Ireland!"

21/9/29

THE TUAM HERALD.
(Ninety-two years established).

In eight years the Tuam Herald will complete its hundredth year of active existence and public utility. During that long stretch of time it was all through considered the leading newspaper of the West. It was so because it was inspired in its policy by the most prominent and trusted men of their day in Irish politics and never shirked its duty. It can therefore boast of a record of patriotic service creditable and unexampled. Even in America and Australia among exiled Connaught men it is read, and whether there or at home it is universally regarded and respected as an outspoken, a fair-minded and an independent organ of Catholic and National opinion.

As an advertising medium its age, its high character and its select circulation give it superior if not exceptional advantages.

For terms of advertising apply to
The Manager,
HERALD OFFICE, TUAM.

21/9/29.

The Tuam Herald

Fiat Justitia Ruat Coelum.

Bidheadh cóir déanta dá d-tuitfeadh neamh.

LET JUSTICE BE DONE THOUGH THE HEAVENS FALL.

Guaranteed to be the best Provincial Advertising Medium in Ireland.

SATURDAY, SEPTEMBER 28, 1929.

THE INDECENCY OF FEMALE DRESS

Some weeks ago the Archbishop of Tuam commented, in deservedly strong language, upon the present indecent dress of young women. The warning and admonition were merited, for really the length to which apparently respectable girls allow themselves to go would shock their grandmothers and bring the blush of shame to their cheeks. Not many years ago, even on the stage, women's dress was considered indecent that exposed the legs little above the ankles, and so strict and rigorous was the restriction that girls who dared to violate that rule were ostracised. Now dress on the stage, then considered indecent, is universally worn in the crowded streets. It is a deplorable and melancholy exhibition of female independence which, combined with the deplorable habit of abominable cigarette smoking, is repelling men from daring to venture upon the perilous experiment of mating with such extravagance. It is said that smoking amongst women keeps half the tobacco shops going and that often the weekly bill of a single girl amounts to twenty shillings or over £52 a year. Fear of facing such a source of wasteful extravagance and unwilling to have as consorts for life girls who live so extravagantly and who dress so immodestly it is said deters the young men now unhappily going from ever dreaming of marrying, and really when one considers the risks and difficulties of modern life under such conditions we cannot wonder at such reasonable reluctance on the part of young men to take as partners for life girls addicted to such extravagance. Women may glory in their so-called independence and some may think that it is grand to kick over the traces of the old conventions, but they are paying dearly for their indescretions. They are repelling possible partners and committing themselves to a life of single loneliness and the weary misery of cheerless old maidenhood. This, apart from the moral guilt of indecency in itself, as one often wonders if a really innocent mind can so wish it, is the punishment and the penalty for resorting to such vile practices. The beautiful life of a young girl of former days, modest, reserved and gentle in her action, modest and reserved in her dress, are now substituted for a different type of female, the short skirted damosel, with the eternal cigarette in her mouth and with too often a vulgar freedom of speech and a rudeness of manner that are positively repugnant to a refined mind. Recently a friend of the writer visited Las Palmas in the Canary Islands and was struck with the manifest disgust shown by the natives to English women who dressed in so scanty a garment when bathing and otherwise that the natives, who go almost fully dressed into the water, were positively so shocked at their white visitors' indecent dress that they would not bathe with them. When these poor people were disgusted what feelings of regret must the nice and pure-minded experience ? A man in Dublin once was so shocked at the attenuated attire of females in a tram that he asked the conductor to let him out, as he said he had made a mistake in getting in. He wanted, he said, a tram car and found himself in a bathing box. Society has no sanctions in these matters and it is hard to say how these wild, wayward excesses in dress and smoking can be cured, but sooner or later women will find the error of their present wayward ways. We fear, however, before the change comes that much moral mischief will be caused, much harm done ere awakening occurs. The tobacco habit will have become strong and have such a hold over women that it will be impossible for them to give it up and in the meantime much more money will go in smoke and with it the otherwise happy future of a female who if she acted right might be the happy mother of a family and live the innocent life God intended her to live when he sent her into this world.

28 /9/89

BURKES, Dublin Rd.,
GROCERIES, CONFECTIONERY,

GILBEY'S WINES & SPIRITS,
SPORTING GUNS & AMMUNITION.

Select Bar

—.—

FRESH FINNON HADDOCK, KIPPERS
AND FILLETED FISH

Twice Weekly, Wednesdays and Fridays, for
Lenten Season.

—.—

BEST VALUE - SERVICE - ASSORTMENT.

———[o]———

JOHN BURKE
DUBLIN ROAD, TUAM

28/9/29

G. A. A. NEWS.

Tuam Senior and Junior Football teams are again to represent Tuam on Sunday next at Corofin. The Seniors are to play Kilbannon and it is expected that this will be a game worth going to see. The Juniors will play the junior team from Menlough. Considering the strong game Tuam put up against Corofin a few weeks ago they should be able to beat Menlough who were runners up for the Junior District Championship last year.

Time for the Junior game to start will be 3.30 and the Senior game is timed for 5 o'clock.

TUAM STAR F.C.

A meeting was held in the Town Hall on Thursday night last at which a good representative crowd of Gaels assembled. There was a word mentioned by the Secretary that the medals won by the Senior team for last year's championship were now ready, and that it would be a night to celebrate when the players would be presented with them.

The selection of the Senior and Junior teams was drawn up and the following were selected to represent Tuam in the Senior and Junior games in Corofin on Sunday next :-

Senior team — H.Cunningham (Capt.), H.Burke, P.Flanagan, P.Hannon, J.O'Rorke, D.McCormack. M.Mannion, P.Waldron, T.Hughes, P.Kelly, W.Birrell, C.Reide, P.Walsh, M.Stewart, M.Rooney, J.Nohilly, T.Creaven, T.Joyce, Joe Grady.

Junior Team — J.Fahy, J.Farrell, P.Mooney, M.Curran, J.Reilly, C.Kelly, W.Leahy, T.Leahy, Jer Walsh, J.Tighe, J.Rooney, M.Murray, A.Nicholson, T.Connor, P.Quinn, W.Stockwell, P.Donelon, J.Nicholson, J.Forde.

28/9/29

TUAM FIFTY YEARS AGO.

About 50 years ago there visited Tuam, then engaged here in professional work in connection with the Protestant Cathedral, Mr. Edmund Sharp. He is the head of the present well-known monumental works of 42 Pearse Street, Dublin. Mr. Sharp at the time was working for a firm of builders, namely, Messrs. Goode and Sharp. He holds the premier position as an architectural sculptor in ecclesiastical work. One of the most striking proofs of his skill and taste and mastery of design is afforded by the superb marble shrine in the Augustinian Church in Dublin carried out by him. He is a member of the Architectural Association of Ireland and the author of a notable book on ecclesiastical art, entitled "Our Altars and how to select them." Many years after his visit Mr. James Pearse came here. He was an English man and the father of Patrick Pearse, the Irish leader, who was executed after the Rising of 1916, and after whom Great Brunswick Street was changed to Pearse Street. Mr. Pearse, senior, had entered into partnership with Mr. Sharp and subsequently visited Tuam in connection with work in the Protestant Cathedral. His distinguished son took to law and became a barrister, his first case being to defend a Kinvarra man for having his name in Irish and not in English on his cart and he made an able defence. He then took to school teaching. Mr. Sharp when first in Tuam lodged with Mrs Patrick White, who lived and kept a lodging house opposite the Grove House at the corner house. She was then a widow, her husband having just died. He was in the employment of the late John and his son, Mr. Peter A. Daly, of the Hotel, as a car driver. He drove for that famous posting establishment, once having twenty cars on the road, for over forty years and a remarkably careful, courteous and safe driver. Mrs White had one son called Bobby who used to give great concern to his devoted mother by his vagaries and particularly by his attempts to run away from home. He usually ran off to Dunmore and had to be brought back by his mother only to go away again on the slightest provocation. At that time Dean Seymour was the clergyman who took an active interest in the work of the renovation of the Church which he helped to erect. The original error of its erection was building it in such a low situation and building it of limestone, as it was destined to be affected with perpetual damp which cannot be effectively checked. The damp consequently injured the beautiful stalls then presented to the Church by the late Miss Cooper, of Markree Castle. She was the grand aunt of Major Bryan Cooper, the popular member of the Dail. Mr. Sharp has vivid recollections of his pleasant sojourn in Tuam and remembers the chief local notorieties whom he met at the time and whom are now all dead. He himself is in the enjoyment of excellent health and of recent years has travelled a great deal—to Spain, the Canary Islands and Italy particularly.

28/9/29

THE LEARNED TRAMP—MR. JOHN GIBBONS.

TO EDITOR TUAM HERALD.
46, Rosebery Gardens,
Crouch End, London, N.8.
21st Sept., 1929.

Dear Sir—I do not know who you are, but I am very grateful for two press cuttings you kindly sent from the TUAM HERALD in very friendly criticism of some stuff I have recently done for London "Daily Express."

They are very valuable from my point of view. A public, you see, is usually almost inarticulate, and you may write stuff to be read by a million or so people, and then not have the faintest idea as to whether the million approve or disapprove. About 2 per cent of them write in.

So if you casually see any more Irish references to my stuff, I'd be most grateful for a few. I don't want scores, and I can't afford to pay a press cutting agency, and I don't care much whether they praise or damn. But I would be obliged for just a few more references if you come across any without trouble to yourself. Then you know next time whether to alter the style or what.

I am of course a Catholic but incidentally I am English, about as English as they make them. So that I saw everything thro' English eyes. But I did try for all that to be civil to Ireland. And I was especially anxious to tell everyone who I was. It isn't fair to take stranger's kindness (and I got a good deal of hospitality in Ireland), and then calmly write them up for a great Daily.

I very much hope that there may be a book to be made out of this trip. "An Englishman looks at Ireland" or something of that sort.

Anyway you're a very Catholic country. I went through France to Lourdes last year, and this spring the "Wide World Magazine" paid me to get thro' Italy to Rome by road, and neither of them came up to the Catholicism of Ireland.

With many thanks, yours very truly,
JOHN GIBBONS.
28/9/29

GALWAY NOTES.
(From Our Own Correspondent)

Mr. John Gibbons, the celebrated Englishman and Catholic, who has been tramping Ireland and whose impressions are appearing in "The Daily Express" of London are so interesting, visited Tuam in the course of his wanderings. This is how his account of this town opens:-

It was near Tuam, I think it was Tuam. Anyway it was the place where the guard came along, and said he would be taking the engine away now. He didn't say where, and he didn't say why, let alone saying whose engine it was or what he was going to do with it, but he just left us there in the rain for about an hour and a half. And when we started again this party got in. There was half a dozen of them, all young men, and each was seen off by half-a-dozen of his family. They were crying, both men and girls, and the exportees were trying to keep very poor spirits up by a bit of singing. No they weren't drunk. Everybody was stone cold sober. Only they were miserable. I'd never seen men kiss each other before except in France and places like that. But this lot were kissing. I wished somehow that I hadn't seen them. I felt a bit mean staring at other people's trouble, only I couldn't help it, standing as I was in the corridor before the press got in and cut me off from getting back into my carriage. A very horrible thing, it struck me as, youth having to leave its own land to travel to find a home in a far America. And when I did get back to my carriage I said so to a man sitting there. But they weren't going to America, he told me. But only to Manchester across in my own England. Only the trouble was that they looked upon England as a country about as alien and pagan as, say, Central Africa. Hang it all! I always thought of London as the world's capital with everybody in the world outside it straining every effort to get there. This seemed at least a new point of view."

Further on he says :-

"All my life I seem to have been reading about Ireland as a thoroughly drunken nation, and only about twice did I see an Irishman badly drunk. And both times it was an elderly man. As far as the younger men are concerned, they seem growing up an almost tee-total race.

"Then, in all those hundreds of miles I never once saw an Irishman with a pipe stuck in his hat. And I particularly looked out for one. They must do it somewhere, because I had seen in a paper only a week or two back that this pipe combination made up Ireland's national headgear. Only somehow I missed it.

"I never saw any potheen. Once, it is true, a man indicated to me by a wink that he knew where some was, but by another wink, only far more complicated, I indicated to him that I guessed it was methylated spirit made in Bermingham, and that anyway I never drank potheen on a Tuesday. But I know that I missed the chance of at least trying it."

This is all very creditable to the country and shows that the old ideas of Irishmen are fast dying out.
28/9/29

DR. MACHALE AND THE LAND LEAGUE.

The crisis of the launching of the Land League movement was solved ay the Westport meeting. Dr. MacHale, the Archbishop of Tuam, whom O'Connell called "the Lion of the Fold of Judah," had set his face very resolutely against the Land League, and the bulk of his priests followed his lead. When the Westport meeting was announced, Dr. MacHale issued a letter through the "Freeman's Journal," denouncing its organisers as "designing men," and calling on his faithful clergy to raise their warning voices against it. Mr. Davitt says this bolt from the blue was launched the day before the meeting was to be held, and he hurried over to Morrison's Hotel in Dublin, where Parnell stayed, convinced that Parnell like the other speakers would find some excuse for staying away. "Will I attend? Certainly. Why not? I have promised to be there, and you can count on me keeping that promise." Davitt says, "This was superb. Here was a leader who feared no man who stood against the people, no matter what his reputation or record might be -- a leader, too, who though a Protestant, might be politically subservient to a great Catholic prelate on public issues than the Catholic Nationalists of Mayo would consent to be in such a democratic cause. It was Mr. Parnell's first step in his progress towards the leadership of a race mostly Catholic, and I have always considered it the most courageously wise act of his whole political career." Dr. MacHale in a letter to a meeting called in Ballyhaunis, renewed his protest, and warned the people "not to find themselves at the tail of a few unknown strolling men, who with affected grief for the condition of the tenantry, sought only to mount to place and preferment on the shoulders of the people." Parnell's strong line was, however, the determining factor. Where Mr. Davitt and the doctrines of the new American apostle of Socialism, Henry George, would not be listened to, Parnell's position and prestige swayed a race at bottom attached to the land as a personal property. Had Davitt's Henry Georgian plan succeeded the land movement was ruined.

THE FAMOUS JOHN REA AND THE IRISH PARTY.

Mr. Davitt in his book "The Fall of Fuedalism," says Jasper Tully, draws attention to a curious point about Parnell's appearance. It is the first time we have seen it noticed in any book or paper. We ourselves had observed it at a small Land League Convention held in the Antient Concert Rooms in Brunswick Street in Dublin a great many years ago, but as no one else drew any attention to it we thought, perhaps, it might have been an optical delusion. It was the size of Mr. Parnell's head. Mr. Davitt's observation arose out of an incident in Sligo Courthouse away back in 1879. Disraeli's Government, then in office, had struck at the infant Land League. Mr. Davitt, Mr. James Daly, of Castlebar, and Mr. Killeen, a Belfast barrister, had been arrested for speeches they had made at the Gurteen meeting, and they were brought up before a police magistrate at Sligo. Mr. Joe Biggar had decided to import for the defence of Killeen an eccentric Belfast attorney, named John Rea. Rea called himself "Her Orthodox, Presbyterian, Britannic Majesty's Orange Fenian Attorney General for Ulster." He used to declare that he would not be alive were it not for his habit of drinking what he called "The Essence of Shamrocks," which was his polite way of referring to Irish whiskey. He would assert that were it not for his love of this, "he would have been in the other world a very unsubstantial Irish-Orange-Fenian angel flying through Purgatory with a plumage of the most dingy hue, or, perhaps, if in favour of St. Peter, of orange, green and crimson, the Irish tricolour." Mr. Davitt describes Rea as six foot high with a massive head, prominent Ulster accent and a provocative manner that would drive a bench of Quakers into a militant mood of retaliation. Rea used to address the presiding magistrate as "Mr. Promoted Policeman," and kept continually interrupting and insulting everybody, and he even had a fling in the true Belfast fashion at "Romish priests and Italian Cardinals" as an extra gag. Rea prolonged the proceedings for days, and at last he found the police magistrate hardly ever spoke. Once when he opened his mouth, Rea challenged his pronunciation of one of the words, and charged him "with murdering the Queen's English." Parnell grew tired of this excellent fooling, and insisted on the case being brought to a close. When the Court proceedings ended, the people cleared out of the Courthouse. It was noticed, however, that Rea had not come out with the rest of the public. Mr Davitt returned to the building, and he found Rea leaning with his back against the Bench, his arms folded across his huge chest, and his head bent down. "What is the matter, John--why don't you come out?" "Only for Parnell, my friend, this thing could have gone on for nearly another week. He has spoiled the play. I don't like him. His head is too small to contain much brains, and he will come to a bad end." Rea added tht he wanted to halt the proceedings as a Contempt of Court prisoner, and in this blaze of glory he would get elected "for the next vacancy in a political Papist constituency, and that nothing could stop his progress to a seat in the House of Commons. "Heavens, how I could help Biggar there, but Parnell has spoiled it all." Biggar's Belfast selections were not always the wisest. He brought an old Presbyterian minister named Isaac Nelson down to Leitrim as a candidate, and as Leitrim would not have him, he split that county for years. Nelson was afterwards imposed on Mayo for one Session, and then they too got rid of him. It is somewhat remarkable that Rea should have drawn attention to the size of Parnell's head. But it is contended by some authorities that some people's heads grow with their years, and that they frequently require bigger and bigger hats. That may have happened in Parnell's case, and may account for observers in later years not drawing attention to it. Apart from this, the fact cannot be denied that Parnell in his quiet, resolute way was the driving force of the Land League from its inception. At that time the bulk of the tenant farming class was wedded to the idea that "they could not live without their good landlords." When the complete abolition of landlordism was preached at the earliest meetings in Mayo, an old peasant cried out, "Arrah, sir, who would we pay our rent to then?" Later on when the Land League doctrines spread more widely, this same peasant was noticed carrying a banner to a meeting with two words printed on it "Pay Nothing."

28/9/29

BERLIN LETTER

By Gunther Gericke

The 10th Anniversary of the adoption of the Weimar Constitution solemnly celebrated in Berlin. Meeting of the International Advertising Congress in Berlin.

Reichspresident von Hindenberg at the Constitution day Celebrations on the 11th August, 1929.

On the 11th August, 1919--at a time of direct distress in Germany--the German Reich adopted its Constitution and thus laid the foundation of a development which led from the collapse of the year 1918 to reconstruction. The German people recalls the ten years which have intervened with feelings of profound earnestness when remembering the gravity of its experiences, but also with the cheerfulness born of confidence in a better future. The tenth anniversary of the day on which the text of the Constitution was ratified in Weimar, the native town of Goethe, was worthily celebrated in all parts of Reich.

In the German capital, which had been decked for the occasion with flags and flowers, two impressive ceremonies took place: the March past of the Reichsbanner, a union of all republican ex-service men, in the historical state street, "Unter den Linden," and a "popular festival of youth" in the Stadion. Beneath a sky of cloudless blue 30,000 spectators witnessed a Children's Fete which concluded with the formation of a living flag by 1,000 girls and boys dressed in the national colours, while a squadron of aircraft with fluttering banners manoeuvred overhead.

The principal event of the Constitution celebrations was again this year the solemn ceremony in the Reichstag, at which Germany's venerable chief, Reichpresident von Hindenburg was present. Nothing can provide clearer evidence of the consolidation of internal conditions in Germany and nothing underlines the political importance of the celebrations on the 11th August more strongly than the fact that Hindenburg--true to his oath--recognises the Constitution. The commander of the imperial army, the monarchist who was staunchly loyal to his prince for half a century, has answered the call of the German people and given his services to the new State, thus creating the national republic. The well-known historian Hans Delbruck, who died recently, called Hindenburg "the reality of the union between old and young," thus expressing the fact that the man who had taken part, as a young soldier, in the German people's struggles for unity felt himself linked in his innermost being with Germany's past and is yet the emblem of Germany's future. The respect for the human greatness of this personality was expressed by the representative of the German Reichschancellor, at the conclusion of this year's ceremony in the Reich Parliament House, in the following words : " We bow in veneration before the present Reichs-president, who was our leader in the hardest times and whose life and work will also be our symbol in the future."

After the ceremony, the Reichspresident descended the great flight of steps—greeted with tumultuous applause by the many thousand spectators—and inspected the Guard of Honour of the Reichswehr. On the morning of Constitution Day, Hindenberg had been present at Divine Service in Trinity Church, that old Berlin house of prayer from the pulpit of which Schleirmacher once appealed to the German people to search their hearts and renew their determination. It is in accordance with the whole character of the man, who has recognised the development of life and the value and worthlessness of all things human, that he began the day that was a day of festival for his country by putting aside all temporal things and manifesting his faith in God. The 11th August, 1919, and the 10th anniversary of Constitution Day can become milestones on the German nation's road to internal freedom, for the Weimar charter provided Germany with the possibility of electing Hindenberg President.

28/9/29

GAELIC NATIONS LEAGUE.

We understand that a league of Gaelic nations is the ideal of the leaders of the language movement in Ireland, and the development of the Cumann Gaedhealach, or Gaelic Society in Scotland is regarded as being a move in this direction. It is pointed out that, thanks to the pressure of this society, the Scottish Education Act of 1918 provides for the teaching of Gaelic in the Gaeltacht, or Gaelic speaking districts, and it is now taught in 270 schools in those districts, while Gaelic committees have been formed to extend the benefits of the Act. Another method of spreading the language in Scotland is by holding of national and provincial Mods, correspomding to Feiseanna in Ireland, at which competitions exclusively Gaelic are held in story-telling, dialogue, oratory and music.

The Gaelic Society of Scotland has branches in all parts of the world, and descendents of Scots who emigrated to Nova Scotia more than a century ago speak as good Gaelic as that spoken by their ancestors when they were at home.

Yet another link between Ireland and Scotland is the Scottish national game of camanachd, or shinty, which is practically the same as hurling in Ireland.

The Gaelic League headquarters in Ireland have recently proposed unification of the two codes. This, it is believed, would lead to international matches between Ireland and Scotland, thus bringing the people of the two countries into closer contact, and eventually leading to the establishment of a league of Gaelic nations.

Mr John Keane, the celebrated Hon. Sec. of the Gaelic Athletic Association, has just retired after a long and creditable connection with that body. He was the moving soul of it for years here and abroad. His increasing business as a corn factor has obliged him to take that step. He has extensive stores at Blackhall Place, Dublin, and has done a growing business in the buying of corn, potatoes and hay all over the whole country, North as well as South. He is one of the best known public men in Ireland and universally esteemed. He was in his day a noted athlete, a great runner and a fine high jumper, doing a record jump of six feet. He took an active and prominent part in recent political events.   28/9/29

TOWN HALL, TUAM.

Wednesday 9th —— 3 Nights Only.

Special Flying Visit on our way to Cork.

DOROTHY GRAFTON'S
REPERTORY COMPANY
In a round of NEW and UP-TO-DATE DRAMAS and COMEDIES direct from Opera Houses, Cork, Derry, Dublin, Limerick, etc.

The Company includes MISS DOROTHY GRAFTON, daughter of Madame Louise Grafton, MR. GEORGE P. WHITE, a Man of Many Parts, supported by a full company of Selected Theatre and Variety Artistes.

The Plays to be presented include the following:— First Night—A New Drama by Louis J. Walsh, D.J. :-

NOTHING IN HIS LIFE.

This is a play quite unlike any other by this famous Irish author. It is a gripping and deeply interesting story that rises to very emotional and tragic scenes at times, and keeps the audience full of wonder as to how it will end.

The scenes are laid in a country doctor's dispensary during 1911, and ten years afterwards, during the "Black and Tan" time. It is purely Irish and Catholic in character, and truthfully portrays the real national spirit of Irishmen that is so frequently distorted in plays that usually hold up the Irish character to ridicule.

Quotations from "Derry Journal" of 27th September, 1929, on Production :-

" The acting all through was superb- Miss Grafton was the perfect heroine- fair to look on, beautiful of voice and gesture, and with extraordinary sincerity of emotion- Mr. Walsh said that he had rarely seen acting of such a high order."

Dorothy Grafton as "Norah," Mr. G.P. White as "Dr. Armour."

Each evening the Performance is preceded by a Variety Entertainment.

Doors Open at 7.30.   Begin at 8 p.m.
Admission : 2/4, 1/6, 9d (Including Tax.)
Seats may be reserved at the Hall from 12 to 1.
The Management reserve the right to refuse Admission.   5/10/29

GALWAY, Oct. 15

S.S. "THURINGIA"

Will Sail From

GALWAY, OCTOBER 15,

to

HALIFAX, BOSTON and NEW YORK.

Fares—3rd Class, £18 15s 0d ; Cabin Class, £29.

Excellent Meals——-Comfortable Cabins---Music——Cinemas on Board Dances——Irish Matron on Board---Every facility for celebrating Holy Mass.

HAMBURG-AMERICAN LINE

Apply Wm.H.MULLER & CO., (London) Ltd.,

COBH (Queenstown),
And all Principal Passenger Agents.
5/10/29

FILM.

Some idea of the profits made by the film makers is conveyed when it is stated that the Fox Co. have secured the services of Count John McCormack, the world famous tenor for the "talkies" his fee being some thousands of pounds. Mr. McCormack visited, says the "Observer," the Claddagh last week and has selected it for a film depicting Irish life. He will return to Galway next week. The great tenor is no stranger to the city. It is more than twenty golden years ago, before fame had come his way, that he sang in the old court theatre here. Old patrons like Jimmy Madden recall the great reception he received on that occasion. He afterwards married a Miss Foley who was with the Ludwig company. Mr. Ludwig has long since joined the majority. A powerful basso Ludwig was very popular with the music loving public in Dublin and the big towns in Ireland. After operatic selections a humourous number of his that was very popular was "Lord Waterford is dead says the Shan Van Vocht."

Eileen Bohan, a highly intelligent little girl of ten summers residing in Corrib Terrace, Galway, recently wrote to Buckingham Palace, London, inquiring after King George's health and wishing him a speedy recovery. A couple of days after she posted the letter she received an acknowledgement by command of the King from his Secretary. 5/10/29

SAD DEATH OF MRS TULLY.

We deeply regret the sad death of Mrs Helen Tully, wife of Mr. Geo. Francis Tully, the well-known actor, a native of Galway. She was fatally injured in a motor accident at Glynde, near Lewes, on the Eastbourne to Brighton road. She was aged 51. Mr Tully was driving a two-seater car with his wife seated beside him, and Mr. Lawson Lambert, manager of the Brighton Theatre Royal, in the back seat, when the car ran into a ditch and overturned, all three occupants being thrown out. Mrs Tully was dead when she was removed to Lewes Victoria Hospital, and Mr Lambert was detained suffering from head injuries. Mr. Tully, later taken to Brighton, suffered injuries to the right arm and face.

He was born at Balla, Co. Mayo, in 1876, where his mother was temporarily staying at the time with her parents, Mr. and Mrs. Fitzpatrick, but his father and brother were resident at Galway, where his father William Tully was Inland Revenue Officer. He was educated at the Jesuits' College, Galway, and at the age of 20, made his first appearance on the London stage at the Court Theatre in 1905 as John Coneely in "The Pot of Broth." He has appeared in many well-known plays, including "A Messenger from Mars," "Her Temporary Husband," "Out to Win," "When Knights Were Bold," "General John Regan," "Quality Street," "Bric-a Brac," and "General Post." 5/10/29

FORD
THE UNIVERSAL CAR

ALL NEW FORD MODELS.

Can now be purchased at MORAN'S & CO, TUAM, who requests the kind patronage of intending purchasers.

Service unequalled by Skilled Mechanics Trained Specially at

FORD WORKS, CORK.

Large Quantities of Spare Parts always in stock.

MORAN & CO., TUAM.

5/10/29

Auctioneering Notice.

I, RICHARD O'KELLY, late of Knockavannie, Tuam, now Hy-Many, Tuam, wish to inform the public that I have taken out an Auctioneer's Licence, and any business given me will have my best attention together with prompt settlement.

RICHARD O'KELLY,

Hy-Many, Tuam.

We are pleased to see that last week there were some good herring catches in Galway Bay. On Tuesday morning the steam drifter "John Summers," the property of Mr. Martin Mc Donagh, T.D., landed 26 thousand herrings at Galway Docks. In Dublin and at Howth there were no herrings and the fishing a failure.

5/10/29

IRELAND'S POPULATION.

Some interesting facts are brought to light in the report of the Register-General of the Free State of births, marriages, and deaths for the quarter ending June 30 last, which was issued recently.

The marriages, numbering 3,336 are below the average for the corresponding quarter of the last ten years. More than 3,000 of them were between Catholics, and 255 related to persons belonging to other denominations.

The registered births for the whole country were 15,363, and of this number 7,777 were girls. Here again the rate is below the average for the proceeding ten years. While the number of boys born all over the Free State is greater than the number of girls, the figures are reversed for the Dublin registration area, for of the 2,986 births in the area 1,512 were girls and 1,474 boys.

The death rate all over the State was also lower than in the preceeding ten years, and of the 10,877 registered deaths 5,450 were of females and 5,427 males. In the Dublin registration area, the deaths of males exceeded those of females.

The deaths in the Dublin area and ten of the principal urban areas were 14.7 per thousand of the population. Kilkenny has the lowest rate—11.1, then follow Dundalk (11.4), Galway (14.9), Cork (16.1), Limerick (16.2), Waterford (16.5), Wexford (16.8), and Drogheda (17.0)

Pulmonary tuberculosis continues to lay a heavy toll on the population. The annual rate for the eleven towns in the aggregate was 1.66 per 1000 of the population.

The deaths included those of three men and five women more than ninety years of age.

In a table showing the mean temperature for the quarter, we find that not only is Dublin the driest spot in Ireland, but that it had more sunshine and less rain than Greenwich, Glasgow, or Edinburgh. The mean daily number of hours of bright sunshine recorded at Dublin during the thirteen weeks was 6.5; at Cork 6.3; at Greenwich 6.4; at Glasgow 5.6; and at Edinburgh 5.9.

The rainfall at Dublin in the same period measured 4.17 inches; at Cork 7.72 inches; at Greenwich 4.22 inches; at Glasgow 6.47 inches; and at Edinburgh 5.51 inches.

5/10/29

TUAM TOWN COMMISSIONERS

The monthly meeting was held on Tuesday evening last.

Mr. P.J.Byrne, Chairman, presiding.

Other members present - Messrs P.J.Dwyer, Jas. Moran, Pat Walsh, John Byrne, Simon Fahy, J.H.Corcoran, P.Gibbons, T.Wilson, W.Holian, M.W.Cahill, J.Burke.

THE TOWN BOARD RATES.

In reviewing the finance, Demand Notes for Rates on the Board's property for year were received as follows :- First moiety £94 10s 7d, second moiety £94 10s 6d.

CO-OPTING A MEMBER

Mr. Dwyer proposed the co-option of Mr. John O'Toole, Shop Street, in room of Mr. Cooney, resigned.

Mr. Fahy seconded, and Mr. O'Toole was unanimously elected, Messrs. Moran, Holian, Cahill, and other members expressing their approval of the selection.......

THE FIRE HOSE.

Mr. Corcoran said that some time ago he happened to be passing and he saw the Commissioners' men using linseed oil in lubricating the hose. That was not the proper material to use. They should get dobbin.

Mr Dwyer called attention to the necessity of replacing defective portions of the hose and also having it in a place easily accessible in case of fire. At a recent fire no one seemed to know rightly where the key was or whether the hose was stored at the back of the meat stalls or in the Turf Shambles. He suggested that it be kept in the Turf Shambles and that a key be left in the Civic Guards Barrack. He also suggested that some new lengths of hose be got to replace the defective parts.

Some members having expressed the opinion that the Town Board was not responsible for the upkeep of the hose, or for procuring new hose, that it was the Waterworks Committee under the Board of Health, it was decided to refer the matter to that body. Meantime it was ordered that the keys suggested be procured and one left at the Guards Barrack.

A VIGOROUS OFFICIAL

Reports were received from Mr John Hession, the new Town Surveyor, calling attention - 1st. To obstruction caused by a certain street trader who on Saturdays and fair days takes up position at Meagher's corner on the Shop St. side, causing an obstruction. He suggested that the most suitable place for the man to stand would be near the Cross or crane, when the corn and potato market was over. 2nd. That a building on the Galway Road overhangs the street and is in danger of collapsing at any moment to the danger of passers by or to those selling bonhams on market days. 3rd. That he visited most of the shopkeepers in town and asked them to remove boxes and other articles from the streets or footpaths which might be likely to cause an obstruction, and all were agreeable to comply with the order, except two, one of whom refused to remove an oil drum cabinet from the front of his premises, and the other refused to remove a hay rake and weighing machine in front of his premises. The Town Surveyor also submitted a formidable list of damages and breakages in the different rooms of the Town Hall, keys and electric bulbs missing and breakages to windows etc.

The Town Surveyor's reports were discussed at length and generally approved of, and in the case of street obstruction he was given power to prosecute should the parties persist in their action.

TARRING THE STREETS

It was decided to proceed with the tarring and sanding of the streets of the town as suggested by Mr Kennedy Co. Surveyor. 5/10/29

GALWAY NOTES

The Kirwans, as I said, nearly three hundred years ago came out from Galway City where they were, like all the Galway aristocracy, leading merchants and traders. The first of them to come out to become resident gentry were those who came to Lough Hackett and there built the house which they uninterruptedly continued to occupy for 300 years, sad to have to say that it was destroyed during the awful period of devastation we passed through and in its destruction many famous old relics of the past perished in the flames. Here was the head and principal bones, I believe, the skeleton of the famous Race horse that once won the principal race at the Curragh which it was said, saved the then heavily encumbered estate. Nay more, it was generally believed by the people round about that the horse was ridden by a "fairy", for the Kirwans and the "good little people" were always on the best of terms and the greatest friends. The firm belief in the fairies living in the recesses of Knock Ma survived until recent days and was a pleasing and harmless illusion. The fairies it was thought and believed came out every night from under the famous and historic hill called after Queen Maev, Knock Ma. She was supposed to have been the Queen of the Fairies and is believed to have been buried under the cairn of stones that to this day is on the summit. The fairies went all over the country on their midnight excursion and of course frequently called at Castlehackett always, it was said, to receive there a hearty welcome. But these beliefs are now dissipated and the upspringing generation do not believe in fairies and we do not think they are the better for casting away the old customs and beliefs. There was a respectable woman in Tuam whom forty years ago every one in the town believed to have been once in the fairies, carried away for seven years and a person like her in all respects left in her place. There were people then living who would assert they often saw the fairy lights around the hill and the little men in green moving to and fro. Such was Castlehackett, hallowed by such fairy traditions and consequently the last place it was thought the devouring torch would be put to was that fairy haunted house which was supposed to be specially guarded and protected by them.

******

About forty years ago there was a terrible hub bub up at Ardacong, Tuam, near the old Gurranes Race Course. The place was known for generations as the Fairy Mills, and one day—it was Sunday—mysterious noises were said to have been heard and hundreds of the simple folk of Tuam in those happy days went out there and hundreds from the neighbourhood to hear and marvel at those strange subterranean sounds. Undoubtedly this was the noise of running waters and the credulous people believed that the fairies were busy at work grinding their corn. The real fact was that the ground all over the whole district being limestone and full of holes and caverns the water freely flowed through them and when in flood made this great noise. The entire county is of such cavernous formation. Up at Gort the river sinks into the bottomless, seething pool, called the Devil's Punch Bowl, situated in the demesne of Lord Gough at Lough Cutra, and comes out miles away at the Lake of Coole. There again disappearing underground the water comes out ultimately at the bridge, four miles away, at Kinvarra, where it finally enters the sea. For nearly a half mile out in the Bay the water is fresh and not salty, but it gradually mixes with the sea and acquires its saltiness. That was the natural explanation, but the majority of people then still adhered to the belief that it was the fairies that were at work underground and the reason for their belief was that the place was so called Fairy Mills, and must be so, and such it was in their simple faith in these simple and happy days.

******

There is an old De Burgo castle on the hillside at Castle Hackett, and around it still left is a fair quantity of timber planted originally by the Kirwans who were an improving class of land owner, the leading of their class indeed. Denis Kirwan was the first gentleman to introduce the growing of swede turnips. He ran a kind of agricultural farm for years at Caltra under an experienced Scotchman, Mr. Abner Baillie, who cultivated some hundreds of acres and grew the best oats, potatoes and barley in the county. He was a respectable and popular man, greatly liked by his neighbours. Another family at Castlehackett well known and respected were the Blighs. Patrick Bligh resided at a house near the Hill and he married the widow of a Mr. Kelly of Tuam. Her son was the famous Colonel Kelly who commanded the 69th Regiment in the American War of 1864-67. He succeeded in that post the distinguished Thomas Francis Meagher. By Mr. Bligh his wife had also two sons who became the leading doctors in Liverpool of their day. Both are dead now. They were Dr. Alexander and John Bligh. They were educated at Galway Queen's College and there they got their medical degrees. They went to Liverpool and soon reached the top of their profession. Dr. John Bligh lived at Mount Pleasant, and all during his life the late Bishop of Clonfert-- he being formerly as P.P. of Cummer and the great friend of the Blighs as of every other family--Dr. Duggan, had a room specially set apart for his reception at that hospitable house of Dr. Bligh. A son of Dr. Bligh is now following the same profession as his illustrious father and being equally esteemed. Alexander, the other brother, or Sandy, as he was familiarly called, had also a son, John Murray Bligh. He is Senior Hon. Physician of the David Lewis Northern Hospital and Lecturer and Examiner in Clinical Medicine at the University of Liverpool. His mother was a daughter of the late Philip Brady of Dublin. His father was an Alderman of Liverpool for years, and both Blighs T.P.O'Connor's strongest supporters. Both were fellow students of his at Galway and did not forget the old days there. Mr. Bligh of Castlehackett had also two other sons, the best known being Matthew, deceased some years, whose widow resided in the old Bligh home until she sold out and went with her family to live in England. She was a widow of Richard Prendergast, who was born in Tuam and whose mother resided on Circular Road some forty years ago. A daughter of Mrs Bligh married Michael Lynskey of Caltra, one of the Ashgrove family, but all are dead now.

*****

We are pleased to see that Salthill at Galway will have its hotel running again. Mrs Emerson, Dominick St., who has taken over Eglinton Hotel, Salthill, has employed Mr. Dooley, a local building contractor to carry out extensive repairs to the building, and to install all modern conveniences. When the work is completed the hotel will be found to suit every requirement of the tourist and will supply a long felt want in that salubrious district. The Salthill season this year was one of the best for years past. The excursion trains every Sunday brought thousands of visitors to Salthill and the shopkeepers and boarding house owners benefitted considerably.
5/10/29

"AN OLD MAN'S MUSINGS."
[From "Derry Journal."]

A BUBBLE BURST.

The publication of the lists for the Saorstat Intermediate Certificate Examination, 1929, has burst not one, but a whole crock-full of bubbles. Since An Roinn Oideachas set itself to work out in detail its educational policy, we have been tired listening to shrieks from all the avowed and covert enemies of Irish nationalism, and from all the backboneless invertebrates amongst us, who take their cue from the remnants of the Protestant Ascendancy to whom they still slavishly look up, that the study of Irish was standing in the way of progress in more useful subjects, and was going to overwhelm the Saorstat in an overwhelming educational disaster. I don't say that all the people who said this really believed it. Many of them were far too intelligent. Those who hate the whole national ideal, and who are in their hearts absolutely imperialistic and pro-British, are naturally and rightly opposed to the spread and encouragement of the national language. For they know, as Edmund Spencer did in Queen Elizabeth's time, that "the speech being Irish, the heart must needs be Irish." If I believed myself that Ireland's best and proper destiny was to be a "contented province of the British Empire," I would oppose Irish for all I was worth, no matter what I thought was its educational value. The same must be true of intelligent people amongst genuine Irish Unionists. They know as well as I do that you could hardly find a more fitting instrument for sharpening the brains of Irish children than to teach them their national speech. But knowing what the language would mean as a bulwark of nationality, they are determined to oppose it to the death. They don't deem it politic to give their real reason for doing so, and, besides, they require the votes and influence of the invertebrates. So they have invented these sham educational ones, which any genuinely educated person can see through, but which are good enough for those, amongst our people, who cannot think, and are victims of generations of vitiated educational systems.

THE PREPARATORY COLLEGES.

The success of the Preparatory Colleges in the recent Intermediate examinations has been so remarkable, however, that it is difficult to see how even the stupidest person amongst us could be any longer deceived by the "educational" nonsense that is written in the "Irish Times" or delivered in the form of speeches at "Church of Ireland" synods, or at a distribution of prizes in Protestant schools. For not only is Irish made the chief study in Preparatory Colleges but everything else is taught through the medium of Irish, and Irish is made the ordinary language of the school, alike at prayer, work and recreation. Well, now, how have these schools fared in comparison with those in which, what the "Irish Times" would call, those "mind-killing and soul-killing" methods of education did not prevail—that is to say, where Irish was only taught perfunctorily or not at all ? In the boys' section, Colaiste Caoimhin, Glasnevin—one of the Preparatory Colleges,—heads the list by a long lead of all the other boys' schools in the Saorstat. It presented 53 pupils, of whom 46 got honours and 7 passed, thus giving a total of 53. The next best total in the Saorstat was only 18. In the girls' section the superiority of the Preparatory Colleges was no less marked. The college at Rockhill, Letterkenny, and the other Preparatory College at Falcarragh are miles ahead of all the other girls' schools in the Saorstat. Rockhill got a hundred per cent. pass result, presenting 52 pupils, and getting them all through, with the extraordinary number of 45 "honours." In Falcarragh one girl got sick during the examination, and there, too there would probably have been a 100 per cent pass list. As it was the college had, out of 42 entries, 28 "honours" and 13 "passes." The next best result in the girls' section is for the Protestant Preparatory College at Glasnevin, where Irish is also made the principal study!

REMARKABLE RESULTS.

These totals are very remarkable in themselves; but when one examines the results in individual subjects, the case usually made against Irish by the "Irish Times" and its correspondents appears still more ridiculous. So far from the intensive study of Irish preventing progress in other subjects, the good Irish students showed that they were more than able to hold their own with all comers. Thus, first place in English was actually won by a student of the Rockhill Preparatory College—Siun Ni Ghabhainn—with 345 marks out of a possible 400. Another pupil of the same college (Sile Ni Chiardha) accomplished the extraordinary feat of getting full marks in mathematics (600), while first place in one of the science courses was won by Maire Nic Ghiolla Pheadair, of the Falcarragh College, with 267 marks out of a possible 300. With results such as these in subjects like mathematics and science, taught through the medium of the national language, what becomes of the nonsense we have been hearing about the impossibility of using Irish for technical and scientific purposes ?

WHERE IRISH IS TABU.

But to see the matter in its true perspective, one has to compare those results with those of institutions in which Irish is more or less tabu. Thus, take that famous seat of learning—St. Columba's College,

Rathfarnham. This is a well known Protestant school, the warden of which—the Rev. Mr. Armstrong, I think his name is—is, or was, one of the most doughty opponents of "compulsory Irish." In a long and somewhat pompous article in the "Irish Times," he once demonstrated, to the joy of all the breakfast tables of the Saorstat rectories and of all our Masonic Lodges, that our educational policy was hopelessly and completely wrong, and that Irish was ruining the study of all the useful languages and sciences. Let us now examine the results for this school. Nobody would suggest that Irish would be allowed to "ruin the study" or other subjects in a place like this select Rathfarnham institution. In fact, only three boys out of the school presented Irish, and two of them failed in it—so that not much time is wasted on that subject, of which Mr. J. Allen Osborne, solicitor, Milford, says he feels so "blissful" because of his ignorance of it. Now, St. Columba's appear to have had 15 entries—out of which it secured one "honours" and two "passes." More remarkable still was the fact that the only boy amongst them who got "honours" on the whole examination was the only boy in the school who got a good mark in Irish and passed in it. The highest mark in the school in mathematics was 487, secured by the boy who did Irish reasonably well, whereas in the Preparatory College, Glasnevin, where everything is taught through the medium of Irish, several students are well over 500 in the subject, one being as high as 563, and on the same paper the Rockhill girl got the full 600 marks assigned to the subject. On the other hand, in the Protestant Alexandra School, the principals of which for some time recognised the educational value of the national language, and where it appears to be reasonably well taught, there were four honours and seven passes out of 15 entries, and the school obtains sixth place amongst the girls schools in the Saorstat. All the Alexandra girls presented Irish, and a big number of them passed it. All of which proves that the study of Irish so far from being an obstacle to progress in other subjects, even English, is a distinct help to it.

THE SIX COUNTIES.

If the Saorstat schools had been directly competing with the Six Counties' schools, I think it is fairly certain that the point I have been making would have been still more emphasised, and that the schools in which everything is taught through the medium of Irish would have swept not only the Saorstat, as they did, but the whole country. Because it will hardly be disputed by educationalists, capable of making proper comparisons, that the standard for the Saorstat examinations is higher than is the case across the Border. A Saorstat College Professor, for instance, once told me that he found that his junior class could have passed on a Belfast Senior Mathematics paper on which he tried them. But I do not wish my word to be taken for the difference in educational standards in what is quaintly called "Northern Ireland" and in the Saorstat. For we are told by the Belfast "Northern Whig," that during the hearing of a school attendance case no less a personage than Sir Robert Kennedy made a statement to this effect. He said, according to the "Whig" report, "that an eminent military authority had informed him that a large number of recruits were obtained both in the North and South, and on joining the army had to undergo an educational test. According to the results of the examination they were classified in order of merit—A. B. C. D. E.—and a significant fact, which struck him very forcibly, was that the large percentage of the Southern recruits were placed in B. and C. classes, whilst those of the North, whose knowledge seemed to be more limited, were for the most part allotted to the two latter classes." These would be the products of the primary schools; but readers of the Belfast Unionist Press will be familiar with the complaints from those who know, and who are genuinely interested in the welfare of the Belfast Government, of the state of affairs that prevails in many of the secondary schools. Thus, from a letter in last Saturday's "Northern Whig." I cull these doleful sentences : "A careful study of the pass lists of the 1929 junior certificate examination, recently issued by the Ministry of Education (Northern Ireland), must bring grave disquiet to all lovers of our language and our literature. For, if the marks are a criterion, the teaching of English in Northern Ireland is in a deplorable condition." Only five boys in the Six Counties' intermediate certificate obtained 75 per cent. in English, whereas in one small school in the Saorstat, where everything is taught through the medium of Irish—namely Rockhill Preparatory College—I find no less than four girls with much over seventy-five per cent. in English, one of them, as I have said, obtaining 345 out of a possible 400. If things continue to go as they seem to be going, the only way to save the tongue of Shakespeare in Belfast will be to bring over a few girls out of the Rockhill or Falcarragh Preparatory Colleges to teach English to the children of the merchant princes of the Malone Road through the medium of Irish! Amongst the Six Counties' schools themselves, it is the ones in which Irish is best and most extensively taught that the most satisfactory all-round results are obtained. Thus, we are all proud of the extraordinarily fine achievements of St. Columb's College, Derry, this year, where Irish is splendidly taught. The capture of almost all the scholarships given by the local authority in Derry shows that St. Columb's stands head and shoulders above all its rivals in that part of Ireland.

ONLY WHAT WAS EXPECTED.

If education is deteriorating in the Six Counties, outside the Catholic Schools, it is only what a good psychologist would expect. The Belfast educational authorities are making the mistake that "Mr. Bounderby" and "Mr. Gradgrind" of Dickens' famous educational satire made before them. They think that the way to educate a child is to stuff him with "facts," whereas the true educational objective should be to develop the child's taste and sense of appreciation and to teach him how to think and use his brains. You must appeal, too, to his imagination, and to his emotions, and above all teach him self-respect. Take, for instance, that subject on which the Belfast educational "realists," as they would describe themselves, set such store. That is geography. Most of the facts that are learned so painfully in that subject are of no use to the average Irish boy. Even if he is destined to go abroad or to have trade relations with other countries, he will easily find out, when he requires to do so, all the information that will be of any service to him. That is why it would pay him far better in any walk of life to have had his mind developed by the study of such an apparently useless subject as Ancient Greek—always provided that he was able to make such substantial progress in the language that he could understand and appreciate its subtleties and enjoy its great literature. Because mere poking at a language is of little educational value. Which is why Irish is of tremendous educational importance. Because Irish is actually learned as a living language by everybody, whereas there are little opportunities and hardly any incentive for boys and girls to make the same progress with any other modern language except English.

THE SAORSTAT'S EDUCATIONAL POLICY.

That is why I am convinced that the Saorstat's educational policy is going to produce very big results in Ireland, when it has time to work itself out. I see evidence of it already. If Viscount Charlemont or the editor of the "Irish Times" are betting men, I will let them select at random any bilingual primary school, say, in the Rosses, and compare it with a school of the same size, where Irish is not taught, also selected at random, in rural Antrim, and I will give ten to one on the Rosses school for all-round efficiency. Similarly I will take St. Louis' Convent, Monaghan, where so much time has always been given to Irish, and I will guarantee it to beat hollow any similar establishment in Viscount Craigavon's wide dominions—in spite of all his Educational Acts and Regional Committees. The revival of the teaching of Irish in the Irish schools is going to have the most stupendous results in about twenty years' time for those of us who live to see them. *Cormac MacAirt.*

P.S.

When I am on the subject of results, I would like to congratulate the President and Professors of St. Eunan's College, Letterkenny, on their great success in the Saorstat examinations this year. As St. Eunan's College is a comparatively small college in comparison with the big boarding schools of the South, it is a tremendous achievement for it to have been amongst the first twenty boys' schools in the Saorstat. Irish is strong in St. Eunan's.

C.MacA. 5/10/29

TUAM GREAT OCTOBER FAIRS.

Tuesday,   October 15th --- Sheep
Wednesday, October 16th --- Cattle
Thursday,   October 17th --- Horses
Friday,   October 18th --- Pigs.

Tuam Great October Fairs being considered the largest and best in Connaught in the years past this year is expected to beat all records.

Buyers will be numerous, including Cross Channel and otherwise.

By Order Tuam Town Commissioners.

J.P.WHYTE, Town Clerk.

TRANSFERRED.

Mr. M. Keegan, Gaelic Teacher, Tuam, has been transferred to Ballinasloe. Mr. Keegan was very successful with his pupils in Tuam. Many of them got the fainne during his time, and his students in Irish dancing and singing carried off numerous prizes at the Feiseanna in Galway and Mayo.

Mr. D.F. Langton, Manager, National Bank, Dunmore, has been changed to the head office, Dublin. He has been changed by his own request. He was an extremely popular and efficient manager and highly esteemed.

INVITING AMERICAN TOURISTS.

In its advertisement of invitation to Irish American tourists to visit Ireland the White Star Line says:-

"Dublin! The social and intellectual centre of Ireland. Walk along its stately O'Connell Street---where an impressive monument to the great Emancipator holds sway. Within easy distance are sea, mountain lake and river---calling the sportsman and seeker of beauty." It adds, "Daily celebration of Mass on board."

The Cunard Co. has its inviting notices also, and so has the Hamburg-American line which has an altar for the celebration of Mass and "an Irish matron to care for the comforts of the women and children.

5/10/29

GALWAY NOTES.
(From our own correspondent.)

An interesting article on the "Gordon Bennets" and American Journalism, appears from the cultured pen of T. Mc Cullagh in the pages of this quarter's "Studies." He speaks of the old Bennet and his erratic son, Gordon, the latter, he says, a man of many whims and fancies but a prince in paying for what he wanted. There we learn a curious fact, that the original proprietor of the once famous "New York Herald," James Gordon Bennett, was a Catholic and an Irishman. He never practised his religion. Half Irish and half Scottish, his father being Scottish and his mother Irish, he was a true Celt in every respect. The old man married Miss Henrietta Agnes Crean, a lady from the West of Ireland—probably Mayo—and one of the Crean Lynch family, of which the present Attorney General for the Free State is the principal representative. There were members fifty years ago of the Crean Lynch family living near Tuam, and we believe some are there still. There was a Captain Crean Lynch of Dugara whose son was George so well known in Tuam. Miss Lynch came to the United States in 1838 and was supporting herself there as a composer of music when she met the elder Bennett and he married her. The son, Gordon, has been described as "having the worst qualities of the two races to which he belonged, the Scotch and the Irish," and unfortunately there is some truth in this. The Irish half of him was, says the writer of that wild Galway type that Lever is so fond of depicting, but in 1915 a "Herald" man fresh from Paris being asked about him in New York, replied as follows— "He's dead. The old drunken, money spending Tim Bennett, is dead. In his place has come a Scottish miser." It would take an Arabian Nights volume to chronicle all the mad doings of the young man. His expenses in Paris were enormous. He had several houses splendidly furnished, and a printing press, and a palatial country seat, and a steam yacht which cost him a fortune alone to keep in commission. He kept a house in New York, a large mansion in Washington Heights, and a villa in Newport, although he never spent any more than three months at any one time in the States. A nephew of the second Gordon Bennett was at one time—some thirty years ago—the popular Master of the Blazers, Mr. Bell. He left this to take up mastership of the Kilkenny Hounds, but always regretted his departure from Galway as did his friends here regret his departure. He was a genial, good natured gentleman, with no side or nonsense. The Gordon Bennets are now either extinct but at any rate not what they were, while the "Herald," at one time the most enterprising and remarkable paper in the world, is now joined with the "Times" but not what it once was.

***

In the pleasant pages of "The Book Lover" which he helped some 30 years ago to start and ran for over a quarter of a century at his own expense, Dr. J. S. Crone refers to Ballinrobe printing and says that in that town in 1868 the Query and Presentment for the Co. of Galway was printed by Gore Kelly, the Jury and Voters Lists by John MacDougall, and the contract for the advertising in the four county papers—the TUAM HERALD, The "Western Star", published at Ballinasloe, the "Galway Vindicator" and "Galway Express," was taken out by Richard Kelly.

***

The foreman of the Co. Galway Grand Jury in 1868 was William Henry Gregory, M.P., of Coole Park, Gort, whose widow, Lady Gregory, still lives. He was appointed Governor of Ceylon in 1870 and knighted. He was the best Governor they ever had in Ceylon and to this day the memory of him lingers. He was a decidedly able man and very nearly rising to great political prominence. He had by Miss Persse, of Roxboro, one son, a gallant young man who was killed in the war. He was in the British Air Force on the Italian side when he was shot down and killed. His widow and a son survive.

***

In the current issue of "Studies," in which appears the article I referred to on the Gordon Bennetts of the famous and far famed "New York Herald," is a very learned and interesting article on Ephesus by Professor Michael Tierney the popular Professor of Greek at University College, Dublin, and a native of this county. He is full of the Greek spirit and in this respect a worthy successor to Professor Mahaffy of Trinity College who was the most distinguished scholar of his day and a man of universal fame as such. Our county man bids fair to equal him in his profound and extensive knowledge of Greek classical literature and history.

***

I see it rumoured that Castlehackett, the famous residence of the Kirwans, who up to thirty-five years ago lived there for over two hundred years, and later on occupied it as the heirs and descendants, being the children of the late Percy Broderick Bernard, Esq., has been acquired as tenant by Mr. Henry MacDermott, K.C. the well-known Solicitor of Galway. He is son of the late lamented and distinguished lawyer, The MacDermott, K.C., who was for years and until his death, the universally admitted and acknowledged leader of the Irish Bar when there were intellectual giants at it. Mr. Mac Dermott is a keen sportsman and Castlehackett is an ideal centre for the county hunting. 5/10/29

PARS OF LOCAL INTEREST.
(From Our Own Correspondent.)

SUCCESSFUL HOCKEY WHIST DRIVE.

A very successful Whist Drive organised by the Tuam Ladies Hockey Club was held in the Town Hall on Sunday evening. The large prizes attracted a good crowd.

The lucky prize-winners were as follows:—

1st. Men's Prize, £2 10s 0d—Mr Edward Kirwan, Gardenfield.

1st Ladies' Prize, £2 10s 0d—Mrs Finucane, Bank of Ireland.

2nd Men's Prize, Safety Razor—Mr. Hurley, Shop Street.

2nd Ladies' Prize, Electric Comb—Nurse O'Sullivan.

There was a box of cigarettes and a box of chocolates given at half time to the losing pair at a certain table. These were won by Mr. S. Hehir and Miss Kenny.

A gold pencil presented at the end to the lowest score in the room was won by Mr. Carroll, High Street.

The Whist Drive was followed by a short dance from 11 o'clock until 2.

PIONEER HALL.

The Tuam Pioneer Hall, adjoining the Cathedral Gate, was formally opened on Sunday last. Rev. Father Fergus and Rev. Father Killeen, C.C., (the new Spiritual Director of the Association in Tuam) were in attendance. Games were played during the day and in the evenings since, and the hall has been well patronised by the members. It is expected that within the next week or ten days a span new billiard table with all the needful accessories will be installed and in full playing order. This hall should prove a great centre of attraction and amusement for the members of the Tuam Pioneer Association.

THE G.A.A.

Two challenge matches for sets of medals are announced to come off in Parkmore on to-morrow (Sunday). The Galway Commercials are to meet the Tuam St. Jarlath's in hurling at 3 o'clock, and the Galway Gaels v Tuam Seniors in football at 4.30.

It is expected that both matches will be well contested, though in the hurling bout the odds are in favour of Galway, but they are reckoned to hold no advantage in football.

VICTORY DANCE.

A victory dance will follow in the evening in the Town Hall at which the presentation of medals to the Tuam Senior Football team will take place. To know those in charge of the arrangements is to anticipate a gala night's amusement. A splendid band has been engaged   12/10/29

CHRISTMAS CARDS.

We have received some excellent specimens of Christmas Cards and Calendars artistically printed. An Irish Dominican priest who saw the new Christmas Cards issued by Brian O'Higgins for the coming season wrote of them: " 'Noble' is the only word I can think of that describes them." They mark a big advance on anything issued up to the present, and we venture to say they will be more popular than any Irish Christmas Cards have ever been. They are in four classes, and all the designs are exquisite and the greeting verses worthy of the designs. There are twelve single cards in five colours, all different designs, and each with a miniature of some famous Christmas picture. These are prayer book size, and are especially suitable for priests and nuns. The price is one penny each. There are twelve twopenny four-fold cards (2 wholly in Irish) in Celtic designs also and in very chaste colours. Twelve threepenny cards come next. The entire series of 48 Cards and 12 Calendars will be sent post free to any address for 21/-, but smaller quantities will be sent. A descriptive list of all, with prices marked, will be sent post free to readers of this paper on application. Lists for friends will also be sent by Brian O'Higgins, Stormanstown, Glasnevin, Dublin.

THE PRICE OF PROHIBITION.

The "Commonweal," an excellent, outspoken American Catholic weekly, says:—

Since the passing of the national prohibition law, the annual per capita consumption of alcohol has about doubled; crimes of violence have increased; the official figures for arrests for drunkenness have climbed yearly, the additions showing mainly in the categories "women" and "young persons"; large numbers of working people are undermined morally and physically by drinking the undiluted spirits which are the principal commodity dispensed by bootleggers; the average of community health has been lowered "by increased records of chronic drunkenness, delirium cases and alcoholic insanity"; a considerable section of the population have given up reputable occupations to work as distributing agents in "the vastly more lucrative liquor trade"; among the priveleged classes, to whom dining is both an occupation and an art, the law is commonly and elaborately broken, but is held to be "like religion, a very good thing for the masses"; a government commission, after a searching investigation, returned a general report embodying a set of unmitigatedly depressing statistics, and is supplemented by two independent personal reports, of which the following statements are typical: "Apparently we have a long, hard way before us before we reach the condition of temperance existing before the war. The misuse of medical prescriptions has turned out to be an unprecedented scandal. The application of the law disregards the moral standards of criminal law in general."   12/10/29

The Tuam Herald.

Saturday, October 12th, 1929.

WOMEN SMOKERS.

The late war is accountable for many evils and bringing in its wake more trouble and worry to humanity than can well be conceived, and one of the many resultant effects of that world-moving catastrophe is the habit of smoking and dressing adopted by women, which habits newly acquired by them are supposed to be the outcome of the new era of independence and equality which they want to enjoy and which they are supposed to have achieved for themselves by their participation in the war in giving help in hospitals and in the work of the preparation of munitions. The vicious habit of smoking is one of the evils that have sprung up among the other sex and it has led to a great deal of extravagance and the injury to the health which, if not checked, will become very serious and in the end do infinite harm. The expense of female indulgence in cigarette smoking is growing to be a very important matter and it cannot be too soon exposed and condemned. We have been informed since our last article on the subject of indecent and immoral dress that often young girls spend from one pound to twenty-five shillings and sometimes more on cigarettes and the sex are now considered the main source of custom at tobacco shops. We simply must pity the unfortunate young man who taking one of these as a partner for life on a slender income he has, must support such useless extravagance on the part of his wife and at the same time bring up a young family, a matter which in these days when education for the upper middle classes has become so heavy an item, being double what was paid twenty years ago at the schools, must cripple and beggar him. But what we wish in all sincerity and desire to reform, a growing passion, is the physical danger of excessive smoking to women. The habit is undoubtedly calculated to increase their growing nervousness and other forms of indelicacy and to unfit them for their real duty in life, that of being mothers of healthy children. We have had our attention called to a remarkable letter which has just appeared on that important subject in a leading American journal. It is written by Dr. Barry, a well known American physician, and it gives the experience of a lady smoker. It appears in the "Brooklyn Tablet," once the great organ of Catholicity in the States, and is so serious, weighty and important we give it in all its details. The writer gives an account of her efforts to curb the passion for the cigarette and states her belief in what injury it did and was calculated to do to her. She says :—

"When I first started to smoke it seemed as if I was committing a crime against all womanhood. But the constant urging of my friends—"Go on, smoke, everybody smokes now" led me on. At other times these so-called friends would say : "Do you think you are better than anybody else ? Why don't you like to smoke ?" So it was a case of smoke or lose my friends, except one. That one seemed too quiet to consider, so I smoked.

"I smoked and smoked until my fingers were a disgusting sight. They were stained orange brown. My teeth were yellow and black. My throat was forever full of mucus. My nerves were shaky and my head had a tight feeling. When I walked my steps were irregular. Yet I continued smoking until the nerves of my limbs started to twitch, with pricking pains, and my head jerked at times. At night I could not sleep. Darting thoughts of fear would shoot through my brain, and I dreaded going to sleep, for fear of jumping up suddenly and throwing myself out of the window. Then it became impossible for me to go anywhere, because I was constantly thinking of horrifying accidents. I suffered so much from these anxieties or fears that I thought I was going crazy. I dared not tell any one, lest my husband hear of it and park me in the bug house.

"One day that quiet friend of mine brought me a clipping from Dr. Brady's column on the tobacco habit. I almost fainted with fear when I read it, and all that night I had hallucinations of smoke. Toward 4 a.m. I fell asleep. Awakening an hour later from a dreadful nightmare, I had violent nausea. The very thought of a cigarette increased the nausea. This nausea stayed with me for three months, then slowly passed away. I have never smoked since and never will again.

"The fears are all gone now and my nerves are as steady as ever. My mouth has its natural clean taste, and my steps are sure and regular. My teeth are white, my fingers clean, and I am not afraid of anybody noticing an odor on my breath. At night I quickly fall asleep and nary a bad dream.

"Had my quiet friend not brought me that clipping I believe I would have been in the bug house by this time, or maybe dead. For my recovery I thank God and Dr. Brady.

"Yes, it is no irreverence to observe God is nearly always with me when the applause begins, maybe from the very beginning, but what I mean is that God gets the credit and I receive honourable mention.

"At that I can't imagine what I ever said about the tobacco habit that would scare a poor girl like this. If I knew just what it was, or just how I said it, you may be sure I'd see that it never happened again.

"There are two points to the ladies confession that deserve special emphasis. First, why should a girl or woman succumb to such appeals as this woman's friends made—must she do something or not do it merely because 'everybody else' does it or does not do it. ? Does a woman lack the moral courage to hold out for her own wish or preference even though every other woman in the gang fails before the 'everybody's doing it' appeal ? And second, it is probably the greatest valid objection against smoking by women, that when a girl or woman does take to smoking she is quite likely to indulge to excess.

"I believe temperate smoking is as harmless for a woman as it is for a man, but the evidence seems to indicate that it is more difficult for women to avoid subjection to the habit than it is for men. Perhaps that is partly due to the insidious influence of cigarettes, compared with the benignant pipe that the true devotee of tobacco enjoys.

"I may be narrow and provincial about this, but I hate to see a woman smoking in any public place, and most of all in a restaurant, particularly before the eating is finished. This means excessive indulgence, of course, and excess in the use of tobacco is so ruinous to the health and beauty of a woman that it makes the sight an unpleasant one for me.

"Any smoking that the smoker craves or wants in the middle of work or play hours, in the middle of the day, is probably excessive. It amounts to craving for a drug, a pick-me-up, a substitute for natural or healthful stimulation, an expedient to cover or conceal, ennui, embarrassment or the inferiority complex. It is bad medicine, no matter whether the smoker be man, woman or child.

"A temperate use of tobacco means, for instance, one or two cigars after the day's job is finished; or three or four cigarettes; or two or three pipefuls. Smoking time comes once a day for the temperate smoker. For the excessive smoker any time one can't think of anything better to do is smoking time.

"I have reported here, from time to time, such evidence of the effects of tobacco on various classes of users as seemed to me sound and reasonably well established scientifically. I don't know that tobacco can cause arteriosclerosis (hardening of the arteries), in any circumstances, though I suspect it may have a good deal to do with this state in many instances. I don't know. but strongly believe, that excessive smoking may cause a form of angina indistinguishable from true angina pectoris, and this is notoriously a fatal disease. I accept the opinion of physicians of large experience with a peculiar type of gangrene of the legs known as thrombo-anglitis obliterans that this is caused by excessive cigarette smoking; the trouble seems to be almost if not wholly confined to Jewish men who are heavy cigarette smokers. There seems no logical reason why Jewish men should suffer gangrene of the legs, so I believe the excessive smoking is the essential cause of thrombo-anglitis obliterans.

"All physicians and surgeons recognise the constant and prolonged irritation of burns or of the hot smoke as at least an exciting factor of cancer of lip or throat.

"We may set down at once as the explanation for the terrible voices to which the public is exposed in the talkies, on the radio and in vaudeville the excessive use of cigarettes by women. Perhaps tobacco is as injurious to a man's voice as it is to a woman's, but to the untrained ear the coarsening or deadening effect on the feminine voice is more apparent.

"Even if there was no question of injury to health involved, it is still a desirable thing to keep the habit under control and to make sure that he or she will not become a slave to the habit."

This testimony is so truthful, so telling and important that we give it in full with no words of commendation on our part. We let the communication speak for itself. It well merits serious consideration at the hands of young female smokers and those who have any control over them if such really exists to any effective extent.

VETERINARY PREPARATIONS

LUNGTOL, for Timber Tongue in Cattle.
3/6 & 7/- per bottle, 6d postage.

BLACKQUARTER PREVENTATIVE For Blue Leg in Cattle.
Bottles :-- 1/6 & 2/6, postage 6d extra.

BLACKLEGOIDS in tubes of 10, 6/6 each, postage 3d.

AGENT :

STAFFORD,

CHEMIST,
VICAR STREET, TUAM.
Branches : DUNMORE & MOUNTBELLEW
12/10/29

MISCELLANEOUS.

We are told that "if the Free State Government had only sufficient pluck to compel millers in Ireland to mix 15 per cent. of home-grown grain with the foreign maize used in the country we could stop emigration almost completely," as Mr. Frank Aiken, T.D., declared at a meeting at Hagardstown (Co. Louth). "If this proposal was carried through it would mean that 74,000 extra acres of tillage would be required in a year, and £11,000,000 of Irish money, which is at present paid to foreign farmers, could be kept at home. The real Irish people, for whom the Government should legislate, are the tillage farmers and the labourers." It was deplorable, he said, year after year to see people leaving for America, while they could be living in peace and security, and with a certain amount of prosperity, in their Irish homes. Ireland's main hope was to keep the working farmer on his land and to make it profitable for him to work at home. 12/10/29

****

At the meeting of the Galway County Committee of Agriculture, Mr. Gerald Bartley properly enquired what was being done for afforestation in Connemara. Mr. McNicholas, Instructor, stated that £75 was allocated for shelter beds for the whole county, and they had put down a number of them in the western area. Mr. McGovern, Inspector, stated that in addition any farmer could get trees at cheap rates through the committee.

****

We are pleased to see that Lieutenant-Colonel Denis J.C.K.Bernard,C.M.G.,D.S.O., who this month will leave Aldershot to take up charge of the station at Belfast, is the son of the late Mr. Percy B.Bernard, J.P., D.L., of Castle Hacket, County Galway, and is a relative of the Earl of Bandon, who is the head of the Bernard family. Colonel Bernard, who was born 47 years ago, was educated at Eton, and went on to Sandhurst for his military studies. He took a commission in the Rifle Brigade in1902, and reached his captaincy ten years later. He rendered distinguished service in the European War, and in 1927 held the command of the 1st Battalion of the Royal Ulster Rifles. From 1915 until the close of the war he was General Staff Officer. He received the D.S.O. in 1917 and the C.M.G. in 1919.

Colonel Bernard's father and grandfather, the late Percy B. Bernard and the Bishop of Tuam, were undoubtedly in their day the most popular gentlemen in not only the county but in Ireland. Every one liked Percy Bernard. When he was getting married first to a beautiful young English lady, a fair blonde, as he was dark, the Tuam people got up a subscription—all classes and creeds joining and presented him with a wedding present which took the shape of a piece of plate which we believe was burned when Castlehackett was raided. The Hon. Secretaries to that popular movement were Messrs. Denis J. Kirwan, then of Tuam, and subsequently of Dalgan, and Mr. R.J. Kelly, now of Dublin. Both these gentlemen were at the head of every popular project and took an active part in getting up the agitation that led to the building of the railway connection between Tuam and Claremorris which the selfish policy of the Midland Company prevented for twenty-five years. The connection was ultimately made despite all those mean efforts and for that good work Mr. Kirwan and Mr. Kelly deserve praise, as do also the late John Bermingham, of Millbrook, who actually drew the first plans and surveyed the line. He is now forgotten, but a more remarkable man could not be imagined. Self-taught, he became so distinguished an astronomer that on the best map of the Moon are one or two seas or mountains called after him. He catalogued the Red stars and got the Royal Irish Academy silver medal and the recognition of every astronomer of his day for so doing. He was a great man in every respect and quiet, simple and unobtrusive. He could write well and contributed many articles of literary merit to the TUAM HERALD. He could also write beautiful poetry and composed a long poem called Anglicania, or the conversion of England, which was printed and had a wide circulation. He once delivered a learned lecture at St. Jarlath's College on a then little known science, "Spectrum Analysis." He had a splendid observatory at his place at Millbrook, a mile outside Milltown, beside Dalgin, where his cousin, Mrs. Kirwan lived. This was the third or fourth largest in Ireland, Lord Rosse's being the largest, not only in Ireland but in the world, until the Lick observatory was built. There night after night he sat watching the stars, following their mysterious movements, observing their changes and taking elaborate and careful notes which were afterwards published. And to add to his manysidedness he was a Poor Law Guardian and attended the Tuam Board almost every meeting day of importance.

****

These beauty competitions are vulgar and offensive. A Dublin paper tried to run them but had to desist. We agree with Mussolini who says:— "We have abolished beauty contests in Italy. The physical charm of woman is too sacred a symbol of feminine virtue and love to be placed on parade. It is not a thing of gilded brass, shameless to hypocritical admiration. Oriental slave girls exhibited in the market place of the East try to hide themselves from shame but the 'beauty queens and princesses' discard the blush of womanhood for the icy stare of the graven image." 12/10/29

PARS. OF LOCAL INTEREST.
(From Our Own Correspondent.)

INJURY TO THE WATERWORKS MACHINERY.

Early this week the pumping apparatus for driving water from the well to the reservoir got out of order, one of the cogs breaking off and carrying with it the spur wheel and pinion wheel and rendering the pumping machinery useless. A meeting of the Waterworks Committee was held immediately, and as it was not found possible to get the necessary repairs effected locally the Committee instructed Mr. Shine, Waterworks Superintendent, to telegraph to London for new parts. This, it is understood, will take at least ten days, and as there is grave danger of a shortage of water if the parts do not come to hand within that time people ought to be careful to waste as little as possible. At the beginning of this week there were 8 feet of water in the reservoir, but as a good deal of that must have been consumed during the fair people should be very careful of what remains or they may find themselves without water within the next week or two.

***

NEW BUSINESS OPENING.

During the week Mr. John J. Waldron opened his new hardware and provision store on Bishop Street adjoining the Square. It is, for its size, as pretty and well laid out a business house as could be found outside the city of Dublin and reflects credit on the contractor, Mr. David Dwyer. The window dressing and goods displayed inside were in keeping with the beautiful appearance of the shop, and all concerned are to be congratulated on the taste displayed. It is splendidly lighted and when lit up each evening crowds may be seen gathered around the windows admiring all the beautiful articles displayed therein. Mr. John Waldron is one of our most popular young townsmen and his hosts of friends wish him success in his undertaking.

***

MORE HOUSES NEEDED.

The Tuam Town Commissioners on Monday evening deputed a committee to meet the owner of the plot adjoining the four houses just completed on St. Paul's Terrace. If this can be secured at a reasonable figure the intention is to build at least 5 or 6 more houses there. Already there are 15 houses constructed and finished in that locality and in some degree the want of housing accommodation is less keenly felt on that account. There is still the need in Tuam for at least 50 more houses, and some go so far as to say that the town will not be right until all the thatched cottages in it are knocked down and rebuilt— that they are antideluvian, unsanitary and unhealthy.

WANTED,

HALL KEEPER and BILLIARD MARKER required for Tuam Pioneer Hall.
Apply to J.J. Waldron, Hon. Sec., stating salary expected, on or before Tuesday, 22nd inst.
Applicant must be a Pioneer.

19/10/89

TUAM OCTOBER FAIR.

THE SHEEP FAIR.

The sheep fair on Tuesday, which is practically a wether fair, was much larger than last year—though not as large as the September one which now takes from the October fair, as in September farmers purchase mainly for breeding purposes. Very few ewes were exhibited or sold on Tuesday except by local people. However, there was an all-round improvement over last year both in price and the quantity and quality of sheep sold. There were 50 wagons more railed this year than last year.

Quotations—2 year old wethers, 72/- to 80/- ; 1 and a half year olds, 60/- to 70/-.

THE CATTLE FAIR.

The cattle fair on Wednesday was very large and in that respect showed an improvement also over last year. The quality of cattle exposed showed superiority and nearly all were in good condition. For good, "warm" cattle there was an immediate sale, but the few backward in condition had a slower sale. The conditions at the station for railing were fair and a special more than last year was railed. A feature of this year's fair was that bullocks were equal in demand and prices with heifers.

Quotations—3 year old, £18 to £22 ; 2 and a half year old, £14 to £17 10s ; 1 and a half year old, £11 10s to £13 10s; springer cows ranged from £17 to £18, to £27 for the " pick of the basket."

HORSE FAIR.

The horse fair on Thursday was well supplied as usual with foals, which for animals of good quality sold well. For 1 year to 1 and a half year olds prices averaged £12 to £15, and for younger ones £6 to £9.

THE PIG FAIR.

There was a very large pig fair on Friday and prices were most satisfactory. There was an almost complete clearance before 10 o'clock. Prices averaged 65/- to 66/- per cwt.

19/10/29

GALWAY NOTES.

Dr Walter Starkie, F.T.C.D., the only son of the late Dr. Starkie, for some time President of University College, Galway, and afterwards Resident Commissioner of National Education, who has recently returned to Ireland from a most picturesque and original tour among the gypsies of Bohemia, where he has been collecting folk music by going among them disguised as an itinerant musician, is one of the most distinguished Catholics in Trinity College, Dublin. He obtained his Fellowship there some years ago. He had shown such promise as a violinist as a boy before the war that he thought of devoting himself entirely to music. But his academic attainments led to his competing for the Trinity Fellowship, which his father had also held, and he has since made an international reputation as one of the most brilliant young scholars in Spanish literature. As a public lecturer he has had great success in the United States, and he is one of the most popular social figures in Dublin under the new regime.

***

I find now that it was Mrs. Beddington, who lived near Athlone, in the King's County, and was a Miss Mulock, who first discovered that the famous tenor, Count MacCormack, had that superb voice he has delighted the world with. His father was foreman in the woolen mills at Athlone. In 1905 she discovered that fact and we are indebted to her for his coming so soon into prominence. He first appeared in public at the annual Feis Exhibition then held at the Rotunda and the song that charmed every one was "The snowy breasted Pearl," sang as only he could. He next went through Mr. Vincent O'Brien's hands and he went with him as his accompanist all over the best part of the world--to America and Australia. He has made millions by his voice and is the owner of the castle of the O'Moore's in Queen's Co. and of thirteen highly bred race horses.

Mr. Vincent O'Brien also brought to the forefront Walter MacNally, also a Connaught man and a native of the Co. Mayo, from which county comes Margaret Burke Sheridan, who was born in Castlebar and educated at the Dominican Convent, Eccles Street. She was sent there by her guardian--her mother and father being dead--the late Canon Lyons, P.P., who was recommended that excellent school by Mr. R.J.Kelly, K.C., his lifelong and esteemed friend. He (Mr. Kelly) had at the time six daughters and one son going to the Eccles St. Convent Schools and he well knew and appreciated the value of the excellent training and teaching imparted then and since has done with such marked and brilliant success.

***

Mrs. Beddington comes of a famous Irish family, the Mulocks of the King's County. She tells us that she "has more ink than blood in her veins," for her mother's aunt was Miss M.E. Braddon, the great novelist, and her father's second cousin was no less a person than Dinah Mulock, the author of "John Halifax, Gentleman," and one of her father's sisters married Alfred Austin, the poet Laureate, but why he was so appointed as he wrote excellent prose, but nothing that could be called poetry, is now told us by Mrs. Beddington. It was because he would take no other reward or recognition from Lord Salisbury.

***

We see that the business premises of Mr Thomas Nolan, Shop-street, Tuam, where for many years a victualler's trade was carried on, was sold on Tuesday, the purchaser being Mr. Martin Rooney, Shop-street, Tuam, for the sum of £700 and auction fees. The auctioneer was Mr. Martin Cooney, and the solicitor having carriage of sale was Mr. Henry Concanon.

19/10/29

TUAM TOWN COMMISSIONERS.
FOR SALE
Four Newly Built Cottages at St. Paul's Terrace, Tuam.

The Tuam Town Commissioners will at their Meeting to be held on Tuesday, November 5, 1929, consider offers for the purchase, singly, of the above Cottages.

The Commissioners reserve the right to accept or reject such offers.

Proposals addressed to the "Presiding Chairman," will be received by me up to 8 p.m. on the above-named day.

By Order, Tuam Town Commissioners,
JOHN P. WHYTE,
Town Clerk.   26/10/29

TUAM.

Candid Comments—Complimentary and Otherwise.

(BY "FIAT.")

The geography tells us that Tuam is an important town in County Galway, the seat of an Archbishop, the Metropolitan of Connacht, and also the seat of a Protestant Bishop. It tells us further that there are two Convents, a Diocesan College and two beautiful Cathedrals, one of them containing an ancient Arch of the Romanesque period. The population is given as 3,287, last census (1926), but of course makes no reference to the population of Tuam having declined 50 per cent. in 70 years. Free trade certainly brought wonderful "blessings" in its train. Tuam's population in 1860 was 6,000. It had a Brewery, Match Factory in the Curragh, and several other local industries on a smaller scale. These have all gone out of existence now, and if the opponents of Protection—there are a few in Tuam—get their way, well—there will be no industries to protect.

The average tourist visiting Tuam is always ready to admit that for neatness, compactness, and general lay-out, Tuam stands alone. The streets radiate from the Square and end in charming suburbs of picturesque terraces and private residences. The Convents with their beautiful grounds, the two Cathedrals, the Christian Brothers' Schools, and that famous "alma mater" of so many prominent Irishmen—clerical and lay—St. Jarlath's College—all these convey to him the importance of the town. The brilliantly lighted streets, the shop windows so tastefully decorated, the businesslike attitude of the people convey a neat city atmosphere. The town has 5 clubs, each complete with Billiard Table, Card Rooms and Reading Room. If a walk is desired in picturesque surroundings, there is a choice of Gardenfield or Togher. Parkmore offers a splendid sportsground, as it is ideal for Football and Camogie purposes. There are two Tennis Clubs, a Golf Club, several G.A.A. Football and Camogie Cumainn, and, of course, a Rugby and Hockey club.

It will be seen, then, that Tuam has all the essentials conducive to the enjoyment of the inhabitants, except—here's the rub—a decent Railway Service. A native wishing to travel to Dublin, do a little business in the city and return the same evening, finds "it can't be done."

The morning train leaving Tuam at 9.20 a.m. arrives at the Broadstone at 1.40 p.m. The traveller must then "rush some" —to use the American expression—as the only train giving a connection to Tuam leaves at 2.35 p.m. In other words, the traveller has only the narrow margin of 55 minutes between arrival and departure of trains in which to transact business.

Here is "a slap" for Tuam : Loughrea, Ballyhaunis, Castlerea, Claremorris and Ballymoe are not nearly so important as Tuam, yet they all have connections with night mail trains leaving Galway at 8 p.m. and the Broadstone at 7 p.m. Tuam is neglected and if the people of Tuam—particularly the Town Commissioners and the merchants—only demanded redress, their demand would command attention. (See footnote).

The HERALD has done good work in protesting against the management of the Irish Railways, and the writer gladly pays tribute to its protests against the singling of the Line to Galway. The HERALD has also in the past pointed out the necessity for a train leaving Tuam at 7.30 p.m. to connect at Athenry with the Galway train to Dublin and take the mails and passengers from the Dublin to Galway night mail. Such a train would arrive at Tuam at 11.15 p.m., thus allowing a traveller over 5 hours stay in Dublin, having left on the 9. 20 a.m. train.

In conclusion, the writer begs to remind the people of Tuam that the Railwaymen have contributed a lot to the town's welfare. The fortnightly wages bill, amounting to no small amount, is spent, *every penny of it* in the town. The Railway employees living in the town pay local and county rates, and are a valuable asset to the town in general. The status of Tuam, as a railway centre, has declined during the past few years, since the Amalgamation of the Railways. Claremorris is now Head Centre between Limerick and Sligo, and if the Tuam people remain apathetic Tuam, after a short time, will be merely a "2 minute halt" instead of a Railway Centre.

Now then, Town Commissioners and Merchants get to work and demand a connection with the night mail from Dublin. Tuam town is the cause of enough merriment already, owing to having no Teachtai Dala and Athenry having two. "Where there's a will there's a way," and if the Commissioners and Merchants show a lead the people will co-operate and bring the matter to a successful conclusion.

(The writer is in a position to state that the granting of a train leaving Tuam at 7.30, returning at 11.15, is not improbable if a proper demand is made. On the occasion of a former demand for such a train, the only stumbling block was Post Office cost of carrying the mails. The writer will be glad to hear from any readers who are interested in the matter, and who are willing to co-operate in having the grievance remedied).

2/11/29

"Need Life Be Dull ?"

TO EDITOR TUAM HERALD.

Sir—I have often heard young and middle aged people complain that life is dull and boring. They complain of having to do too much work, and they also complain that they do not know how to spend their spare time! May I use your valuable space to make a few suggestions to them ? I propose to mention some of the things which have occupied my very limited amount of spare time during the past five or six years. Some of them may interest a few of your readers.

(i). Encouraging boys and young men to take part in athletic sports, cross country running, football, boxing, etc., as well as taking part in sports myself.

(ii). Assisting and organising amateur theatricals, dances, and other entertainments in aid of charitable institutions.

(iii). Excursions to the country and seaside camps for boys and girls from the slums of big cities.

(iv). Excursions to the sea for boys and girls from the country.

(v). The encouragement and development of the Boy Scout movement.

(vi). The provision of sports grounds, playing fields and athletic equipment to those who cannot afford to procure them for themselves.

(vii). Encouraging the thrift movement by acting as hon. sec. to a savings association and selling savings certificates.

(viii). Assisting the unemployed to find work either at home or abroad.

(ix). Collecting funds for sundry charitable institutions.

(x). Organizing debates on subjects dealing with social, political, national and international questions.

(xi). Addressing public meetings in sundry places on the practical application of Christianity to present day social, economic, national and international problems.

(xii). Assisting hospitals, institutions for cripples, imbeciles etc., and the deserving poor (including widows and orphans, the unemployed etc.)

(xiii). Writing letters to sundry newspapers (including the TUAM HERALD) on religious, social, economic, national and international questions.

(xiv). Reading in sundry newspapers and books the views of other people on these matters as well as the daily news.

(xv). Working for the improvement of housing conditions, and roads, and the erection of sign posts and danger signals on the latter.

(xvi). Working for the proper treatment and economical use of animals.

(xvii). The assistance of foreign missions.

(xviii). The improvement of agriculture and trade in Ireland.

(xix). Endeavoring to secure for employees (a) Better wages (b) A share in the profits of the business in which they are employed.

The above summary shows most of the ways in which my spare time has been spent on and off during the past five or six years. Certainly I have never found life dull or uninteresting. My spare time has not only been filled, but I have never been able to do quite as much as I wanted to do.

By my spare time, I mean the hours not taken up with my job, my daily work. I do not find these hours dull either, for I am thoroughly interested in my job, and I try to do it to the best of my ability.

I have written this letter for the benefit of those who find life dull, and who cannot think of any interesting way of spending their spare time. Many people find life dull, I think, because their chief aim in life is to amuse themselves. I believe that in most cases those who find life most interesting are those whose chief aim, with God's help, is to help other people, and to make the world a better, a happier and a brighter place.

Yours etc.,

"Irishman."

Sunday, 27 :10 : 29

2/11/29.

WILLIAM F. DILLON.
CENTRAL CHAMBERS,
15 D'OLIER ST., DUBLIN,
Agent in the Free State, Ireland, for
Cantassium
the Wonderfully Successful remedy for
Treatment of Cancer.
Free Booklet and full particulars to Bona-fide Inquirers.
Spread the Good News--
You may save a human life
2/11/29

UNIVERSITY COLLEGE GRANT.

University College Galway, is getting an additional grant from the Dail of £12,000 bringing its endowments up to £28,000, mainly to encourage the teaching of Irish. It is in a sense a grand idea but as a very thoughtful and independent member of the Dail and a Galway man, Professor Tierney, pointed out, the authorities ought to proceed carefully and cautiously. If it is to teach science, literature and the continental languages through the medium of Irish its professors in these subjects must know Irish thoroughly, not the cram knowledge that satisfies, and it is believed that there are not many on the staff so qualified or many likely to be got outside for years. Too often men are being preferred elsewhere and promoted for an apparent knowledge of Irish but having a painful want of more necessary qualifications. That is the danger ahead. Galway once had great medical and great engineering schools. Has it to-day ? Once its studens were known all over the world. Are they likely to be so in the future ?

ABBEY THEATRE.

With the production of "Ever the Twain" at the Abbey Theatre on Tuesday last, Mr Lennox Robinson celebrated an important event in his career in a very unusual way. The date was the twenty-first anniversary of his *debut* as a dramatist. I wonder whether the date of the first production of this new play was chosen with that event in view, or whether it "just happened" to coincide. Anyway, it is a date on which the dramatist deserves congratulations and the success of "Ever the Twain," although it is hardly his best play, marks a happy "coming-of-age" event. It was on the 8th of October, 1908, that the name of Lennox Robinson—not then known quite by that name—first appeared on a programme at the Abbey Theatre.

DOMINICAN PREACHER.

We notice with pleasure that a Galway Dominican priest has spoken out strongly on female dress. Father Barrett said that the good mother could so mould the minds of her children as to make them model Christians and Catholics. He referred in passing to the emigration evil and declared that he would rather see them starving in Galway than millionaires in a den of iniquity like New York. He spoke as one who had lived in New York, and saw the abomination of that great city. He regretted to have to say that numbers of Irishmen reared in Catholic homes in Ireland lost the faith in the American cities. He next referred to the type of woman to be met to-day who monkey like copied the so-called fashions of England, frequented the dance hall and the cinema and deserted the home. They had no use for that class of person—these so-called ladies who brought disgrace on the country by opening their arms to the foul things sent over by England and America. He described this type as like a modern residence painted in front, shingled behind and with nothing in the attic. He warned his hearers against marrying this class of woman. We must, he concluded, keep out the foul things England imports—immodest, and a hundred and one other things. Have we, he asked forgotten the Black and Tans. We must forgive England but we can never forget. 2/11/29

EXCITING SCENES.

A sensational account from its active Galway correspondent appears in Tuesday's "Irish Times" of exciting scenes witnessed last Sunday evening in the hurling final in Galway between Galway City and Claddagh for a cup and medals, presented by the Galway Hurling League. After two minutes' play the referee, Mr. Seamus Malone, Kilrush, ordered off M.Cunningham, Galway City, and D.Curran, Claddagh, for endeavouring to fight on the field. The game was continued for twelve minutes and Edward Moore, Claddagh, was injured. Then a Galway City player was seen to strike a a Claddagh player with a hurley. Immediately there was pandemonium.

The crowd numbered over six thousand, including almost every inhabitant of the Claddagh fishing village. Some of them rushed on to the field, and one of them was struck on the head with a hurley. An attempt was made to attack a Galway City player, who was immediately surrounded by Civic Guards and players from his own team and escorted off the field. Clergymen endeavoured to restore order, but without success.

The referee awarded the match to Claddagh, but for a time the cup could not be found, and a rumour was circulated that it had been stolen. Eventually it transpired that the man in charge of it was on the ground, but that as a City player had threatened to smash it if the game was not continued, the Guards had protected it. The cup was then taken to the dressing room, where a conference took place between the members of the League Committee, and it was decided to adhere to the referee's decision and give the cup to Claddagh.

This news was received with great jubilation by the Claddagh followers, and the captain and members of the team were carried shoulder high through the city and back to the village, where bonfires were lighted.

People who had paid for admission to see the game passed sarcastic comments upon the whole affair, and some tried to get back their money, but as a large section of the crowd had scaled the walls and secured free admission this was impossible.

Among the spectators were some officers and men of the British destroyer, Sea Wolf, which was in Galway on an unofficial visit. 9/11/29

NATIONAL THRIFT MOVEMENT.

Savings Committee Appointed in Tuam.

Revd. P. Kelly, Adm., presided at a public meeting in the Town Hall, Tuam, on Tuesday evening, when a committee was appointed under the scheme of National Thrift Saving.

There were present—Rev. J. O'Dea, Diocesan Secretary, St. Mary's College, Galway ; Very Revd. Dean Lendrum, Tuam ; Messrs J. J. Quinn, Solr.; F.B.McDonogh, Solr.; J.O'Toole, T.C.; W.Holian,T.C.; W.F.Purcell, Manager National Bank; Ml.Heskin, M.J. Walsh, D.J. Butler, and Mr. Anderson, Postmaster, Tuam.

Mr. Seamus O'Sullivan, State Savings officer, said: This Savings Committee, which is now established in Tuam, is a branch of the Central Savings Committee, and like that body it is representative of all classes. The aims of this Committee will be to promote the ideals of the thrift movement in and around Tuam. Saving confers a double benefit. In the first instance it benefits the indvidual by providing for future needs, the education of children, helping their start in life, providing against bad times, etc. Secondly, it broadens the base of national welfare by facilitating regular investment of the people's small savings. Thrift helps to form character and makes for good citizenship. This movement encourages constructive thrift. Thoughtful spending of money is bound to have a good effect on trade. The Savings Association, a group of people banded together for saving co-operatively, is the basis of the movement, and it is the object of the Central Savings Committee to start these associations in every school, workshop, factory, or anywhere people may be associated for a common purpose. It is very pleasing to note that excellent work has been done in the schools of Tuam and the country generally. There is room for many adult Savings Associations in this district. One of the functions of this Committee would be to issue an appeal to employers and employees with a view to having these associations formed. There is no doubt that, if workers are thrifty, they are most likely to be more contented and more efficient. The material instrument of the thrift movement is the Savings Certificate, which is a State guaranteed security earning 5 and a quarter per cent compound interest free of Income Tax. It can be cashed at any time. The Savings Association enables the investor to purchase these certificates by instalments, and they may be purchased privately either by instalment or in full at any post office.

"The schools scheme under the movement," he added, "had already been established in over 2,000 schools in the country and there were 300 adult associations in large business bonuses."

Father O'Dea said that the object of the movement is not to make them a nation of money grabbers or to develop any principle that would change their Constitution of hospitality and generosity. The fundamental aim and object was to instil into the people a spirit of thrift and wise saving. He thought if there were two national vices they were laziness and pride. The climate may have something to do with it, but it was a well-known fact that they did not make as much use of their opportunities as people of other countries. There was a great deal of waste in the country.

It may be cynical to talk about things in the West of Ireland where the struggle for a living is hard, but at the same time there is a certain amount of spare money which could be put by for the occasion when better use could be made of it. A beginning must be made somewhere and by somebody. The saving of money develops a spirit of independence and industry will then enable the people to stand on their own feet and not be depending on doles or on their friends in America to keep them going. The second and perhaps the most important result that may come from this movement is the fact that the money so saved may be ultimately used in local industries. A large amount of money was invested in banks which in turn invested in industries. If the people invested their money in Savings Certificates there would be no need to worry or suffer from night mares of Hatry collapses, etc., and they would have the satisfaction of knowing that while their money was absolutely safe for them it was utilised for the benefit of local industries, the improvement of works and general benefit to the country.

The main idea of the organisation was to have each district committee appointed under a County or Regional Committee. It was important to have every interest, particularly labour in all classes represented on the Local Committee. If the object is achieved the Local Committee can do a lot of work and coordinate the different classes of workers, shop assistants, railway workers, and any other organisation that might be made nucleus of a club. There was a certain amount of self-sacrifice and unselfish work required of members of the committee who are called on to do voluntary work for the general good of the country. A great patriot had said that patriotism to be firm did not depend on the way a person declared it but the service in which it was rendered. The greatest service they could do to make their people independent to find emloyment for themselves was to support the Thrift Movement by local Saving Committees, representative of the people doing the work allotted to them. Politics in this country had become a fetish. Everybody was entitled to have his opinion, they all had them, but a good many suffered from the delusion that this Thrift Movement was a party stunt and that it is a monoply of the Government in power at present. That was not so, anything that would tend to make the country as a whole independent was not a matter for party and he thought it would be a great thing if politicians dropped some of their sneers and became willing to co-operate to do something for the people as a whole. It was due to the country, and they should all do something to make it independent financially and so save people the necessity of having to go to other countries to earn a living.

The organiser, Mr.O'Sullivan, said it was the intention to hold an All-Ireland Conference in future at which representatives would attend from all district committees. The main function of the district committee was to invite representatives of local clubs, societies and organisations to encourage the Thrift Movement amongst the members. They had already been very successful in the schools, the teachers having gone to an extraordinary amount of trouble to facilitate the work. In one of the Convents in Tuam - the Presentation, the scheme was very successfully carried out, and they hoped to have the same to say of the other Convent shortly. In many other schools in the district Savings Associations have been working for many years.

Mr.Quinn said it would be a good thing to have the teachers represented on the committee.

The Organiser said that the National School Teachers had no representation on the committee but that he had invited Mr. M.O'Connell, N.T., Tuam, to the meeting.

Asked how they could get labourers to join this movement, Mr.O'Sullivan said that in Messrs. McDonogh's of Galway there were 35 employees who had kept up the Savings Association since it was formed in 1925, and those people had a good sum now to their credit. There were very few people who could not save a 1/- or 2/- a week and in this way could get certificates by instalments.

Mr.Quinn proposed and Mr.McDonogh seconded, "That a Savings Committee be established in Tuam."

Dean Lendrum suggested that the heads of business firms in the town be brought in to encourage the movement amongst their employees. A good deal also depended on how the schools took it up. This would be the work of the committee for the promotion of the scheme. They wanted people on the committee who will work and further this most excellent cause, and there is no doubt they wanted thrift in this country. He was very much in favour of the movement and hoped they would get on the committee people who will work and make it a success.

It was decided to nominate those present at the meeting as members of the committee with power to co-opt, and to invite the different clubs, organisations, in the town to nominate representatives for appointment on the committee.

Mr. John P. Whyte, Town Clerk, was appointed hon. secretary to the Committee.

On the proposition of Rev.P.Kelly, Chairman, a vote of thanks was passed to Fr. O'Dea for his trouble in coming from Galway for the meeting and giving them a most interesting address on the objects of the Thrift Movement.

Fr. O'Dea returned thanks.

9/11/29

TUAM NOVEMBER FAIRS

Tuesday, Nov. 12th—Sheep and Cattle
Wednesday, Nov. 20th—Pigs

Farmers would be well advised to bring in their stock to this fair, as sheep and cattle are in great demand at the present time.
Don't forget to bring your pigs to this fair, as the last Pig Fair beat all records for good prices, etc.

By order Tuam Town Commissioners,
JOHN P. WHYTE,
Town Clerk.

9/11/29

TUAM TOWN COMMISSIONERS.

The monthly meeting was held on Tuesday evening last.

Present—Messrs. P.J Byrne (presiding), S.Fahy, W.Holian, Pat Walsh, P.J.Dwyer, T.Wilson, Jas. Moran, M.W.Cahill, J.O'Toole, John Byrne, P.Gibbons, J.H.Corcoran, J.Burke.

Two tenders were received and accepted for the 4 cottages advertised, No. 3 at £215, and No. 4 at £210.

Mr. F.B.McDonogh, Solr., represented both purchasers.

The Chairman said that the committee appointed to purchase a new site had agreed with Mr. Moran for a sum of £95 to be paid for the plot adjoining the 4 cottages recently erected, subject to the approval of the Board.

This was agreed to and the Clerk directed to submit the agreement to the L.G.D.

Plans were put in from from the engineer, Mr. Kennedy, showing that the site would allow of 7 more cottages and also that the road could be widened at that particular point—the well there to be closed up.

A NIGHT MAIL FOR TUAM.

Mr. Dwyer proposed and Mr. Fahy seconded the following resolution, asking for a Night Mail to Tuam, which was passed unanimously :

"That we demand that the G.S.R.Company run a train from Tuam to Athenry each evening at 7.30 p.m. to connect with the Galway night mail and also to take passengers and mails off the night mail from Dublin to Galway, which arrives at Athenry at 10.30 p.m. Other towns of much less importance than Tuam, have a connection with the Dublin to Galway night mail, and we call upon the G.S.Rly. Coy. and the Minister for Posts and Telegraphs to give our demand their immediate attention."

Mr. Corcoran drew attention to the heavy rates being charged on the Tolls. It absorbed more than a third of the amount. They should seek to have it reduced.

It was decided to apply for a revision of the rates charged on the Tolls.

A DRINKING TROUGH FOR ANIMALS.

A letter was read from Mr. R.M Burke asking the Board if they were prepared to accept his offer of a drinking trough for animals to be erected at some convenient part of the town. It would be given free.

It was decided to give a place for the trough convenient to the Weigh House on the Square.

URBAN POWERS.

A letter was received from the Co. Galway Board of Health in reply to an enquiry from the Board as to why the proposed latrine was not being erected, stating that they (the Board of Health) had applied for urban powers to the L.G.D., and that until they had received those powers the latrine could not be erected.

It was decided unanimously to send a strong resolution to the L.G.D. protesting against any such powers being delegated to the Board of Health, and on the suggestion of Mr. Dwyer the Loughrea Town Commissioners were asked to make a similar protest.

TUAM WATERWORKS COMMITTEE.

Meeting of above was held on Thursday evening, Very Rev. Canon Walsh presiding. Two tenders were received for the supply of paraffin oil to the waterworks engine for the coming six months. The I. and B. Petroleum Co. tendered at 1s. a gallon (less 1d per gallon rebate), and the Texas Co. tendered to supply the oil at the schedule price ruling on date of delivery (less 1d per gallon rebate).

Mr. J.H.Corcoran proposed that the contract be given to the Texas Co. and Mr. O'Malley seconded.

Mr. Cahill proposed the contract be given to the I. and B.P., but there was no seconder and this proposition fell through, Mr. Corcoran's proposition being carried.

Mr. Collins, B.E., was instructed to prepare an estimate of the cost of working the engine with crude oil. The committee gave instructions to have the water cut off at 9 o'clock each evening, as the engine was not working, to give a full supply to the town.

A letter was read from Messrs. Conway and Quinn, Solicitors, relative to the flooding of the land of Mr. C.T.O'Rourke, Bermingham, requesting to be informed whether or not the committee will proceed with the cleaning, otherwise they were instructed to take proceedings for damage.

The chairman said the order made at the previous meeting in this matter was that Mr. O'Rourke be asked to point out on the map the part of the river that he wanted cleaned, and the committee was still waiting for an answer.

The Secretary said that Mr. Comerford, Solr., told him that he did not know of any agreement between Mr. O'Rourke and the committee.

Mr. O'Malley said that the river had been cleaned very often in the past, but the question was whether the committee were liable.

Mr. Cahill—There would be floods there if there never was a waterworks in it.

Mr. Daly said there was an arbitrator's award and the question depended on the terms of that award.

The same order as that made at the last meeting was again made—to find out what part of the river was to be cleaned by the committee. 9/11/29

An Coiste Ceard-Oideachais, Condae na Gaillimhe.

COUNTY GALWAY COMMITTEE OF TECHNICAL INSTRUCTION.

The above Committee has arranged (by kind permission of the Christian Brothers) for a short course of

INSTRUCTION IN WOODWORK

To be held in

THE MANUAL TRAINING ROOM OF THE CHRISTIAN BROTHERS' SCHOOLS

TUAM.

The opening meeting will be held on **WEDNESDAY, 13th NOVEMBER, at 7.30 p.m.,** when the Instructor, Mr. N.P. HARTNETT, will be in attendance to explain details and make full arrangements for the work.

The classes are primarily intended for men and boys who have left school.

The instruction will be of a practical nature calculated to train the eye and hand and will consist of simple drawing, the use of tools, lectures on various kinds of timber and the making of useful articles.

As the course must necessarily be short, all wishing to take advantage of it should be in attendance from the outset.

A nominal fee of One Shilling will be charged for the course.

S. O BAOIGHILL,
Runaidhe,
Co. Galway Technical Committee Office,
Prospect Hill, Galway.

9/11/29

FOR SALE
MORRIS OXFORD FOUR SEATER,
Good Running Order, Owner Driven.
£70,
M.GUNNING,
National Bank, Tuam.

9/11/29

MISCELLANEOUS

Six Catholic women, each the mother of 13 children, were decorated with gold medals at St. Columbkill's Church on the occasion of the blessing of the babies of the parish at Dubuque, Ind. U.S.A. The blessing was a feature of the eight-day dogmatic mission conducted by the Rev. Thomas J.S. McGrath, S.J., of Shreveport, La. Father McGrath had announced that a solid gold medal of Christ and his Mother would be presented to the mother of the largest number of children. At the blessing ceremony the missionary asked from the altar if "there is in the church a mother of 20 children ?" From that number he came down the line until he got to 13, when the six women approached the altar. At the blessing 153 children were present, ranging in age from less than 2 weeks to 6 years. The silver medals of the Immaculate Conception, offered for the youngest boy and girls present, went to Arthur Francis Houselog, born Sept. 22, and Elizabeth Jane Cosley, born Sept. 19.

9/11/29

GUINNESS'S PORTER.

Guinness is again, thanks to the judicious and extensive advertising, coming into favour again in England and the exports from Ireland are growing every week. The advertisements are well designed. We find in the London dailies a quarter page advertisement giving the following advice to readers :-

"Guinness is of great value in Neurasthenia, and its action appears to nourish the brain cells."
L.R.C.P.

"Guinness is a most valuable combined tonic and food, especially applicable to Neurasthenia and neurotic patients of the thin or emaciated type."
L.R.C.P., L.R.C.S.

"I am convinced that Guinness taken regularly at dinner time has prevented many people - especially business men - from having a serious breakdown."
M.D.

Extracts from three of the thousands of communications received by Messrs. Guinness from Doctors.

16/11/29

CHRISTIAN BROTHERS RAFFLE.

For a Solid Silver Watch.
Winning No. 3850—Francis Burke,
Ratesh,
Kilconly, Tuam.

16/11/29

KEEP THE IRISH YOUTH AT HOME.

By Cornelius O'Donovan, Promoter of the Statue of Erin at Cork Harbour.

The Irish people have been lured away from their native land by insidious immigration propaganda, put out by Steamship Companies seeking lucrative business from the people of Ireland in the past era - through oppression, political turmoil, fued and poverty.

That era has passed.

It now behoves Ireland to retain its people within herself, as its high time that all will think; and that public organisations both governmental and commercial should make a serious effort to retain the Youth of Ireland, its brains, and its man power, to their native land.

Very often the Canadian press has Headlined Editorials entitled :- " Keep the Canadian Youth at home," and the necessity for keeping them is stressed for the development of that Dominion ; and while officials there estimate an immigrant an asset worth 1,500 dollars each, this should be taken into consideration what Ireland is losing. Consider what Ireland has lost by emigration ?

Those reasons prevail far more strongly in the case of Ireland - a nation just coming into its own.

Countries that are progressive as Germany and Italy, are very drastically enforcing this idea of keeping its man power within themselves ; but of course I do not advocate governmental interference with the freedom of the Irish people to go wheresoever they please; but the Government and other Organisations might educate the people on the folly of Emigration.

16/ 11/ 29

TAIBDHEARC NA GAILLIMHE.

Searching for a suitable play to produce at Taibdhearc na Gaillimhe (Galway Gaelic Theatre) Michael MacLiammhoir was in town a few weeks ago and solved the problem by writing one. The result is " Lulu " which no one who enjoys dramatic art or who wishes a laughter tonic - be he or she Irish-speaking or not should have missed seeing. " Lulu " and a '98 play by the late Father Tom Kelly, were produced at a matinee on Sunday, and Monday and Tuesday nights. The little theatre is beautifully lighted and heated and there is the added attraction of Miss May Brown's band. Those who may not like plays but who are fond of music should hear this altogether delightful orchestra. It is a well-balanced and harmonious combination and is a decided acquisition to the Irish theatre. The music was as refreshing and pleasant as anything to be found in metropolitan houses.

16/11/29

NOW IN FULL SWING

HIGGINS'S RECREATION HALL.

JACK HIGGINS wishes to announce to his numerous Friends and Patrons that he has now started his YOUNG MEN'S RECREATION HALL ON THE GALWAY ROAD, five minutes' walk from Town and three minutes' walk from the Railway Station. FIRST CLASS BILLIARD SALOON, GAMES, etc, Also attached

High-Class American Ladies' and Gents'

HAIR DRESSING SALOON.

Shingling, Waving, Dyeing, Tinting, etc., etc.
Expert Workmanship and Cleanness
a speciality

16 /11/29

CHRISTMAS IN ROME.

Private Pilgrimage under Priest Leadership
LEAVES LONDON DECEMBER 21st.
FARE 21 GUINEAS.
Also with Extension to the Riviera,
7 Guineas Extra.

OBERAMMERGAU, 1930

Send in your application for illustrated booklet giving full details of the Passion Play and how to get there.

CATHOLIC TRAVEL BUREAU,

19, James Street,

Phone : 98 Bank. Liverpool.

16/11/29

BASIC SLAG
"ANCHOR" BRAND
GROUND AT

SLIGO BASIC SLAG MILLS.

*45 per cent, 40 per cent & 35 per cent Total Phos
Delivery at any time during the Season at a moment's notice.
Packed in New Bags, Analysis Branded on Every Bag.
Uniform Quality Guaranteed.*

ARTHUR JACKSON & SON, Ltd., SLIGO.

16/11/29

TUAM TOWN COMMISSIONERS.

A special meeting, convened by requisition, was held on Wednesday evening to consider the advisability of setting or letting the two new houses left after last sale.

There were present—Messrs P.J.Byrne (presiding), W.Holian, S.Fahy, Pat Walsh, J.Moran, J.Byrne, M.W.Cahill, J.O'Toole, J.H.Corcoran, J.Burke.

After a long discussion, in which some of the members declared their opposition to setting any of the houses in the event of a failure to sell, it was decided unanimously to again invite tenders for purchase at a price not lower than £210 each, and that if there was no purchasers at that price the houses to be let.

URBAN POWERS.

A letter was read from Mr. Gallagher, Sec., Board of Health, declaring that his Board in applying to the L.G.D. for Urban Powers did so for the sole reason of being empowered to erect the latrine in Tuam, and that they had no intention of using such powers for any other purpose.

It was decided to accept the explanation, Mr. Gallagher's letter to be entered on the minutes, and to withdraw opposition to the Board of Health being granted Urban Powers under the circumstances.

MACHALE TERRACE AGAIN.

Mr. Hession, Town Surveyor, reported that some houses on MacHale Terrace were badly in need of repair, the down-pipes being broken and defective in some places. He also reported the sewerage there was again a source of trouble and that the man-holes should be sealed down.

Mr. Hession was ordered to prepare an estimate of the repairs required and the probable cost and to have same for next meeting.

16/11/29

THE COUNTY GALWAY HUNT.
(" The Blazers.")
NOVEMBER MEETS, 1929.

Monday,	18th	Cregg Castle.
Wednesday,	20th	Dunsandle.
Friday,	22nd	Castle Hackett.
Monday,	25th	Monivea.
Wednesday,	27th	Eastwell.
Friday,	29th	Tullira Castle.

At 11 o'clock.

BOWES DALY, M.F.H.

A GRAND OLD TUAM LADY.

The Hon. Miss Katherine Plunket, whose claim to be the oldest inhabitant in the British Isles is not contested, celebrated her 109th birthday at her home, Ballymascanlon House, Co Louth, on November 22.

Miss Plunkett was born in 1820 at Kilsaran, Co. Louth, when her father, who afterwards became the second Baron Plunket, was curate there. Her father, who was born in 1792, was consecrated Lord Bishop of Tuam, Killala and Achonry in 1839. She lived her early years in Tuam where her father was Bishop.

She was six years old when her grandfather, the first Lord Plunket, received his peerage upon his appointment as chief justice of the Court of Common Pleas. She has survived five holders of the barony, the present peer being the sixth Bishop Plunket.

Her grandfather on her mother's side was John Foster, M.P. for Fanevalley, Co. Louth, the last speaker of the Irish Parliament, before the Act of Union, after whom Foster Place in this town is called.

****

The late Father Gormally, P.P. of New Inn, in this county, laboured for forty-seven years in New Inn and Bullaun, and his death has caused universal regret amongst his parishioners. He was born in 1854. Having completed his secondary education, in 1875, passed on to Maynooth, where he was ordained in 1882. He then went as curate to New Inn, and as curate worked there for eleven years, afterwards in 1893 succeeding to the late Father Head as parish priest of New Inn and Bullaun. Father Gormally, therefore, spent the whole of his missionary life in one parish, a fact which is unique in the life of any secular priest.

****

The D'Olier Music Co. Dublin, have issued a 6d edition of "Let's Dance the Old Waltz," song-waltz, and "Kelly's Cow has got no Tail", Fox-trot Comedy song. Both numbers have been written, composed and sung by Patrick Kavanagh, "Dublin's Popular Entertainer," and owing to their popularity recently recorded by the Parlophone Co. The D'Olier Music Co. are open to consider songs, sketches, and plays by Irish Authors for publication.

THE MISSIONARY SISTERS OF THE HOLY GHOST want postulants for their Order in San Antonio, Texas.
Apply to:
Mother Francis Hughes, c/o Mrs. P. Pettit,
Ballygar, Roscommon.   23/11/29

EMPIRE THEATRE, GALWAY,
for Six Nights, Commencing Monday,
Nov. 25th, at 8.15.
Syncopation 100% All Talking and Singing Picture, featuring MORTON DOWNEY, Broadway's Silver Toned Tenor. Matinee, Saturday, 30th, 3.30. Seats booked by letter enclosing postal order.
Prices — 2/4; 1/10; 1/3.
23/11/29

TUAM MARKETS.

Hay	— 3s 6d to 4s 3d per cwt
Straw, wheaten	— 4s 0d per cwt
Oaten	— 3s 6d per cwt
Oats	— 1s to 1s 1d per st.
Potatoes	— 6d to 7d per stone
Turnips	— 1s 6d per cwt
Geese	— 3s 6d to 4s 6d each
Turkeys	— 1s per lb
Pigs	— 60s per cwt l.w.
Bonhams	— 60s to 67s
Wool	— 1s 4d per lb

23/11/29

CONNRADH NA GAEDHILGE.

At a meeting of Tuam Feis Committee held in the Library on Tuesday night, P.Breathnach, vice-chairman, presiding.

The following were present—M.O'Conaill, O.S., cisteoir; Seamus O'Maoldhomhnaigh, O.S.; P. O'Puirséill, O.S.; Tadh De Bri, O.S.; P.Grealish, Seán O nAthchair, Pádraig O'Máille, Runaidh.

It was decided to start the work of Feis 1930 immediately, for which a general meeting will be held in the Town Hall on Sunday, 8th December, at 4 o'clock.

There will be a Ceilidh Mór in the Town Hall that night from 8—12 at which the delegates will attend. Some of the best known artistes in Connacht will also be present—Runaidhe.

Beidh Eire fós ag Cáit Ni Dhuibhir.
30/11/29

GALWAY'S FIRST "TALKIE."

If all the "talkies" booked for the Empire Theatre, Galway, are shown with the same clarity and synchronisation as "Syncopation" was shown last week, the management need have no qualms about the success of their enterprise in being the first to have talkie apparatus installed in any theatre in the west.

Usually when the talkies are being shown on a newly installed apparatus there are several hitches, but "Syncopation" was as perfect in reproduction at the Empire as any apparatus yet devised could make it.   30/11/29

NEXT FIRST FRIDAY
HOLY MASS WILL BE OFFERED FOR YOU
ON THE TOMB OF OUR LORD JESUS CHRIST AT JERUSALEM
ON THE ALTAR ON MOUNT CALVARY THAT STANDS WHERE JESUS WAS NAILED TO THE CROSS.
IN THE GARDEN OF GETHSEMANE WHERE HE LAY IN HIS AGONY.
ON THE ALTAR AT PARAY-LE-MONIAL, WHERE THE SACRED HEART APPEARED TO ST. MARGARET MARY.

Holy Mass Will Also Be Offered For You

In the Stable at Bethlehem on 25th of each month.
On the Tomb of Pope Pius X., St Peter's, Rome, on the 20th of each month.
On the Tomb of St. Peter, Rome, on the 29th of each month.
On the Incorrupt Body of St. John Baptist Vianney, the Cure of Ars, at Ars, France, the 3rd of each month by the present Cure of Ars.

Who help by NO MATTER HOW SMALL AN ALMS, the REV. FATHER MARTIN POWER, P.P., BIRCHES HEAD, STOKE-ON-TRENT, to clear the heavy debt off the new Catholic Church which has been opened in the parish of poor Irish miners -Irish by birth or descent - owing to the fewness of their numbers and their poverty are unable to undertake the onerous task themselves. Having hitherto nobly responded to our Appeal and thereby enabled us to build this beautiful home for Jesus in the Blessed Sacrament, we continue to Appeal to your generosity to help us to remove this heavy burden of debt and have our Church consecrated.

Father Power has arranged to have all the above Masses said monthly
FOR THE INTENTIONS AND DECEASED FRIENDS OF ALL HIS BENEFACTORS
whose donations will be most thankfully received and acknowledged by
THE REV. FATHER MARTIN POWER, P.P., BIRCHES HEAD, STOKE-ON -TRENT, ENGLAND.
A MEDAL, which has been placed on Calvary, the Holy Sepulchre, and all the Holy places in Palestine will be sent to each subscriber.

30/11/29

40 MASSES
a Year for Ever

will be offered for all who send donations to **REV. WM. BROWNE, ST JOSEPH'S BURSLEM, STOKE-ON-TRENT,** towards paying off the heavy debt on his New Church. Give your departed ones a share in these *perpetual* Masses by sending a small offering on their behalf. Registration card and coloured picture of Pius X sent by return. Also six novenas of Masses each year. Send your intentions with small offering.

30/11/29

EMPIRE THEATRE, GALWAY.
Week Commencing Dec. 2nd,
at 8.15,
THE SINGING FOOL,
Starring Al Jolson.
Hear him sing
"SONNY BOY,"
"THERE'S AN ANCHOR ROUND MY SHOULDER,"
And
"IT ALL DEPENDS ON YOU."
Matinee, Thursday, 4 p.m., and Saturday, 3.30.
Prices — 2/4; 1/10; 1/3; 8d

30/11/29

The Tuam Herald.
Saturday, November 30, 1929.

CITY AND COUNTRY.

The citizens of Dublin are rightly complaining of the heavy tax before them in the coming year to meet the demands of the State authorities to provide unemployment benefit for the growing population of workless in the capital. The normal population there is increasing by leaps and bounds and this influx is due to the crowds denied or prevented from emigrating to America who are coming up from rural parts. This exodus is becoming a serious matter economically, as the rural parts are fast denuding themselves of sufficient labour to adequately run the country's chief industry, that is its agriculture. In consequence of this deplorable depletion the farmers are finding it impossible to get young persons, even of their own families, to turn to the ways of industry at home. They prefer, with the natural inclination of the Irish man or woman, pleasant if precarious employment in the city, to steady, proper, useful and healthy work on the land. The country is accordingly suffering and must suffer more materially from the drain on its labour resources and the only present or probable advantage the city can gain by it is the addition to the burdens of its taxpayers. So great is this invasion of Dublin that its population is being appreciably increased by thousands and bids fair to run to figures which will be a quarter in advance of what, in ordinary and normal circumstances, it should reasonably be or expect to be. Houses of a kind are being built by the thousand in every quarter and still the cry is for more such. We trust these new dwellings will prove durable and lasting, for constructed as they seem to be they don't so look, so that the occupants who in nearly every case have purchased them must out here find them a serious loss to keep in repair once deterioration and decay set in. Built as they are, mostly in a hurry, with no proper provision for the ordinary wear and tear, in some cases with no adequate scientific supervision and constructed of materials, in the main wasteful, unsuitable and not lasting, their chances of being long habitable are not very bright. However, that is only a side issue and a future source of public trouble. The present and pressing matter of complaint and consideration is the serious growing increase of the civic population of Dublin which, in the conditions of business and employment at present, or as in the near future it is likely to be, must be burdens upon the rates and perpetual objects for unemployment benefits which now add so considerably to the rates as to become a very serious problem and indirectly in itself a cause of producing more unemployment and driving many householders out of their employment. It is hard to say what can be done to remedy this alarming state of things. As at present measured it will, it is calculated, mean an addition to the already high city rates of 5s to 6s in the pound, a heavy burden considering the present high rates. The granting of the demoralising dole should be controlled more strictly and the circumstances and conditions of every member of a family relieved taken into consideration. There are cases, we hear, where the wife of a man in the present receipt of hundreds a year, because she happened to lose a casual job, gets unemployment herself, and other cases where members of the family, being employed, some one or two without employment, get benefits although their aggregate earnings, all living together, come to hundreds a year. Dublin, like all cities, has its attractions, its dissipations, its cinemas and its dances alone of themselves bring girls and boys up from the country. The girls won't go to any work such as domestic service and so relieve a want, but if they cannot get work as typists they go into the tobacco works, or in some such daily employment, or they do nothing but idle. A ring fence cannot be drawn around the city and no person allowed in, as in the case of entry now to the United States, but those sure of employment and capable of work, but it is hard on Dublin to have to suffer from this invasion from the country and harder on the rural parts of the country to lose the labour they have and which could be more profitably employed on the land and so help to develop the resources of a country which is so capable of development but which so far is behind its possible development.

GRANTS FOR HOUSES

In helping to build houses of the value of £180 in the Gaeltacht region, which of course includes these parts, the Government is going to give a free grant of £80 which is a considerable aid. We hope that no house will be allowed to be erected which is not on an improved plan and to save expense the Government should provide free plans and specifications of a common style applicable to all such construction. No house should be built without at least a half an acre of land included and every house should have a garden or plot available for crops and the occupant should be helped to grow fruit trees and obliged to keep them protected. No house should be given to a single man, as the country is overburdened with bachelors who are, generally speaking, the most useless sort of citizen.

YOUNG TRAVELLER.

The youngest traveller is probably Joseph W. Hughes, a two-month old baby, who travelled unaccompanied to his grandmother in Ballyglunin from New York on board the s.s. Karlsruhe. Miss McMorrow, the matron of the s.s. Karlsruhe, took care of the baby during the voyage to Galway.

30/11/29

Come and See Our New Stocks of
WOLSEY

We recommend to our customers only those articles which we know will give every satisfaction, and we, therefore, have every confidence in recommending WOLSEY UNDERWEAR and HOSIERY, including Men's Cardigans and Pullovers; Ladies Winter Hose, Gaiters, Golf Sox; Children's Jerseys, etc.

WINTER OVERCOATS

We are offering Wonderful Value in Men's and Boy's Winter Overcoats and Ready-to Wear Suits. Agents for the Famous

"Sandom" Style Coats.

MENS OUTFITTING

We have a complete range of HATS, CAPS, SHIRTS, TIES, etc.
HOUSEHOLD GOODS—Blankets, Quilts, Rugs, Flannels, Linens, etc.
SUITING AND SERGES IN GREAT VARIETY.

WINTER FOOTWEAR.

Offered at Bargain Prices, every pair guaranteed to give satisfaction. Agents for "Moccasin," "C.R." "Gipsy Queen," "Holyrood" brands of ladies shoes.
Latest in colour, Latest in Style, and the Last Word in Foot Comfort.

XMAS GOODS — UMBRELLAS, GLOVES, DRESSING CASES, HANDKERCHIEFS, BRUSH SETS, SLIPPERS, ETC.

WE have a varied Selection of all the above, and
We cordially Invite You to Come and See Them.

J. CUMMINS,
Bishop Street, Tuam.

7/12/29

THE SCHOOLS IN TUAM A HUNDRED YEARS AGO.

We are indebted to the learned labours and researches of Mr. O'Duffy, a Dublin resident but a native of Co. Roscommon, for the following interesting details and particulars of the good old schools and schoolmasters and the places where the schools were held in Tuam one hundred and five years ago. These were the "so called hedge schools" which it was the fashion to disparage, depreciate and so describe, but they were excellent means of education and whatever they taught they certainly taught well and thoroughly and no boy or girl leaving them ever failed in being well acquainted with the essentials and fundamentals of education—a proficiency in the three R's—Reading, Writing and Arithmetic. They wrote a good hand, they could make up any sum in addition or in any branch of lower mathematics and they knew English grammer well and they could write English better than the boys and girls of the present day with the majority of whom, we regret to say, handwriting and the other necessary knowledge seems to be becoming a lost art. Later on we had in Tuam the splendid ladies' school on the Circular Road, where the Post Office now stands, taught by the two Misses Gannon—Miss Bedelia and Julia—and as we all know no boy or girl (and they taught boys in their early age) who were under them ever failed to write a good hand and to behave themselves properly for these good ladies, above all other things, inculcated the necessity of good behaviour or "deportment" as it was then called. The old schools and the old teachers of them in Tuam should never be forgotten, and with extreme pleasure we do our part in printing their names and so keeping alive their cherished memories. God be with them and the good old times is the constant and sincere aspiration of thousands to-day. These good men and women were as follows:—

1823-1824.

Dublin Road—Beech Sandford and Alice Sandford, Protestants, Pay School.
Bishop Street—Terence Foley and Margaret Foley, Protestants, Free School.
St. Jarlaght's Seminary, Bishop Street—
Mr. Thos. Feeney, Principal, (R.C.)
Mr. John Harris, Professor, ,,
Mr. Thos. Kielty, ,, ,,
Mr. John Morris, ,, ,,
Mr. M. Magee ,, ,, Pay School.
Galway Road—John Donnellan, R.C. Free School.
Julia Jackson, R.C. Free School.
Tullynadaly Road—Francis Slattery, R.C. Pay School.
Vicar St.—Nicholas Lynatt and Eliza Lynatt, R.C. Pay School.
The Mall—Chas. O'Callaghan and Cathe. O'Callaghan, R.C. Pay School. Patk. and B. Murray, R.C. Pay School.
Frasers Lane—F. Ryan and Isabella Ryan, R.C. Pay School.
Bishop Street—Widow Flinn, R.C. Pay School.
Carricreen—Patrick Hopkins, R.C. Pay School.
Carrareagh-beg—James Mc Donnell, R.C. Pay School. 7/12/29

A NEW FAVOUR FOR THE M.D.D.C.

MESSAGE FROM HIS HOLINESS.

RENEWAL OF THE APOSTOLIC BLESSING.

The following gracious reply has been forwarded by His Eminence Cardinal Gaspari, Secretary of State to His Holiness, to the members of the Irish Modest Dress and Deportment Crusade, Mary Immaculate Training College, Limerick, in acknowledgement of the congratulations offered by them to the Holy Father on His Golden Jubilee :-

Dal Vaticano, November 11th, 1929.
Secretario di Stato
di Sua Santita.

Dear Members—The Holy Father was very grateful for your expression of homage and devotion and of congratulations on his Golden Jubilee. His Holiness was pleased to learn of the remarkable increase in membership in the Irish Modest Dress and Deportment Crusade.

His Holiness gladly renews the Apostolic Blessing to all members of the Staff and the Students of Mary Immaculate Training College and to all those who are members of the campaign for the preservation of Christian modesty.

Very Sincerely yours in Christ,
P. CARD. GASPARI (Signed).
To the Members of the
Irish Modest Dress and Deportment Crusade,
Mary Immaculate Training College, Limerick.

All those who wish to become members of the above Crusade and thereby share in the Apostolic Blessing, are requested to communicate with the Registrar of the M.D.D.C., Mary Immaculate Training College, Limerick.

The purpose of the Crusade is to combat the rapidly increasing demoralisation resulting from immodest dress and deportment. 7/12/29

DEANTA I NGAILLIMH.

Galway Woollen Manufacturing Co.

*Save 25 per cent Duty
By Purchasing Direct from the Manufacturers*

YOUR TWEEDS RUGS BLANKETS FLANNELS, FRIEZES &c,
At THE WOOLLEN DEPOT,
39 Shop St., Galway.

Suits to Measure £4 to £5 15 0.
Clean Washed Wool taken in Exchange
or Part Payment.

Woollen Depot Galway.
7/12/29

EMPIRE THEATRE, GALWAY.

Monday, Tuesday, Wednesday,
Dec. 9th, 10th, 11th,
WILLIAM BOYD
The Scathernech.
Talking-Singing Picture.

Thursday, Friday, Saturday,
MOLLY AND ME,
Talking-Singing Picture.

PIGS put on flesh at an amazing speed when given **Wilson's Canadian Pig Powders**

Trade Mark
The Pig That Went to Market

Wonderful for every ailment.
6d, 1/-, 2/9, 8/- packets & 21/- tins.
Agents Everywhere.
STEPHEN WILSON,
7 & 8 BACHELOR'S WALK, DUBLIN
7/12/29

TUAM XMAS FAIRS,
will be held on
Monday, December 16th---Pigs,
Tuesday, Dec., 17th---Sheep and Cattle.

This being one of the oldest Fairs in the West, it is expected there will be a record supply of stock.

Buyers will be numerous from Cross-Channel and other places, so Farmers bring in your Stock to this Fair in large numbers and don't disappoint the Buyers as you did the November Sheep and Cattle Fair.

By order Tuam Town Commissioners,
JOHN P. WHYTE, Town Clerk.

Teachers and other young ladies desirous of consecrating their lives to the glorious work of teaching the little "Black Lambs" of "Christ the King" in the island of Jamaica are invited to communicate with Mother M. Magdalen, who is staying for a few days at Sisters of Charity, Seville Place, Dublin. 7/12/29

As a milk substitute for calf rearing, there is nothing so reliable and effective as LACTIFER, Thorley's Cooked Calf Meal.-- Sold by agents everywhere, or direct from Joseph Thorley, Ltd., King's Cross, London, N.1.

TUAM 50 YEARS AGO.

Fifty years ago there were many living in Tuam who remembered '98 and the coming of the French. Dr. MacHale, as a boy, hid from them as they passed his father's house at Tubbernavin, concealing himself in a potato dyke. In the English Army were the Fraser Fencibles (the last regiment to retreat after the Battle of Castlebar). They were embodied at Inverness by the veteran Colonel Fraser of Belladrum, and they soon went to Ireland. The regimental uniform was the Highland garb, with belted plaid and philabeg of the red Fraser tartan. The name of "Fraser" was borne by 300 of the recruits from Stratherrick and Aird, and the rest were also Highlanders—except 48 old soldiers who were Lowlanders and English and Irish. The Frasers were small men, well made and active, and they were already marchers, never leaving a straggler on the quickest and longest march. They were self-respecting, obedient and trusty, well-conducted and incorruptible. The regiment—then commanded by Fraser of Lovat—was stationed in Tuam when the French landed at Killala, and a detachment marched to Castlebar two days before the battle. The Fraser Fencibles and the Galway Yeomanry formed the second line of the army that met the 900 blue-coated veterans of France on the hills on the morning of the 27th of August, 1798. When the redcoats fell back, a few of the Frasers and Kilkenny Militia—under fire from the houses and roads—held the bridge of Castlebar against the charging French Hussars until half of the defenders fell. The British Army, leaving 53 dead, retired thirty miles and reached Tuam on that night. A Fraser Highlander was the sentry at Castlebar Prison, and his retreating comrades could not persuade him to quit his post on a little flight of steps. When the enemy came, he loaded and fired his musket five times, killing a French soldier with every shot. Then they rushed on him, beat out his brains, and threw him down the steps, with the sentry-box on his body. A week later the Frasers returned to Castlebar, which, after another week, they defended against the gallant Mayo Gaels. On the 23rd September the Frasers and Mayomen met in the last battle on the seashore at Killala.

There were, however, some men in Tuam who went down to Killala to join the French and remained with them until they surrendered at Ballinamuck to superior forces, and one of those was Hugh Delap who died, and for years before he died was Workhouse porter. His sons went to Brisbane and settled there, and none of the name is now to be found in these parts. There were Frasers here, and a lane called Frasers lane, but we do not think it was so called after the Fraser Fencibles, not that those of the name had anything to say to the soldiers who fought against the native Irish in 1798. One William Fraser lived over at Cloontoo and his daughter married John Hopkins. He was a respectable, kindly old man, and the last of his race and name in Tuam, but Fraser's Lane remains a relic of the old days.

A correspondent writes :- Mention in the Press of the Governor-General's visit to Galway Gaelic Theatre brings to mind the memory of the late Professor Tom O' Kelly, of Galway University College, who was the author of the Irish play, "The Harvest," produced before His Excellency. Father Tom O' Kelly was Professor of Education in Galway College. In very truth an O' Kelly of "Hymaine, " he wrote, with great fertility, poetry, newspaper articles, books, plays. and an opera or two, all in Gaelic, and the offering of his deep love for the language to whose rescue and enthronement he devoted the intellectual resources of his gifted and active life. It is sad that Father O' Kelly should not have lived to see his play produced under such auspices in the Galway which he loved; it is, perhaps, sadder still to think on his lonely death at Nice a few years back, where he contracted pneumonia while on holiday. Buried as an unknown, he was subsequently identified, disinterred, and reburied in Cockade Cemetery, Nice, where his grave is marked by a Celtic cross. It is interesting to note that among his effects, which fortunately were taken possession of by the British Consul at Nice, was a bulky manuscript, described by the officials as "A book in an unknown language." It was sent home by the Consul and proved to be the MS. of a valuable Gaelic compilation, "The Music of the Isles," which is now in the press of the National Manuscripts Commission in Hume Street. Father O' Kelly was the first librettist of an Irish opera, viz.---"Eithne," and of "Sruth na Maoile," which was produced at the Dublin Theatre Royal a few years ago. He also wrote variously in collaboration with Mr. W.B. Yeats, Mr. Perceval Graves, Professor Robert O' Dwyer and others.

Kensal Green, in London, where T.P.O' Connor was buried, is the last resting place of many Irish celebrities. Samuel Lover, poet, painter, novelist and composer, who died in 1869, is there interred. Catherine Hayes, Ireland's "Queen of Song, " whose death ocurred in 1861, was buried there. Ireland's two greatest composers, William Vincent Wallace and Michael William Balfe, who died, respectively, in 1865 and 1870, lie side by side in Kensal Green. Two of Ireland's eminent painters, William Mulready, R.A., whose demise took place in 1863, and Daniel Maclise, R.A., who passed away in 1870, also rest there, the latter with his father, mother brothers and sisters. Feargus O'Connor the Chartist leader, who died in 1853, and John Francis O'Donnell, one of Ireland's greatest poets of the second half of the 19th century, who died in 1874, likewise sleep in Kensal Green.   7/12/29

THE HOUSE FOR VALUE.

WE
Extend to You a Cordial Invitation to Visit Our Stores and See
OUR XMAS DISPLAY of

Fruit   Toys   Presents

Groceries, etc

Irish and Imported Bacon, Hams, Gammons. Currants, Muscatels, Sultanas, Lemon, Orange and Citron Peels, Almonds, Nutmeg, Cinnamon, Spice, Syrup, Jams, Jellies, Custards, Blanc Manges, Jacob's Biscuits, My Lady Fruits, Xmas Crackers, Xmas Stockings, Boxes of Chocolates in great variety.

Christmas Decorations.

Tensil Stars, Strings, Balls, Paper etc. Lanterns, Cribs, Wall Pockets, Flowers, Crepe Paper, Paper Bats.

China.

Tea Sets in various designs and shapes from 7/6 to 32/6. Fancy Teapots, Vases, Coffee Sets, Fruit Sets, etc.

Electroplated Goods.

Jam Dishes, Cruets, Butter Coolers, Sweet Dishes, Cake Dishes, Biscuit Barrels, Sandwich Sets, Sugar Sifters, Espergnes, Souvenir Spoons, Toast Racks, Cake Stands, Cigarette Cases, Money Boxes, Silver Neck Chains, Claddagh Rings.

Christmas Presents.

Manicure Sets from 1/3 to 15/-. Leather Dressing Cases from 8/6 to 35/-. Brush and Comb Sets from 2/6 to 15/- each. Shaving Sets from 4/6 to 15/- each. Leather Pocket Wallets from 1/- to 12/6 each. Ladies Hand Bags from 1/- to 10/6 each. Prayer Books from 6d to 10/6 each. Mother o' Pearl Beads, 1/3 to 8/6 each.

Toys.

Dolls from 6d to 8/6 each, Dolls Prams 2/- to 8/6 each, Plush Teddy Bears, Dogs and Cats 6d to 8/6, Trains on Tracks from 1/- to 8/6, Scooters 1/6 each, Violins complete with bow 2/- and 4/6 each, Melodeons, 10 keys 1 stop, 4/6 each, Mouthorgans from 3d to 4/6 each. Wood Horses 1d to 2/- each, Horses and Cars 6d to 1/- each, Dolls Tea Sets 6d, 1/-, 2/6 each, Assorted Games, Building Blocks, Carpenters Sets, and Toy Reins 6d to 1/-, Cap Guns and Water Pistols from 1d to 1/-, Carded Guns from 6d to 2/-.

ASSORTED TIN TOYS.

Motor Cars, Engines, Post Vans, Lorries, Aeroplanes, Trains, at 1d, 2d, 3d and 4d each.

MECHANICAL TOYS.

Saloon Motors, Fire Engines, Lorries, Steamboats, Furniture Vans, Racing Cars, etc., 6d and 1/- each, Mechanical Toys 2/- each, Comic Figures, "Busy Lizzie," "Stepping Harry," "Barney Google," and Sparking Plug Aeroplanes, Steamroller, Tin Buses, Motor Lorries, Vans, 16" long, 3/- each, Kay Don Racing Car 2/6 each, Saloon Cars with electric head lights 3/9 each, the Powerful Latunka, 2/-, miniature Rolls Royce 12" 3/6 each, Whistling Engines 2/- each, tip off Motor Lorry 2/9 each, Celluloid Dolls, Bugles, etc.

Cutlery.

SPECIAL LINE.—

Half dozen Stainless Knives (Sheffield) dessert size, Xyto handle in rack box at 5/11 per box. Half doz. Stainless Table Knives (Sheffield) Xyto handle in rack box at 7/6 per box. Half dozen Barber's Stainless Knives, mirror polished, dessert size, in rack box at 9/- per box. 6 E.P.N.S. Teaspoons and Tongs, in Plush Case, at 5/-. Half dozen Stainless Knives and Forks, in Plush Case, at 21/-. Also Bread Knives and Carvers.

We have the largest selection of Toys in the West. And our prices range from a penny to a pound.

You are welcome to stroll through our Stores; no "pressing to purchase" except the silent appeal of the goods themselves.

Your complete satisfaction is a matter of personal importance to us.

Note Address :—

J.J. WALDRON & CO.

WHOLESALE   CENTRAL STORES   GROCERY
&   PROVISIONS
RETAIL   TUAM   DYES
EARTHENWARE
CHINA
GLASS
HARDWARE
&
FANCIES

14/12/29

CATHOLIC BOY SCOUTS OF IRELAND

Movement Inaugurated in Tuam.

A Branch of above was organised in Tuam under the care of the St. Vincent De Paul Society, six of whom form the Troop Committee.

It is well in this first report to explain to your readers what this great Association stands for and to give some of the rules.

The Association has been approved of by the Cardinal, Archbishops, and Bishops of Ireland.

The aims of the Association are to promote the methods, principles, and exercises of scouting among the Catholic boys of Ireland; to apply these methods, principles and exercises according to Catholic ideal and teaching, so as to cultivate, train, develop and strengthen all the faculties, physical, intellectual, moral and religious which constitute in the boy nature and human dignity to form him to be true to himself and of service to others. In a higher conception to elevate his present life and thus prepare him for the life to come.

The 3 principles are;
1. A Scout glories in his Holy Faith.
2. A Scout loves his country.
3. The duty of a Scout begins in his own home.

POLICY.

[A] The Association is not to take the place of the Religious Sodalities, or in any way to be detrimental to their success but shall encourage boys to become Members of such Organisations as a means of becoming better Scouts.

[B] The Association is strictly non-political. Its members are forbidden to take part in any political activity when in uniform. Political discussions are forbidden during any scout exercises.

[C] The Association is strictly a Civil Oranisation, with no military tendencies whatever. Drill is but a means for attaining physical development and discipline, not an end in itself.

MEMBERSHIP.

The Association is composed of Active and Honorary Members;

[A] Active Members are;- the Members of the National Council, Diocesan and District Councils and Troop Committees, the Chief Scouts, Chaplains, Commissioners, Scout Masters, Instructors and Scouts of all grades and categories.

[B] Honorary Members

[a]. Benefactors - those donating an annual subscription of £10.

[b]. Donors - those donating an annual subscription of £5.

[c] Participants - those donating an annual subscription of £2.

[d] Adherents - those donating an annual subscription of £1.

The National Council reserve the right to refuse donations for a reason.

SCOUT RANKS.

Catholic Boy Scouts of Ireland are organised into [a] Scouts; [b] Knights Errant, all of which are grouped into Patrols and Troops.

A Patrol consists of not more than 8 boys, which include a Patrol Leader and an Assistant Patrol Leader.

A Troop consists of not more than Ten Patrols with a Scout Master and at least One Assistant Scout Master.

There are three classes of Scouts -

[1] Rawley Scouts; [2] 2nd Class Scouts; [3] 1st Class Scouts.

RAWLEY SCOUTS.

The requirements necessary to become a Rawley Scout are:-

A boy must be at least 11 years of age on day of admission. A request for admission must be made in writing to the Troop Chaplain or Scout Master by the boy and endorsed by his parents or guardian. He must be recommended by 2 boys of the Troop.

After admission he must then study and has to do an examination before allowed to wear his uniform.

The 1st Troop have taken the name of the Patron Saint of Tuam, " St. Jarlath," and their colours are purple, as they are to be known as "The Archbishop's Own."

The 1st Patrol are known as " The Lion Patrol," with shoulder colours of Yellow and Scarlet.

The 1st Investiture Ceremony of St. Jarlath's Troop took place in the Town Hall on Sunday evening, December 8th. This Feast Day is also one of the principal Feast Days of the Association and each scout is to receive Holy Communion on that day.

The ceremony started at 6 o'clock. Very Rev. Father Kelly, Adm., Troop Chaplain, officiated.

Mr. R. K. Browne, Chairman, Troop Committee, presided, assisted by Messrs. Byrne, Hehir, Madden and Cummins, members of the Troop Committee.

The Rev. Chaplain first presented a Scout Badge to each member of the Committee.

Mr John Fahy was then called and after receiving the Chaplain's Blessing recited the Scout Promise. Then the Rev. Chaplain presented him with with his Commission as Scout Master, 1st Tuam Troop.

The candidates were then presented, and having answered the questions of the Rev. Chaplain and Chairman, each came separately to receive the Chaplain's Blessing. Then after having recited the Scout Promise, the candidate was invested with the Rawley

Badge by the Chaplain, then the neckerchief, hat and staff.

The last being invested, the Chairman addressing them said:- " By virtue of the power vested in me by the National Council Catholic Boy Scouts of Ireland I now declare you Rawley Scouts."

They were then given over to the charge of their Scout Master, who shook hands with each, giving the Scout Salutations— Our Guardian Angels, the Scout answering— May they guide us both.

The Rev. Chaplain then addressed the Scouts and congratulated them and urged them to be good Scouts and they would be good Catholics and good Irishmen.

The Chairman then read the following message from the Chief Scout, Mr. John O'Neill, Dublin :-

Please tell the Scout Master and each Scout how glad I am to welcome them into the C.B.S.I., and my hope they will find considerable pleasure in carrying out the Scout Law. My message to them is : " The greatest pleasure they will find in life is in the knowledge of that in their work they are helping others."

After this all in the Hall stood and joined in the singing of " Faith of Our Fathers."

The Scouts marched to the Cathedral for Devotions, and a beautiful sermon, most appropriate to the occasion, was delivered by the Rev. Fr. Jennings, St. Jarlath's College—" Mary Immaculate."

Benediction was afterwards given by the Troop Chaplain, the Scouts joining with the choir in the singing of the Benediction Service.

Before leaving the Cathedral the Scouts sang "Faith of Our Fathers."

They went to St. Vincent's Hall after Devotions where the Chaplain and members entertained them to tea.

This being over there was a little concert, all doing their bit. At 9.50 all joined in the singing of the Scout Anthem, "My Land," when all went home at 10 o'c.

The members of the Invested Scouts are— Vincent Stockwell, Frank Egan, Patrick Costelloe, Michael Bray, Gus Stockwell, Jack White, Jarlath Burke, Raymond Canney, Joseph McElgunn, Jack Garvey.

The Troop Chaplain and Committee are very grateful to Mr. Garvey, The Mall, for the use of the Hall for the occasion.

TOWN TENANTS ASSOCIATION.

A meeting to organise the Town Tenants Association will be held in the Town Hall on to-morrow (Sunday, 15th) at 12.30. All interested in the movement are invited to attend.   14/12/29

Town Commissioner's Building Scheme Held Up.

The scheme whereby the Tuam Town Commissioners hoped to complete a second street of houses by the erection of 7 more in addition to the 15 already completed on the Church Fields, has been held up by the action of the Local Government Department.

A letter was received during the week refusing their sanction to the proposed extension of building in that locality on the grounds that the place is unsanitary and unsuitable for building, and that the amount proposed to be paid (£90) for the site was too high.

Following the receipt of the letter a special meeting of the Commissioners was held on Monday evening when there were present—Messrs. P.J.Byrne (Chairman), presiding ; W.Holian, Pat Walsh, John Byrne, James Moran, John O'Toole, M.W.Cahill, P.Gibbons, J.Burke.

The letter from the L.G.D. having been fully considered, it was decided to draft a reply stating that the new site was much superior in position and elevation to that on which the 15 houses had been already erected and which had been approved by the L.G.D. Inspector, and that the Board did not consider the amount for the new site too high considering its advantageous position, and as to the place being unsanitary the Board were of opinion that the site was not more or less unsanitary than any other part of this town of Tuam would be until such time as a proper scheme of sewerage was constructed to meet the wants of its growing population. The L.G.D. was asked to withdraw its interdict and allow the Board to proceed with its building programme and so improve that portion of the town.   14/12/29

The Christmas Fowl Market.

There was a large display of fowl—geese and turkeys—exposed for sale on Saturday last. So large indeed was the display that the Turf Shambles being crowded there was an overflow market stretching along Vicar Street on the one side and on to Dublin Road and the Market Square on the other. But prices were very low, and buying so slack that a number of turkeys were carried home unsold. First class turkeys could be had for 6 1/2d and 7d per lb. The buying for geese was a little more spirited and prices ruled fair enough, some fetching as much as 7s and 7/6 each. At Wednesday's market there was a smaller supply, but a welcome increase in the price for turkeys, the price varying from 8d to 9d per lb.

21/12/29

Tuam Harrier Club

Up to the present Tuam Harrier Club has not been formed for the Cross Country events which will be coming off early in the New Year. As already noticed in the public Press Tuam is honoured this season with two fixtures. The first will be held in Parkmore on Sunday, January 19th, under the auspices of the Galway Co. Board N.A.C.A., to run the inter-Club contest of the County.

This will be held for the purpose of selecting a team to represent the County in the Healy Cup Competition. This contest which is carried out by the Connaught Council N.A.C.A. will be held on Sunday, February 9th, and the honour has also been given to Tuam by having the event in Parkmore.

With these two events coming off Tuam intends to place a team on the field, and a start will be made on Sunday next, December 22nd, with a cross-country practice.

The meet will be at Mr. Eddie Cooley's Garage, Tullinadaly Road, where all members and intending members are requested to turn out at 12 o'clock.

21/12/29

Russian Ruffianism.

There is no doubt but that the ruffian hand at present unhappily in control in Red Russia means, if it can, to exterminate all visible signs and evidence of Christianity. They are tearing down crosses and turning churches into cinemas and murdering priests. An excellent agitation has been started in England under the aegis of "The Morning Post" and Lord Glasgow to prevent the British Government from entering into diplomatic relations with these savages and even trading with them. Famine is impending and all the godless want is to attract English money to enable them to continue their cursed campaign against Christianity. But in vain. The gates of Hell shall not prevail. This sort of thing is an old game and was tried by abler men and better brains than the craven caitiff crew of degenerates who are now attempting the task which presumptious man in his little feebleness so often in vain has tried. All credit to the "Morning Post" and to the organisation under Lord Glasgow and may they succeed.

Bolshevism's outrageous persecution of religion already has been reported from the many sections of Russia, but information which has just come to hand from an absolutely authentic source shows clearly that the desperate measures being taken against all Christian Churches in Soviet Armenia equal, if they do not surpass in cruelty, the outrages elsewhere.

In Soviet Armenia churches have been desecrated; priests have been whipped, publicly humiliated and reviled, and in at least one case buried alive. The residences of Apostolic Administrators have been broken into and papers confiscated, translated and published in an effort to embarrass priests. Mock processions have been staged with hoodlums dressed as Jesuits and Dominicans, and others wearing sacred church vestments. Extreme measures have been resorted to to break down the children's faith in Christ and to build up a reverence for Lenin.

My information has come from a distinguished Armenian, a dealer in precious stones, a man of culture, whose word is absolutely dependable. Conditions in the Soviet States, which threaten not only my informant, but also the members of his family with dire and barbarous punishment if his name became known, compel me to keep his identity a secret. I have been able, however, to corroborate the entire truth of his statements with the aid of documents.

"My profession," said my informant, "takes me on long journeys all over my native country, from the Caucasus to far beyond Erzerum. In this way, I have been, in the last few years, the witness of a history of suffering which for my whole nation has been written in blood and tears. The lot of the Christian Churches, the Orthodox, to which I belong, and the Armenian united with Rome, as well as the two Georgian Churches, are equally unfortunate. The lot is made bright only by the many confessors and martyrs who sacrificed liberty and their lives for their faithfulness in Christ.

CHURCHES IN RUINS.

"The Orthodox Armenian and the Georgian Churches are to-day heaps of ruins. All the once beautiful domed churches erected for soldiers in the gardens of the various garrison towns have been transformed into clubs and places of amusement. The crosses fixed in the domes have been replaced by stars and these are illuminated at night, lest the triumph of impiety be forgotten even then. Inside the churches the heads, hands and feet of saints in mural paintings, which in many cases, were very valuable, have been cut off and obscene illustrations and descriptions put on.

"In the time of Diocletian no more human beings fell before the executioner than during the Russian religious persecutions. Archbishop Gjud, one of the most eminent linguists in Armenia, was dragged from the Edmiadsin Monastery at Erwian by the Cheka and put in prison. He was subjected to such cruel tortures there that when he was released some six months later he was mentally unbalanced and died a short time afterwards."

21/12/29

SANTA CLAUS

Invites You
to the Grand Array of Xmas Novelties now on view

AT THE ARCADE

There are Presents Suitable for every age & TASTE

FRIENDS AT HOME AND OVERSEAS

it is to your interest to visit our various
Departments and compare our prices
before purchasing elsewhere.

ARCADE DRAPERY CO.,

(Bulk Buyers Manufacturers' Samples)
(And Bankrupt Stocks.)

Shop St., Tuam

21/12/29

A Beautiful Crucifix

Much interest was created in Tuam when it became known that some anonymous donor had presented the Very Rev. Canon Walsh the new crucifix to be erected over the High Altar in the Cathedral. The crucifix has now been set up and has attracted a great deal of attention. It is of a type unusual in this country, but strictly in accordance with the rubrics of the church. Instead of standing on the altar in the ordinary way the crucifix is suspended by gilded chains from the canopy which is over the High Altar.

The crucifix is about 5 feet in length and is Gothic in style to accord with the architecture of the church and the altar; it is made of Austrian oak, covered and gilded and decorated in the mediaeval manner; the heraldic colours, puce, vermillion, azure, blue, gold, silver and a little black, being exclusively used. This heraldic combination of colours so usual in the churches of the middle ages is all too rarely seen at present in spite of the rich and pleasing effect it produces. The cross itself is of the Latin form, about 5 feet long and well proportioned; the figure of Our Lord is treated in more or less naturalistic colouring, the rich gold and silver of the cross providing an effective background. The four arms are terminated by panels of Gothic design, carved, decorated and gilded with the symbols of the Evangelists.

The crucifix, which was supplied by Messrs. Bull, Dublin, reflects great credit on the designer, Professor R.M.Butler, A.R.H.A., Dublin.

A Christmas Appeal

The following Christmas Appeal has been issued by St. Jarlath's Conference, Tuam, of St. Vincent De Paul Society :-

The Society again appeals to the generosity of its patrons for financial aid to alleviate the sufferings of the deserving poor of this district.

The prevailing condition of unemployment entails increased expenditure. Funds are urgently needed. It has been a severe drain on our resources to provide even the bare necessities of life for many. The winter so far has been severe, and the colder period has yet to come. We appeal for aid, however small, to help brighten the Christmas for God's Poor.

HON TREASURER.

21/12/29

AN ADVENT PASTORAL.

The Most Rev. Dr. Gilmartin, Archbishop of Tuam, in an Advent Pastoral to his people, says "Universe," dealt with the doctrine of the Immaculate Conception, the Feast Day of which on Sunday was noteworthy in all the dioceses in Ireland for an increased fervour of devotion and for the number of Holy Communions. His Grace said it is incumbent on all, priests, parents, guardians and writers, to leave nothing undone under new conditions and dangers to keep up the high standard of morality which is the greatest glory of this ancient Catholic nation. One of the most efficacious of means is devotion to the Blessed Mother of God which more than any other can be called an Irish national devotion. The dangers of bad books, indecent pictures, and suggestive conversation were pointed out. "We cannot," said his Grace, "keep our young people in glass houses, but parents and masters should see that those under them keep proper hours and should warn the innocent against the dangers that lurk in certain kinds of company keeping. The tone of our Irish newspapers is, on the whole, healthy, but unfortunately our people too often prefer foreign papers."

Irish human nature is at bottom, said the Archbishop, as weak as any other human nature. If historically we have a good moral character it is largely because we have been cut away from the current of vice that circulates through bad literature, gathers strength from luxury but dries up under the practice of religion. 28/12/29

" Conal Cearnac."

The lamented Dr. O'Connell, a gifted native of this county, whose father is Archdeacon of Tuam and Rector of Clifden, was one of the best known writers of modern Irish. Using the pseudonym "Conal Cearnach," he edited Gaelic selections from Keating's History of Ireland and from the same author's "Three Shafts of Death." He also edited the well-known poem. 'The Midnight Court," besides many other well-known works in the Irish language. He also had written several works in English criticism, of which the best known is "The Poetry of Koran." He was credited with being the fluent speaker of fourteen languages.

PAPAL NUNCIO.

The Most Rev. Paschal Robinson, O.F.M., whose selection as Apostolic Nuncio to the Irish Free State has been announced here, will reside in the Under-Secretary's Lodge at Phoenix Park, which was donated for his use by the Government. The Papal Nuncio will enjoy precedence over all other foreign representatives in the Free State.

REVIEW.

The "Call to Arms," by Esther Graham, the new Irish novel of the season, is a delightful story of the Irish Land War. The writer tells a tale of Irish life during that period, in the 70's and 80's, when the people all over the country, weary of the old political party in the Westminster Parliament, were aroused to action by the few Irish members, led by Charles Stuart Parnell, who rebelled against the old system, and called on the country to rise and defend their birthright—the land. The scene of action is Dublin, carried as the story proceeds to the West of Ireland, and among other places to Gort, where Michael Davitt, stirred by the conditions after '48 and '67 and the burnings and evictions of the Irish homes, advises the unfortunate sufferers to make a blow for their rights against the Landlords.

Esther Graham, with her facile pen, draws a charming picture of simple family life in the old Dublin of the day, and of a warm hearted people struggling for an ideal of a free Ireland against the domination of Dublin Castle and Buckshot Forster's regime.

In the romance we get a most thrilling and vivid picture of the events of history which followed the disappointment of Isaac Butt, and the appointment as leader of the people of Charles Stuart Parnell. We are carried through scenes of the troubled times, when the whole country rallied to the younger statesman. We see hoary Irish patriots and young men battling behind the great figure in his determination to win, where others had failed, when Archbishop Croke, the young priests, laymen, Protestant and Catholic alike, were banded together in a solid force in the great National fight. We see Parnell, at the height of his strength, and follow him to Kilmainham, where the famous treaty was signed.

This is a sufficient outline for our readers who will themselves read the book with intense enjoyment. It is Esther Graham's first novel, and is full of promise. The book is published by Messrs. Brown and Nolan (3/6 net). 28/12/29

THE LAND ANNUITIES FRAUD.

"This campaign against land annuities is an evil omen. It is the first time in our history that an attempt has been made to identify the flag of Ireland with brazen dishonesty. That was not the way of our fathers, nor is it the way to national well-being."

Such is the opinion of Most Rev. Dr. Fogarty, Bishop of Killaloe, and that of every honest man who has his country's good name at heart.

28/12/29

Christmas in Tuam

Not for a great many years past was such boisterous weather experienced around Christmas as this year. On Christmas Eve a fierce gale blew accompanied by vivid flashes of lightning and torrential rain. Fortunately there was no harm done in the town or suburbs, although the gale was at times almost terrifying.

IN THE CATHEDRAL.

The Christmas ceremonies started with first Mass at 7.30 celebrated by His Grace the Archbishop, and a second Mass immediately after celebrated by him also. There was a very large congregation present, and it was a most edifying sight to see the large number that approached the altar rails -practically every one of those present receiving Holy Communion.

At 9.30 the congregation was if anything larger, and the greater number also received. At 11.30 there was Solemn High Mass followed by Benediction. His Grace the Archbishop presided. Rev. Father Killeen, C.C., preached an eloquent sermon on the coming of the Divine Child.

THE CRIB

at Our Lady's Altar was, as usual, a great centre of attraction for young and old, and there was scarcely an hour of the day or night that it had not its group of devout visitors.

IN THE TOWN.

Business in the town had an unusual appearance of livliness, and it is pleasing to be able to record a much better Christmas in the business line than we have had for a considerable time past. On the days before the great festival the streets were thronged with country people intent on securing the Christmas goods and the shops did a roaring trade. Let pessimists say what they will about the days of the small town being gone owing to the prevalence of the lorry trader, Tuam is not to be counted amongst the number and is more than holding its own, a proof of which is to be found in the number of new business houses opened in every quarter of the town, and old ones rehabilitated, since this time twelve months. Some think that if our commercial people could be got to come together and show more enterprise by offering inducements to purchasers to come here (as is done elsewhere) the business of the town could be increased greatly. Tuam has potentialities and prospects which have never been fully developed.

ST. VINCENT DE PAUL SOCIETY.

The good working members of the St. Vincent De Paul Society left nothing they could possibly do undone to alleviate the lot of the poor and helpless. Their charity was not given in a careless or perfunctory manner, but by sympathetic and careful visitation of the young men those most in need were found and succoured and their Christmas brightened.

THE BANKS AND POST OFFICE.

The Banks and Post Office were kept busily engaged with the amount of business to be transacted. There was a very large mail - especially the American mail. All was handled expeditiously and carefully by the capable staff of the Tuam P.O.

THE WAITS AND MUMMERS.

The waits were in evidence for the week or two previous to Christmas, and some how or other are welcome as a reminder of the happy time, but the mummers, which for the last few years seem to increase every Christmas, are in a different category and their vulgar displays are not worthy of support.

THE CASSIDY NAME.

The Cassidys of County Cavan are in a state bordering on revolt. There are hundreds of them all over the county, and in every one of them there is surging an outraged indignation.

Superstition is the cause of all the trouble. There is a belief in the county that the best way to cure a sick animal is to burn a rag from the clothes of a Cassidy under its nose.

Consequently, when any of the farm stock goes ill the cry at once goes round, "Go for Cassidy's rag." The nearest owner of the name is approached and asked for a piece from his clothes. It is stated that when the cloth is burned as stated the ailing animal invariably recovers.

Recently, however, there has been more trouble than usual with the farm stock, and the Cassidy's have been so much pestered by the superstitions that they are now beginning to tire of their fame.

One bearer of the name told me that he was thoroughly sick of the superstition.

"If I gave generously to every one who asked for a piece of cloth I would hardly have a stitch left in the house," he declared. "I generally use old suits for the purpose, but recently even this supply has been exhausted." "Indeed." he added. "I have been thinking seriously of making a bit of money from the belief and selling rags to the farmers."

The origin of the superstition is stated to be due to the fact that the Cassidys were a noted medical family in the county many centuries ago. Their powers of curing all kinds of ailments were believed to have been handed down to each generation, until today their curative skill is associated even with the garments of any bearer of the name.

28/12/29

GALWAY NOTES
(From Our Own Correspondent.)

It was a sad vicissitude of Fortune to read of the announcement of the sale of Kilcornan of the entire furnishing of that once hospitable and well equipped house of the Redingtons, now, alas, without one of the name in, or we believe, out of the county. It is a melancholy reflection to see a once socially great family disappear and leave but a cherished memory of goodness and kindliness behind. The late Christopher Talbot Redington was for twenty years or more one of the leading Catholic gentry of this county. He was the son of Sir Thomas Redington, who was Under Secretary for many years and esteemed as a zealous, high minded official. It is strange that he should have been succeeded in that once important post by another Galway county gentleman, Thomas Henry Burke, of Knocknagur and Glynsk, who by the way was born in Waterslade House, in this town, where his family then lived and which they owned, as they did the broad acres about Knocknagur, near Milltown. He was basely murdered in the Phoenix Park by the Invincibles and a public meeting in Tuam, held in the Court House and presided over by the late Archbishop MacEvilly, gave voice to the general feeling of indignation felt over the country. The statue which stands in the Tuam Cathedral grounds to commemorate the charity of William Burke, of Curraleigh, is an exact likeness of the murdered official, as Sir Thomas Farrell, who carved it, told those who asked him. He said the reason was that no one could produce a photograph or painting of William Burke, for his portrait was never taken and one could not carve a statue to an ideal man, so it occurred to the sculptor to suggest the most prominent of the name then in Ireland, and Dr. MacHale, who knew Sir Thomas and also knew William Burke, consented, and so the statue in the Cathedral grounds is that to William Burke but not of William Burke but of Sir Thomas Burke. There was another Connaught man Under Secretary, the late Lord MacDonnell, a native of Mayo but educated at Queen's College, of whom great things was expected. The last to fill the post was a former Secretary in the Post Office, but he was a mere automaton and ran no risk, while the real work of administration was done by two others in the Castle.

***

Two prominent and popular members of the excellent Community of Christian Brothers stationed in Ballinrobe have recently died at other places where they were changed to. The last was Brother Walshe who died at Tralee this week quite suddenly. The other was Brother Gallagher who died at the Brothers' Retreat a Baldoyle. Both had led active lives in the educational world and were favourites in all the centres they were engaged in and highly thought of in Ballinrobe. The Christian Brothers in Ballinrobe were established there by the late Dean Ronayne, a great educationist and administrator, and to him the Ballinrobe people are indebted for the boon. There was an interesting newspaper correspondence at the time in our columns arising out of the remarks alleged to have been made by a respected and energetic Inspector of Schools, the late Mr. James William Greer, who was said to have declared that Ballinrobe was already educationally well provided for by the National School it had been running there and that the people did not wish or want the Brothers and to be obliged to support them when they had free schools already. The Dean, who could make use of a powerful pen, took the Inspector to task. It was a nine days' wonder, but it excited great interest in these parts at the time. Before going to Ballinrobe, where he succeeded Father Hardiman as P.P., the Dean was Administrator in Westport. There he succeeded Father Francis J. McCormack. He was appointed from being C.A. in Westport to be Bishop of Achonry. This unprecedented step was mainly brought about by the action of the late Cardinal Cullen to whom the sterling qualities and excellent priestly virtues of Father McCormack were made known by the Cardinal's sister, the late Mother Paul. She was Reverend Mother of the Convent of Mercy in Westport for nearly 50 years and was one of the ablest women of her time in religion. She certainly was a true sister of a very able Churchman, as Cardinal Cullen was undoubtedly. He was misunderstood and misrepresented by the Fenians who were then strong in Irish politics and intolerant. But when his Life comes to be written and published, as we believe it is being now underaken by a capable hand, the distinguished clergyman, Monsignor Walshe, P.P., D.D., who wrote the successful Life of Dr. Walshe, Archbishop of Dublin, it will be seen and recognised that in addition to being a great Churchman, whom all the world so recognised, Cardinal Cullen was also a good Irishman and lover of his country and due justice will be done to his memory. No one did more for the spread of religion in his day and deserves more honour for his work.

***

We all know in Galway, when he visited us as a sympathetic visitor and later spent two months at Her Majesty's Hotel, the County Gaol, the distinguished Englishman of high lineage and high character, Sir Wilfrid Blunt. He visited the Clanricarde estate and was inveigled into attending a midnight meeting at Portumna and burning the Queen's Proclamation -- a silly proceeding, inspired by William O'Brien. For

this he got two months. He went through the two months like a man, never grumbled or bemoaned his lot, but he never visited Ireland afterwards or showed the slightest interest in its welfare. He evidently was sick of the theatricals that went on. He was married to the only daughter of Lord Byron, the Poet, and he was a cousin of Mr. George Wyndham, the best Chief Secretary Ireland ever had. In his book he throws a new light on the descent of Gladstone. The family came from the Lowlands of Scotland, and the first of them to come into notoriety spelled his name"Gladstan". He was a baker, and he was convicted in the Scotch Courts for selling lightweight bread. Mr. Blunt was a Catholic, and in his Irish visit he called on Dr. Duggan, the famous Bishop of Clonfert. He also called on Archbishop Croke. He says they discussed the whole morality of agrarian crime. "And it is clear", he continued, "that they in their hearts hold the same view as Dr.Duggan, of those things being really acts of war, and so they really are. It is absurd to argue that the landlord, who destroys a hundred families by evicting them, is guiltless because his act is legal, and that the peasant who resisted or retaliates is a murderer because his blows are illegal. There must be a principle of justice underlying the law, or the law itself is a crime". Dr. Croke explained to Blunt that his bellicose attitude in politics came of his Protestant Blood, his grandfather having been a Protestant Saxon, but he had an uncle whose portrait he showed me, who brought him up a Catholic. He has travelled all the world over, and been a Bishop in New Zealand. I had sooner be on his side than against him in a row. According to Mr. Blunt, Archbishop Croke was a strong personality, a shrewd, hard-bitten, fighting Prelate, and he should say an unsparing enemy. His Grace was no lover of the Land League when it started, and there were some brushed between himself and Davitt as well as Parnell. The Land League had come out of Connaught, and it had survived the opposition of Dr.MacHale, of Tuam. That may, perhaps, explain some of his Grace's views about Connaught, as related by Mr. Blunt. "Here in Munster," Dr.Croke said, "they had broken the power of the landlords, because they had stuck together; and he spoke with contempt of the Connaught men, who had given in and taken to petty outrages. The Connaught men are good for nothing, he declared, but to take money and pay it over to their landlords. They had £80,000 given them from the Land League funds, yet when the Parnell memorial was being raised, only £400 were subscribed in Connaught. Talking of the project of repeopling the plains with peasants from the mountains, he said it would not succeed; the peasants would no more migrate from one county to another than from Ireland to America; where they were born, they would die; a Connaught man would be chased out of Munster like a fox by the Munster men".
28/12/29

NOTES.

GALWAY FORGING AHEAD.

This week there arrived in Galway three Atlantic liners with Christmas excursion parties from the United States. The first, the Hamburg-American liner Cleveland (17,000 tons) disembarked a large number of passengers and Christmas mails destined for almost every county in Ireland. The Cleveland in March will engage on a monthly westward and eastward-bound service between Galway and the United States. The Cunard liner Laconia and the North German Lloyd liner Stuttgart arrived in Galway on Friday with 300 passengers to spend the Christmas in Ireland. So despite all Galway is holding its own and advancing in favour.

PASSION PLAY.

The 300 inhabitants of Oberammergau who are to take part in a Passion Play are engrossed in learning their roles. Full rehearsals began on Christmas Day. The first presentation is scheduled for May 11. The cost of the 1930 production is estimated at close to a quarter of a million dollars. At least 300,000 spectators are expected from every quarter of the world.

NOBEL PRIZE.

For the first time since 1912, the Nobel prize has been awarded a German writer. Thomas Mann, author of "Buddenbrooks", in the three volumes of which life in North Germany is faithfully depicted, was born at Lubeck in 1875. At the age of 29 years he came to Munich where he was employed by an insurance company. He also contributed articles to various journals including "Simplicimus." The winner of the Nobel prize has a brother, Heinrich, who is well known both at home and abroad for his fiction of a political tendency.
28/12/29

TUAM TOWN COMMISSIONERS

NOTICE TO BLACKSMITHS

Tuam Town Commissioners will at their meeting to be held on Tuesday, January 7th, 1930, consider tenders for keeping their horse shod for one year from 10th Jan., 1930.

The lowest or any tender not necessarily accepted. By Order Tuam Town Commissioners,

JOHN P. WHYTE,

Town Clerk.

28/12/29

Death of a Tuam man and a Distinguished Christian Brother.

We regret to record the death of a Tuam man and distinguished Christian Brother. There died at Richmond Street School, Dublin, on Wednesday last, the 19th inst., Brother James Canice Craven. He was in his 76th year of age and in the 60th of his religious profession. He was born at Cloonkeen, Cloonascragh, near this town and he got his first training at the Christian Brothers here under that excellent teacher and guide of Tuam's youth for a quarter of a century, the revered Brother Lowe. Brother Craven left Tuam when a lad to go to the Christian Brother Novitiate in Richmond St., Dublin, along with several other Tuam boys of the same age the chief being a Mr. Moylan, who afterwards became the Superior General of the Order, Mr Conway, who went to Australia, and Mr. Mullens. While in Dublin and Belfast, where he subsequently was, Brother Craven led a very active life as a teacher. He also went into journalism and established the popular publication associated with the Order, "Our Boys", and brought it to the very successful stage which it now enjoys. He was a very energetic and active minded man and a great educationist. In Belfast he was for years well known for his educational activity and highly esteemed by the Catholics of that city. He was a man of strong views but of unceasing energy and never wearied doing good. He turned out many pupils who owe much to his sound training. He established a Trade School at Belfast which was a great success and still running. Being a practical and useful work it supplied the wants which Technical Schools are now so efficiently fulfilling all over the country. He was undoubtedly a well known personality in educational and Catholic centres and highly thought of. His journalistic work in the starting and editing of "Our Boys" showed that he had the talent for such work. He conducted that juvenile monthly paper for several years and made it a success. He displayed marked ability in its conduct.

A correspondent in "Independent" speaks of Brother Craven in those flattering terms:-

The death of this distinguished religious closes a long life of sterling service to God and Ireland. An able educationist, many noted men in the public life of Ireland to-day pursued their early studies under his rule. He will be specially remembered in Belfast, where he laboured for many years, opening there the first Trades Preparatory School in Ireland, which has since become such a notable success.

Indeed, the fruits of his work in the Northern Capital may be said to have opened up a new prospect for the rising generation there. His interest in his pupils did not cease when they passed from his classroom. His guiding and helping hand was ever at their service, and through the medium of his influence among employers he planted the feet of very many of his boys in useful careers.

He will probably be longest remembered, however, as editor of "Our Boys". In his sphere he did a man's part to uphold National and Christian ideals.

His was a labour of love. He worked with the zeal of an apostle. A man, in his prime, of powerful physique, he spent his power ungrudgingly. His strength failed about a year ago, and though he still worked on, the end approached inevitably. His death was peaceful - a quiet close to a life of unremitting labour.

The remains after Requiem Mass were interred in the community grave in Glasnevin.

28/12/29

Note:
In 1916 the managing director of Harland and Wolff, J.W. Kempster, complimented the Belfast headmaster, Brother J.C.Craven:
"The Christian Brothers deserve the thanks of the community for having attacked with no little success that important educational problem which is involved in a general primary education followed by a training in science of a character suited to boys whose parents could not otherwise well afford to give them a higher education whilst the Brotherhood, as might be expected, fully realise the ethical value of Christian influence.
(Source : Letter to the Editor, Irish Times, March, 1991, from G. Allen, Blackrock, Co. Dublin.)

Swearing is a habit. It does not make conversation more expressive. It does not lend emphasis. It does not convey an idea any better. Profanity is the product of a cheap course mind. It is not only inelegant, but usually emanates from a mind rough and uncouth, and is never heard coming from a person well bred or educated.

28/12/29

---

247 EGGS from seven birds in the awful wet and cold January and February convinces me that **OVUM**, Thorley's Poultry Spice, is the cause of such good results.—Sold by **Cahill & Co.**, Wholesale Grocers and General Merchants, Mitre Buildings, Tuam.   28/12/29

The Tuam Herald.
Saturday, December 28th, 1929
THE PARTING YEAR.

The year 1929, which is just taking its place in the records of Time so far as doing its part to make history, has been, in its way, a memorable one. It has seen much in its twelve months' span and its story will when written register many useful changes and some decided progress towards peace and a rehabilitation of the shattered fortunes of the war devastated countries that eleven years ago concluded a peace that ended the most disastrous and exhausting war which man has yet embarked upon in his blind passion for domination and terrible lust for power. In all these countries some advance has been made towards more stable conditions and men can feel more confidence in the future. Great Britain is, however, sadly troubled with serious Labour questions and the most formidable is perhaps the vast and increasing numbers of unemployed it has been nurturing by its degrading dole policy and burdening its resources so heavily that it is eating into its very entrails economically. It has also had vast financial failures and frauds and millions have been lost in wild speculation. Similarly in America the United States has had even a worse experience in these money matters and the losses incurred are almost incredible, certainly so to our ordinary capacity for understanding figures, accustomed as we were to moderate and easily comprehended amounts and fairly honest transactions. All this is owing to the growing lust for wealth to be got at any cost and the reckless passion for getting rich in a hurry, which never succeeds. Thousands are sufferers from this speculative passion and there are some in this country even who are heavily dipped in the London crashing operations. Their misfortune should make reasonable people more careful and more cautious and less ready to put money into wild schemes proposed by company schemers with director decoys who have no capacity for direction and simply deceive the people by their titles. They and such like are incapable of being good judges of business or reliable guides in money matters. England is also now grappling with its eternal coal difficulty and we may expect as a certain result of any settlement a further increase in the price of that article. Hence the less dependent we in Ireland are upon imported coal the better. Our Shannon project is in operation and working well. Every day sees further progress in its extended use in every walk of life with advantage to all.

Abroad several events concerning our religion have occurred of immense and enduring advantage and singular importance. The Roman question is satisfactorily settled after for 59 years being a vexed and vexing one. The Pope has now secured to him his city and surroundings as the Vatican territory and the arrangement has given universal satisfaction. The happy historical event has been fitly celebrated by the universal church. It has been accompanied by the celebration of the Jubilee of the present illustrious occupant of the See of St. Peter. By his calling to the Sacred College the Archbishop of Armagh to fill the place vacant by the lamented death of Cardinal O'Donnell the Pope has given one more proof of his deep and active interest in this country and its spiritual welfare. We all in Ireland and wherever Irishmen are, wish Cardinal Mac Rory long years of health and strength to discharge the duties of the high position he has been called upon to fill. In addition to this signal mark of appreciation the Pope sends, as his special Nuncio to Ireland, a distinguished Dublin man and Franciscan, Monsignor Robinson, who will next week be warmly welcomed in his native city by all Catholic Ireland. It is a significant and a great historical event and one which will have done much to bring Ireland before the world and to make it less provincial and more generally known abroad.

***

But with all these pleasing events there unhappily is going on in Russia a systematic, a fearful deliberate and truly diabolical campaign by the Soviet Scoundrels, who have by force assumed control there against every form of Christian belief. Churches of all denominations are being desecrated and being turned into the basest uses. Every thing that the devil's ingenuity could devise is being done to bring religion into discredit and a generation is growing up to whom all divine matters is unknown and forbidden and who have the most awful ideas of everything hitherto held in reverence by all creeds all over the world. In England the conscience of the British people is being aroused to protest against the Red War upon Religion in Russia and we trust and pray that the agitation may grow in strength and that it will spread all over the civilised world. It is sad to think that England or any civilised country should in such circumstances, for the mere sake of greed and gain, or to get some problematical little trade, should recognise a Government so committed to war upon religion as such and destitute of any claim to human respect or recognition. Thanks to the vigorous and creditable action of the "Morning Post", a feeling of just indignation is being aroused which may have its effect even upon the low consciences of the craven crew of degenerates that now unfortunately rule in Russia and who are the devil's own statesmen in every sense. We, in Catholic Ireland, trust and pray that the God of the Christians will hear the prayer of the Christians of all denominations, and indeed of all who acknowledge a Supreme Being, and bring a ray of reason and sense into the black hearts of the base, brutal, bloody Bolshevists now let loose from Hell upon that unfortunate country.   28/12/29

NAMES

Joe Shaughnessy, C2
Michael Hanley, C4
John Hession, C3
Mick Griffey, D4
Johnny Griffey, D4
Joe Reilly, D3
Paddy Brady, D3
Dermot Mulryan, D2
Tom Mulryan, D2
Jimmy Flanagan, D1
Jarlath Forde, D4
Mick Kemple, D2
Terence Kelly, D6

Ted Reynolds, D5
Jack Monahan, D5
Eddie Cooley, D5
Johnny McGrath, D4
Peter Barratt, D4
Jimmy O'Rourke, D4
Richie Walsh, D3
Tommie Garvey, D3
Maggie Keegan, D2
Bridget Curley, D2
Rose O'Dea, D1
Paddy Mooney, E2
Paddy Kelly, E1

Stephen Keane, E4
Mrs McCormack, E3
Dan McCormack, E2
Johnny Ryan, E2
Mrs Cunningham, E2
Johnny Cunningham, E1
John Geraghty, F6
Fanny Tighe, E5
Kathleen Bane, E5
Mr Kennedy, E5
Jim Maloney, F5
Malachy Duggan, F5
Johnny Walsh, F4

Johnny Kelly, F4
Mick Kelly, F4
Albert Madden, F4
Fr. Killeen, F4
Fr. Higgins, F4
(Kilbannon)
John Waldron, F3
Joe Hurley, , F3
Mrs Hurley, F3
Joe McElgunn, F1

The Market Cross, Tuam